RICHMOND

NOW YOU!

CB134827

Richmond

TEACHER'S BOOK 1

WELCOME TO NOW YOU!

Richmond NOW YOU! is a four-level English Secondary course which takes students from A1 to B1+ of the Common European Framework. The course features an eclectic approach which takes the best of the latest developments in ELT teaching methodology and carefully interweaves them within a communicative framework.

Learning threads

The course makes use of these **learning threads** to help streamline the learning and teaching experience and **increase learning efficiency** while also **motivating the students** to connect with the learning process.

Learner-centred approach

Personalisation exercises throughout the course make every student the focus of their own learning journey and help to consolidate language and skills. **Learning to learn tools** provide students with tips and tricks for more effective learning.

Vloggers

In every level of the course the student is accompanied by three vloggers who introduce the context of each unit in their **Vlogs**. The vloggers also narrate the **Culture videos**, creating a cultural link between the unit content and the wider world.

Flipped Learning

There are many tools at the teacher's disposal for implementing Flipped Learning with **NOW YOU!**, such as the fun **Grammar animations** which accompany every grammar point and table. The **Vlogs** with their worksheets also present a great opportunity for introducing the lesson content outside of the classroom.

Project-based Learning

Multi-student **Project tasks** are staged across two units and brought together in a **Final task**. Students recap on the tasks, prepare for a presentation and focus on **21st century skills**. Students are also asked to think carefully about the format of the project and to evaluate themselves and their peers, encouraging **Collaborative Learning**.

Attention to values

Reading content is further explored with speaking tasks, in which students focus on and discuss a specific **Core value**.

Mediation

Project tasks throughout the book and information gap **Pairwork** activities for each unit presented at the end of the book combine unit content with practice of **CEFR mediation** activities and strategies.

External exam preparation

The **Review** pages at the end of each book combine course content with **external exam practice questions**, ensuring students are familiar with the format and can apply their knowledge in an exam context.

For the Student

Student's Book

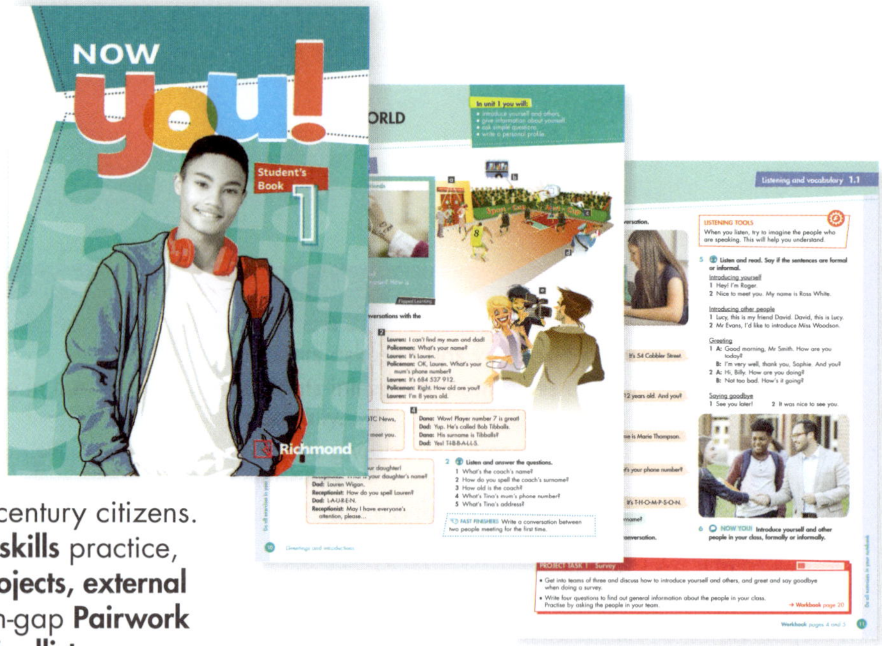

The **NOW YOU! Student's Book** is a dynamic, attractive course book with clear lesson objectives, a wide variety of interesting material for students to engage with and a strong focus on developing skills to help students become confident and competent users of English and well-rounded 21st century citizens. The **Student's Book** includes **integrated skills** practice, **Learning to learn** tools, **Core values, Projects, external exam practice Unit reviews,** information-gap **Pairwork activities,** a **Grammar reference** and **Wordlists**.

Workbook

The **NOW YOU! Workbook** is a **full-colour** resource with more engaging material to complement the **Student's Book**, handy **guided notes pages** for the Writing lessons and Projects, **extra practice for the Grammar reference and Wordlists** and a **Reflect on your learning section** to encourage learner autonomy. Access to **extra interactive practice** based on real-world situations is also available with the **Workbook**.

Workbook Audio

LISTEN ON Spotify

Also available to listen to and download on the **Richmond***Learning***Platform**.

All videos and worksheets available on the **Richmond***Learning***Platform**

For the Teacher

Teacher's Book

The **Teacher's Book** is your comprehensive guide to teaching **NOW YOU!** and the key methodologies on which the course is based. For each unit of the **Student's Book** there is an **overview** for fast lesson planning, plus complete **teaching notes**, audio **transcripts** and **answer keys** for the student's material.

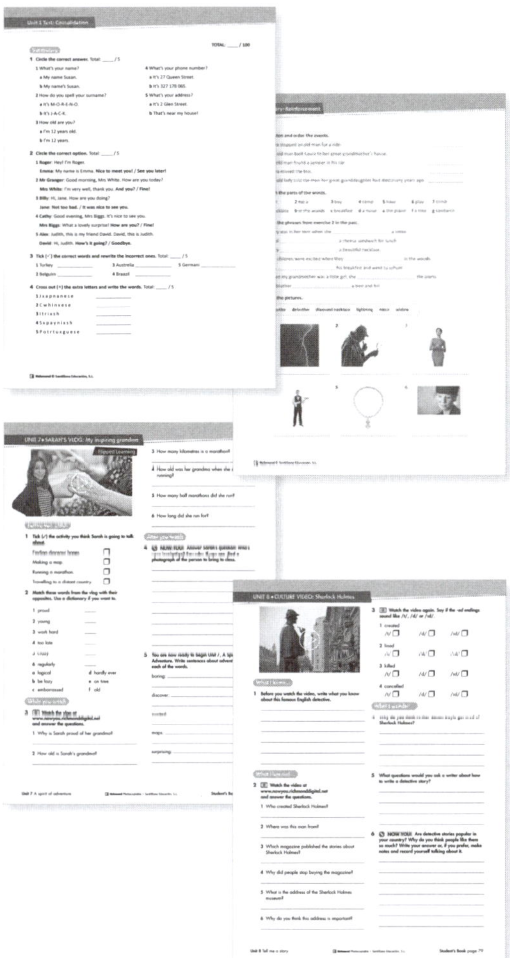

Teacher's Resources

Available on the Richmond *Learning* Platform

A wide range of ready-to-print and editable material is provided to complement and enhance your teaching.

- **Vocabulary worksheets** at 3 levels of difficulty
- **Grammar worksheets** at 3 levels of difficulty
- **Diagnostic**, **Unit**, **End-of-term** and **End-of-year tests** at 2 levels of difficulty
- **Vlog Flipped Learning worksheets**
- **Culture video worksheets**
- **Essential maps** for each unit

Teacher's Audio

Available on the Richmond *Learning* Platform

All audio for listening exercises used in the **Student's Book**, **Workbook** and **Teacher's Resources** is available to listen to and download.

All videos and worksheets available on the Richmond *Learning* Platform

NOW YOU! DIGITAL

For the Student

Student's i-book

The **NOW YOU! Student's i-book** is an online multi-device version of the **Student's Book** to enable students to access the course material at home. It includes:

- All **videos**
- All **Student's Book audio**

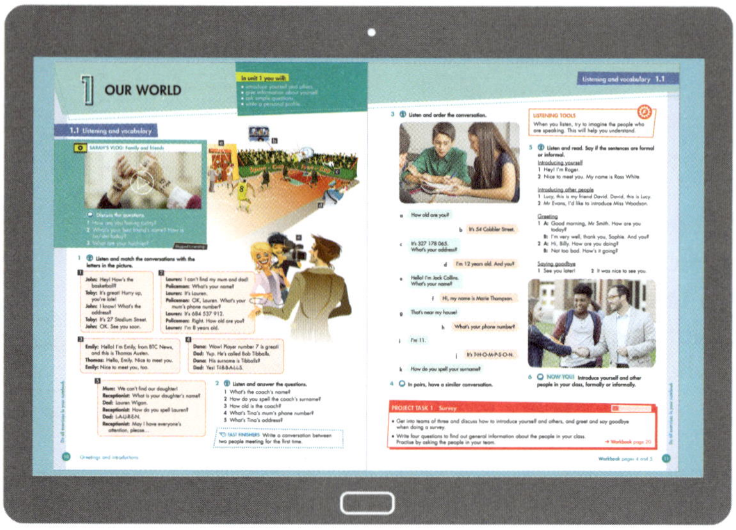

Videos

Three different types of videos (see **Video material** pages 18-19) help teenagers engage with the language in a way that is relevant to their lives outside the classroom.

Vlogs

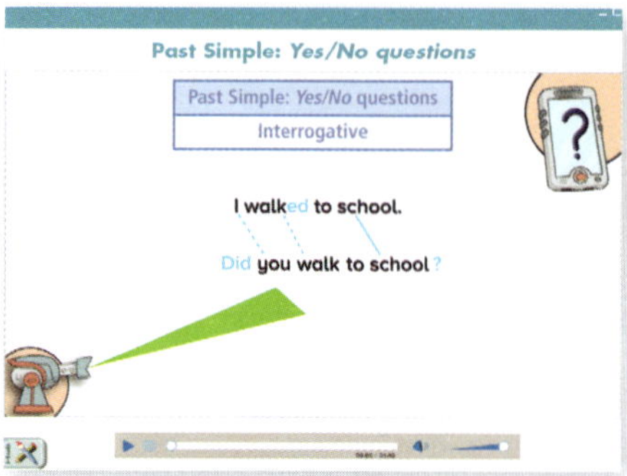

Grammar animations

Culture videos

Student's Interactive Practice

There is also additional interactive practice to consolidate the course content and to develop the concept of English for life. The activities are contextualised in real-world situations. This helps to make the acquisition of language more meaningful for the students.

The **Student's Interactive Practice** includes learning progress and it is ideal for fast finishers or for homework.

Also available to purchase
A fully interactive, **digital version of the Student's Book and Workbook** which provides a complete tracking of the students' progress.

Free App

RICHMOND NOW YOU!

For the Teacher

Offline and online multi-device versions available

Teacher's i-solutions

The **NOW YOU! Teacher's i-solutions** for the classroom include the **Teacher's i-book**, as well as all the resources for the print version of the **Teacher's Book**.

In the **Teacher's i-book** every lesson in the course is presented in the form of a **Learning path**, a step-by step lesson plan that works as a quick lesson guide where the teaching sequence is clear at a glance. All the teaching and learning materials in the course are included and the **resources are colour-coded** to identify what is **core material** and what is **optional**. Teachers can therefore choose activities according to the time available and **tips** for all the material are available **at the click of a button**.

Richmond Test Manager

An online interactive tool to create and assign tests.

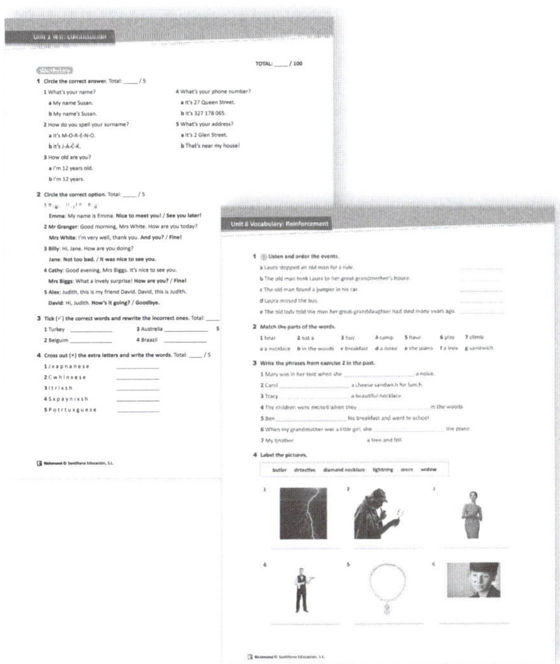

Downloadable material

Teacher's Resources available:

- **Vocabulary worksheets** at 3 levels of difficulty **(PDF and Word format)**
- **Grammar worksheets** at 3 levels of difficulty **(PDF and Word format)**
- **Diagnostic**, **Unit**, **End-of-term** and **End-of-year tests** at 2 levels of difficulty **(PDF and Word format)**
- **Vlog Flipped Learning worksheets**
- **Culture video worksheets**
- **Essential maps**

All videos and worksheets available on the **Richmond** *Learning* **Platform**

UNIT WALKTHROUGH

LESSON 1 Grammar, Vocabulary and Listening

1 The **unit menu** outlines the key learning aims of each unit. The four points outline the general communication goal, the central grammar points and the writing task genre. This provides both teacher and student with a clear learning map for the unit.

2 The **lesson focus** tags highlight the main skills focus of each page.

Lessons 1 and 2 provide **grammar**, **vocabulary** and **listening** input. Speaking exercises throughout give students opportunities to practise the key grammar points and vocabulary sets.

Lesson 3 provides **reading** input with a focus on deepening the students' understanding of the unit language in an authentic context.

Lesson 4 guides **writing** output, putting the students' knowledge to practical use.

Lesson 5 is a **culture and communication** page where students are encouraged to recognise their place in global culture and interact with the world around them.

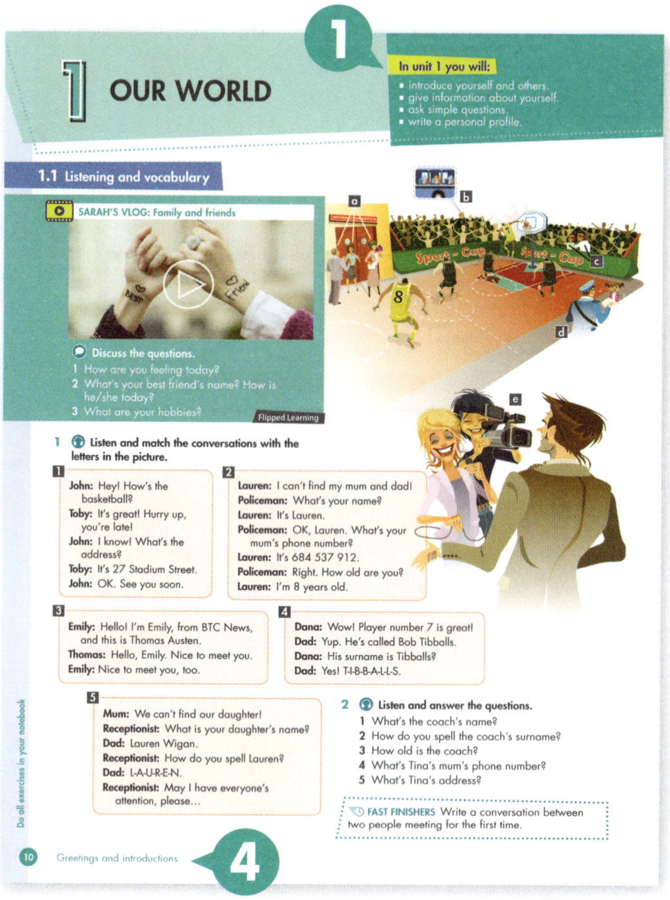

1 OUR WORLD

In unit 1 you will:
- introduce yourself and others.
- give information about yourself.
- ask simple questions.
- write a personal profile.

1.1 Listening and vocabulary

SARAH'S VLOG: Family and friends

Discuss the questions.
1 How are you feeling today?
2 What's your best friend's name? How is he/she today?
3 What are your hobbies?

Flipped Learning

1 Listen and match the conversations with the letters in the picture.

1
John: Hey! How's the basketball?
Toby: It's great! Hurry up, you're late!
John: I know! What's the address?
Toby: It's 27 Stadium Street.
John: OK. See you soon.

2
Lauren: I can't find my mum and dad!
Policeman: What's your name?
Lauren: It's Lauren.
Policeman: OK, Lauren. What's your mum's phone number?
Lauren: It's 684 537 912.
Policeman: Right. How old are you?
Lauren: I'm 8 years old.

3
Emily: Hello! I'm Emily, from BTC News, and this is Thomas Austen.
Thomas: Hello, Emily. Nice to meet you.
Emily: Nice to meet you, too.

4
Dana: Wow! Player number 7 is great!
Dad: Yup. He's called Bob Tibballs.
Dana: His surname is Tibballs?
Dad: Yes! T-I-B-B-A-L-L-S.

5
Mum: We can't find our daughter!
Receptionist: What is your daughter's name?
Dad: Lauren Wigan.
Receptionist: How do you spell Lauren?
Dad: L-A-U-R-E-N.
Receptionist: May I have everyone's attention, please...

2 Listen and answer the questions.
1 What's the coach's name?
2 How do you spell the coach's surname?
3 How old is the coach?
4 What's Tina's mum's phone number?
5 What's Tina's address?

FAST FINISHERS Write a conversation between two people meeting for the first time.

Do all exercises in your notebook

10 Greetings and introductions

3 Three **vloggers** provide an engaging context for the unit content.
The optional **Flipped Learning** tasks encourage students to take control of their learning by beginning the learning process outside of the classroom. For information about Flipped Learning, see pages 20-23.

These **Vlogs** provide exposure to the unit language aims and can be re-watched in order to capitalise on the content, but students can answer the discussion questions and complete the unit without having watched them.

Unit walkthrough

LESSON 1 Grammar, Vocabulary and Listening

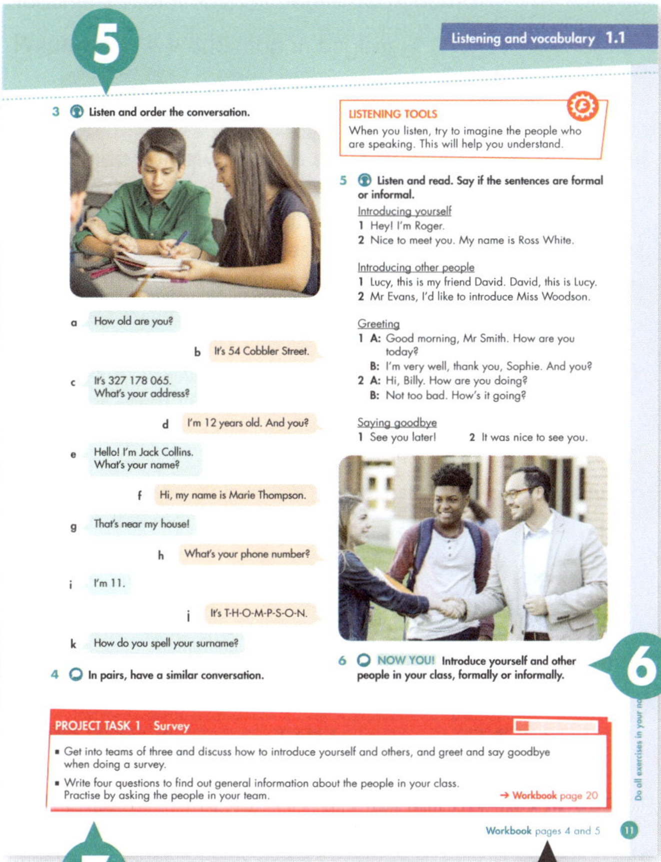
Listening and vocabulary 1.1

3 Listen and order the conversation.

a How old are you?
b It's 54 Cobbler Street.
c It's 327 178 065. What's your address?
d I'm 12 years old. And you?
e Hello! I'm Jack Collins. What's your name?
f Hi, my name is Marie Thompson.
g That's near my house!
h What's your phone number?
i I'm 11.
j It's T-H-O-M-P-S-O-N.
k How do you spell your surname?

4 In pairs, have a similar conversation.

LISTENING TOOLS
When you listen, try to imagine the people who are speaking. This will help you understand.

5 Listen and read. Say if the sentences are formal or informal.

Introducing yourself
1 Hey! I'm Roger.
2 Nice to meet you. My name is Ross White.

Introducing other people
1 Lucy, this is my friend David. David, this is Lucy.
2 Mr Evans, I'd like to introduce Miss Woodson.

Greeting
1 A: Good morning, Mr Smith. How are you today?
B: I'm very well, thank you, Sophie. And you?
2 A: Hi, Billy. How are you doing?
B: Not too bad. How's it going?

Saying goodbye
1 See you later! 2 It was nice to see you.

6 NOW YOU! Introduce yourself and other people in your class, formally or informally.

PROJECT TASK 1 Survey
- Get into teams of three and discuss how to introduce yourself and others, and greet and say goodbye when doing a survey.
- Write four questions to find out general information about the people in your class. Practise by asking the people in your team. → Workbook page 20

Do all exercises in your notebook.

Workbook pages 4 and 5

11

6 The **NOW YOU!** exercises at the end of the lesson challenge students to put their knowledge to practical use in the form of personalised speaking or writing exercises.

7 **Project tasks** develop and build towards a final presentation over two units. These tasks draw on the content of the lesson and promote collaborative work. The bar helps students know how many tasks they have completed and have left to complete the project.

In unit 9 students are given **Review tasks** which encourage them to reflect on what they have learnt from units 1 to 9 and develop revision strategies.

8 At the end of each lesson students are directed to their **Workbook** for further practice of the unit content.

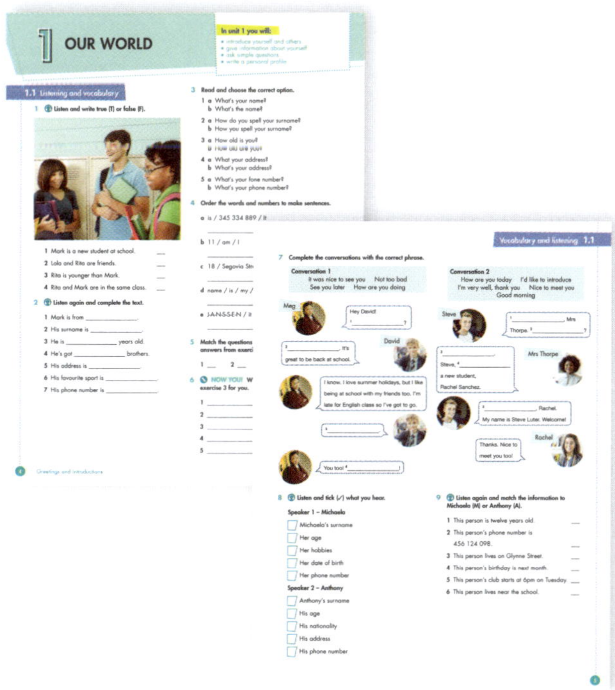
1 OUR WORLD

In unit 1 you will:
- introduce yourself and others
- give information about yourself
- ask simple questions
- write a personal profile

1.1 Listening and vocabulary

1 Listen and write true (T) or false (F).
1 Mark is a new student at school. ___
2 Lola and Rita are friends. ___
3 Rita is younger than Mark. ___
4 Rita and Mark are in the same class. ___

2 Listen again and complete the text.
1 Mark is from ________.
2 His surname is ________.
3 He is ________ years old.
4 He's got ________ brothers.
5 His address is ________.
6 His favourite sport is ________.
7 His phone number is ________.

3 Read and choose the correct option.
1 a What's your name? b What's the name?
2 a How do you spell your surname? b How you spell your surname?
3 a How old is you? b How old are you?
4 a What your address? b What's your address?
5 a What's your fone number? b What's your phone number?

4 Order the words and numbers to make sentences.
a is / 345 334 889 / it
b 11 / am / I
c 18 / Segovia Str…
d name / is / my / …
e J-A-N-S-S-E-N / it …

5 Match the questions … answers from exerci…
1 ___ 2 ___

6 NOW YOU! W… exercise 3 for you.
1 ___
2 ___
3 ___
4 ___
5 ___

4 Greetings and introductions

Vocabulary and listening 1.1

7 Complete the conversations with the correct phrase.

Conversation 1
It was nice to see you / Not too bad / See you later / How are you doing

Meg: Hey David! ¹________?
David: ²________. It's great to be back at school.
Meg: I know. I love summer holidays, but I like being at school with my friends too. I'm late for English class so I've got to go.
David: ³________.
Meg: You too! ⁴________!

Conversation 2
How are you today / I'd like to introduce / I'm very well, thank you / Nice to meet you / Good morning

Steve: ¹________, Mrs Thorpe. ²________?
Mrs Thorpe: ³________, Steve. ⁴________ a new student, Rachel Sanchez.
Steve: ⁵________, Rachel. My name is Steve Luter. Welcome!
Rachel: Thanks. Nice to meet you too!

8 Listen and tick (✓) what you hear.
Speaker 1 – Michaela
- Michaela's surname
- Her age
- Her hobbies
- Her date of birth
- Her phone number

Speaker 2 – Anthony
- Anthony's surname
- His age
- His nationality
- His address
- His phone number

9 Listen again and match the information to Michaela (M) or Anthony (A).
1 This person is twelve years old. ___
2 This person's phone number is 456 124 098. ___
3 This person lives on Glynne Street. ___
4 This person's birthday is next month. ___
5 This person's club starts at 6pm on Tuesday. ___
6 This person lives near the school. ___

5

4 The **lesson objective** clarifies the grammar and vocabulary goals of each lesson. This provides an at-a-glance summary of the lesson for both the teacher and student.

5 The **exercises** give students a variety of ways to practise what they are learning.

Unit walkthrough

LESSON 2 Grammar, Vocabulary and Listening

1 Through the unit students are asked to complete a variety of exercises that build on growing knowledge of the unit aims. Special effort has been made to ensure that all the content is visually appealing to students.

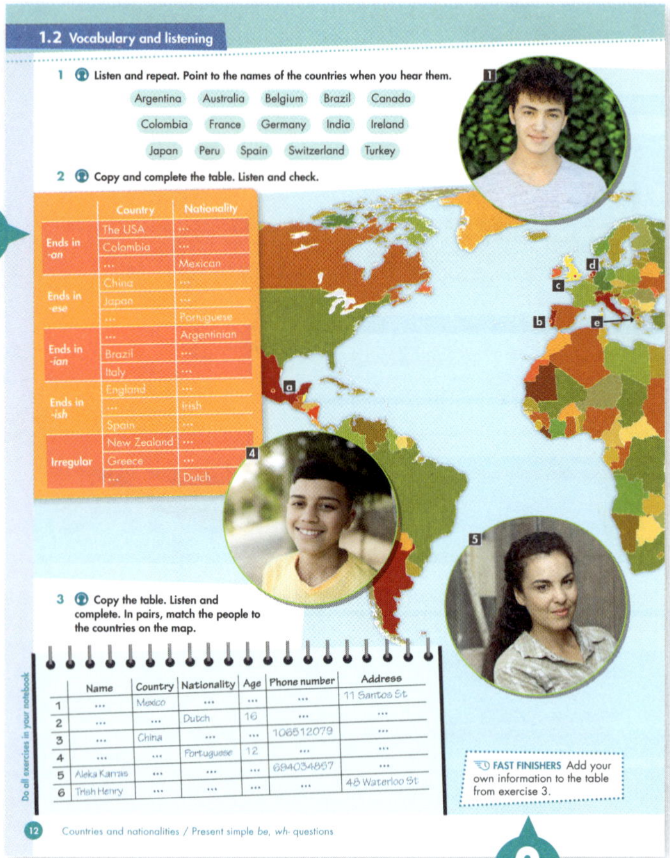

1.2 Vocabulary and listening

1 Listen and repeat. Point to the names of the countries when you hear them.

Argentina Australia Belgium Brazil Canada Colombia France Germany India Ireland Japan Peru Spain Switzerland Turkey

2 Copy and complete the table. Listen and check.

	Country	Nationality
Ends in *-an*	The USA	...
	Colombia	...
	...	Mexican
Ends in *-ese*	China	...
	Japan	...
	...	Portuguese
Ends in *-ian*	...	Argentinian
	Brazil	...
	Italy	...
Ends in *-ish*	England	...
	...	Irish
	Spain	...
Irregular	New Zealand	...
	Greece	...
	...	Dutch

3 Copy the table. Listen and complete. In pairs, match the people to the countries on the map.

	Name	Country	Nationality	Age	Phone number	Address
1	...	Mexico	...	...	...	11 Santos St
2	...	...	Dutch	16	...	...
3	...	China	...	...	106512079	...
4	...	...	Portuguese	12	...	...
5	Aleka Karras	...	...	...	694034857	...
6	Trish Henry	...	...	...	...	48 Waterloo St

FAST FINISHERS Add your own information to the table from exercise 3.

Do all exercises in your notebook

12 Countries and nationalities / Present simple *be*, *wh-* questions

2 There is a **Fast finishers** exercise in lessons 1, 2, 3 and 5 to keep stronger students challenged and engaged if they finish the other exercises quickly. These are short, personalised writing exercises that students can complete alone and could keep as part of a language diary.

3 Each grammar lesson contains a **Grammar table** that shows key structures. These tables show clear models which can be used as a quick reference to complete the accompanying exercises.

The connected **Grammar reference** page at the back of the book includes more detailed explanations of both form and use.

4 The **Grammar animations** present the grammar in an appealing visual format to help to engage the students and consolidate their understanding of the grammatical structures.
These animations also provide opportunities for **Flipped Learning**.

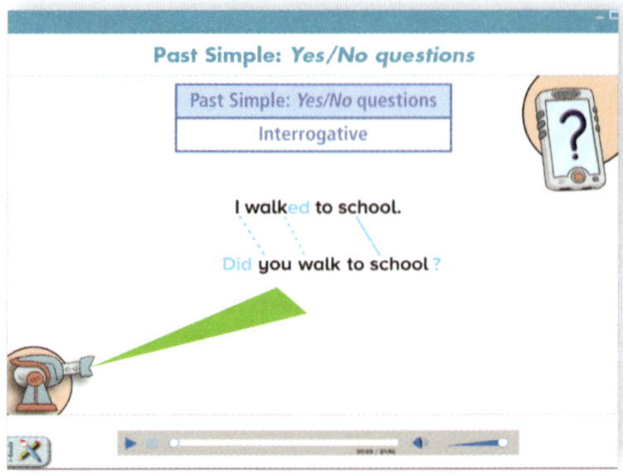

Unit walkthrough

LESSON 2 Grammar, Vocabulary and Listening

Grammar and vocabulary 1.2

PRESENT SIMPLE *BE*

I	am ('m)	from Poland.
He She It	is ('s)	12 years old. French. Monday today.
You We They	are ('re)	16 years old. from Japan. German.

Grammar reference page 107

PRESENT SIMPLE *BE*: *WH-* QUESTIONS

Where is she from? She is (She's) from Ecuador.
Where are they from?
They are (They're) from Portugal.
What is your name? It is (It's) Steven.

Grammar reference page 107

4 **Complete the conversation.**

Sam: Hello, nice to meet you.
Evan: Hi! What [1]… your name?
Sam: My name's Sam. What's your name?
Evan: [2]… Evan.
Sam: How old [3]… you?
Evan: [4]… 12. Where [5]… you from?
Sam: I'm from [6]…. I'm Irish. Where are you from?
Evan: I'm from America. I'm [7]….
Sam: Oh! Maria is American! [8]… from America, too!

SPEAKING TOOLS

To remember the pronunciation of a word, connect it in your mind to another word that sounds the same. For example, *nice* and *ice cream*.

Pronunciation: /aɪ/

5 **Listen and repeat.**

1 I
2 I'm fine.
3 Nice to meet you.
4 I'm from Ireland, I'm Irish.

PROJECT TASK 2 Survey

- In your teams, write two more survey questions. Include a question about nationality.
- Design a form to collect answers. Write your questions on the left-hand side and leave space on the right for your classmates' answers.

→ Workbook page 20

Do all exercises in your notebook.

Workbook pages 6 and 7 13

5 There is a **Learning to learn tool** for each skill across the unit which gives students strategies to help develop their listening, speaking, reading and writing skills, as well their ability to acquire, retain and use vocabulary.
The colour coding helps students identify the skills at a glance:

- Listening tools
- Reading tools
- Speaking tools
- Writing tools
- Vocabulary tools

6 There is a **pronunciation** exercise in each unit to develop students' ability to recognise and produce the different features of spoken English.

7 Further practice of the lesson content can be found in the **Workbook.**

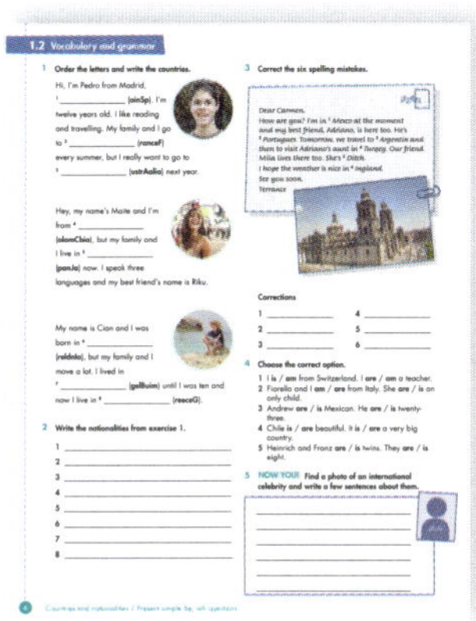

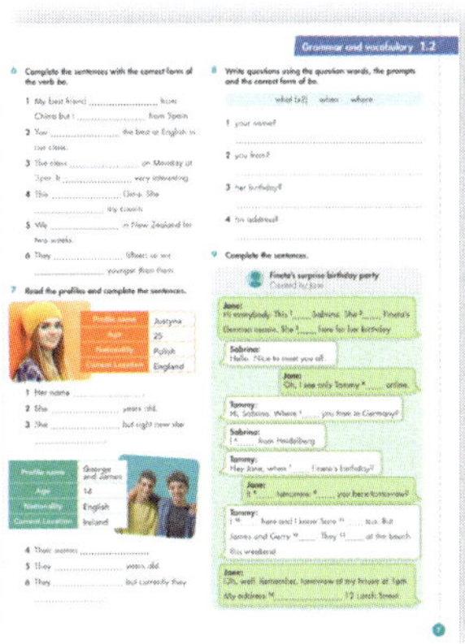

The **Teacher's Resources** provide students with worksheets for further practice of both **vocabulary** and **grammar** at their level — ideal for mixed-ability classes. Each worksheet comes at three levels of difficulty:

- Reinforcement — lower level
- Consolidation — course level
- Extension — higher level

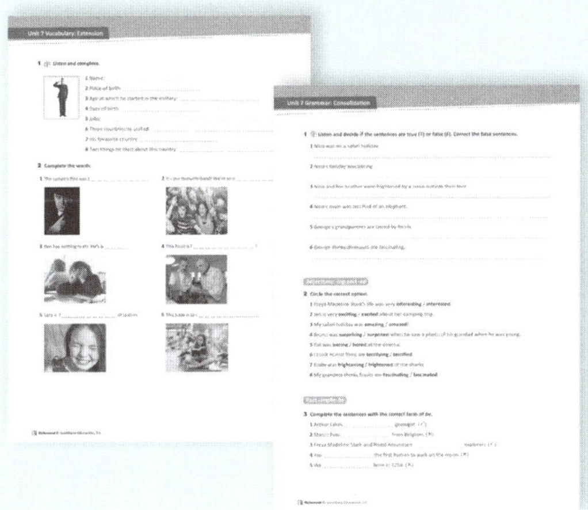

Unit walkthrough

LESSON 3 Reading

2

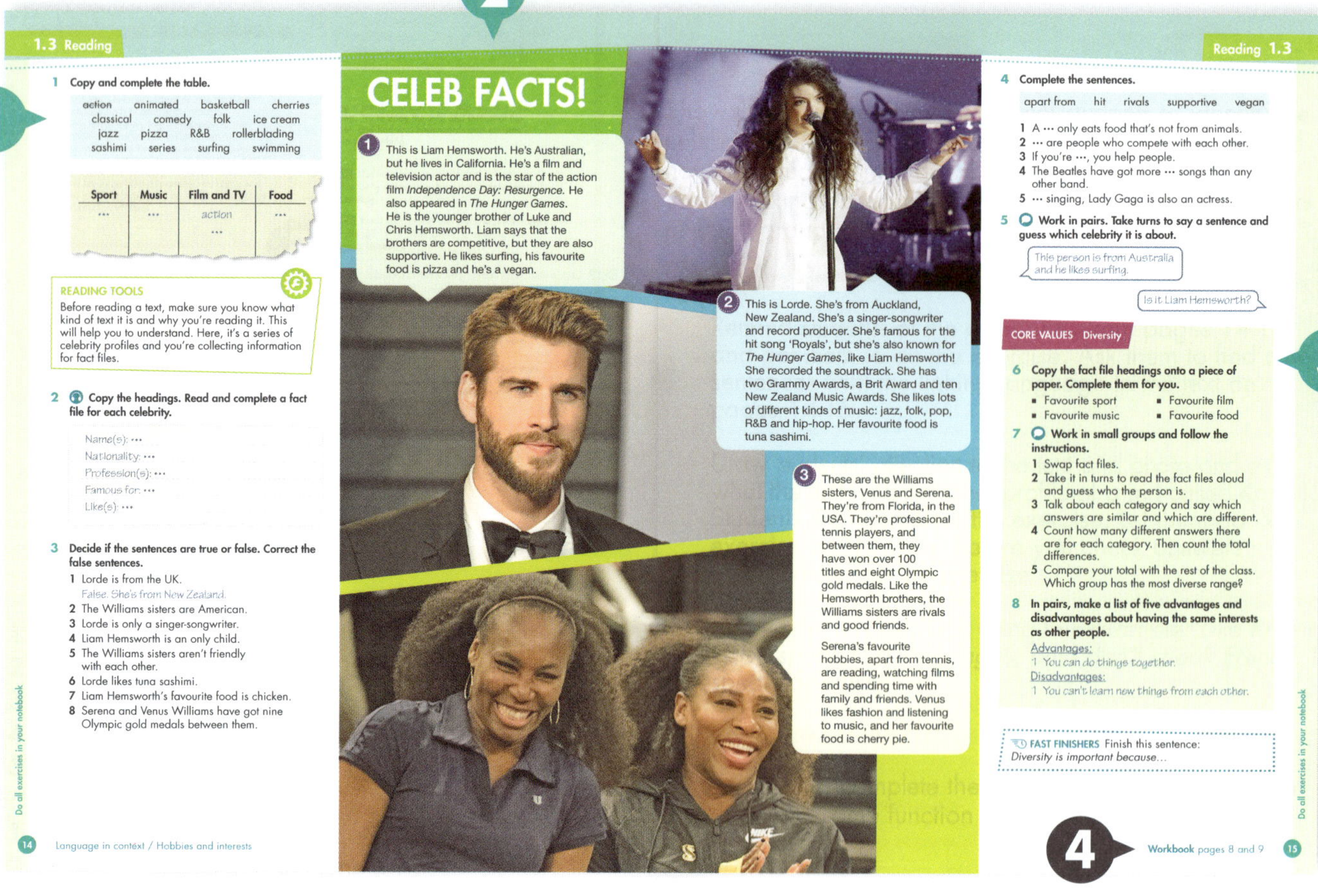

1.3 Reading

1 Copy and complete the table.

action animated basketball cherries classical comedy folk ice cream jazz pizza R&B rollerblading sashimi series surfing swimming

Sport	Music	Film and TV	Food
...	...	action ...	...

READING TOOLS
Before reading a text, make sure you know what kind of text it is and why you're reading it. This will help you to understand. Here, it's a series of celebrity profiles and you're collecting information for fact files.

2 Copy the headings. Read and complete a fact file for each celebrity.

Name(s): ...
Nationality: ...
Profession(s): ...
Famous for: ...
Like(s): ...

3 Decide if the sentences are true or false. Correct the false sentences.

1 Lorde is from the UK.
False. She's from New Zealand.
2 The Williams sisters are American.
3 Lorde is only a singer-songwriter.
4 Liam Hemsworth is an only child.
5 The Williams sisters aren't friendly with each other.
6 Lorde likes tuna sashimi.
7 Liam Hemsworth's favourite food is chicken.
8 Serena and Venus Williams have got nine Olympic gold medals between them.

Do all exercises in your notebook

14 Language in context / Hobbies and interests

CELEB FACTS!

1 This is Liam Hemsworth. He's Australian, but he lives in California. He's a film and television actor and is the star of the action film *Independence Day: Resurgence*. He also appeared in *The Hunger Games*. He is the younger brother of Luke and Chris Hemsworth. Liam says that the brothers are competitive, but they are also supportive. He likes surfing, his favourite food is pizza and he's a vegan.

2 This is Lorde. She's from Auckland, New Zealand. She's a singer-songwriter and record producer. She's famous for the hit song 'Royals', but she's also known for *The Hunger Games*, like Liam Hemsworth! She recorded the soundtrack. She has two Grammy Awards, a Brit Award and ten New Zealand Music Awards. She likes lots of different kinds of music: jazz, folk, pop, R&B and hip-hop. Her favourite food is tuna sashimi.

3 These are the Williams sisters, Venus and Serena. They're from Florida, in the USA. They're professional tennis players, and between them, they have won over 100 titles and eight Olympic gold medals. Like the Hemsworth brothers, the Williams sisters are rivals and good friends.

Serena's favourite hobbies, apart from tennis, are reading, watching films and spending time with family and friends. Venus likes fashion and listening to music, and her favourite food is cherry pie.

Reading 1.3

4 Complete the sentences.

apart from hit rivals supportive vegan

1 A ... only eats food that's not from animals.
2 ... are people who compete with each other.
3 If you're ..., you help people.
4 The Beatles have got more ... songs than any other band.
5 ... singing, Lady Gaga is also an actress.

5 Work in pairs. Take turns to say a sentence and guess which celebrity it is about.

This person is from Australia and he likes surfing.
Is it Liam Hemsworth?

CORE VALUES Diversity

6 Copy the fact file headings onto a piece of paper. Complete them for you.
- Favourite sport
- Favourite film
- Favourite music
- Favourite food

7 Work in small groups and follow the instructions.
1 Swap fact files.
2 Take it in turns to read the fact files aloud and guess who the person is.
3 Talk about each category and say which answers are similar and which are different.
4 Count how many different answers there are for each category. Then count the total differences.
5 Compare your total with the rest of the class. Which group has the most diverse range?

8 In pairs, make a list of five advantages and disadvantages about having the same interests as other people.
Advantages:
1 You can do things together.
Disadvantages:
1 You can't learn new things from each other.

FAST FINISHERS Finish this sentence:
Diversity is important because…

Workbook pages 8 and 9 15

Do all exercises in your notebook

1 The **reading** lesson contains exercises that guide students through the process of effective reading. They include pre-reading exercises, comprehension exercises and follow-up vocabulary and speaking exercises.

2 There are a range of **reading texts** that provide an accessible, authentic context and connect the content of the unit with the world outside the classroom.

3 The **Core values** section provides an opportunity for students to reflect on ideas and beliefs that are considered important in society and the effect these values have on how we behave. The emphasis is on understanding and respecting ourselves and others. This contextualisation of values helps to deepen the students' connection with the reading material and give a clear, communicative resolution to the lesson.

4 More reading practice can be found in the **Workbook**.

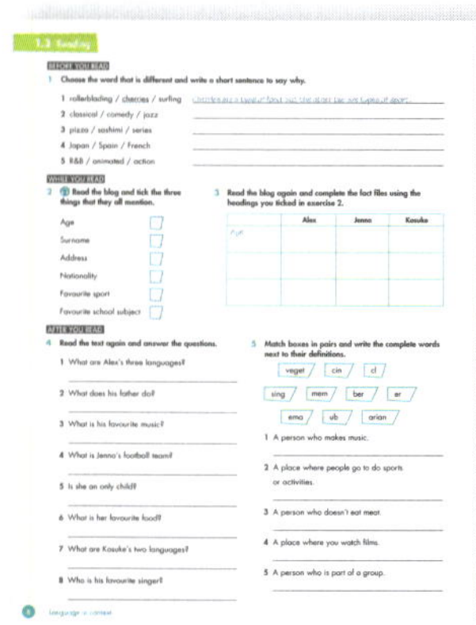

LESSON 4 Writing

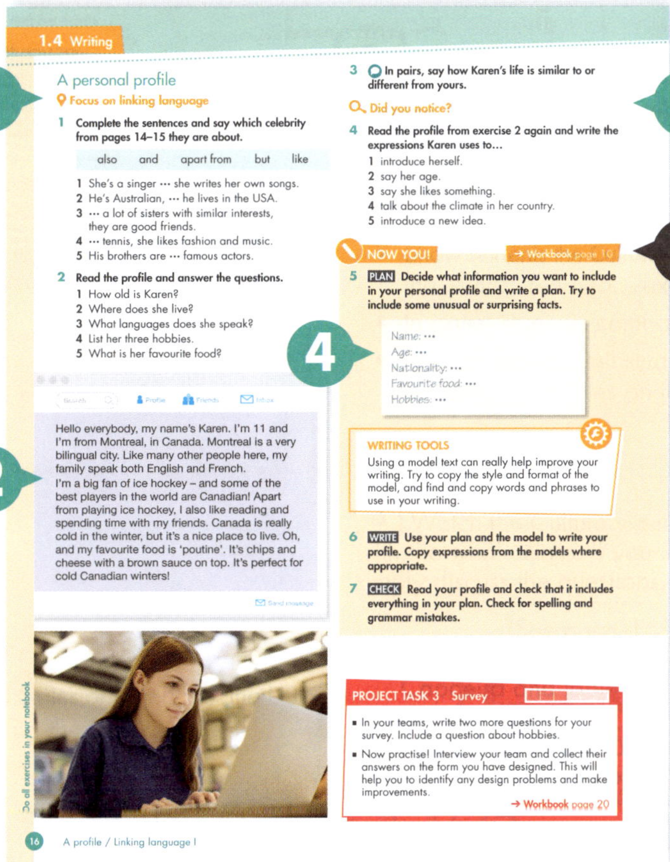
1.4 Writing

A personal profile

Focus on linking language

1 Complete the sentences and say which celebrity from pages 14–15 they are about.

also | and | apart from | but | like

1 She's a singer ··· she writes her own songs.
2 He's Australian, ··· he lives in the USA.
3 ··· a lot of sisters with similar interests, they are good friends.
4 ··· tennis, she likes fashion and music.
5 His brothers are ··· famous actors.

2 Read the profile and answer the questions.
1 How old is Karen?
2 Where does she live?
3 What languages does she speak?
4 List her three hobbies.
5 What is her favourite food?

Hello everybody, my name's Karen. I'm 11 and I'm from Montreal, in Canada. Montreal is a very bilingual city. Like many other people here, my family speak both English and French.
I'm a big fan of ice hockey – and some of the best players in the world are Canadian! Apart from playing ice hockey, I also like reading and spending time with my friends. Canada is really cold in the winter, but it's a nice place to live. Oh, and my favourite food is 'poutine'. It's chips and cheese with a brown sauce on top. It's perfect for cold Canadian winters!

3 In pairs, say how Karen's life is similar to or different from yours.

Did you notice?

4 Read the profile from exercise 2 again and write the expressions Karen uses to…
1 introduce herself.
2 say her age.
3 say she likes something.
4 talk about the climate in her country.
5 introduce a new idea.

NOW YOU! → Workbook page 10

5 PLAN Decide what information you want to include in your personal profile and write a plan. Try to include some unusual or surprising facts.

Name: ···
Age: ···
Nationality: ···
Favourite food: ···
Hobbies: ···

WRITING TOOLS
Using a model text can really help improve your writing. Try to copy the style and format of the model, and find and copy words and phrases to use in your writing.

6 WRITE Use your plan and the model to write your profile. Copy expressions from the models where appropriate.

7 CHECK Read your profile and check that it includes everything in your plan. Check for spelling and grammar mistakes.

PROJECT TASK 3 Survey
- In your teams, write two more questions for your survey. Include a question about hobbies.
- Now practise! Interview your team and collect their answers on the form you have designed. This will help you to identify any design problems and make improvements.
→ Workbook page 20

Do all exercises in your notebook

16 A profile / Linking language I

1 The **Focus on** section gives students an opportunity to revise language they have learnt that will be useful in completing the writing task.

2 A **model text** of the same type required in the writing task provides students with an appropriate scaffold of structure, style and language. The texts are of a range of genres and cover text types and linguistic conventions required in external exams.

3 The **Did you notice?** section highlights contextualised language, style and structural features of the model text for the students to include in their writing.

4 The **NOW YOU!** writing task has **Plan**, **Write** and **Check** exercises to give students a step-by-step guide to producing an appropriate written text, drawing on language they have learnt.

5 The **Workbook** contains a dedicated area per unit for students to complete the writing task. This allows students to build up their own portfolio of writing work.

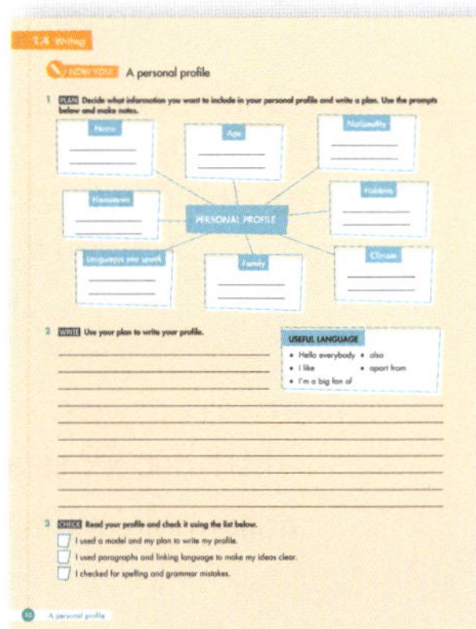

Unit walkthrough

LESSON 5 Culture and Communication

1 The lesson starts with a **Culture video** introduced by the unit vlogger that gives students a window on the world from a cultural perspective using natural language.

As with the **Vlog** at the beginning of the unit, students' responses to the discussion questions will be informed by the content of the video; however, the questions can also be answered by students who have not seen the video.

Understanding of the video is consolidated in the optional **Culture video worksheets** available in the **Teacher's Resources**.

2 Themed sets of **Idioms and expressions** highlight natural, everyday language and phrases. This increases students' confidence by deepening understanding of English as spoken by native speakers and developing fluency.

3 The **Pairwork** exercises provide communicative tasks which practise the target language in line with **CEFR mediation descriptors**. Students analyse, interpret and exchange information using key language from the unit.

Culture and communication 1.5

Irish dancing

Discuss the questions.
1 What are your hobbies?
2 What do you like most about them?
3 How often do you do or practise them?
4 Do you do them with other people?

1 Listen and complete the information.

1 Name: ··· Country: ··· Favourite part of hobby: ···

2 Name: ··· Nationality: ··· When he practises: ···

3 Name: ··· Age: ··· Who she plays with: ···

Idioms and expressions for determination

Idioms and expressions

2 Match the expressions you heard with their meanings.
1 reach for the stars
2 throw in the towel
3 practice makes perfect

a To do something many times, until you are very good at it.
b To be ambitious and aim to do something difficult.
c To stop doing something because it's too difficult.

SPEAKING TOOLS
Listen to audios a few times while you read, and say the words at the same time in your head. Can you say the words in the same way?

3 Read and choose the correct option. Listen and check your answers.

My name's Sarah. [1] I'm / She's from England. I like dancing to hip-hop. [2] We're / It's not easy to learn the dance moves, but practice makes [3] perfect / good! Hip-hop's main instruments are drum machines and synthesisers. I like hip-hop lyrics about politics and family.

My best friend is Lisa. She's from Ireland. [4] He's / She's 13 years old, like me! Lisa plays the guitar really well. She likes reggae. She practises every day and she never [5] throws / puts in the towel. She wants to be famous. I believe she can do it. Reach for the [6] stars / sun, Lisa!

4 NOW YOU! Tell your partner about your hobbies. Try to use the new expressions in exercise 2.

PAIRWORK
Student A: go to page 99
Student B: go to page 103

Unit 1 Review • page 90
Wordlist • pages 117–120

Workbook page 11

17

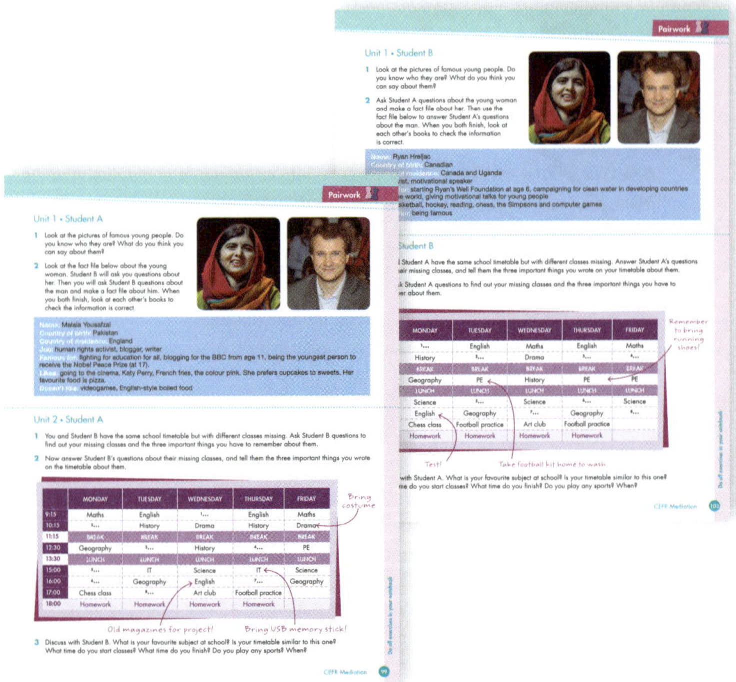

LESSON 5 Culture and Communication

4 The **Unit reviews** help students to revise the language from the unit and practise for external exams. The reading, writing, listening and speaking tasks mirror external exam format and provide comprehensive exam practice.

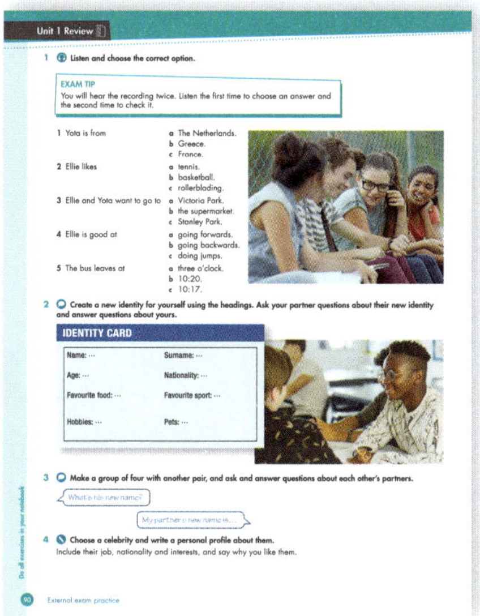

5 The **Wordlist** for each unit helps students to revise the main vocabulary from the unit. The wordlists include key and high frequency words from the unit. There is also an irregular verb list for reference.

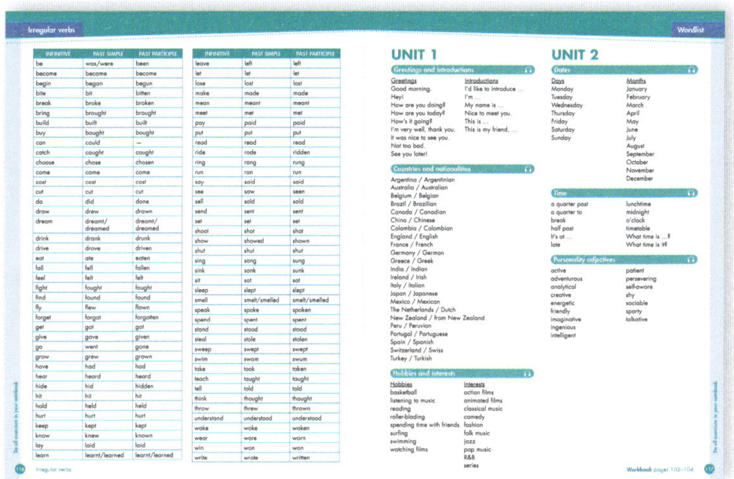

6 In the **Workbook** students will find further practice of the **Idioms and expressions** along with a **Reflect on your learning** table for them to assess their progress using 'I can' statements.

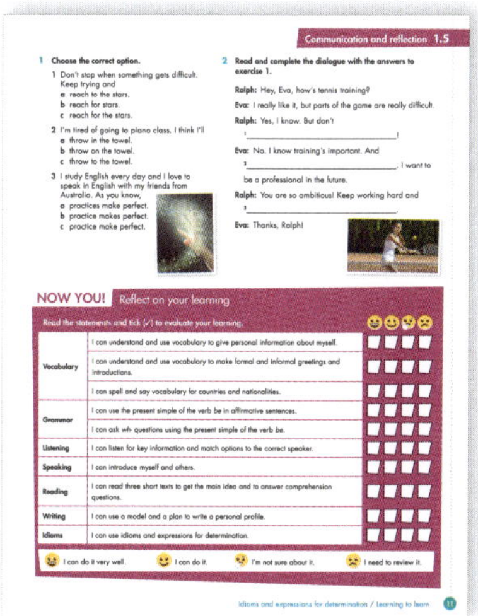

The **Teacher's Resources** contain **tests** which can be used at the end of every unit, term and year. Students can be tested on their knowledge of vocabulary and grammar along with their skills development at two levels of difficulty:

- Consolidation — course level
- Extension — higher level

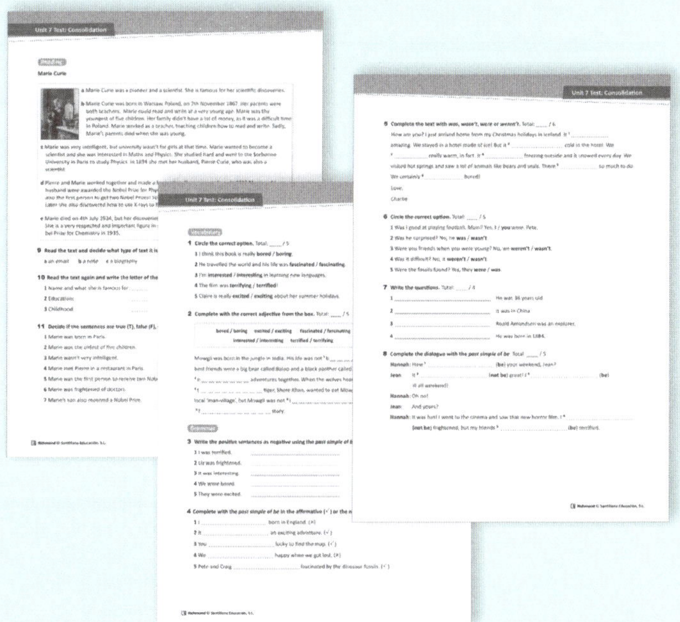

Unit walkthrough

PROJECT

1 At the end of lessons 1, 2, and 4 of each unit students complete a project task. There are six tasks spread over two units. These tasks build towards a final project. The **Recap** section reflects on the six project tasks students have undertaken over the course of these units.
Each of these tasks requires students to apply the knowledge they have acquired in each lesson, which helps boost their motivation.

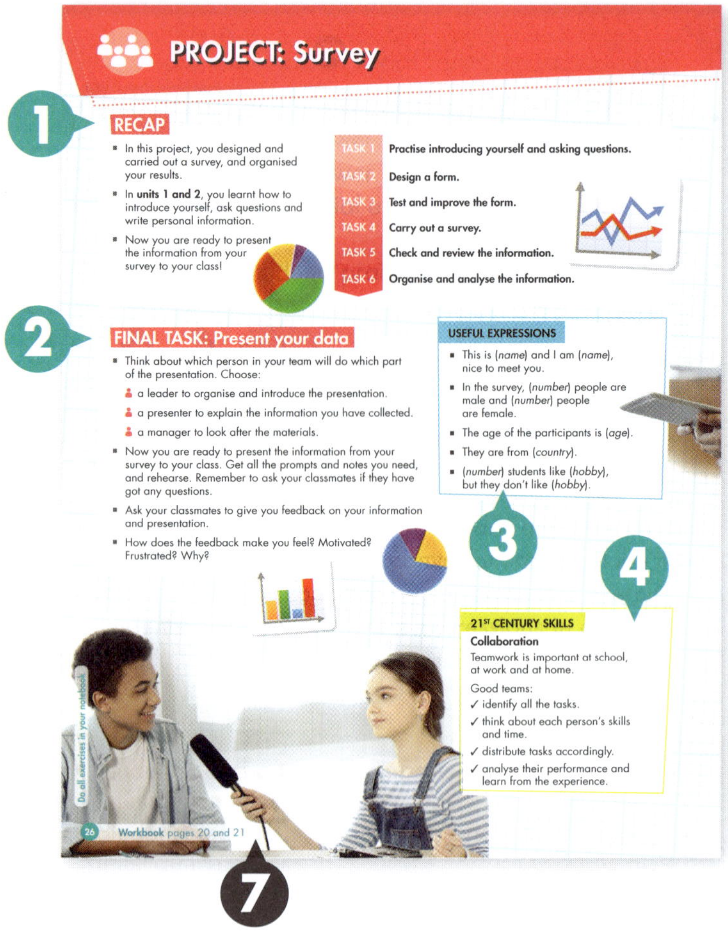

PROJECT: Survey

1 RECAP

- In this project, you designed and carried out a survey, and organised your results.
- In **units 1 and 2**, you learnt how to introduce yourself, ask questions and write personal information.
- Now you are ready to present the information from your survey to your class!

TASK 1	Practise introducing yourself and asking questions.
TASK 2	Design a form.
TASK 3	Test and improve the form.
TASK 4	Carry out a survey.
TASK 5	Check and review the information.
TASK 6	Organise and analyse the information.

2 FINAL TASK: Present your data

- Think about which person in your team will do which part of the presentation. Choose:
  - a leader to organise and introduce the presentation.
  - a presenter to explain the information you have collected.
  - a manager to look after the materials.
- Now you are ready to present the information from your survey to your class. Get all the prompts and notes you need, and rehearse. Remember to ask your classmates if they have got any questions.
- Ask your classmates to give you feedback on your information and presentation.
- How does the feedback make you feel? Motivated? Frustrated? Why?

USEFUL EXPRESSIONS

- This is (*name*) and I am (*name*), nice to meet you.
- In the survey, (*number*) people are male and (*number*) people are female.
- The age of the participants is (*age*).
- They are from (*country*).
- (*number*) students like (*hobby*), but they don't like (*hobby*).

3

4

21st CENTURY SKILLS

Collaboration

Teamwork is important at school, at work and at home.

Good teams:

✓ identify all the tasks.
✓ think about each person's skills and time.
✓ distribute tasks accordingly.
✓ analyse their performance and learn from the experience.

Do all exercises in your notebook

26 Workbook pages 20 and 21

7

2 The **Final task** is where students come together to organise, refine and present their work. The projects are conceived as multi-skill activities that develop students' ability to collaborate and to express their knowledge, aptitudes, interests and feelings.

3 The **Useful expressions** are a list of phrases that students can incorporate into the final presentation.

4 The **21st century skills** box shows students how the soft skills they have developed during the project can be useful to them outside the classroom. This helps the students to see how they can apply broader skills they have developed in the classroom to the real world.

PROJECT

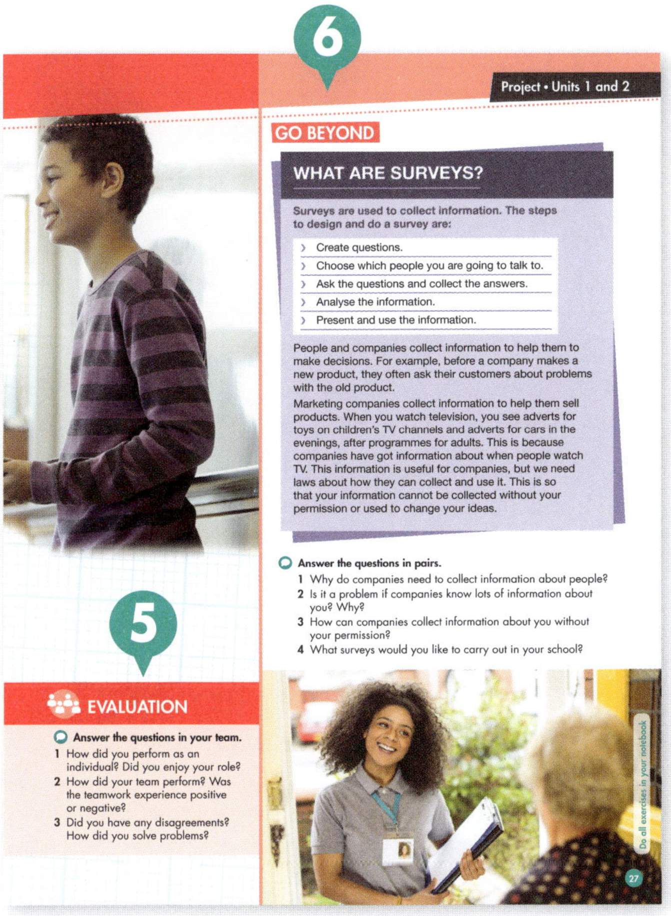
Project • Units 1 and 2

GO BEYOND

WHAT ARE SURVEYS?

Surveys are used to collect information. The steps to design and do a survey are:

- Create questions.
- Choose which people you are going to talk to.
- Ask the questions and collect the answers.
- Analyse the information.
- Present and use the information.

People and companies collect information to help them to make decisions. For example, before a company makes a new product, they often ask their customers about problems with the old product.

Marketing companies collect information to help them sell products. When you watch television, you see adverts for toys on children's TV channels and adverts for cars in the evenings, after programmes for adults. This is because companies have got information about when people watch TV. This information is useful for companies, but we need laws about how they can collect and use it. This is so that your information cannot be collected without your permission or used to change your ideas.

Answer the questions in pairs.

1 Why do companies need to collect information about people?
2 Is it a problem if companies know lots of information about you? Why?
3 How can companies collect information about you without your permission?
4 What surveys would you like to carry out in your school?

EVALUATION

Answer the questions in your team.

1 How did you perform as an individual? Did you enjoy your role?
2 How did your team perform? Was the teamwork experience positive or negative?
3 Did you have any disagreements? How did you solve problems?

Do all exercises in your notebook

27

5 The **Evaluation** questions help students to evaluate individual and team performance from the context of the 21st century skills. This process of reflection promotes a thoughtful approach to the learning process.

6 The **Go beyond** section takes a closer look at an aspect of the project theme. This can be used as a vehicle for class discussion or as a fast finishers activity for students who complete the final task ahead of time.

7 In the **Workbook** the students are provided with a **project notes** organiser to complete each of the project tasks. This ensures that students have all the notes and ideas at hand, creating a portfolio of their work which they can look back on for evaluation purposes.

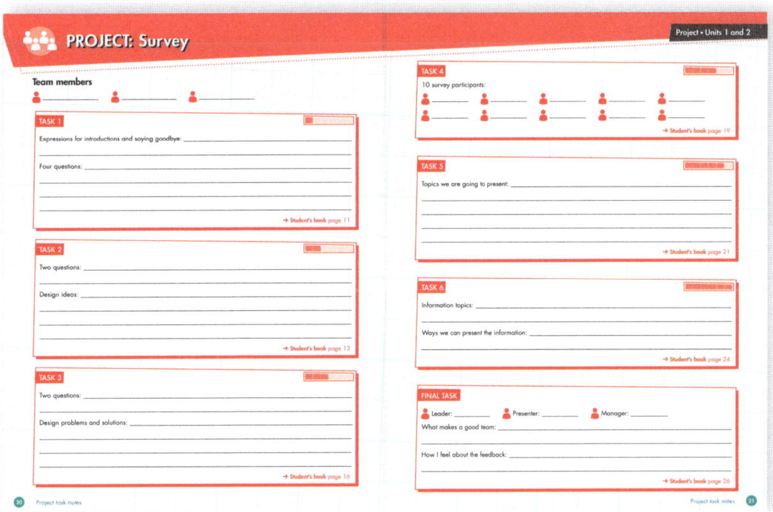
PROJECT: Survey

Project • Units 1 and 2

Team members

TASK 1
Expressions for introductions and saying goodbye:
Four questions:
→ Student's book page 11

TASK 2
Two questions:
Design ideas:
→ Student's book page 13

TASK 3
Two questions:
Design problems and solutions:
→ Student's book page 16

TASK 4
10 survey participants:
→ Student's book page 19

TASK 5
Topics we are going to present:
→ Student's book page 21

TASK 6
Information topics:
Ways we can present the information:
→ Student's book page 24

FINAL TASK
Leader: Presenter: Manager:
What makes a good team:
How I feel about the feedback:
→ Student's book page 26

Project task notes

Video material

The benefits of learning through video

Video is an essential tool in today's ELT classroom and should be embraced as one of the most important resources for learning by both teachers and students alike. Not only does video offer many benefits for students, it is also the **preferred medium of content** for teenagers all over the world. Videos allow students to engage and **connect with English** in a way that written texts do not. This feeling of connection is one of the most **powerful motivational tools** available when learning a language.

Language input and review

Video is a useful tool **for introducing new language** – grammar, vocabulary and functional language. It provides a natural, more complete context for the language, which helps students develop a more **thorough understanding of how the language is used**. Videos give students information about register and pronunciation, as well as lots of audiovisual clues to aid understanding like tone of voice, gestures and facial expressions. This also helps **memory retention**, especially when language is reviewed in subsequent videos. Videos are a very **dynamic review tool**.

Video is also a vital resource for **Flipped Learning**, a dynamic educational model whereby students begin learning new structures by watching a video at home. This is particularly useful for mixed-ability classes because students can learn at their own pace. For more on **Flipped Learning**, see pages 20-23.

Key competences

Video material is also an excellent opportunity to instil **Key competences for lifelong learning**, which encourage students to become responsible citizens in 21st century communities (see **Key competences** pages 42-43). As well as **Linguistic competence**, video helps build these two competences:

- **Cultural awareness and expression:** videos show students how people live and express themselves around the world, thus promoting cultural empathy.
- **Digital competence:** students can gain confidence using digital technologies for learning. This is particularly relevant for students who may be at risk of digital exclusion.

The **videos in NOW YOU! have been specifically designed to appeal to teenage students** of English. They are presented in formats that teenagers enjoy and are familiar with. There are three types of video, as outlined below and explained in more detail on the next page.

NOW YOU! videos at a glance

VLOGS

- A **Vlog** about the daily life of the vlogger at the start of every unit.
- **Teacher's Resources** include a **Vlog worksheet** to be completed in class or at home (**Flipped Learning**).

CULTURE VIDEOS

- A **Culture video** narrated by the vlogger to extend the students' knowledge of the world.
- **Teacher's Resources** include a **Culture video worksheet** to be completed in class or for homework.

GRAMMAR ANIMATIONS

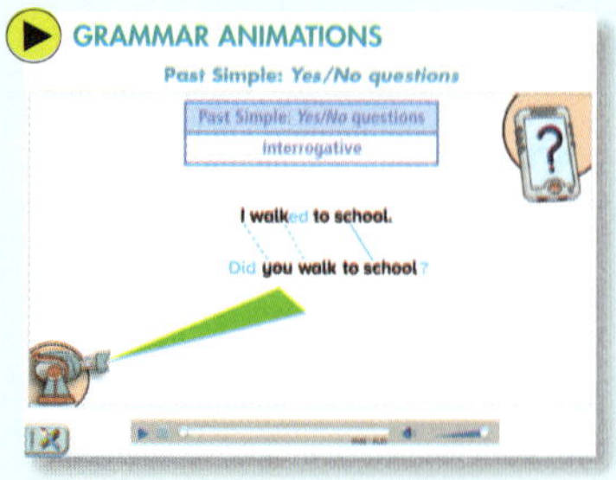

- A **Grammar animation** for every **Grammar table**.
- To be watched either in class or at home (**Flipped Learning**).

How the NOW YOU! videos work

Vlogs and Culture videos

The **Vlogs** and **Culture videos** are used to present and review unit themes and key language, and reflect the way teenagers engage with the world around them. Both videos revolve around **three age-appropriate teenage characters** who are dealing with **authentic, relevant topics** that students can easily identify with. Students hear the unit language being used naturally in context by a native speaker, with visual support from **gifs, emoticons, key words** on screen and, of course, **subtitles**.

The characters' stories evolve throughout the course, from the **Get started!** unit, where students meet the characters, to **Unit 9,** where they say goodbye to them for the summer break. This continuity creates anticipation for the next unit and serves as a memory aid for previous units. There are worksheets to help students get the most out of the videos in the **Teacher's Resources**. Both **Vlog** and **Culture video worksheets** can be used in class and both include exercises to prepare students to watch the videos, to guide them as they watch and to consolidate what they have watched in a way that is personal and accessible to students at all levels of competence. The **Vlog worksheets can also be flipped** (see **Flipped Learning** pages 20-23).

Grammar animations

The **Grammar animations** are a series of fun animations that bring grammar to life for young digital natives. They feature a character called Grammar Gadget, an enthusiastic smartphone in training. It interacts with a group of teenagers on a wide variety of **digital platforms** such as chats and apps. Through their interactions, Grammar Gadget **learns new grammar**, saving it onto its system and **building on it as the level progresses**. Grammar Gadget breaks down each grammar point on screen, so that **students learn along with it**. There are often **multiple grammar animations for each grammar point**. This allows students to focus on each grammar point individually before using them together in subsequent activities. **Like the Vlogs, the Grammar animations can be watched in class or flipped** (see **Flipped Learning** pages 20-23).

All videos and worksheets available on the Richmond*Learning***Platform**

Flipped Learning

What is Flipped Learning?

Flipped Learning is an educational model originally developed by Aaron Sams and John Bergmann, two high school teachers in the US, as a strategy for meeting the needs of students who could not attend class. They started by sending them informative videos so that they did not fall behind in their studies. They realised that by providing such videos to all students before class, students could spend class time discussing content, experimenting with the material and receiving assistance from their teachers. Little by little, teachers discovered the benefits and possibilities offered by this model and it was perfected and extended over time.

In a traditional class, teachers first explain new material to their students in the classroom and students subsequently apply that information to class work or homework. In a **Flipped classroom**, this order is reversed or 'flipped'; students first engage with the new material at home and then apply their newly learnt knowledge in the classroom. This approach was born in the digital age and has become increasingly relevant to the challenges facing students preparing to become citizens of the of the 21st century and their teachers. Today, students can access educational content more easily than ever before, and because of this, the teacher's role is no longer merely to transmit content but to be a guide in the education process, awakening the students' curiosity for learning and helping them to develop the skills that will allow them to become more autonomous learners.

Flipped Learning benefits

The benefits of **Flipped Learning** can be divided into three main areas.

Competences and skills

- It develops the student's **Digital competence** and **audio-visual language**.
- It works as an **initial, autonomous evaluation of the student's understanding of vocabulary and grammar**.
- It promotes the development of the student's **Learning to learn competence**.
- It **promotes creativity**.

Methodological and pedagogical

- It allows the teacher to **save class time** and thus significantly increases opportunities to reinforce the key content and **complete tasks in the classroom**.
- It anticipates the context of the lesson and ensures that **each student can work at their own pace** to get ready for the class.
- It maximises the use of the course resources.
- It allows **multidimensional work** through video images and audio to encourage the student's **comprehension** and **memory**.
- It allows the teacher to include a **wider diversity of tasks** that promote different **thinking skills** and richer access to learning.

Emotional

- It helps **build confidence** by giving students a more active role in their own learning.
- It **motivates** students because it brings classroom work into their real lives. This allows students to **link what they are learning to their emotions, feelings and experiences**.
- It **personalises learning** so that each student can access the new content as often as needed without restriction.
- It provides a space for work on content and pronunciation **in a climate of safety and trust**.

Flipped Learning in NOW YOU!

NOW YOU! has two main resources that favour **Flipped Learning**. These resources can be used to promote change in the English classroom in order to **motivate students** to participate actively in their own learning process and take responsibility for it.

They can also be used to anticipate the content of the next lesson. This encourages **meta-learning** and helps the students to be aware of what will happen in the classroom later. This awareness promotes **security** and **confidence** in our students.

The **Vlog** at the start of every unit anticipates and facilitates the introduction of both the unit theme and the new vocabulary in an engaging context.

SARAH'S VLOG: Family and friends

All the **Grammar animations** can be used to anticipate the presentation of the key grammar structure or structures of each unit. **Grammar Gadget** presents the grammar rules in a very **systematic and standardised** way to facilitate the understanding of each rule and improve the **student's long-term learning and memory**.

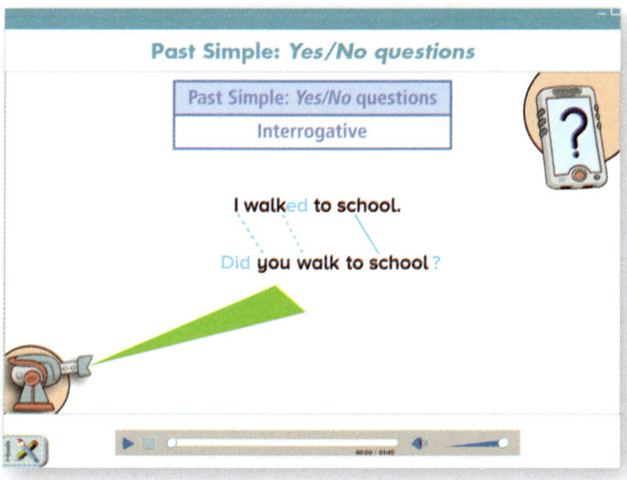

How to get started

Using **Flipped Learning** involves a **commitment on the part of both students and teachers**, each one accepting their role and responsibility. It is advisable that the **starting point** be to **inform the students about this approach** before beginning to use the dynamics of **Flipped Learning** in **NOW YOU!** It is very important that students understand **the benefits that Flipped Learning brings to their global learning process**.

In order to help teachers explain to students how the model works, the **Flipped Learning visual guide** below can be downloaded and printed from the **Richmond***Learning***Platform** to be given out to students during setup.

All the students need to have **access to a computer or mobile device, and internet connection at home**.

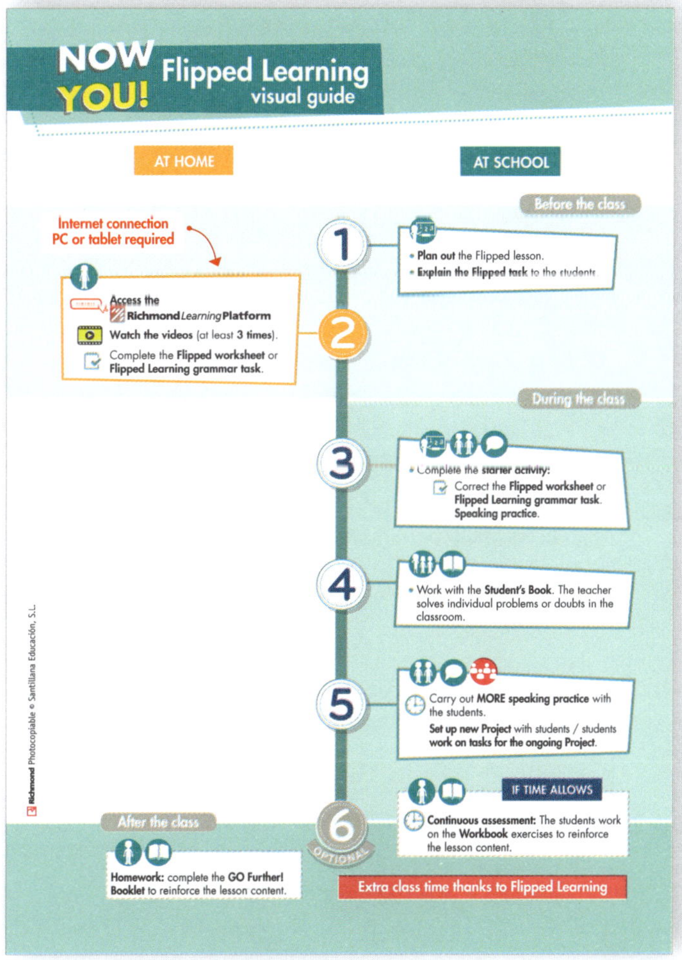

Flipped Learning

How to flip the Vlog

The unit theme is introduced by **watching the Vlog from Lesson 1 at home**. Not only is the content specifically tailored to the relevant age group, the videos are also based on popular formats the students are familiar with and will therefore easily hold their attention.

The videos are available for students on the **Richmond***Learning***Platform**, in a section called **Flipped Learning**. Explain to the students that they have to register on the platform using the **access code included in their Student's Book**. The videos can be viewed from any device, whether it be a computer, mobile or tablet.

SARAH'S VLOG: Family and friends

Before the start of a new unit, the students take home a task that will promote participation and autonomous learning. **Explain the task** in advance in class as follows:

1 **Give a copy of the Flipped worksheet** to each student so they can complete it at home. Make sure it is clear what they have to do. The worksheets are available for teachers in **PDF** format in the **Teacher's Resources** on the **Richmond***Learning***Platform**.

AT HOME

2 The students read all the exercises to get an overall vision of the task and then **complete the** Before you watch section in the **Flipped worksheet** that was given out in the previous class. These worksheets are also available for the students on the **Richmond***Learning***Platform**.

3 The students watch the **Vlog** at least 3 times:

- **A first time** where the video is played all the way through.
- **A second time** stopping at moments of interest to answer the questions in the While you watch section in the **Flipped worksheet**.
- **A third time** to check that the content has been understood. This time it is also played without stopping and students should be encouraged to practise the pronunciation of key words while they watch it.

If there are students who need to watch the video more than 3 times, encourage them to do so. The important thing is that **each student can work at their own pace and come to the next class prepared.** This approach adapts to the learning process of each student.

4 The students complete the After you watch section in the **Flipped worksheet**. The worksheet must be returned to the classroom so the teacher can check that the initial work with the new unit has been done.

AT SCHOOL

5 Once in the classroom, the starter activity of the unit will be to check that the video has been watched, the **Flipped worksheet** completed, and the content understood. This starter activity practises speaking skills and the students use the completed **Flipped worksheets** to participate.

6 After this starter activity has been carried out, the new content is then used in more complex, communicative and active ways during the rest of the class. Some of the **Student's Book** exercises can then be skipped to save time for the **Project tasks**.

Flipped Learning

How to flip a grammar lesson

The **animated grammar presentations** in **NOW YOU!** provide **clear step-by-step explanations** for all the grammar rules covered in the course, ensuring **students can work autonomously**.

Any grammar lesson in the Student's Book can be flipped. However, if teachers have already used the Flipped Learning approach for the start of the unit, it is advisable to flip the grammar presentation in Lesson 2. Remember the videos are available for students on the **Richmond***Learning***Platform**, in a section called **Flipped Learning**.

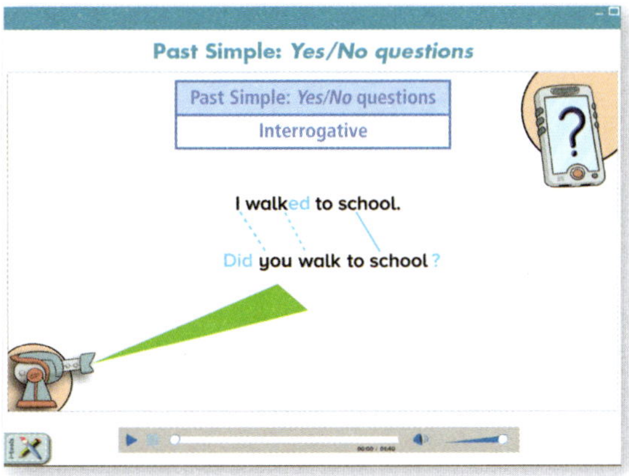

1 **Before the start of Lesson 2**, give students one of these **Flipped Learning grammar** tasks to complete at home:

- Write five true/false sentences using the grammar structure to be shared in class.
- Write five sentences with a word missing for a classmate to complete.
- Write a short dialogue to perform with a classmate in class.
- Write a short quiz of 5 questions and the answers to be shared in class.
- Write a short message for a classmate to reply to using the grammar structure.

AT HOME

2 The students watch the animated grammar presentations before the start of the grammar lesson. Note there may be more than one video for each key grammar structure in the **Student's Book**. The students should **watch each video at least 3 times**:

- **A first time** where they watch the presentation all the way through without stopping.
- **A second time** stopping the presentation several times in order to focus on the most important aspects and write down questions to take to class.
- **A third time** to check that the content has been understood. They watch without stopping while trying to practise the pronunciation and intonation of questions and statements.

If there are students who need to watch the video more than 3 times, encourage them to do so. The important thing is that **each student can work at their own pace and come to the class prepared**. This approach adapts to the learning process of each student.

3 The students **complete** the **Flipped task** that was explained by the teacher in the previous class. The **Flipped task** must be seen in the classroom so the teacher can check the student's understanding of the grammar rule shown in the video(s).

AT SCHOOL

4 When teaching the lesson where the grammar table appears, check that the grammar presentation(s) have been watched at home, the **Flipped task** completed and the content understood.

5 Resolve individual queries and help the students who still have problems with the grammar structures while the rest of their classmates focus on the **Student's Book** exercises individually or in pairs.

Projects

Project-based Learning

Project-based Learning is a method in which students learn through completing real-world projects. The project is completed over a period of time and is an opportunity for students to demonstrate their knowledge and skills and apply them in a practical context, as well as learning from each other.

During the project, the students also learn new skills through the vehicle of the project itself. These skills include not just linguistic skills, but also **higher-order thinking skills** such as **reasoning**, **problem solving** and **critical thinking**, and equally importantly **soft skills** such as **communication** and **collaboration**.

Collaborative Learning

Collaborative Learning is an approach in which groups of learners work together to complete a task, solve a problem or create a product. Collaborative tasks can be outlined and explained to the student; however, the responsibility for checking that tasks are understood and completed appropriately lies with them. Similarly, each participant in the group is responsible for not only their own actions, but the completion of the final product. This in turn encourages exploratory talk within the group into how the work will be completed.

Students are encouraged to **formulate and challenge ideas**, learn to manage and deliver **feedback** and develop **time management skills**. Group members work together to accomplish the shared learning goal, which encourages students to respect the abilities and contributions of their peers.

Unlike more dictated structures of team-based learning, consensus building in collaborative learning relies on cooperation by group members and their identification of the personality types in their group. This method empowers the students to take responsibility for their own learning process and develop their ability to communicate with others.

Project-based Learning and Collaborative Learning in NOW YOU!

Based on the principle that students learn best when engaged in meaningful tasks which involve knowledge, comprehension and production skills, **NOW YOU!** includes many activities which motivate students to use language meaningfully, communicatively and cooperatively.

Each **Project** in **NOW YOU!** is a natural space for **Project-based Learning** and **Collaborative Learning** skills. Students are asked to think carefully about the format of their project and to evaluate themselves and their peers, encouraging them to see the importance of effective collaboration. The tasks draw on the content of the lesson and in this way, students understand the purpose of the target language they are learning rather than understanding it as an isolated verbatim linguistic structure.

By drawing the students' attention to the accumulative nature of their work and the ways in which their own performance affects the members of their group, they also develop metacognitive skills. Students will become aware of their progress, and they will also be presented with concrete examples of how their new knowledge is useful to them.

Challenge-based Learning

Challenge-based Learning is a collaborative experience in which students identify and propose a solution, then implement and evaluate it, finally culminating in a public presentation of a final product. The holistic process encourages students to identify their approach to a problem, develop the material and then reflect on their learning process.

The framework for **Challenge-based Learning** was developed with a focus on real-world challenges. However, this specific skills process can be developed through any task which calls for students to reflect on the key steps involved in solving a problem. Students are called upon to identify an issue, ask appropriate questions to develop their understanding and then develop a method to complete the task. When faced with a challenge, successful groups are able to use their relevant experience, identify and employ available resources, develop a plan and find the best solution to the problem that is posed.

Challenge-based Learning in NOW YOU!

The **Projects** can be used as a vehicle for **developing Challenge-based Learning skills**. In order to do this, the teacher should invert the sequence of the presentation of the project tasks to the students as outlined below. In this way, students are encouraged to understand the importance of both the content and the method by which the final product is created. This will motivate the students' learning experience, help to develop their relevant soft skills and create learner autonomy. This method will also help the students to connect with the language they learn as they begin to understand the learning process as delivering them with useful building blocks for communication and not isolated linguistic content.

Using Challenge-based Learning skills to frame the Project experience

Before beginning each pair of units, direct the students to the **Recap** and **Final task** boxes on the **Project** pages (see the **Project** section of the **Unit walkthrough** on pages 16-17). Promote a discussion either as a class or in small groups about the **Final task** the students will be working towards. Encourage the students to think about the materials, knowledge and the types of personal qualities that will best help them to complete the task.

On page 26 you will find a list detailing ways in which the **Project tasks** can be adapted. This list can be shared with the students, and as a class they can decide the best way to complete the tasks for each particular project.

Once the students have engaged with the **Final task** and method in which they will complete the tasks, direct their attention back to the first lesson of the pair of units. Before you begin teaching each lesson, ask the students to read the contents of the **Project task** box. By framing their learning experience in this way, the students will come to understand their language learning in terms of its real-world application.

Projects

The benefits of projects

Encouraging students to work effectively in groups towards a final product has many benefits. The structured and practical tasks give students an immediate opportunity to practise the language and structures they have learnt during the lesson, which develops their **confidence** and **fluency**. These tasks also improve **motivation** due to the immediate, real world application of skills students have learnt on the page.

Projects provide a natural space for the development of **Mediation skills** (see pages 30-33). As students think together and work together in order to complete a project, they are given a space to grow their **social competence** and **self-esteem**. As students reflect on their contribution to the group's success or failure, they are also made aware of the need for **positive, supportive interactions**. Finally, the structure of the tasks themselves encourage **responsibility, learner independence** and **time management skills**.

How to use NOW YOU! Projects

The **Project tasks** that are woven through **NOW YOU!** can be found at the end of lessons 1, 2 and 5 of each unit. There are six tasks which are then brought together in a **Final task** which can be found on the **Project** pages at the end of the two units. Each **Project task** consolidates the material presented to the students during the lesson.

The instructions included in the task boxes outline the type of group the students will work in for the particular **Project**.Throughout the **Student's Book** there is a combination of group sizes, from pairs to groups of four. This is intended to encourage different group dynamics and avoid students working with the same classmates each time.

The **Projects** are themselves **optional, flexible, integrated** and **adaptable**. They are separated into these six, bitesize tasks so that the students are able to complete the **Project** in a controlled and efficient way, integrated into their class time. The tasks can, however, be used in various ways in class, as outlined in the following list.

Ways to use the Project tasks in class

- Students can complete each **Project task** as indicated in the **Student's Book**, consolidating the content of the lesson and building steadily towards the **Final task**.
- As above, but the teacher can choose to miss out or adapt **Project tasks** as dictated by available class time.
- Students can complete all three **Project tasks** together at the end of each unit as a method of reviewing the content, followed by the **Final task**.
- Students can complete all six **Project tasks** and the **Final task** together in one block of work after the two units.
- Teachers can use a discussion of the **Project tasks** as a vehicle for developing **Challenge-based Learning** skills; students will then complete them using their chosen method.
- All or some of the **Project tasks** can be completed by the groups outside of class time and later brought together or presented in the classroom.
- Alternatively, the **Project tasks** can be avoided altogether, in the case that students do not have available class time. This does not affect the progression of the material in the **Student's Book**.

The Final task

The culmination of the Project is the **Final task**, which consists of a **Recap** and **task summary**, instructions for the **Final Task**, a **Useful expressions** box, **21st century skills** and **Evaluation** boxes and a **Go beyond** section (see the **Project** section of the **Unit walkthrough** on pages 16-17).

The **Recap** section helps students understand the practical use of the grammar and vocabulary structures they have learnt. Similarly, the **task summary** in this initial section helps students to recall the material they have created. Teachers may wish to read this section with their students as they begin **Project task** 1 in order to motivate the students and help them understand their work in relation to the final product.

The **Final task** is the moment when students are encouraged to review, edit and refine the work they have completed over the previous two units. A **Useful expressions** box provides students with relevant language structures that will enable them to present their final product with confidence.

When students have all completed the **Final task**, they are provided with material which encourages them to reflect on their experience. This material can be found in the **21st century skills** and **Evaluation** boxes. For more information on how to use the **21st century skills box**, see pages 28-29. The rubric in the **Evaluation** box directs students to answer the questions included either in their groups after the **Final task** or during the presentations of their peers. This section encourages students to evaluate their individual or group performance and reflect on the learning process.

Finally, the **Go beyond** section includes a short text related to the material that the students have completed in order to bring a broader, real-world context to the content or form of the work they have created. This text can be used to stimulate further class discussion on the **Project** content.

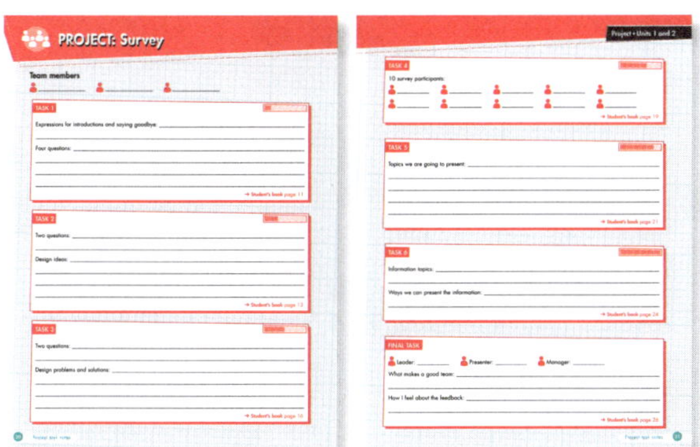

The **Project notes** pages in the **NOW YOU! Workbook** work as an organiser and provide students with a visual presentation of how their work culminates to create the final product. This gradual building of a portfolio of work means that students can also compare their progress over the school year by looking back over the **Projects** they have completed.

21st century skills

What are 21st century skills?

Our world is changing before our eyes. Technological advances, societal and economic developments and a hyper-connected globalisation mean that our students face an exciting yet unpredictable future. The new technologies and types of employment they will encounter are unknown both to them and to us – the adults that shape their education. This poses the question: how can we effectively prepare our students for success in a future we cannot predict?

In answer to this question, educators and academics have identified certain skills as **21st century skills**; that is, soft skills which we can teach our students in order to better prepare them for the future, whatever it may hold.

A quick online search will render multiple definitions of the key **21st century skills**. However, most commonly these are understood in terms of **the 7 Cs**.

The 7 Cs of 21st century skills

- **Collaboration:** Teamwork, adaptability, cooperation, etc.
- **Communication:** Information literacy, ability to share thoughts and ideas, etc.
- **Creativity:** Innovation, productivity, identifying solutions, etc.
- **Critical thinking:** Problem solving, analysis, linking learning across subjects, etc.
- **Career and learning self-reliance:** Responsibility, initiative, self-direction, etc.
- **Computing:** Digital literacy, effective use of electronic tools, etc.
- **Cross-cultural understanding:** Respect for diversity, effective social interaction, etc.

21st century skills in NOW YOU!

Natural spaces for the development of these seven skill sets exist throughout **NOW YOU!**, for example in the **Culture videos** (cross-cultural understanding), **Project tasks** (collaboration) and **NOW YOU! exercises** (communication).

However, a clearly identified **21st century skills box** can be found on the **Project** pages. Here, a specific **21st century skill** that the students have developed during the completion of the **Project tasks** is identified and presented to the student, and the student's attention is drawn to the ways in which it is useful to them outside the classroom. For example, in a **Project** where students are called upon to conduct online research into an individual for a biography, the 21st century skill focus is fact checking.

Teachers who choose not to use the **Project pages** can, however, use this box independently.

In both cases, the teacher should encourage students to read the **21st century skills box** together and discuss their reactions as a class or in small groups. Productive discussion of the themes will include the teacher asking the students to identify their own strengths and weaknesses with regards to the particular skill. Students could also identify ways in which they can develop or apply the skill more effectively in their own lives.

21st century skills from the previous levels are then addressed in the **Get started!** unit of each subsequent level of **NOW YOU!** in order to refresh the student's memory. The connection of the **21st century skill** to a new context also highlights its broader use.

Each skill has been named with the student's understanding in mind, but can also be mapped onto **the 7 Cs** as detailed in the table below.

The benefits of teaching 21st century skills

Aside from the obvious future benefits of teaching students these types of skills, there are also clear implications in terms of **learner motivation**. Encouraging students to recognise and value abilities that are not knowledge-based leads to greater **self-esteem** and **acceptance of diversity**. Furthermore, these skills are intended to promote **learner independence**, develop **positive lifelong learning habits** and place value on **higher-order thinking skills**.

Project	21st century skill	From the 7 Cs
Units 1 & 2: Survey	Collaboration	Collaboration
Units 3 & 4: Scrapbook	Feedback	Communication
Units 5 & 6: Tourist leaflet	Cultural awareness	Cross-cultural understanding
Units 7 & 8: Memorabilia chest	Communication	Communication

CEFR mediation

What is Mediation?

The **Common European Framework of Reference for Languages** (CEFR) in 2001 defined mediation as facilitating cross-linguistic communication; they saw the language learner as a social agent acting between individuals with no common language.

The updated 2018 CEFR, however, gives the skill greater importance and takes a broader interpretation. It sees mediation as those key soft skills required for competent communication, the ability to **reformulate language to facilitate understanding**.

Rather than simply referring to the interpretation or translation of language, mediation is understood as a more meaningful act within the language learning experience. It is an act of interaction that **bridges reception and production**; that interaction can be **between individuals**, **between languages** or **language registers** or in a personal **act of processing language**.

In this way, mediation skills can be developed in a **monolingual learning environment** where use of L1 is not encouraged in the classroom.

The diagram on the next page shows all of the aspects of mediation recognised by the CEFR. There are three main categories of **mediation activities: mediating communication, mediating a text** and **mediating concepts**. Then there are **mediation strategies**, grouped separately because they can be used while doing the mediation activities. As with other skills, there is a range of **CEFR Mediation descriptors** for different levels. For example, in relaying information in speech a language user at B1 level 'can relay specific information given in straightforward informational texts'.

CEFR Mediation in NOW YOU!

NOW YOU! provides opportunities in every lesson for mediation activities and strategies to be developed and has a strong focus on mediation in the **Projects** and **Pairwork** sections.The **overviews** at the beginning of each unit in the **Teaching notes** indicate which **CEFR Mediation descriptors** apply to each lesson (see examples on pages 32-33).

Mediation activities and strategies

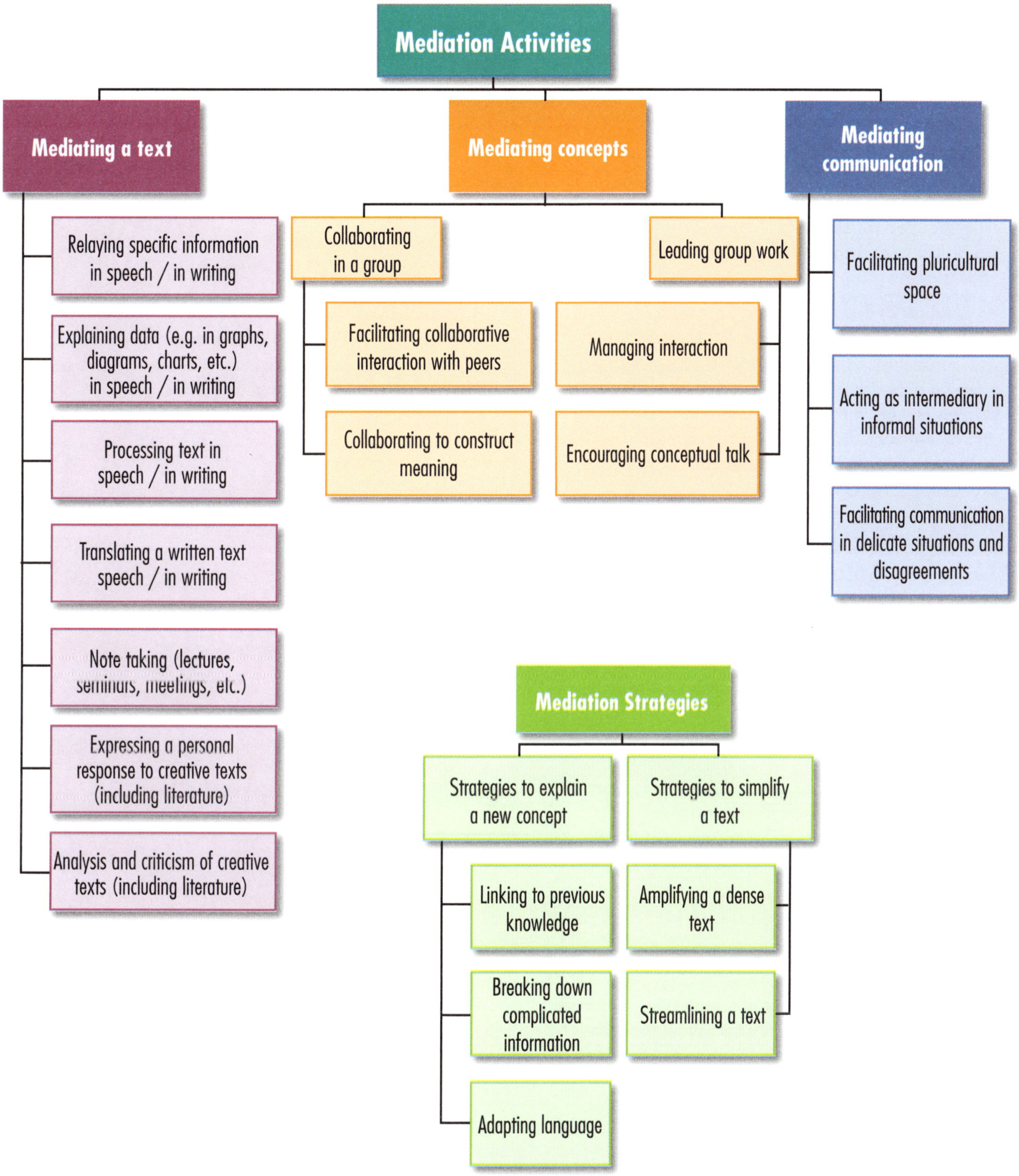

Taken from: Common European Framework of Reference for languages; learning, teaching, assessment Companion volume with new descriptors 2018

CEFR mediation

Main units

All the lessons in the main units of **NOW YOU!** offer students concrete opportunities to develop the **important transferable skills** defined in the **mediation descriptors** in order to become competent, confident communicators, as outlined in the descriptions and examples below.

Lessons 1 & 2 • Grammar, vocabulary & listening

NOW YOU! exercises provide practice for a wide range of mediation skills:
Note-taking
Can make simple notes about familiar subject matter.

Lesson 3 • Reading

Reading lessons develop skills for **mediating a text**:
Expressing a personal response to creative texts
Can describe a character's feelings and explain the reasons for them.
The **Core values** section provides further opportunities:
Facilitating communication in delicate situations and disagreements
Can recognise when difficulties occur in interaction and adapt simple phrases to seek compromise.

Lesson 4 • Writing

Exercises in the **Focus on** and **Did you notice?** sections also develop skills for **mediating a text**:
Processing text in writing
Can pick out and reproduce key words and phrases or short sentences from a short text.

Lesson 5 • Culture and communication

The **Culture video** and **Idioms and expressions** sections provide a space for students to develop skills for **mediating communication**:
Facilitating pluricultural space
Can help to develop a shared communication culture by exchanging information in a simple way about values and attitudes to language and culture.

Projects

The **Project tasks** and the **Final project** are a natural vehicle for Mediation skills concerned with **mediating concepts**; these are further divided into **collaborating in a group** and **leading group work**.

The below tables illustrate the integration of these and other **mediation skills** into the **NOW YOU! Projects**.

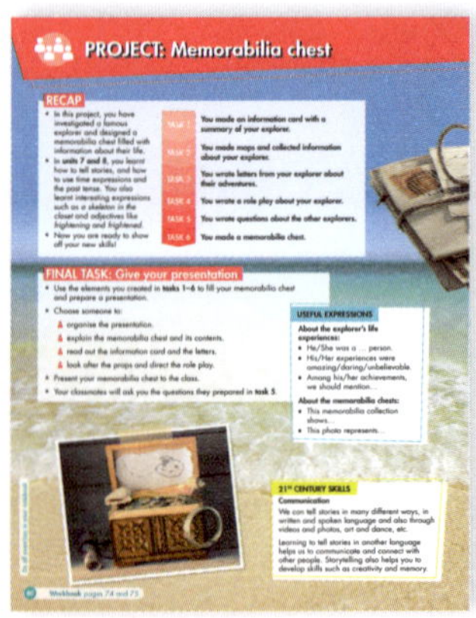

Projects • Student's Book 1	
Project	**A1 / A2 CEFR Mediation descriptors**
Units 1 & 2 Survey	Explaining data in speech Can interpret and describe simple visuals on familiar topics.
Units 3 & 4 Scrapbook	Encouraging conceptual talk Can ask questions to invite people to clarify their reasoning.
Units 5 & 6 Tourist leaflet	Relaying specific information in writing Can relay in writing specific information contained in short, simple informational texts.
Units 7 & 8 Memorabilia Chest	Facilitating collaborative interaction with peers Can invite others' contributions to very simple tasks using short, simple phrases.

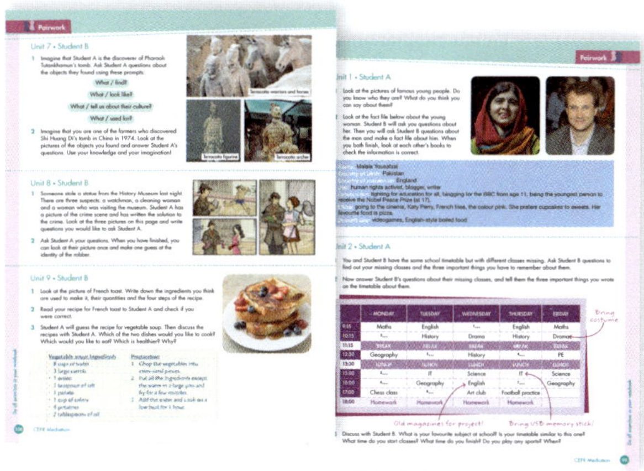

Pairwork

The communicative, interactive nature of the **Pairwork section** creates a natural space for the development of **Mediation skills**.

Pairwork • Student's Book 1	
Unit	**A1 / A2 CEFR Mediation descriptors**
Unit 1 Exchanging personal information	Overall mediation Can convey relevant information contained in clearly structured, short, simple, informational texts, provided that the texts concern concrete, familiar subjects and are formulated in simple everyday language.
Unit 2 Interpreting a timetable	Relaying specific information in speech Can relay simple, predictable information about times and places given in short, simple statements.
Unit 3 Describing people	Collaborating to construct meaning Can express an idea with very simple words and ask what others think.
Unit 4 Requesting information	Processing text in speech Can report in simple sentences the information contained in clearly structured, short, simple texts that have illustrations or tables.
Unit 5 Comparing hobbies and interests	Adapting language Can repeat the main point of a simple message on an everyday subject, using different words to help someone else understand it.
Unit 6 Describing daily routines	Relaying specific information in speech Can relay specific, relevant information contained in short, simple texts, labels and notices on familiar subjects.
Unit 7 Interpreting information	Collaborating to construct meaning Can express an idea with very simple words and ask what others think.
Unit 8 Analysing clues	Generating conceptual talk Can ask what somebody thinks of a certain idea.
Unit 9 Describing a recipe	Facilitating collaborative interaction with peers Can collaborate in simple, shared tasks, provided that other participants speak slowly and that one or more of them help him/her to contribute and to express his/her suggestions.

Plurilingualism

What is plurilingualism?

The **Common European Framework of Reference for Languages** defines plurilingualism as the ability of an individual to call flexibly upon an inter-related repertoire of linguistic experience and strategies to resolve a communicative situation in a given cultural context.

Because it is called on in a given cultural context, the CEFR points out that 'Plurilingualism has itself to be seen in the context of pluriculturalism. Language is not only a major aspect of culture, but also a means of access to cultural manifestations.'

Consequently, an individual will be competent in plurilingualism when he/she develops the ability to use all his/her linguistic knowledge and experience to achieve effective communication with an interlocutor that takes into account their cultural and linguistic background.

Plurilingualism at secondary level

Because of the transversal nature of plurilingualism, it is not considered necessary to define assessable competences at the level of compulsory secondary education, but it is important to **highlight plurilingual strategies** alongside other linguistic competences.

On the basis of the above, in compulsory secondary school we should focus on the development of plurilingualism in two areas:

1 a **knowledge of culture and traditions** in English-speaking regions (mealtimes, customs, habits, etc.)

2 **experience of communicative success** when an individual overcomes his/her fear of oral and written comprehension and expression

Plurilingualism with NOW YOU!

There are several features of **NOW YOU!** that offer students the opportunity to work on developing their plurilingual competences.

Culture and communication

These lessons offer students an opportunity to develop their plurilingual competences by **watching and responding to videos** about various different aspects, features and events of English-speaking cultures throughout the world, including Irish dancing, the Edinburgh Fringe Festival and the American barbecue. The lessons also include listening exercises involving **short talks and conversations** using frequent English **idioms** and a chance to practise the idioms in short **personalised speaking exercises**. Thus both aspects of plurilingualism as outlined above are developed in these lessons.

NOW YOU! exercises and Pairwork

The **NOW YOU! exercises** throughout each unit and the **Pairwork** activities at the end are designed to develop students' ability to communicate effectively in spoken and sometimes written English. In these exercises, students do activities like comparing what they do in their free time, describing other people, using newly acquired expressions in a conversation and writing a description of someone they admire, among others.

Point out to students that these are not just exercises for putting their linguistic knowledge into practice, but also for **building confidence** in and developing their ability to **communicate and interact** with each other using all their linguistic and communicative resources. In the spoken activities, encourage them to participate **without fear of embarrassment** and using whatever language and communicative strategies they have, including **paralinguistic strategies** like gestures and facial expressions, and asking a speaker to slow down to give them the chance to check that they have understood what the speaker is saying.

Projects

The **Projects** require students to collaborate to prepare and then present a final product. Providing students with this challenge **facilitates the transferral of communication strategies** learnt in their own language (and any other languages they speak) over to their English language competence and vice versa. These strategies, which are necessary for effective completion of the project, help build students' ability to communicate more effectively and confidently **in a range of real-life contexts** involving any language.

Other activities you can do in class to develop your students' plurilingual competence include:

- Showing them **TV programmes**, **films** or **plays** with a strong cultural element.
- **Extending speaking activities** in class to include longer class discussions and **other types of discourse** not already featured in the course: role-plays, formal interviews and debates, etc.
- Asking students to **identify similarities in grammar and vocabulary** between English and their own language (and indeed other languages) to help their linguistic ability and confidence.
- Using **digital communications resources** (like Skype, Zoom, Microsoft Teams, etc.) to help develop communication with students from other countries.
- Encouraging students to get involved in **collaborative projects with students or NGOs in other countries** to put the strategies they have learnt into practice in real-life situations.

Literature

What do we mean by literature?

Literature can be defined as the creative production and comprehension of written, spoken and audiovisual texts in an attempt to produce an emotional and/or intellectual reaction in the reader, listener or viewer.

Written literature at secondary level includes novels, short stories, written plays and essays, as well as comics, articles and blog entries.

Oral literature includes all recited or interpreted texts, such as poems, songs, dramatizations (sketches and short plays), and even tongue-twisters, rhymes, sayings and jokes.

Audiovisual literature refers to works that combine images and spoken or written text, such as cartoons, films, series, advertisements, videoclips, trailers, etc.

The benefits of teaching literature at secondary level

Literature provides us all with a **sense of community** and our place within it, and gives us tools to **express ourselves effectively** to other members of the community to **strengthen bonds** between us and help build our **sense of identity**, both individual and communal. Living in a global and multi-lingual community makes this more of a challenge but also more rewarding.

Focusing on English-language literature at secondary school helps students develop this sense of community and their **understanding of the world**, their **own culture** and their **own identity**.

It also helps develop their **skills** in and **enjoyment** of **reading**, **writing** and other forms of communication, as well as stimulating **creativity** and developing **critical thinking**.

At secondary level, students need to learn to **understand** and **assess** a variety of **literary texts** both adapted and authentic, and to be able to **orally reproduce literary texts** (oral literature) both adapted and authentic. They also need to be able to **express themselves** in ways that show an **awareness of literary culture** as defined above.

Literature in NOW YOU!

There are several features of **NOW YOU!** that offer students the opportunity to develop a healthy relationship with literature and to build on their literary skills.

Reading and Writing lessons

In the **Reading** and the **Writing** lessons, students encounter various **different text types**, including articles, stories, blog entries and descriptions of people and artworks, throughout the course. Both lessons provide students with the opportunity to **offer personal responses** to the texts. To help develop their literary skills, use this opportunity to **highlight literary devices and features** of the text, starting with those they found effective and pointing out any that you think worth remarking on. The **Writing lesson** has a specific **Did you notice?** section to help them **develop literary awareness** and to guide them in using relevant features of the model text to produce their own effective writing.

Vlogs and Culture videos

The **Vlogs** and the **Culture videos** are both typical examples of **21st century audiovisual literature**. They also include personal and cultural anecdotes, jokes and sayings to help students develop their knowledge of global literary culture, and the accompanying material gives them the opportunity to share their responses.

To **further exploit** the literary element of these videos videos, prepare extra questions that encourage students to respond to the content with reference to their own experience and cultural and literary knowledge, with a view to **preparing their own videos**, based on the content they have just seen and heard. Give them time to write scripts, prepare questions for other students to answer and then record themselves. Encourage them to include some literary content (even a joke or an anecdote) and to ask questions that require comprehension and interpretation of that content, as well as giving them the chance to express their opinions, feelings and thoughts in response to the videos.

You could also get students to **find a simple literary text** that is related to one of the videos and get them to **recite** or **dramatize** it. This could be a short poem or rap involving rhyme and metre, which help develop good word stress and pronunciation. Encourage supportive and constructive class feedback.

Graded readers

Richmond offers **a wide range of graded readers**, including adaptations of **classic literature** and **original short novels**, each with **audio CD, glossary** and **activities** designed to help comprehension and generate meaningful and informed responses to the content.

You could have your **class choose a reader** for everyone to read and dedicate some class time to do the related activities and discuss the story. We recommend that you encourage them to **discuss excerpts** that they have read or listened to, offering them whatever support they need to do this effectively. Provide them with valid models of literary assessment so that you can help them **develop literary assessment skills**. You could also get students to do **rewriting activities** to help build confidence and as basic training for more **independent writing**. Such tasks could include varying words or phrases, rewriting an excerpt as a different text type (e.g. a play or a speech), writing part of the story from a different character's perspective or writing an alternative ending.

The learning and interest acquired from lessons based around the one reader you chose as a class could then be used as a springboard for students to **each choose a reader or another literary text** to share with the class as a whole or in smaller groups. They could simply **give an assessment** of the work to share and discuss in order to see if it generates interest among their classmates, or perhaps **recite or interpret** it and prepare activities for their classmates to do in response. Encourage them to find something of particular interest to them individually and in any format and using whatever platforms they want, as long as it doesn't make it impractical for them to share their assessment in class.

Mixed-ability classes

The basics of Mixed-ability classes

To some extent, all classes are of mixed ability. Students have different levels of **knowledge** as well as **ability** and learn at **different speeds** and in **different ways**. It can be a challenge to manage a class where these differences are pronounced, a challenge that many teachers have to face. Some students may become stressed and demotivated because they find the class difficult while others in the same class are bored or frustrated because they find it easy and perhaps finish exercises very quickly. However, with a bit of planning, a few helpful strategies and judicious use of resources, teaching a mixed-ability group can be very rewarding for teachers and students alike.

Mixed-ability in NOW YOU!

The Student's Book

Collaborative Learning

With its strong focus on **Collaborative Learning**, **NOW YOU!** helps highlight the idea of language as a tool for communication, and communication as a collaborative activity with **all parties taking responsibility** for its success. With this methodology as the basis, the **Student's Book** provides a range of tools to develop students' skills across various levels and abilities.

The **The Projects**, **Pairwork** activities and **NOW YOU! speaking exercises** all help emphasise broader **communicative criteria** rather than just language accuracy as a way to grade speaking performance (see **Assessment** pages 40-41 for ideas on assessment criteria). They also **help identify students' strengths and weaknesses** and to help them recognise them **without fear of judgement**. For these activities, giving confident and strong students roles that enable them to share their knowledge and understanding with others gives students the **opportunity to help each other**. Students who are less confident can be encouraged to ask questions to check their understanding. Additionally, students who are confident in their knowledge are not always right and if other students are **encouraged to question their knowledge** it can help check accuracy, and develop critical thinking skills **and reinforce what students have learnt**.

Make students aware **all roles are important** in any group activity, for example timekeeper, materials distributor, note-taker, spokesperson, a nominated person to keep the group on task, etc. **Let them assign roles** within their groups where possible. This can be based on their strengths at first, but then encourage students to **swap** roles regularly so that all students can **learn a variety of skills** by practising them themselves and by observing their classmates demonstrating them. Offer and encourage support to all members of a group as much as possible.

Independent Learning

The **Student's Book** also contains tools to allow students to help themselves and to take ownership of their own learning journey.

For students at a lower level, the **Grammar tables** and **animations** provide a reference point when unsure or underconfident against which to check their learning. Similarly, the **Learning to learn tools** offer students strategies for developing their weaker skills. Make sure to always draw students' attention to these tools and encourage independent learning outside of the classroom. For students at a higher level, the **Fast finishers** exercises in lessons 1, 2, 3 and 5 of every unit give further personalised practice for students who finish exercises before the rest of the class. Check the work students produce in these exercises to make sure they are making the most of them and consider asking them to share their work if it could be of interest or use to rest of the class.

Flipped Learning

The integration of the **Flipped Learning** methodology throughout **NOW YOU!** provides students with further opportunities to **take control of their learning**, and to assimilate knowledge **at their own pace** and in their **own way** (see pages 20-23).

The Workbook

The **Workbook** contains lots of extra practice to help students **consolidate their knowledge**, including **more personalised NOW YOU! exercises** for students to write sentences at their own level of complexity to consolidate language points, and specific sections with **extra practice** for the **Grammar reference** and **Wordlist** at each level, which is ideal for mixed-ability classes. It also includes a **Reflect on your learning** section at the end of each unit so that students can **identify their own strengths and weaknesses** and know when and where to ask for guidance.

Teacher's Resources

The **Teacher's Resources** include **Grammar** and **Vocabulary** worksheets for each unit at **three levels**: Revision, Consolidation and Extension, from lowest to highest. There is also a series of tests including a **Diagnostic test** and then **tests at two levels** after each unit, each group of three units and at the end of the year (see **Assessment** pages 40-41). Thus a teacher can **determine their students' levels** at the start of the year and give them **level-appropriate tests** to monitor them throughout the year in a way that gives students a **sense of confidence and progress**. The worksheets are all also **editable** so they can be tailored to the needs of specific students or groups of students.

Assessment

The basics of assessment

In the context of secondary level English language learning, students can be assessed on their performance and progress by **regular tests and exams**, **continuous teacher assessment** and **self-assessment**. In the 21st century language classroom, students should be assessed not only on their language skills, but also on their **ability to use their language skills** in a wider context and on their capacity for **independent learning**, i.e. their ability to learn how to learn.

Assessment in NOW YOU!

Regular tests

The **Richmond Test Manager** offers a comprehensive battery of tests. There is a **Diagnostic test** you can use at the start of the year to assess students' knowledge and use of vocabulary and grammar before they start the course. Then there are **Unit tests**, **End-of-term tests** and an **End-of-year test** to assess students' vocabulary and grammar, as well as their listening, reading and writing skills. These exist at two levels (Consolidation and Extension) and each have a marking scheme that gives a total of 100. There are also **Speaking tests** at the same intervals. These have no marking scheme so as to allow flexibility in using them, but the following criteria could be used to give a mark: overall task completion, fluency, interaction and language (range, appropriacy and accuracy of vocabulary and grammar).

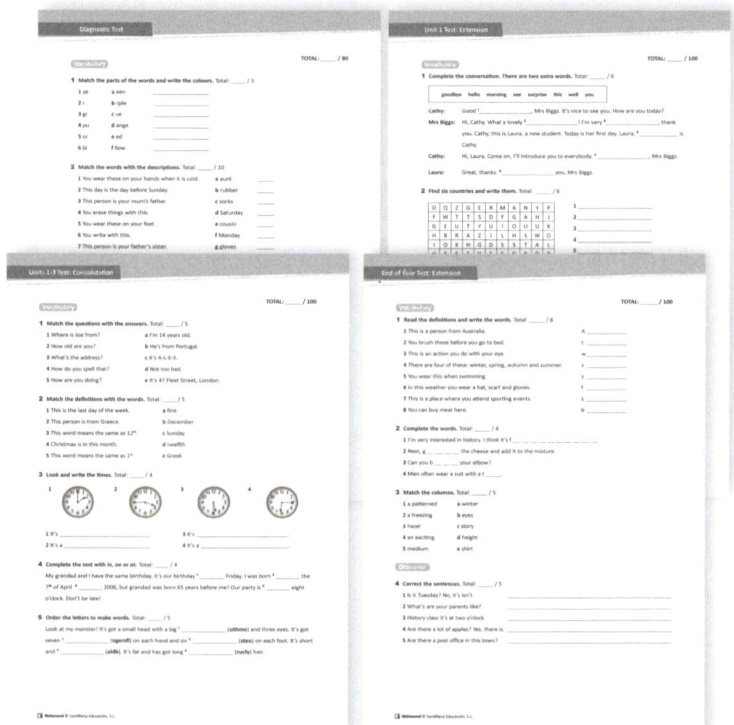
Diagnostic Test

Unit 1 Test: Extension

Units 1-3 Test: Consolidation

End of Year Test: Extension

At the end of the main units in the **Student's Book**, there is also a **Review** for every unit. These offer further assessment of the language content of the unit in the **format of external exams** at the appropriate level.

Continuous assessment

For every lesson there is a **Continuous assessment** footer in the **Teacher's book** for the teacher to be mindful of as students go through the lesson. These are connected to the language and skills objectives of the lesson as outlined in the **overviews** at the start of each unit in the **Teaching notes**. It is a good idea to observe and keep records of all of the students' performances as best you can and offer support to those who need it. The **Writing** lessons require students to produce texts that can also be assessed more formally, perhaps using criteria you set specifically for each writing task or more general criteria you apply throughout, such as task completion, structure/linking, style, language range and language accuracy.

Self-assessment

At the end of every unit in the **Workbook**, there is a **Reflect on your learning** section in the **Communication and reflection** lesson. It offers students an opportunity to **assess their own abilities** in the relevant language points and skills areas. Make sure they understand that the purpose of this is to **build their confidence** in their knowledge and use of English and to **help improve** any areas of weakness. Use their assessments to offer material to help them in these areas. The **Teacher's Resources** offer such material at different levels to suit different students' support needs.

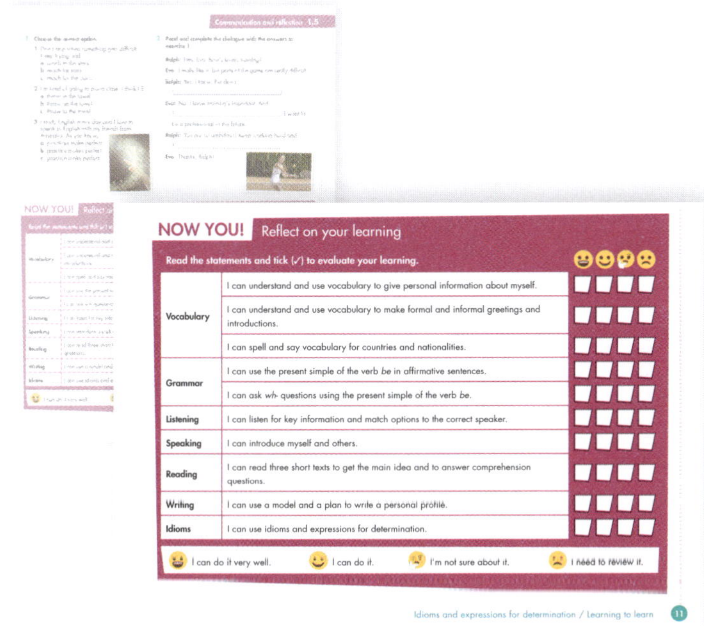

NOW YOU! Reflect on your learning

Read the statements and tick (✓) to evaluate your learning.

		😀	🙂	😕	🙁
Vocabulary	I can understand and use vocabulary to give personal information about myself.				
	I can understand and use vocabulary to make formal and informal greetings and introductions.				
	I can spell and say vocabulary for countries and nationalities.				
Grammar	I can use the present simple of the verb *be* in affirmative sentences.				
	I can ask *wh-* questions using the present simple of the verb *be*.				
Listening	I can listen for key information and match options to the correct speaker.				
Speaking	I can introduce myself and others.				
Reading	I can read three short texts to get the main idea and to answer comprehension questions.				
Writing	I can use a model and a plan to write a personal profile.				
Idioms	I can use idioms and expressions for determination.				

😀 I can do it very well. 🙂 I can do it. 😕 I'm not sure about it. 🙁 I need to review it.

Idioms and expressions for determination / Learning to learn 11

There is also an opportunity for students to self-assess more informally in the **Evaluation** section of the **Project**. These activities allow students to **assess individual and team performance**, as well as their personal experience of bringing the project to completion.

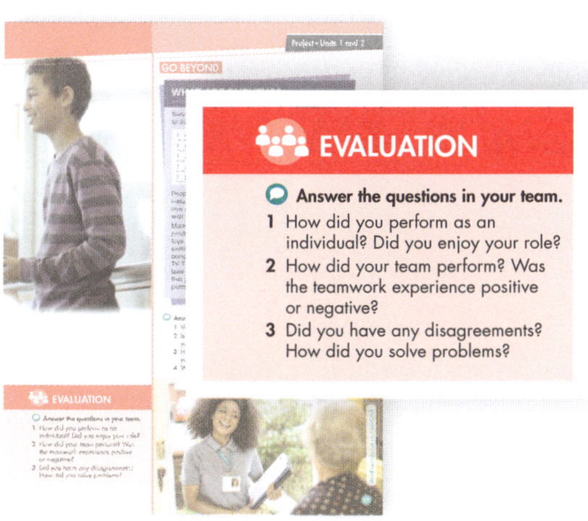

EVALUATION

Answer the questions in your team.

1 How did you perform as an individual? Did you enjoy your role?
2 How did your team perform? Was the teamwork experience positive or negative?
3 Did you have any disagreements? How did you solve problems?

It is a good idea to get students to keep a **self-assessment diary**, and their discussions in the **Project Evaluation** could be an opportune moment for them to start and continue the diary.

This diary could include a range of criteria on which students could assess themselves, including linguistic skills as well as other broader skills that **NOW YOU!** helps teach students.

These include the **21st century skills** on the **Project pages**, **the Core values** in the **Reading lessons**, **Learning to learn tools** throughout the book and **mediation skills** from the unit overviews in the **Teacher's Book**. You could make a list of these and get students to write what knowledge and skills they have acquired and developed, and which they want to work on. Encourage them to write how they feel about their learning and progress too. Collect these diaries at intervals to monitor students' awareness of their abilities, performance and development, as well as their morale and motivation.

Key competences

What are the Key competences?

Key competences combine the **knowledge**, **skills** and **attitudes** necessary to develop and achieve success as well being active **in all areas of social and civic life**. Each of the competences is equally important, and for that reason there are many shared goals which support and underpin one another. The basic skills of language, literacy, numeracy and information and communication technologies provide the foundation blocks for critical thinking, creativity, taking initiative, problem-solving, decision-making and management of feelings.

NOW YOU! works on these **Key competences** as set out by the European Commission.

Linguistic competence

LC

This competence develops the use of language as a tool for communication. It involves understanding and producing oral and written messages and requires knowledge of vocabulary and grammar. The focus here is on understanding, expressing and interpreting a range of facts, opinions, thoughts and feelings in a variety of different contexts. Language skills students learn when studying a foreign language can be transferred to their native language and use of other languages, which enhances their plurilingual abilities.

Mathematical competence and basic competences in Science and Technology

MST

The use of mathematical thinking to solve problems in everyday situations, scientific knowledge to explain the natural world and an understanding of technological principles are the focus of this competence. An awareness of the world around us and the effect we have on it are at the core. Introducing these competences into the language learning environment enriches the students' learning experience.

Digital competence

DC

Digital competence involves the use of information technology as a way of researching, presenting and exchanging information. Students use computers, the internet, the interactive whiteboard, audiovisual material and other multimedia resources to enhance their own learning experience. They also learn to critically evaluate different information technologies and the content they provide access to.

Social and Civic competences

SCC

These competences equip students with the necessary skills to participate fully in social and civic life on both a personal and interpersonal level. On a personal level, students focus on those skills needed to function effectively and constructively in everyday life, skills such as being able to know, express and assert themselves. Students also focus on values such as diversity, tolerance and understanding, which will help them become an active part of the local and wider community.

Cultural awareness and expression

CAE

Studying a foreign language involves an awareness of the culture of the people that speak it, including their art, their food, their festivals and their customs, as well as a general sense of global culture. By learning about other cultures through reading texts, videos and discussions to share different cultural experiences, students also become more aware of their own culture and learn to express themselves creatively in a way that shows awareness of their cultural context, reinforcing their sense of the world and their place in it.

Learning to learn

LL

Students need to develop effective strategies to improve their ability to learn independently. This means trying a variety of strategies to find ones which suit them and their learning styles, evaluating their own progress and thinking of ways to improve their ability to gain new knowledge and skills. Many of these strategies can be transferred to other subjects and learning contexts.

Sense of initiative and entrepreneurship

IE

Creativity, innovation, risk-taking and the ability to plan and manage projects in order to achieve objectives form the core of this competence. Collaborative projects give students a range of contexts in which to demonstrate and develop these abilities. Success in this competence gives students skills that are transferable from the classroom directly to the workplace.

Key competences in the Student's Book

Linguistic competence

Every page of the **Student's Book** is dedicated to this competence.

Mathematical competence and basic competences in Science and Technology

Get started page 7
Unit 1 pages 10-12
Unit 2 pages 18, 20, 22-23
Unit 3 pages 28, 29, 32, 33
Unit 4 pages 40-42
Unit 5 pages 47, 49, 52
Unit 6 pages 54, 56, 58, 59, 61
Unit 7 pages 66-69
Unit 9 pages 82, 83, 86, 87

Digital competence

Get started page 6
Unit 1 pages 10, 17
Unit 2 pages 18, 24, 25
Unit 3 pages 28, 35
Unit 4 pages 36, 38, 43
Unit 5 pages 46, 48, 49, 53
Unit 6 pages 54-56, 61
Unit 7 pages 64-66, 71
Unit 8 pages 72, 79
Unit 9 pages 82, 89

Social and Civic competences

Get started pages 6-9
Unit 1 pages 10-17
Unit 2 pages 18, 21-23, 25
Unit 3 pages 29, 32, 33, 35
Unit 4 pages 39-43
Unit 5 pages 47, 49, 51-53
Unit 6 pages 54-61
Unit 7 pages 65, 67, 69-71
Unit 8 pages 73, 75, 76, 78, 79
Unit 9 pages 82, 83, 86 89

Cultural awareness and expression

Get started pages 6-9
Unit 1 pages 10, 12-17
Unit 2 pages 18, 21, 25
Unit 3 pages 28, 29, 31, 34, 35
Unit 4 pages 36, 37, 40, 41, 43
Unit 5 pages 46, 49, 50-53
Unit 6 pages 54-61
Unit 7 pages 64, 69, 71
Unit 8 pages 76, 77, 79
Unit 9 pages 82, 89

Learning to learn

Get started page 7
Unit 1 pages 11, 13, 14, 16, 17
Unit 2 pages 21, 22, 24, 25
Unit 3 pages 30-32, 34
Unit 4 pages 36, 37, 39, 40, 42
Unit 5 pages 47, 49, 50, 52
Unit 6 pages 55, 56, 59, 60
Unit 7 pages 65, 68, 70, 71
Unit 8 pages 72, 75, 76, 78, 79
Unit 9 pages 83, 85, 86, 88, 89

Sense of initiative and entrepreneurship

Unit 1 pages 11, 13, 16
Unit 2 pages 19, 21, 24
Unit 3 pages 29, 31, 34
Unit 4 pages 37, 39, 42
Unit 5 pages 47, 49, 52
Unit 6 pages 55, 57, 60
Unit 7 pages 65, 67, 70
Unit 8 pages 73, 75, 78
Unit 9 pages 83, 85, 88

CONTENTS NOW YOU! 1

• Saxon genitive • Articles • Punctuation

GET STARTED

At the start of each unit and lesson, explain to the students what the objectives are.

Language objectives

Grammar

Prepositions of place
- Students review and practise prepositions to show spatial relationships.

Possessive pronouns and the Saxon genitive
- Students review and practise possessive pronouns and -'s to show possession.

Articles
- Students review and practise *the*, *a* and *an*.

Punctuation
- Students review the uses of capital letters.

Vocabulary

Classroom language and objects: *bin, board, borrow, classmate, clock, cupboard, desk, exam, hall, head teacher, highlighter, library, listen, marker, notebook, pen, pencil case, repeat, rubber, ruler, schoolbag, sharpener, study, whiteboard*
- Students review and practise vocabulary related to the classroom.

Family: *aunt, brother, child, cousin, father, grandparent, mother, neighbour, parent, pen-friend, sister, teenager, uncle*
- Students review and practise vocabulary related to family.

Jobs: *astronaut, athlete, babysitter, business owner, dentist, doctor, journalist, lawyer, librarian, mechanic, police officer, president, teacher*
- Students review and practise vocabulary for a range of jobs.

21st century skills objectives

Learning to learn
- Students reflect on the importance of learning to learn more effectively.

Self-confidence
- Students reflect on self-confidence and factors that influence it.

Citizenship
- Students reflect on the value of citizenship and the rewards of different jobs.

Audiovisual objectives

Meet the vloggers: Students watch and listen to Emma, George and Sarah talk about the summer holidays and the people they spent them with.

Key competences

LC **Linguistic**
pages 6-9

MST **Mathematical and Science and Technology**
page 7

DC **Digital**
page 6

SCC **Social and Civic**
pages 6-9

CAE **Cultural awareness and expression**
pages 6-9

LL **Learning to learn**
page 7

→ See pages 42-43 **Key competences**

CEFR Mediation

Facilitating collaborative interaction with peers
Can collaborate in simple, shared tasks.
Can help work towards a common goal by asking and answering straightforward questions.

Relaying information in writing
Can relay specific information contained in simple spoken texts on familiar subjects.

Collaborating to construct meaning
Can make simple remarks and pose occasional questions to show that he/she is following the conversation.
Can make suggestions in a simple way to move the discussion forward.

Encouraging conceptual talk
Can ask what somebody thinks of an idea.

→ See pages 30-33 **Mediation**

Remind students to do all the exercises in their notebook

Language review

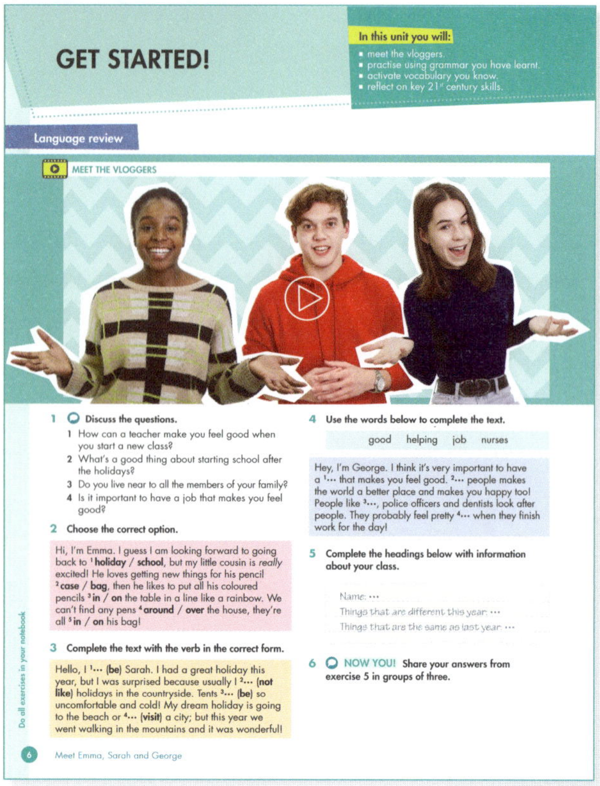

GET STARTED!

In this unit you will:
- meet the vloggers.
- practise using grammar you have learnt.
- activate vocabulary you know.
- reflect on key 21st century skills.

Language review

MEET THE VLOGGERS

1 Discuss the questions.
1 How can a teacher make you feel good when you start a new class?
2 What's a good thing about starting school after the holidays?
3 Do you live near to all the members of your family?
4 Is it important to have a job that makes you feel good?

2 Choose the correct option.

Hi, I'm Emma. I guess I am looking forward to going back to [1] **holiday / school**, but my little cousin is *really* excited! He loves getting new things for his pencil [2] **case / bag**, then he likes to put all his coloured pencils [3] **in / on** the table in a line like a rainbow. We can't find any pens [4] **around / over** the house, they're all [5] **in / on** his bag!

3 Complete the text with the verb in the correct form.

Hello, I [1]··· (**be**) Sarah. I had a great holiday this year, but I was surprised because usually I [2]··· (**not like**) holidays in the countryside. Tents [3]··· (**be**) so uncomfortable and cold! My dream holiday is going to the beach or [4]··· (**visit**) a city; but this year we went walking in the mountains and it was wonderful!

4 Use the words below to complete the text.

good helping job nurses

Hey, I'm George. I think it's very important to have a [1]··· that makes you feel good. [2]··· people makes the world a better place and makes you happy too! People like [3]···, police officers and dentists look after people. They probably feel pretty [4]··· when they finish work for the day!

5 Complete the headings below with information about your class.

Name: ···
Things that are different this year: ···
Things that are the same as last year: ···

6 NOW YOU! Share your answers from exercise 5 in groups of three.

Do all exercises in your notebook

6 Meet Emma, Sarah and George

LESSON FOCUS

Grammar Review and consolidation of basic structures covered in a primary syllabus

Vocabulary Review and consolidation of basic vocabulary covered in a primary syllabus

Speaking Sharing observations and comparing this school year and the last

Resources

Teacher's i-solutions, Student's Book audio, Vlog and worksheets

MEET THE VLOGGERS

Video and worksheet available on the Richmond Learning Platform

- In pairs, ask students to complete the *Before you watch...* exercises on the vlog worksheet.
- Show students the vlog and ask them to complete the *While you watch...* exercises on the worksheet.
- In pairs, students compare answers.
- In small groups, tell students to complete the *After you watch...* exercises on the worksheet.

ANSWER KEY

Page 6

1 *Student's own answers*

2
1 school
2 case
3 on
4 around
5 in

3
1 am / 'm
2 do not / don't
3 are
4 visiting

4
1 job
2 Helping
3 nurses
4 good

5 *Student's own answers*

6 *Student's own answers*

Warmer

Tell students that you are going to tell them 3 simple things about yourself but that one is a lie and they have to guess the lie. Put the students in pairs or small groups to repeat the activity.

1 Get the students to leave their books closed and dictate the questions. Then ask them to open their books and check their questions before asking them in pairs or small groups.

2, 3 and 4 Put students into groups of three. When they've finished, write the answers to all three exercises on the board and get them to write them in their notebooks. Then each group of three could test how much the person who did the exercise remembers of the text with his/her book closed, using their books to prompt him/her. You could also get them to test each other's memory of all of the vloggers by reading facts about them for the others to guess the vlogger.

5 Encourage students to write as many things as they can and help them with any vocabulary they need.

6 **NOW YOU!** Ask students to swap seats with another student, so that they're not next to their usual partner. See what sentences they have in common.

Remind students to do all the exercises in their notebook

 CONTINUOUS ASSSESMENT Students can understand written texts about school and holidays.

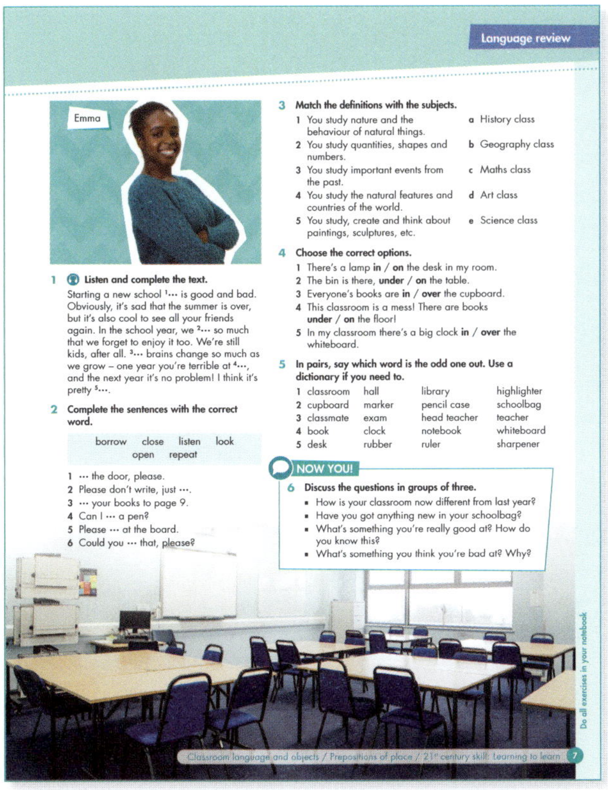

Language review

Emma

1 Listen and complete the text.

Starting a new school [1]··· is good and bad. Obviously, it's sad that the summer is over, but it's also cool to see all your friends again. In the school year, we [2]··· so much that we forget to enjoy it too. We're still kids, after all. [3]··· brains change so much as we grow – one year you're terrible at [4]···, and the next year it's no problem! I think it's pretty [5]···.

2 Complete the sentences with the correct word.

borrow close listen look open repeat

1 ··· the door, please.
2 Please don't write, just ···.
3 ··· your books to page 9.
4 Can I ··· a pen?
5 Please ··· at the board.
6 Could you ··· that, please?

3 Match the definitions with the subjects.

1 You study nature and the behaviour of natural things.
2 You study quantities, shapes and numbers.
3 You study important events from the past.
4 You study the natural features and countries of the world.
5 You study, create and think about paintings, sculptures, etc.

a History class
b Geography class
c Maths class
d Art class
e Science class

4 Choose the correct options.

1 There's a lamp **in** / **on** the desk in my room.
2 The bin is there, **under** / **on** the table.
3 Everyone's books are **in** / **over** the cupboard.
4 This classroom is a mess! There are books **under** / **on** the floor!
5 In my classroom there's a big clock **in** / **over** the whiteboard.

5 In pairs, say which word is the odd one out. Use a dictionary if you need to.

1	classroom	hall	library	highlighter
2	cupboard	marker	pencil case	schoolbag
3	classmate	exam	head teacher	teacher
4	book	clock	notebook	whiteboard
5	desk	rubber	ruler	sharpener

NOW YOU!

6 Discuss the questions in groups of three.

- How is your classroom now different from last year?
- Have you got anything new in your schoolbag?
- What's something you're really good at? How do you know this?
- What's something you think you're bad at? Why?

Do all exercises in your notebook

Classroom language and objects / Prepositions of place / 21st century skill: Learning to learn 7

ANSWER KEY

Page 7

1 **1** year
2 study
3 Human
4 something
5 interesting

2 **1** Close
2 listen
3 Open
4 borrow
5 look
6 repeat

3 **1** e **2** c **3** a **4** b **5** d

4 **1** on
2 under
3 in
4 on
5 over

5 **1** highlighter
2 marker
3 exam
4 clock
5 desk

6 *Student's own answers*

LESSON FOCUS

Grammar Prepositions of place
Vocabulary Classroom language and objects
Listening Listening and completing a text
Speaking A discussion about the classroom
21st century skills Students reflect on the classroom environment and their own academic strengths.

Resources
Teacher's i-solutions, Student's Book audio

Warmer

Put students in pairs and ask them to write down the names of as many things as they can see in the classroom. Give them a time limit and see who can come up with the most names written correctly. You could give them one point for correct items and two points for items that no one else has listed, and then calculate total points.

1 1.1 (See page 168 for transcripts) Tell students that they will listen to Emma speaking about starting school. Give them time to read the text and tell them there is one word missing in each gap, that they have to listen for. Answer any vocabulary questions to make sure they understand. Alternatively, you could get the students to close their books and listen first to take notes about what she says about starting school. Ask them if they agree with what she says.

2 Ask students who they think would say the sentences (a teacher or a student) before they do the exercise. You could get them to test each other with one student saying key words from a sentence and the other trying to remember the whole sentence.

3 To extend the exercise, ask students to write definitions for other subjects.

4 Introduce this exercise by placing a classroom object (e.g. a pen) on the desk and asking where it is and then placing the object in different places to elicit a variety of prepositions of place.

5 Elicit the first answer as an example and encourage students to give reasons for their answers.

6 **NOW YOU!** Tell students you will ask members of the groups to give answers from their group to encourage them to give extended answers and listen carefully to each other. When they've finished and you've discussed some answers, point out the importance of the skill of learning to learn; remind them that the more responsibility they take for their own learning, the more effectively they will learn.

Remind students to do all the exercises in their notebook

CONTINUOUS ASSESSMENT Students can understand classroom language and objects, and prepositions of place.

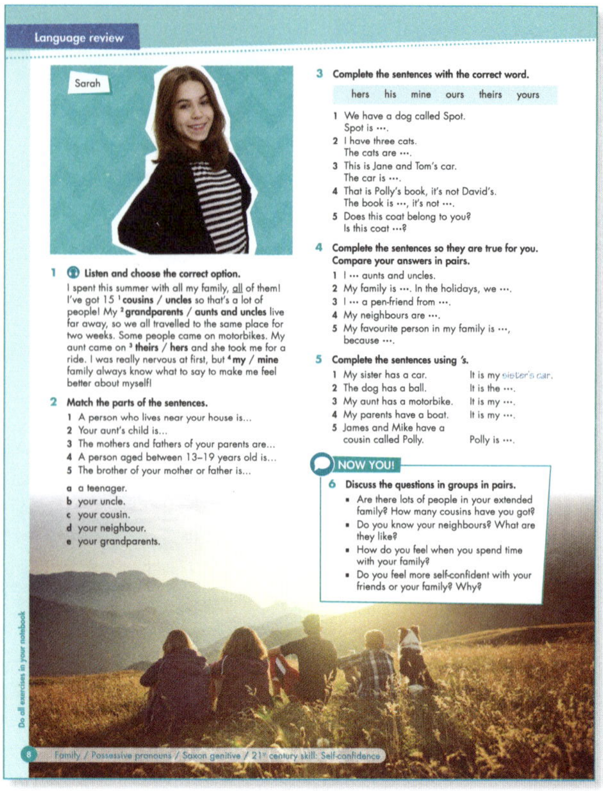

Language review

Sarah

1 Listen and choose the correct option.

I spent this summer with all my family, all of them! I've got 15 [1] **cousins / uncles** so that's a lot of people! My [2] **grandparents / aunts and uncles** live far away, so we all travelled to the same place for two weeks. Some people came on motorbikes. My aunt came on [3] **theirs / hers** and she took me for a ride. I was really nervous at first, but [4] **my / mine** family always know what to say to make me feel better about myself!

2 Match the parts of the sentences.

1 A person who lives near your house is...
2 Your aunt's child is...
3 The mothers and fathers of your parents are...
4 A person aged between 13–19 years old is...
5 The brother of your mother or father is...

a a teenager.
b your uncle.
c your cousin.
d your neighbour.
e your grandparents.

3 Complete the sentences with the correct word.

hers his mine ours theirs yours

1 We have a dog called Spot. Spot is ⋯.
2 I have three cats. The cats are ⋯.
3 This is Jane and Tom's car. The car is ⋯.
4 That is Polly's book, it's not David's. The book is ⋯, it's not ⋯.
5 Does this coat belong to you? Is this coat ⋯?

4 Complete the sentences so they are true for you. Compare your answers in pairs.

1 I ⋯ aunts and uncles.
2 My family is ⋯. In the holidays, we ⋯.
3 I ⋯ a pen-friend from ⋯.
4 My neighbours are ⋯.
5 My favourite person in my family is ⋯, because ⋯.

5 Complete the sentences using 's.

1 My sister has a car. It is my sister's car.
2 The dog has a ball. It is the ⋯.
3 My aunt has a motorbike. It is my ⋯.
4 My parents have a boat. It is my ⋯.
5 James and Mike have a cousin called Polly. Polly is ⋯.

NOW YOU!

6 Discuss the questions in groups in pairs.

- Are there lots of people in your extended family? How many cousins have you got?
- Do you know your neighbours? What are they like?
- How do you feel when you spend time with your family?
- Do you feel more self-confident with your friends or your family? Why?

Do all exercises in your notebook

8 Family / Possessive pronouns / Saxon genitive / 21st century skill: Self-confidence

LESSON FOCUS

Grammar Possessive pronouns; Saxon genitive
Vocabulary Family
Listening Listening to choose the correct option
Speaking A discussion about family and community
21st century skills Self-confidence

Resources

Teacher's i-solutions, Student's Book audio

Warmer

Tell the students about your family, writing any family words students need on the board in a family tree format. Then put them in pairs or a small group to talk about theirs.

1 1.2 (See page 168 for transcripts) Tell students they will hear Sarah talk about spending the summer with her extended family. Let them read the text and guess answers before they check with the audio.

2 Check pronunciation as you go through the answers to the exercise.

3 Write the subject personal pronouns on the board and leave a space for possessive pronouns under each one for students to come to the board and complete after the exercise.

4 Complete and read the first sentence out loud as an example for the students. After completing the exercise, ask pairs what they had in common.

5 Draw students' attention back to the sentences in exercise 3 with 's in them to check they understand that it shows possession. After they do the exercise, consolidate by pointing to students' belongings and asking whose they are.

6 NOW YOU! Put students in pairs or groups and ask them to note any interesting or surprising answers. After the discussion, ask volunteers to report answers and use the last question to discuss the importance of self-confidence and of factors influencing it. Remind them that being supportive of others helps self-confidence because supportive people tend to be appreciated and positivity breeds positivity.

ANSWER KEY

Page 8

1 **1** cousins
2 aunts and uncles
3 hers
4 my

2 **1** d **2** c **3** e **4** a **5** b

3 **1** ours
2 mine
3 theirs
4 hers; his
5 yours

4 *Student's own answers*

5 **1** sister's car
2 dog's ball
3 aunt's motorbike
4 parents' boat
5 James and Mike's cousin

6 *Student's own answers*

Remind students to do all the exercises in their notebook

CONTINUOUS ASSESSMENT Students can understand and use possessive pronouns, the Saxon genitive and vocabulary for family.

Language review

George

4 In pairs, copy and complete the table about workplaces.

School	Station	Outdoors	Office	Hospital
teacher	firefighter	gardener	···	···
···	···	···	···	···

5 Copy the text and put capital letters in the correct places. Check your answers in pairs.

my name is george franklin. i'm english and i'm from manchester. my favourite subject at school is french, the classes are on mondays and wednesdays. my teacher's name is marianne, she's from paris.

1 Listen and complete the text.

I had a good summer, but my parents didn't! They work a lot because they've got their own [1]···. I don't think that I would like to have my own business in the future; it's a lot of [2]··· and not a lot of holidays! I wouldn't like to work in [3]··· either. I like to talk to people, not look at [4]··· all day. I would like to help people. Maybe I'll be [5]···.

NOW YOU!

6 Discuss the questions in groups of four.

- Would you prefer to be a lawyer or a police officer? Why?
- Does someone in your family have a good job? What is it?
- Would you prefer to work with people or computers? Why?
- Is it better to work in an office or outdoors? Why?

2 Match the parts of the sentences.

1 Journalists investigate and write…
2 Babysitters look after…
3 Mechanics repair and maintain…
4 Lawyers go to court and protect…
5 Dentists examine, clean and repair…

a your teeth.
b stories for the media.
c people and businesses.
d babies and small children.
e the engines of cars, vans, etc.

3 Complete the sentences with *a*, *an* or *the*.

1 Being ··· doctor and helping lots of people must be wonderful.
2 I wouldn't like to be ··· president of ··· country.
3 My dream is to be ··· astronaut.
4 ··· library is my favourite place, I'd love to be ··· librarian.
5 I go to the gym every day, I want to be ··· athlete!

Do all exercises in your notebook

Jobs / Articles / Punctuation / 21st century skill: Citizenship 9

LESSON FOCUS

Grammar Articles; Punctuation
Vocabulary Jobs
Listening Listening to complete a text
Speaking A discussion of job preferences
21st century skills Citizenship

Resources

Teacher's i-solutions, Student's Book audio

Warmer

Describe a job and have students guess what it is. Encourage them to use the indefinite article in their answers. Get volunteers to come to the front of the class and do the same.

1 1.3 (See page 168 for transcripts) Tell students they are going to hear George talk about work and that they have to complete the text with one or two words in each gap. Let them read and guess answers before playing the audio.

2 Remind students of their descriptions of jobs in the Warmer and get them to complete the exercise.

3 Say 'artist' and ask students whether you would say 'a artist' or 'an artist'; elicit that it's 'an' because it starts with a vowel. Students complete the exercise.

4 Help students with any vocabulary they need, encouraging them to ask you in English: 'What do you call the person who…?'

5 Elicit when we use capital letters, and then ask students to add any categories they forgot after you check the exercise.

6 NOW YOU! Put students into groups and ask them to note any interesting answers from others to tell you afterwards. Ask for volunteers to report interesting answers. Ask what they think the importance of having and doing a good job is, and what they think makes a good citizen: honesty, responsibility, respect, kindness, integrity, etc.

ANSWER KEY

Page 9

1
1 business
2 stress
3 an office
4 a computer
5 a firefighter

2 **1** b **2** d **3** e **4** c **5** a

3
1 a
2 the; a
3 an
4 The; a
5 an

4 *Suggested answers:*

School	Station	Outdoors	Office	Hospital
teacher	firefighter	gardener	journalist	doctor
librarian	police officer	archaeologist	lawyer	nurse

5 My name is George Franklin. I'm English and I'm from Manchester. My favourite subject at school is French, the classes are on Mondays and Wednesdays. My teacher's name is Marianne, she's from Paris.

6 *Student's own answers*

Remind students to do all the exercises in their notebook

CONTINUOUS ASSESSMENT Students can use articles, punctuation and vocabulary for jobs.

1 OUR WORLD

At the start of each unit and lesson, explain to the students what the objectives are.

Language objectives

Grammar

Present simple *be*
- Students practise the affirmative forms of *be* in the present simple.

Present simple *be*: *wh-* questions
- Students practise *wh-* question forms with *be* in the present simple.

Vocabulary

Greetings and introductions: Greetings: *Good morning., Hey!, How are you doing?, How are you today?, How's it going?, I'm very well, thank you., It was nice to see you., Not too bad., See you later!*, Introductions: *I'd like to introduce …, I'm …, My name is …, Nice to meet you …, This is …, This is my friend, …*
- Students practise basic phrases for greeting people and introducing themselves and others.

Countries and nationalities: *Argentina/Argentinian, Australia/Australian, Belgium/Belgian, Brazil/Brazilian, Canada/Canadian, China/Chinese, Colombia/Colombian, England/English, France/French, Germany/German, Greece/Greek, India/Indian, Ireland/Irish, Italy/Italian, Japan/Japanese, Mexico/Mexican, The Netherlands/Dutch, New Zealand/from New Zealand, Peru/Peruvian, Portugal/Portuguese, Spain/Spanish, Switzerland/Swiss, Turkey/Turkish*
- Students practise vocabulary for countries and nationalities.

Hobbies and interests: *basketball, listening to music, reading, rollerblading, spending time with friends, surfing, swimming, watching films, action films, animated films, classical music, comedy, fashion, folk music, jazz, pop music, R&B, series*
- Students practise vocabulary for talking about their hobbies and interests.

Idioms and expressions

Determination: *reach for the stars, throw in the towel, practice makes perfect*
- Students look at idioms and expressions related to determination.

Recycled language

Subject pronouns; Numbers; Letters; Question words

Skills objectives

Speaking

- Students ask and answer basic personal questions.
- Students introduce themselves and others formally and informally.
- Students give basic personal information about celebrities.
- Students discuss their hobbies.

Pronunciation: Students practise the /aɪ/ sound.

Pairwork: Students use various mediation techniques in order to ask and answer questions about famous young people.

Listening

- Students listen to match conversations to elements in a picture.
- Students listen to order a conversation.
- Students listen to help distinguish formal from informal register.
- Students listen to complete vocabulary tables.
- Students listen to idioms and expressions in context.

Reading

- Students read a text to complete a fact file.
- Students read a text in detail to decide if sentences about it are true or false.
- Students read words and expressions in context to determine how they are used.

Core values: Students consider and discuss the importance of **diversity** and the advantages and disadvantages of having the same interests as others.

Writing

- Students focus on the style and format of a model personal profile to copy in their own writing.
- Students plan, write and check a personal profile.

Focus on linking language: *also, and, apart from, but, like*

Remind students to do all the exercises in their notebook

Learning to learn tools

SPEAKING TOOLS Students practise making mental connections between words with similar pronunciation and practise saying expressions to themselves.	**LISTENING TOOLS** Students imagine the speakers to help their understanding.
READING TOOLS Students focus on text type and task purpose to help their comprehension.	**WRITING TOOLS** Students recognise the importance of models to help their writing skills.

Project objectives: Survey

Task 1 Students practise introducing themselves and asking questions.

Task 2 Students design a form.

Task 3 Students test and improve the form.

Audiovisual objectives

Vlog: Students watch and listen to Sarah talk about her family and her best friend.

Culture: Students watch and listen to Sarah talk about Irish dancing.

Grammar animations: Students are presented with visual presentations of the unit grammar.

Key competences

LC **Linguistic**
pages 10 - 17

MST **Mathematical and Science and Technology**
pages 10 - 12

DC **Digital**
pages 10,17

SCC **Social and Civic**
pages 10 - 17

CAE **Cultural awareness and expression**
pages 10, 12-17

LL **Learning to learn**
pages 11, 13, 14, 16, 17

IE **Sense of initiative and entrepreneurship**
pages 11, 13, 16

→ See pages 42-43 **Key competences**

CEFR Mediation

1.1 Acting as an intermediary in informal situations
Can communicate other people's personal details and simple information.

1.2 Facilitating pluricultural space
Can facilitate a simple intercultural exchange.

1.3 Processing text in writing
Can list relevant information contained in short simple texts.

1.4 Processing text in writing
Can pick out and reproduce key words and phrases from a short text.

1.5 Facilitating pluricultural space
Can exchange simple information about values and attitudes to language and culture.

Project Explaining data in speech
Can interpret and describe simple visuals on familiar topics.

Unit review Collaborating to construct meaning
Can make simple remarks and pose occasional questions to indicate that he/she is following.

Pairwork Relaying specific information in speech
Can relay specific, relevant information contained in short, simple texts.

→ See pages 30-33 **Mediation**

Remind students to do all the exercises in their notebook

1.1 Listening and vocabulary

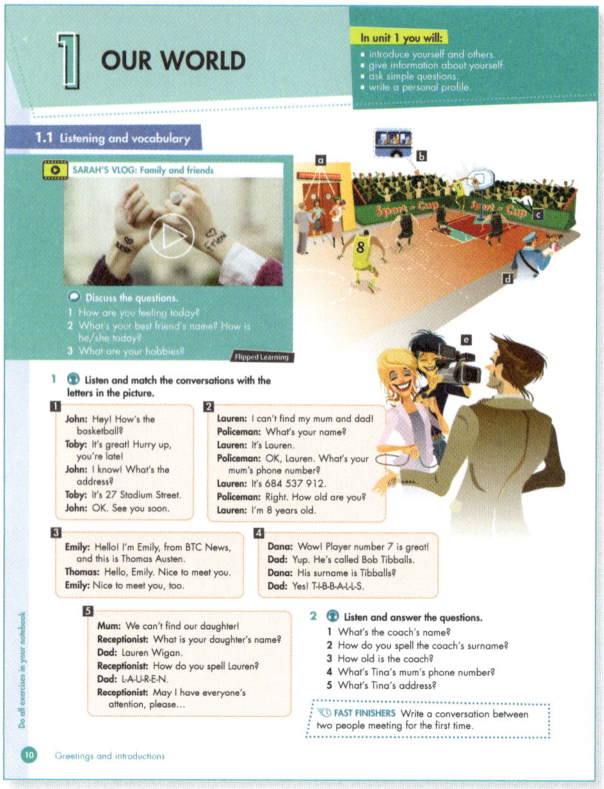

1 OUR WORLD

In unit 1 you will:
- introduce yourself and others.
- give information about yourself.
- ask simple questions.
- write a personal profile.

1.1 Listening and vocabulary

SARAH'S VLOG: Family and friends

Discuss the questions.
1 How are you feeling today?
2 What's your best friend's name? How is he/she today?
3 What are your hobbies?

Flipped Learning

a b c d e

1 **Listen and match the conversations with the letters in the picture.**

1
John: Hey! How's the basketball?
Toby: It's great! Hurry up, you're late!
John: I know! What's the address?
Toby: It's 27 Stadium Street.
John: OK. See you soon.

2
Lauren: I can't find my mum and dad!
Policeman: What's your name?
Lauren: It's Lauren.
Policeman: OK, Lauren. What's your mum's phone number?
Lauren: It's 684 537 912.
Policeman: Right. How old are you?
Lauren: I'm 8 years old.

3
Emily: Hello! I'm Emily, from BTC News, and this is Thomas Austen.
Thomas: Hello, Emily. Nice to meet you.
Emily: Nice to meet you, too.

4
Dana: Wow! Player number 7 is great!
Dad: Yup. He's called Bob Tibballs.
Dana: His surname is Tibballs?
Dad: Yes! T-I-B-B-A-L-L-S.

5
Mum: We can't find our daughter!
Receptionist: What is your daughter's name?
Dad: Lauren Wigan.
Receptionist: How do you spell Lauren?
Dad: L-A-U-R-E-N.
Receptionist: May I have everyone's attention, please…

2 **Listen and answer the questions.**
1 What's the coach's name?
2 How do you spell the coach's surname?
3 How old is the coach?
4 What's Tina's mum's phone number?
5 What's Tina's address?

FAST FINISHERS Write a conversation between two people meeting for the first time.

Do all exercises in your notebook

10 Greetings and introductions

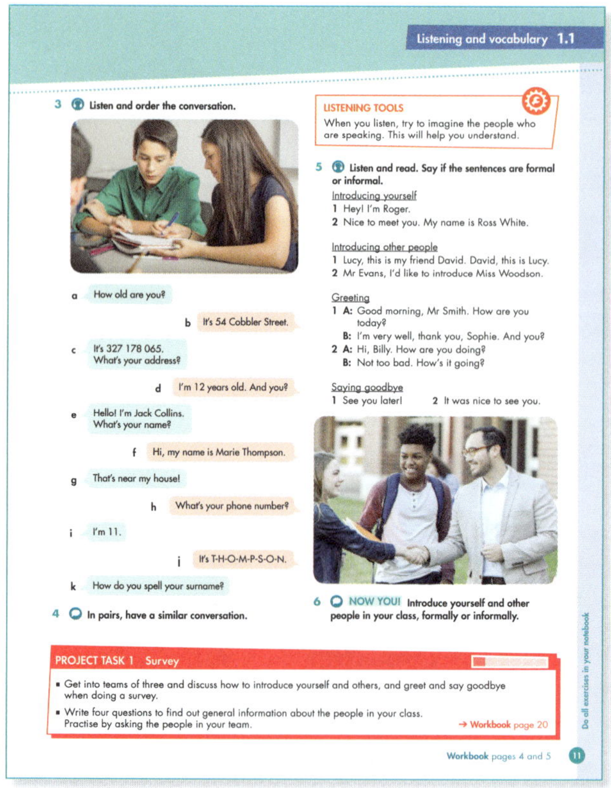

Listening and vocabulary 1.1

3 **Listen and order the conversation.**

a How old are you?
b It's 54 Cobbler Street.
c It's 327 178 065. What's your address?
d I'm 12 years old. And you?
e Hello! I'm Jack Collins. What's your name?
f Hi, my name is Marie Thompson.
g That's near my house!
h What's your phone number?
i I'm 11.
j It's T-H-O-M-P-S-O-N.
k How do you spell your surname?

4 **In pairs, have a similar conversation.**

LISTENING TOOLS
When you listen, try to imagine the people who are speaking. This will help you understand.

5 **Listen and read. Say if the sentences are formal or informal.**

Introducing yourself
1 Hey! I'm Roger.
2 Nice to meet you. My name is Ross White.

Introducing other people
1 Lucy, this is my friend David. David, this is Lucy.
2 Mr Evans, I'd like to introduce Miss Woodson.

Greeting
1 **A:** Good morning, Mr Smith. How are you today?
B: I'm very well, thank you, Sophie. And you?
2 **A:** Hi, Billy. How are you doing?
B: Not too bad. How's it going?

Saying goodbye
1 See you later! 2 It was nice to see you.

6 NOW YOU! **Introduce yourself and other people in your class, formally or informally.**

PROJECT TASK 1 Survey
- Get into teams of three and discuss how to introduce yourself and others, and greet and say goodbye when doing a survey.
- Write four questions to find out general information about the people in your class. Practise by asking the people in your team. → Workbook page 20

Do all exercises in your notebook

Workbook pages 4 and 5 11

ANSWER KEY

Pages 10-11

1
1 b
2 d
3 e
4 c
5 a

2
1 Sam Veasey
2 V-E-A-S-E-Y
3 33 years old
4 932 466 82
5 32 Green Street

3
1 e
2 f
3 k
4 j
5 a
6 d
7 i
8 h
9 c
10 b
11 g

4 *Student's own answers*

5 **Introducing yourself**
1 informal
2 formal

Introducing other people
1 informal
2 formal

Greeting
1 formal
2 informal

Saying goodbye
1 informal
2 formal

6 *Student's own answers*

Remind students to do all the exercises in their notebook

LESSON FOCUS

Grammar Greetings and introductions

Listening Greetings, introductions, saying goodbye and sharing personal information

Speaking Formal and informal introductions

Project task 1 Practise introducing yourselves and asking questions

Resources

Teacher's i-solutions, Student's Book audio, Vlog and worksheet

Flipped Learning

SARAH'S VLOG: Family and friends

- Make sure to set up the **Flipped Learning** work with the students beforehand. **See pages 20-23 for complete Flipped Learning guidelines.**
- Ask students to put the **Flipped Learning worksheets** on their desks and walk around to check how many have completed the Flipped task.
- In pairs or small groups, ask students to compare and check the *Before you watch...* and *While you watch...* exercises on the worksheet.
- Show students **Sarah's vlog** and ask volunteers to provide correct answers and clarify any doubts other students may have.
- Choose three or four students to read aloud their answers to the *After you watch...* exercises on the worksheet and encourage some class discussion.
- Move straight to exercise 1 on page 10.

Warmer

Watch Sarah's vlog and discuss the questions with the whole class. If you don't have video facilities, simply discuss the questions.

1 1.4 (See page 168 for transcripts) Ask students to say what the picture shows, helping them with vocabulary where needed. Students then complete the exercise.

2 1.5 (See page 168 for transcripts) Tell the students they are going to listen to another conversation at the basketball arena. Give them time to read the questions before playing the audio and completing the exercise. If you have time, in pairs get them to take turns to cover the questions and read the answers to remember the questions.

FAST FINISHERS Students can complete this exercise alone or in pairs.

3 1.6 (See page 168 for transcripts) Find the first and second answers together as a class (e and f). Then play the audio, pausing to give time for students to give you the answers. Get students to repeat the conversation.

4 You could write the conversation from exercise 3 on the board with gaps where students have to use their information, and then erase more words so they have to recite more of the conversation from memory.

LISTENING TOOLS

Draw students' attention to the **Listening tool.** Imagining the speaker and the context helps with listening comprehension. Tell students to apply this technique to the next exercise.

5 1.7 (See page 168 for transcripts) Play the audio and have students complete the exercise. Encourage them to tell you anything else about what they think the speakers might be like. Then play the audio again and get them to repeat the phrases, copying the tone.

6 **NOW YOU!** Put students into pairs. They are going to invent new identities for themselves, with a first name and a surname. Say that you're first going to practise informal introductions. Tell them that their pairs have to introduce themselves to as many other pairs as they can and give them a time limit. When you stop, see which pair introduced themselves the most and then repeat the activity with formal introductions and their formal identities. If you have time, repeat again with greetings both informal and formal and see how many students remember the identities of the students they met in the introductions activity.

PROJECT TASK 1 Survey

Organise students into teams of three. Tell students that during this project they will be designing and carrying out a survey and presenting the results to the class.

Remind students that they need to keep their project notes together in their **Workbook** (page 20) or in their own notebook.

→ See pages 24-27 **Projects**

FURTHER PRACTICE

Workbook pages 4-5
- **Grammar reference and practice** pages 84 and 93
- **Wordlist and exercises** pages 98 and 102

Remind students to do all the exercises in their notebook

CONTINUOUS ASSESSMENT Students can use formal and informal greetings and introductions

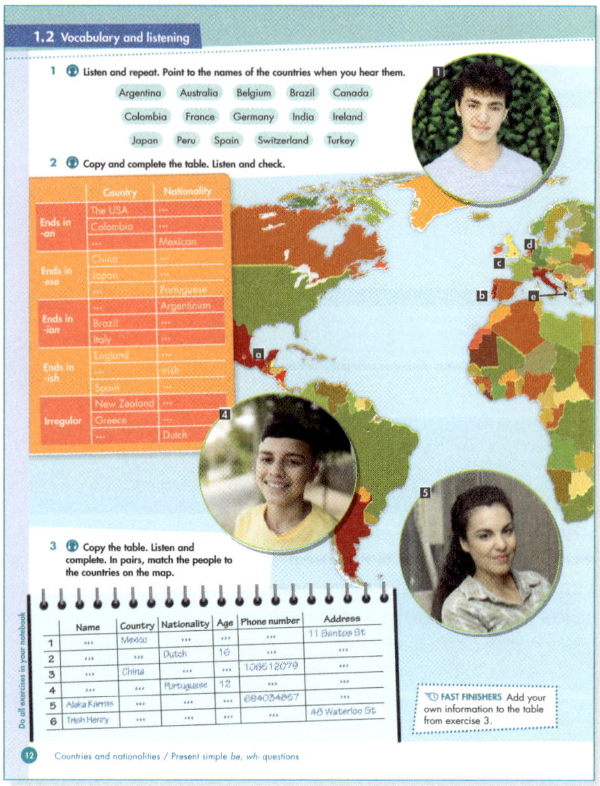

1 Listen and repeat. Point to the names of the countries when you hear them.

Argentina Australia Belgium Brazil Canada
Colombia France Germany India Ireland
Japan Peru Spain Switzerland Turkey

2 Copy and complete the table. Listen and check.

	Country	Nationality
Ends in -an	The USA	...
	Colombia	...
	...	Mexican
Ends in -ese	China	...
	Japan	...
	...	Portuguese
Ends in -ian	...	Argentinian
	Brazil	...
	Italy	...
Ends in -ish	England	...
	...	Irish
	Spain	...
Irregular	New Zealand	...
	Greece	...
	...	Dutch

3 Copy the table. Listen and complete. In pairs, match the people to the countries on the map.

	Name	Country	Nationality	Age	Phone number	Address
1	...	Mexico	...	...	...	11 Santos St
2	...	...	Dutch	16	...	...
3	...	China	...	...	106512079	...
4	...	...	Portuguese	12	...	...
5	Aleka Karras	...	...	...	694034857	...
6	Trish Henry	...	...	...	...	48 Waterloo St

FAST FINISHERS Add your own information to the table from exercise 3.

Do all exercises in your notebook

PRESENT SIMPLE *BE*

I	am ('m)	from Poland.
He She It	is ('s)	12 years old. French. Monday today.
You We They	are ('re)	16 years old. from Japan. German.

Grammar reference page 107

PRESENT SIMPLE *BE*: *WH-* QUESTIONS

Where is she from? She is (She's) from Ecuador.
Where are they from?
They are (They're) from Portugal.
What is your name? It is (It's) Steven.

Grammar reference page 107

4 Complete the conversation.

Sam: Hello, nice to meet you.
Evan: Hi! What [1]... your name?
Sam: My name's Sam. What's your name?
Evan: [2]... Evan.
Sam: How old [3]... you?
Evan: [4]... 12. Where [5]... you from?
Sam: I'm from [6].... I'm Irish. Where are you from?
Evan: I'm from America. I'm [7]....
Sam: Oh! Maria is American! [8]... from America, too!

SPEAKING TOOLS
To remember the pronunciation of a word, connect it in your mind to another word that sounds the same. For example, *nice* and *ice cream*.

Pronunciation: /aɪ/

5 Listen and repeat.
1 I
2 I'm fine.
3 Nice to meet you.
4 I'm from Ireland, I'm Irish.

PROJECT TASK 2 Survey
- In your teams, write two more survey questions. Include a question about nationality.
- Design a form to collect answers. Write your questions on the left-hand side and leave space on the right for your classmates' answers.

→ Workbook page 20

Do all exercises in your notebook

ANSWER KEY

Pages 12-13

1 *Student's own answers*

2

Country	Nationality
The USA	American
Colombia	Colombian
Mexico	Mexican
China	Chinese
Japan	Japanese

Country	Nationality
Portugal	Portuguese
Argentina	Argentinian
Brazil	Brazilian
Italy	Italian
England	English

Country	Nationality
Ireland	Irish
Spain	Spanish
New Zealand	from New Zealand
Greece	Greek
The Netherlands	Dutch

3

	Name	Country	Nationality	Age	Phone number	Address
1	Jaime Ramírez	Mexico	Mexican	18	55 5450 170	11 Santos St
2	Hendrika Jansen	The Netherlands	Dutch	16	20 672 560	75 Albert Street
3	Li Wei Ying	China	Chinese	32	106512079	Renmin St
4	Osvaldo Santos	Portugal	Portuguese	12	21 346 123	17 Farol Street
5	Aleka Karras	Greece	Greek	45	694034857	2 Toro St
6	Trish Henry	England	English	40	020 7980 442	48 Waterloo St

1 a **2** d **3** f **4** b **5** e **6** c

4
1 is / 's
2 It is / It's / My name is / My name's
3 Are
4 I'm / I am
5 are
6 Ireland
7 American
8 She is / She's

5 *Student's own answers*

Remind students to do all the exercises in their notebook

LESSON FOCUS

Grammar Present simple *be*, *wh-* questions
Vocabulary Countries and nationalities
Listening Personal details including nationality
Speaking Practise personal phrases with the /aɪ/ sound
Project task 2 Design a form

Resources
Teacher's i-solutions, Student's Book audio

Preparation A world map in English

Warmer

Put the map somewhere the students can access easily. Put them in groups and get each group to appoint a writer and a runner. Tell them that you are going to ask them to write the names of countries according to your instructions. Tell them the runners can go to the map and find answers, the writers write them and the rest of the group helps. Give them categories like *Countries that begin with 'U'; Countries in the Mediterranean; African countries with no coast.* For each category give them a time limit and see which group can write the most countries correctly.

1 1.8 (See page 169 for transcripts) Get students to go to the map and point to the countries as the class repeats.

2 1.9 (See page 169 for transcripts) Highlight the similarities in stress patterns within nationalities with the same endings and get students to repeat after the audio.

3 1.10 (See page 169 for transcripts) Tell the students that they will hear the people introduce themselves in order and that the last two talk to each other. The students complete the exercise.

FAST FINISHERS Students can complete this exercise alone or in pairs.

PRESENT SIMPLE *BE* AND PRESENT SIMPLE *BE*: *WH-* QUESTIONS

Flipped Learning

Draw students' attention to the **Grammar table**. Remind students that they can use this as a quick reference while completing the exercises.
Show students the **Grammar animation** and/or refer students to the **Grammar reference** on page 107 for further information on form and use.

→ See page 23 for how to flip the **grammar lesson**

4 Get students to refer to the grammar table as they complete the exercise. If there's time, get them to practise the conversation in pairs with their invented identities from page 11, exercise 6.

SPEAKING TOOLS

Get students to read the **Speaking tool** and draw their attention to the countries with the letter 'I' in them in exercises 1 and 2. Ask them which countries have an 'i' as in 'nice' and 'ice cream' (Ireland and China).

Pronunciation

5 1.11 (See page 169 for transcripts) Put the phonetic script /aɪ/ on the board and drill before students complete the exercise. Make sure they pronounce all the /aɪ/ sounds correctly.

PROJECT TASK 2 Survey

Check that students have paper that's big enough and leave enough space for their classmates' answers. Remind students that they need to keep their project notes together in their **Workbook** (page 20) or in their own notebook.

→ See pages 24-27 **Projects**

FURTHER PRACTICE

Workbook pages 6-7
- **Grammar reference and practice** pages 84 and 93
- **Wordlist and exercises** pages 98 and 102

Vocabulary and Grammar worksheets available to download and edit from the **Richmond** *Learning* **Platform**

→ See pages 38-39 **Mixed-ability classes**

Remind students to do all the exercises in their notebook

CONTINUOUS ASSESSMENT Students can talk about countries and nationalities and use *be* in the present simple affirmative and questions

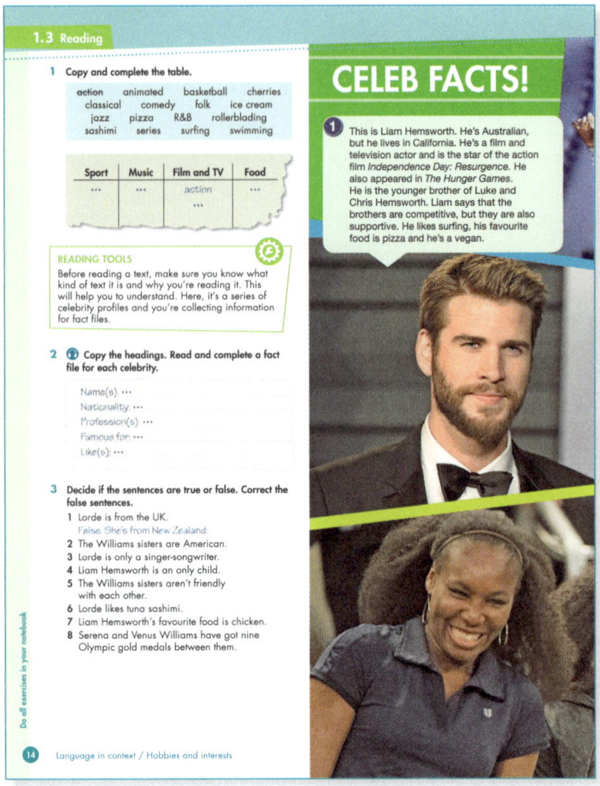

1.3 Reading

1 Copy and complete the table.

action animated basketball cherries classical comedy folk ice cream jazz pizza R&B rollerblading sashimi series surfing swimming

Sport	Music	Film and TV	Food
···	···	action ···	···

READING TOOLS
Before reading a text, make sure you know what kind of text it is and why you're reading it. This will help you to understand. Here, it's a series of celebrity profiles and you're collecting information for fact files.

2 Copy the headings. Read and complete a fact file for each celebrity.

Name(s): ···
Nationality: ···
Profession(s): ···
Famous for: ···
Like(s): ···

3 Decide if the sentences are true or false. Correct the false sentences.
1 Lorde is from the UK.
False. She's from New Zealand.
2 The Williams sisters are American.
3 Lorde is only a singer-songwriter.
4 Liam Hemsworth is an only child.
5 The Williams sisters aren't friendly with each other.
6 Lorde likes tuna sashimi.
7 Liam Hemsworth's favourite food is chicken.
8 Serena and Venus Williams have got nine Olympic gold medals between them.

CELEB FACTS!

1 This is Liam Hemsworth. He's Australian, but he lives in California. He's a film and television actor and is the star of the action film *Independence Day: Resurgence*. He also appeared in *The Hunger Games*. He is the younger brother of Luke and Chris Hemsworth. Liam says that the brothers are competitive, but they are also supportive. He likes surfing, his favourite food is pizza and he's a vegan.

Do all exercises in your notebook

14 Language in context / Hobbies and interests

Reading 1.3

2 This is Lorde. She's from Auckland, New Zealand. She's a singer-songwriter and record producer. She's famous for the hit song 'Royals', but she's also known for *The Hunger Games*, like Liam Hemsworth! She recorded the soundtrack. She has two Grammy Awards, a Brit Award and ten New Zealand Music Awards. She likes lots of different kinds of music: jazz, folk, pop, R&B and hip-hop. Her favourite food is tuna sashimi.

3 These are the Williams sisters, Venus and Serena. They're from Florida, in the USA. They're professional tennis players, and between them, they have won over 100 titles and eight Olympic gold medals. Like the Hemsworth brothers, the Williams sisters are rivals and good friends.
Serena's favourite hobbies, apart from tennis, are reading, watching films and spending time with family and friends. Venus likes fashion and listening to music, and her favourite food is cherry pie.

4 Complete the sentences.

apart from hit rivals supportive vegan

1 A ··· only eats food that's not from animals.
2 ··· are people who compete with each other.
3 If you're ···, you help people.
4 The Beatles have got more ··· songs than any other band.
5 ··· singing, Lady Gaga is also an actress.

5 Work in pairs. Take turns to say a sentence and guess which celebrity it is about.

This person is from Australia and he likes surfing.
Is it Liam Hemsworth?

CORE VALUES Diversity

6 Copy the fact file headings onto a piece of paper. Complete them for you.
- Favourite sport
- Favourite film
- Favourite music
- Favourite food

7 Work in small groups and follow the instructions.
1 Swap fact files.
2 Take it in turns to read the fact files aloud and guess who the person is.
3 Talk about each category and say which answers are similar and which are different.
4 Count how many different answers there are for each category. Then count the total differences.
5 Compare your total with the rest of the class. Which group has the most diverse range?

8 In pairs, make a list of five advantages and disadvantages about having the same interests as other people.
Advantages:
1 You can do things together.
Disadvantages:
1 You can't learn new things from each other.

FAST FINISHERS Finish this sentence:
Diversity is important because...

Do all exercises in your notebook

Workbook pages 8 and 9 15

ANSWER KEY

Pages 14-15

1

Sport	Music	Film and TV	Food
basketball	classical	action	cherries
rollerblading	folk	animated	ice cream
surfing	jazz	comedy	pizza
swimming	R&B	series	sashimi

2 **Name(s):** Liam Hemsworth
Nationality: Australian
Profession(s): film and television actor
Famous for: *Independence Day: Resurgence* and *The Hunger Games*. Also, younger brother of Luke and Chris Hemsworth
Likes: surfing, pizza

Name(s): Lorde
Nationality: from New Zealand
Profession(s): singer-songwriter and record producer
Famous for: 'Royals' and the soundtrack for *The Hunger Games*
Likes: jazz, folk, pop, R&B, hip-hop, tuna sashimi

Name(s): Venus and Serena Williams
Nationality: American
Profession(s): tennis players
Famous for: winning over 100 titles and eight Olympic gold medals
Likes: Serena: reading, watching films, spending time with family and friends
Venus: fashion, listening to music, cherry pie

3 **1** False. She's from New Zealand.
2 True
3 False. She is also a record producer.
4 False. He has two brothers.
5 False. They are good friends.
6 True.
7 False. His favourite food is pizza.
8 False. They have got eight gold medals between them.

4 **1** vegan
2 rivals
3 supportive
4 hit
5 Apart from

5 *Student's own answers*

6 *Student's own answers*

7 *Student's own answers*

8 *Student's own answers*

Remind students to do all the exercises in their notebook

LESSON FOCUS

Language in context Hobbies and interests

Core values Diversity

Resources

Teacher's i-solutions, Student's Book audio

➔ See pages 36-37 **Literature**

Warmer

Put the categories from exercise 1 on the board: *Sport, Music, Film and TV* and *Food*. Put students in pairs or small groups and get them to copy the categories. Shout a random letter and tell students to think of a word that fits in each category and that the first pair/group to have something for all categories is the winner. Let them use names if you think it helps.

1 Students can simply add to their list from the categories game if you've done the activity. Help with any unfamiliar vocabulary by using examples where possible.

READING TOOLS

Ask students what kind of text they see on pages 14-15. Get them to read the **Reading tool** and tell them that they will have time to read in more detail and check unfamiliar vocabulary afterwards.

2 1.12 (See page 169 for transcripts) Start the fact file for Liam Hemsworth together to make sure the students are focused on the task at hand and tell them that you will deal with unfamiliar vocabulary later.

3 Give students more time to complete this exercise. If they ask about unfamiliar vocabulary, encourage them to guess before you explain or let them use a dictionary.

4 Tell students that they encountered all of this vocabulary in the text. For any words or expressions they don't understand, encourage them to find them in the text and guess their meaning from context before completing the exercise.

5 Encourage students to choose information they find interesting and any vocabulary they've just learnt in this exercise.

CORE VALUES Diversity

6 This exercise gives students the chance to respond personally to the text they have read. Point out that they will read each other's fact files in the next exercise and try to guess who wrote each fact file, so they should try and put something interesting and guessable in their fact file.

7 Make sure students show respect for each other's choices. Show interest in any choices that are unusual and ask a question or two to generate interest among the rest of the class.

8 More advantages include that you can share things related to your interest; you can share knowledge and skills; it can give you an identity; it can help you feel like you belong. More disadvantages include that it could be boring if everyone had the same interests; you could miss out on an unusual interest and what it might teach you; the more people have the same interests the harder it can be for people who don't share them.

FAST FINISHERS Students can complete this exercise alone or in pairs.

FURTHER PRACTICE

Workbook pages 8-9

Remind students to do all the exercises in their notebook

CONTINUOUS ASSESSMENT Students can understand vocabulary for hobbies and interests in a text about celebrities.

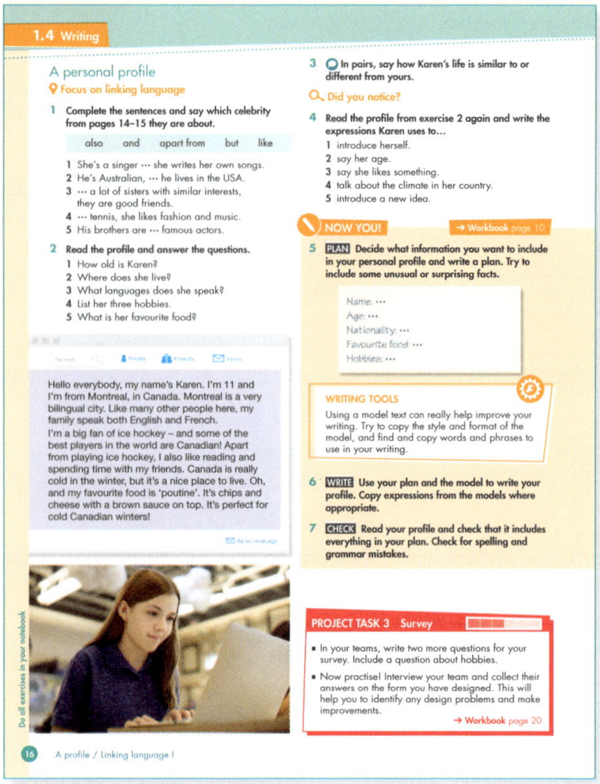

1.4 Writing

A personal profile

Focus on linking language

1 Complete the sentences and say which celebrity from pages 14–15 they are about.

also | and | apart from | but | like

1 She's a singer ··· she writes her own songs.
2 He's Australian, ··· he lives in the USA.
3 ··· a lot of sisters with similar interests, they are good friends.
4 ··· tennis, she likes fashion and music.
5 His brothers are ··· famous actors.

2 Read the profile and answer the questions.
1 How old is Karen?
2 Where does she live?
3 What languages does she speak?
4 List her three hobbies.
5 What is her favourite food?

Hello everybody, my name's Karen. I'm 11 and I'm from Montreal, in Canada. Montreal is a very bilingual city. Like many other people here, my family speak both English and French.
I'm a big fan of ice hockey – and some of the best players in the world are Canadian! Apart from playing ice hockey, I also like reading and spending time with my friends. Canada is really cold in the winter, but it's a nice place to live. Oh, and my favourite food is 'poutine'. It's chips and cheese with a brown sauce on top. It's perfect for cold Canadian winters!

3 In pairs, say how Karen's life is similar to or different from yours.

Did you notice?

4 Read the profile from exercise 2 again and write the expressions Karen uses to...
1 introduce herself.
2 say her age.
3 say she likes something.
4 talk about the climate in her country.
5 introduce a new idea.

NOW YOU! → Workbook page 10

5 PLAN Decide what information you want to include in your personal profile and write a plan. Try to include some unusual or surprising facts.

Name: ···
Age: ···
Nationality: ···
Favourite food: ···
Hobbies: ···

WRITING TOOLS
Using a model text can really help improve your writing. Try to copy the style and format of the model, and find and copy words and phrases to use in your writing.

6 WRITE Use your plan and the model to write your profile. Copy expressions from the models where appropriate.

7 CHECK Read your profile and check that it includes everything in your plan. Check for spelling and grammar mistakes.

PROJECT TASK 3 Survey
- In your teams, write two more questions for your survey. Include a question about hobbies.
- Now practise! Interview your team and collect their answers on the form you have designed. This will help you to identify any design problems and make improvements.

→ Workbook page 20

Do all exercises in your notebook

16 A profile / Linking language I

ANSWER KEY

Page 16

1 **1** and; Lorde
2 but; Liam Hemsworth
3 Like; the Williams sisters
4 Apart from; Venus Williams
5 also; Liam Hemsworth

2 **1** She is 11.
2 She lives in Montreal, in Canada.
3 She speaks English and French.
4 Ice hockey, reading and spending time with her friends.
5 Her favourite food is poutine.

3 *Student's own answers*

4 **1** Hello everybody, my name's Karen.
2 I'm 11.
3 I'm a big fan of…
4 Canada is really cold in the winter.
5 Oh, and…

5 *Student's own answers*

6 *Student's own answers*

7 *Student's own answers*

FURTHER PRACTICE

Workbook page 10

LESSON FOCUS

Focus on Linking language
Writing Personal profile
Project task 3 Test and improve the form from Project task 2

Resources
Teacher's i-solutions

Preparation Pictures of any celebrities you think the students know

Warmer

Show the class the pictures and get students to identify the celebrities. Say a sentence about a person or people and have the students tell you which celebrity or celebrities you're talking about. Students continue the activity in pairs or small groups.

Focus on linking language

1 Remind students of the celebrities from pages 14-15 and get them to do the exercise. Ask them to find other sentences with the linking language in the text on pages 14-15.

2 Draw students' attention to the text and photo and ask what the text is (a personal profile of a girl called Karen). Students then complete the exercise. Let them do this exercise and the next before you check answers to help personalise the exercise.

3 Model this exercise using this example: *Like Karen, I also speak two languages, but I don't speak French. I speak (Spanish).*

Did you notice?

4 As students complete the exercise, elicit other ways of doing the same function (I'm Karen; I'm 11 years old, etc.)

5 **PLAN** Once students have finished their plan, encourage them to talk it through with a partner.

WRITING TOOLS

Point out that the writing pages in the **Student's Book** all have a model text for them to refer to and have them read the **Writing tool**.

6 **WRITE** Before students start writing, make a checklist on the board of any elements related to content, structure, language and style that they should bear in mind.

7 **CHECK** Once students have checked their own profiles, they can swap with a partner and check theirs.

PROJECT TASK 3 Survey

Students will invent more questions for their survey and practise interviewing each other and correcting any problems. Tell students that they need to keep their project notes together in their **Workbook** (page 20) or in their own notebook.

→ See pages 24-27 **Projects**

Remind students to do all the exercises in their notebook

CONTINUOUS ASSESSMENT Students can use appropriate linking language to write a mini-biography.

Culture and communication 1.5

Irish dancing

Discuss the questions.

1 What are your hobbies?
2 What do you like most about them?
3 How often do you do or practise them?
4 Do you do them with other people?

1 Listen and complete the information.

1 Name: ··· Country: ··· Favourite part of hobby: ···

2 Name: ··· Nationality: ··· When he practises: ···

3 Name: ··· Age: ··· Who she plays with: ···

Idioms and expressions

2 Match the expressions you heard with their meanings.

1 reach for the stars
2 throw in the towel
3 practice makes perfect

a To do something many times, until you are very good at it.
b To be ambitious and aim to do something difficult.
c To stop doing something because it's too difficult.

SPEAKING TOOLS
Listen to audios a few times while you read, and say the words at the same time in your head. Can you say the words in the same way?

3 Read and choose the correct option. Listen and check your answers.

My name's Sarah. [1] I'm / She's from England. I like dancing to hip-hop. [2] We're / It's not easy to learn the dance moves, but practice makes [3] perfect / good! Hip-hop's main instruments are drum machines and synthesisers. I like hip-hop lyrics about politics and family.

My best friend is Lisa. She's from Ireland. [4] He's / She's 13 years old, like me! Lisa plays the guitar really well. She likes reggae. She practises every day and she never [5] throws / puts in the towel. She wants to be famous. I believe she can do it. Reach for the [6] stars / sun, Lisa!

4 NOW YOU! Tell your partner about your hobbies. Try to use the new expressions in exercise 2.

PAIRWORK
Student A: go to page 99
Student B: go to page 103

Unit 1 Review • page 90
Wordlist • pages 117–120

Do all exercises in your notebook

Idioms and expressions for determination

Workbook page 11

17

LESSON FOCUS

Idioms and expressions Determination
Listening Taking notes
Speaking Discussing hobbies

Resources
Teacher's i-solutions, Student's Book audio
Preparation Culture worksheet for each student

Irish dancing

Video and worksheet available on the
Richmond*Learning***Platform**

- In pairs, ask students to complete the *What I know...* exercises on the **Culture video worksheet.**
- Show students the **Culture video** and ask them to complete the *What I learned...* exercises on the worksheet.
- In pairs, students compare answers.
- In small groups, tell students to complete the *What I wonder...* exercises on the worksheet.

ANSWER KEY

Page 17

1 **1**
Name: Trish
Country: America / the United States of America / the USA
Favourite part of hobby: eating the food
2
Name: Jacob
Nationality: South African
When he practises: every day from Monday to Friday
3
Name: Joanna **Age:** 14
Who she plays with: her cousin

2 **1** b **2** c **3** a

3 **1** I'm **3** perfect **5** throws
2 It's **4** She's **6** stars

4 *Student's own answers*

FURTHER PRACTICE AND UNIT ASSESSSMENT

Unit 1 Review **Student's Book** page 90
Workbook page 11
- **Reflect on your learning** page 11
- **Grammar reference and practice** pages 84 and 93
- **Wordlist and exercises** pages 98 and 102

Tests available to download and edit from the
Richmond*Learning***Platform**

→ See pages 40-41 **Assessment**

Warmer

Watch the Culture video and discuss the questions with the whole class. If you don't have video facilities, simply discuss the questions.

1 1.13 (See page 169 for transcripts) Ask students if they can identify the hobbies in the pictures (cooking, Capoeira and table tennis). Confirm if they guess correctly but, if not, let them listen to the speakers name them in the audio. Then have them complete the information in the exercise.

Idioms and expressions

2 Ask students if they remember how the expressions were used in the listening exercise. This should help them to guess the meaning.

SPEAKING TOOLS

If you can, play the audio for exercise 1 again, pausing after each speaker and checking students' pronunciation. Then get them to read the **Speaking tool**.

3 1.14 (See page 170 for transcripts) Get the students to identify the names of the two people featured, their relationship and the activities they're doing and then complete the exercise.

4 **NOW YOU!** Give students time to think how they will use the expressions. You could get them to take notes about a hobby to talk about without naming it and have their partner guess what it is.

PAIRWORK **Student's Book** pages 99 and 103
See **Teacher's Book** page 62 for more information.
→ See pages 30-33 **Mediation**

Remind students to do all the exercises in their notebook

CONTINUOUS ASSESSMENT Students can use idioms and expressions for determination

Unit 1 Review

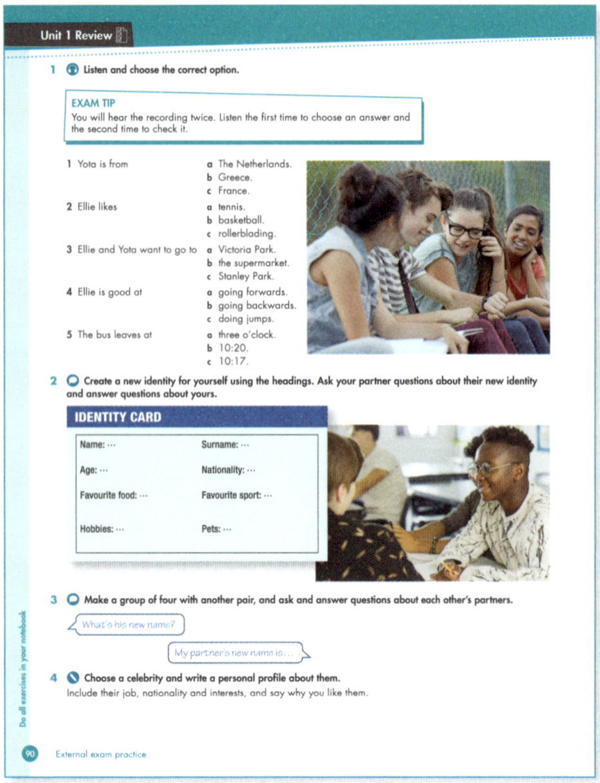

Unit 1 Review

1 Listen and choose the correct option.

EXAM TIP
You will hear the recording twice. Listen the first time to choose an answer and the second time to check it.

1 Yota is from
a The Netherlands.
b Greece.
c France.

2 Ellie likes
a tennis.
b basketball.
c rollerblading.

3 Ellie and Yota want to go to
a Victoria Park.
b the supermarket.
c Stanley Park.

4 Ellie is good at
a going forwards.
b going backwards.
c doing jumps.

5 The bus leaves at
a three o'clock.
b 10:20.
c 10:17.

2 Create a new identity for yourself using the headings. Ask your partner questions about their new identity and answer questions about yours.

IDENTITY CARD

Name: ···	Surname: ···
Age: ···	Nationality: ···
Favourite food: ···	Favourite sport: ···
Hobbies: ···	Pets: ···

3 Make a group of four with another pair, and ask and answer questions about each other's partners.

What's his new name?

My partner's new name is…

4 Choose a celebrity and write a personal profile about them.
Include their job, nationality and interests, and say why you like them.

Do all exercises in your notebook

90 External exam practice

Student's Book page 90

ANSWER KEY

See page 180 for transcripts

1 2.41
1 b
2 c
3 a
4 a
5 b

2 *Student's own answers*

3 *Student's own answers*

4 *Student's own answers*

Pairwork

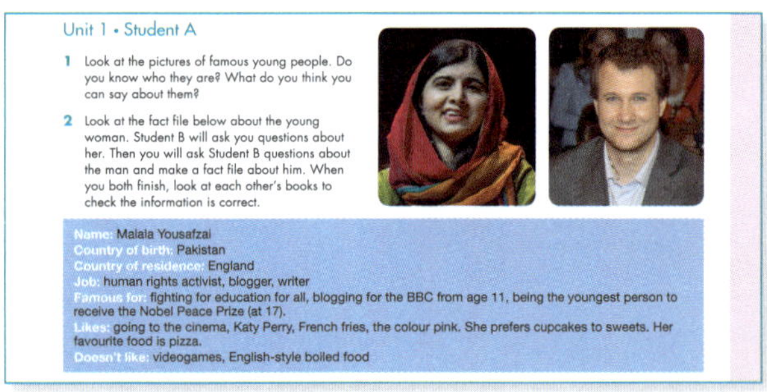

Unit 1 • Student A

1 Look at the pictures of famous young people. Do you know who they are? What do you think you can say about them?

2 Look at the fact file below about the young woman. Student B will ask you questions about her. Then you will ask Student B questions about the man and make a fact file about him. When you both finish, look at each other's books to check the information is correct.

Name: Malala Yousafzai
Country of birth: Pakistan
Country of residence: England
Job: human rights activist, blogger, writer
Famous for: fighting for education for all, blogging for the BBC from age 11, being the youngest person to receive the Nobel Peace Prize (at 17).
Likes: going to the cinema, Katy Perry, French fries, the colour pink. She prefers cupcakes to sweets. Her favourite food is pizza.
Doesn't like: videogames, English-style boiled food

Student's Book page 99

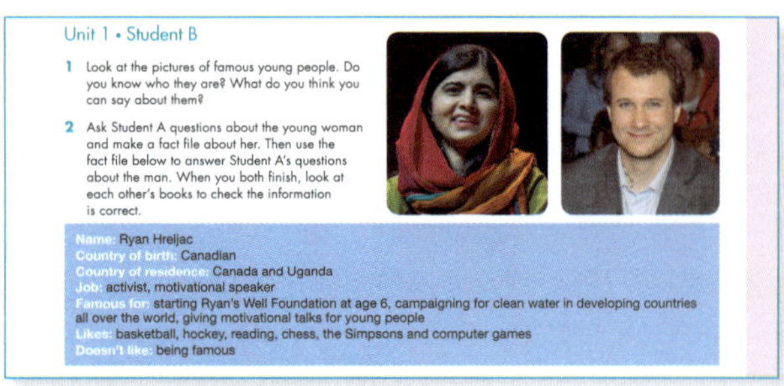

Unit 1 • Student B

1 Look at the pictures of famous young people. Do you know who they are? What do you think you can say about them?

2 Ask Student A questions about the young woman and make a fact file about her. Then use the fact file below to answer Student A's questions about the man. When you both finish, look at each other's books to check the information is correct.

Name: Ryan Hreljac
Country of birth: Canadian
Country of residence: Canada and Uganda
Job: activist, motivational speaker
Famous for: starting Ryan's Well Foundation at age 6, campaigning for clean water in developing countries all over the world, giving motivational talks for young people
Likes: basketball, hockey, reading, chess, the Simpsons and computer games
Doesn't like: being famous

Student's Book page 103

CEFR MEDIATION DESCRIPTOR

- **Overall mediation**
Students can convey relevant information contained in clearly structured, short, simple, informational texts, provided that the texts concern concrete, familiar subjects and are formulated in simple, everyday language.

- **Exchanging personal information**
Tell Student A and B that they each have information about a different person and that they are to ask each other questions to write fact files on the people they don't have information for.

Remind students to do all the exercises in their notebook

Present simple *be*

I	am ('m)	from Poland.
He She It	is ('s)	12 years old. French. Monday today.
You We They	are ('re)	16 years old. from Japan. German.

We use the verb ***be*** to talk about nationalities, jobs, to make general statements and to give descriptions. We generally use the contracted form of the affirmative.

We'**re** happy.

My mother'**s** an engineer.

Edinburgh **is** in Scotland.

Present simple *be*: *wh-* questions

What	is ('s)	your name? the answer? the most difficult language?
When	is ('s)	your birthday? English class? George's party?
Where	are	they from? the new books? Sarah and Emma?
Which girl	is ('s)	his sister? the tallest? your friend?
Who	is ('s)	your favourite actress? the author? Michael's best friend?
Whose	are	these shoes? those tickets? those cars over there?
Why	are	you sad? your parents angry? bicycles better than cars?

We use *wh-* questions to ask for specific information. *Wh-* questions begin with a question word.

We use ***what*** to ask about a thing.

What is your name?

It's Steve.

We use ***when*** to ask about a time or date.

When is your birthday?

It's in April.

We use ***where*** to ask about a place.

Where are they from?

They are from Portugal.

We use ***which*** to ask about a thing from a small number of choices.

Which girl **is** his sister?

She is the one with the brown hair.

We use ***who*** to ask about people.

Who is your favourite actress?

It's Salma Hayek.

We use ***whose*** to ask who something belongs to.

Whose are these shoes?

They're Tom's.

We use ***why*** to ask about a reason.

Why are you sad?

I'm sad because my dog is lost.

Be careful, don't confuse ***whose*** with ***who's*** (***who is***); they sound very similar!

We use ***how old*** and the verb ***be*** to ask about someone's age.

How old is she?

She's 14 years old.

NOT ~~How many years has she? She has 14 years.~~

Do all exercises in your notebook

Workbook pages 93–96 107

Student's Book page 107

Wordlist

UNIT 1

Greetings and introductions

Greetings	Introductions
Good morning.	I'd like to introduce …
Hey!	I'm …
How are you doing?	My name is …
How are you today?	Nice to meet you.
How's it going?	This is …
I'm very well, thank you.	This is my friend, …
It was nice to see you.	
Not too bad.	
See you later!	

Countries and nationalities

Argentina / Argentinian
Australia / Australian
Belgium / Belgian
Brazil / Brazilian
Canada / Canadian
China / Chinese
Colombia / Colombian
England / English
France / French
Germany / German
Greece / Greek
India / Indian
Ireland / Irish
Italy / Italian
Japan / Japanese
Mexico / Mexican
The Netherlands / Dutch
New Zealand / from New Zealand
Peru / Peruvian
Portugal / Portuguese
Spain / Spanish
Switzerland / Swiss
Turkey / Turkish

Hobbies and interests

Hobbies	Interests
basketball	action films
listening to music	animated films
reading	classical music
roller-blading	comedy
spending time with friends	fashion
surfing	folk music
swimming	jazz
watching films	pop music
	R&B
	series

Do all exercises in your notebook

Workbook pages 102–104 117

Student's Book page 117

2.47 2.48 2.49

Remind students to do all the exercises in their notebook

2 TIME FOR SCHOOL

At the start of each unit and lesson, explain to the students what the objectives are.

Language objectives

Grammar

Present simple *be*: negative, *yes/no* questions

- Students focus on the negative forms of *be* and the use of *be* in *yes/no* questions and short answers.

Prepositions of time

- Students practise the prepositions *in*, *on* and *at* with expressions of time.

Vocabulary

Dates: Days: *Monday, Tuesday, Wednesday, Thursday, Friday, Saturday, Sunday;* Months: *January, February, March, April, May, June, July, August, September, October, November, December*

- Students practise using dates in English.

Time: *a quarter past, a quarter to, break, half past, It's at …, late, lunchtime, midnight, o'clock, timetable, What time is …?, What time is it?*

- Students practise expressions for telling the time.

Personality adjectives: *active, adventurous, analytical, creative, energetic, friendly, imaginative, ingenious, intelligent, patient, persevering, self-aware, shy, sociable, sporty, talkative*

- Students practise adjectives for describing personality.

Idioms and expressions

Time: *take time out, just in time, time flies*

- Students look at idioms and expressions related to time in the context of three short talks.

Recycled language

Present simple affirmative, *Wh-* questions

Skills objectives

Speaking

- Students ask and answer questions about dates.
- Students ask and answer personal *yes/no* questions.
- Students ask and answer questions about timetables.
- Students discuss special events at their school.

Pronunciation: Students practise the unvoiced /θ/ and voiced /ð/ sounds

Pairwork: Students use various mediation techniques in order to complete a timetable.

Listening

- Students listen to complete a calendar and a timetable.
- Students listen to complete conversations about the time.
- Students listen to complete a multiple-choice exercise.
- Students listen to idioms and expressions in context.

Reading

- Students read a text to compare ideas about intelligence with their own.
- Students read to match descriptions with types of intelligence.
- Students read a text to match adjectives and definitions.

Core values: Students do an activity to encourage their **self-awareness** and discuss how important it is to be self-aware.

Writing

- Students focus on paragraph structure in the context of an email.
- Students plan, write and check an email to a friend to tell them about their school.

Focus on punctuation: apostrophes, capital letters, commas, exclamation marks, question marks

Learning to learn tools

SPEAKING TOOLS Students practise copying language from a question to help their fluency, range and accuracy.	LISTENING TOOLS Students practise focusing on listening for specific information without needing to understand everything.
READING TOOLS Students practise using cognates to help their comprehension.	WRITING TOOLS Students practise planning a clear paragraph structure.

Project objectives: Survey

Task 4 Students carry out a survey.

Task 5 Students check and review the information.

Task 6 Students organise and analyse the information.

Audiovisual objectives

Vlog: Students watch and listen to George talk about a typical day at his school.

Culture: Students watch and listen to George talk about the Edinburgh Fringe Festival.

Grammar animations: Students are presented with visual presentations of the unit grammar.

Key competences

LC **Linguistic**
pages 18-25

MST **Mathematical and Science and Technology**
pages 18, 20, 22-23

DC **Digital**
pages 18, 24, 25

SCC **Social and Civic**
pages 18, 21-23, 25

CAE **Cultural awareness and expression**
pages 18, 21, 25

LL **Learning to learn**
pages 21, 22, 24-25

IE **Sense of initiative and entrepreneurship**
pages 19, 21, 24

→ See pages 42-43 **Key competences**

CEFR Mediation

2.1 Relaying specific information in writing
Can list the main points of simple messages and announcements.

2.2 Relaying specific information in speech
Can relay simple information about times and places in short, simple statements.

2.3 Encouraging conceptual talk
Can ask what somebody thinks of a certain idea.

2.4 Processing text in writing
Can use simple language to render short texts on familiar themes.

2.5 Facilitating pluricultural space
Can ask for clarification and express agreement and interest.

Project Explaining data in speech
Can interpret and describe simple visuals on familiar topics.

Unit review Collaborating to construct meaning
Can make simple remarks and pose occasional questions to indicate that he/she is following.

Pairwork Facilitating collaborative interaction with peers
Can help work towards a common goal by asking and answering straightforward questions.

→ See pages 30-33 **Mediation**

Remind students to do all the exercises in their notebook

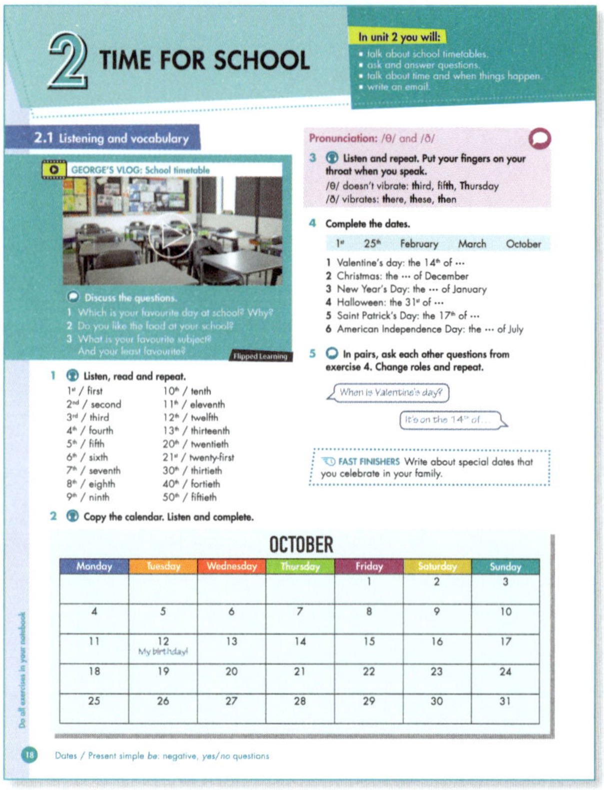

2 TIME FOR SCHOOL

In unit 2 you will:
- talk about school timetables.
- ask and answer questions.
- talk about time and when things happen.
- write an email.

2.1 Listening and vocabulary

GEORGE'S VLOG: School timetable

Discuss the questions.
1 Which is your favourite day at school? Why?
2 Do you like the food at your school?
3 What is your favourite subject? And your least favourite?

1 Listen, read and repeat.

1st / first	10th / tenth
2nd / second	11th / eleventh
3rd / third	12th / twelfth
4th / fourth	13th / thirteenth
5th / fifth	20th / twentieth
6th / sixth	21st / twenty-first
7th / seventh	30th / thirtieth
8th / eighth	40th / fortieth
9th / ninth	50th / fiftieth

2 Copy the calendar. Listen and complete.

OCTOBER

Monday	Tuesday	Wednesday	Thursday	Friday	Saturday	Sunday
				1	2	3
4	5	6	7	8	9	10
11	12 My birthday!	13	14	15	16	17
18	19	20	21	22	23	24
25	26	27	28	29	30	31

Pronunciation: /θ/ and /ð/

3 Listen and repeat. Put your fingers on your throat when you speak.
/θ/ doesn't vibrate: third, fifth, Thursday
/ð/ vibrates: there, these, then

4 Complete the dates.

1st 25th February March October

1 Valentine's day: the 14th of …
2 Christmas: the … of December
3 New Year's Day: the … of January
4 Halloween: the 31st of …
5 Saint Patrick's Day: the 17th of …
6 American Independence Day: the … of July

5 In pairs, ask each other questions from exercise 4. Change roles and repeat.

When is Valentine's day?
It's on the 14th of…

FAST FINISHERS Write about special dates that you celebrate in your family.

Do all exercises in your notebook

18 Dates / Present simple be: negative, yes/no questions

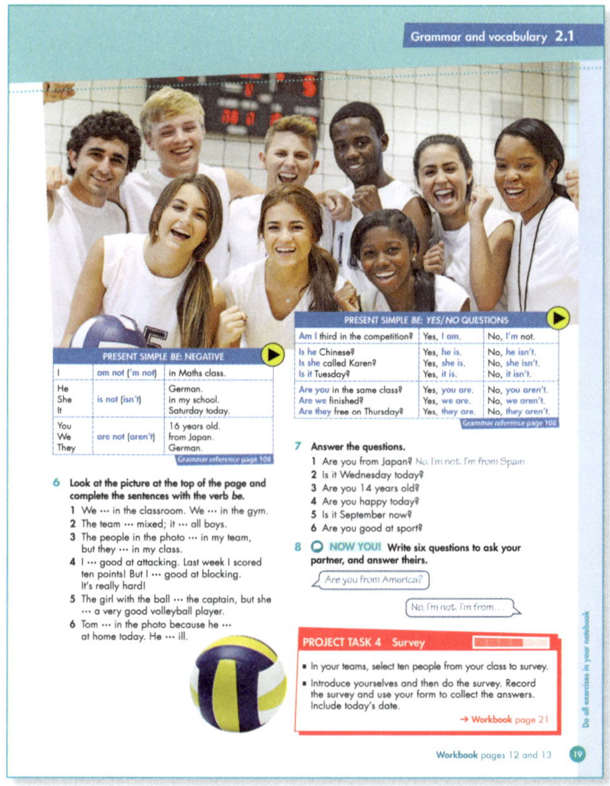

Grammar and vocabulary 2.1

PRESENT SIMPLE BE: NEGATIVE

I	am not ('m not)	in Maths class.
He / She / It	is not (isn't)	German. in my school. Saturday today.
You / We / They	are not (aren't)	16 years old. from Japan. German.

Grammar reference page 108

PRESENT SIMPLE BE: YES/NO QUESTIONS

Am I third in the competition?	Yes, I am.	No, I'm not.
Is he Chinese? Is she called Karen? Is it Tuesday?	Yes, he is. Yes, she is. Yes, it is.	No, he isn't. No, she isn't. No, it isn't.
Are you in the same class? Are we finished? Are they free on Thursday?	Yes, you are. Yes, we are. Yes, they are.	No, you aren't. No, we aren't. No, they aren't.

Grammar reference page 108

6 Look at the picture at the top of the page and complete the sentences with the verb be.
1 We … in the classroom. We … in the gym.
2 The team … mixed; it … all boys.
3 The people in the photo … in my team, but they … in my class.
4 I … good at attacking. Last week I scored ten points! But I … good at blocking. It's really hard!
5 The girl with the ball … the captain, but she … a very good volleyball player.
6 Tom … in the photo because he … at home today. He … ill.

7 Answer the questions.
1 Are you from Japan? No, I'm not. I'm from Spain
2 Is it Wednesday today?
3 Are you 14 years old?
4 Are you happy today?
5 Is it September now?
6 Are you good at sport?

8 NOW YOU! Write six questions to ask your partner, and answer theirs.

Are you from America?
No, I'm not. I'm from…

PROJECT TASK 4 Survey
- In your teams, select ten people from your class to survey.
- Introduce yourselves and then do the survey. Record the survey and use your form to collect the answers. Include today's date.

→ Workbook page 21

Workbook pages 12 and 13 19

ANSWER KEY

Pages 18-19

1 *Student's own answers*

2

Monday	Tuesday	Wednesday	Thursday	Friday	Saturday	Sunday
				1	2	3
4	5	6	7	8	9	10 Today
11	12 My birthday	13	14	15	16	17
18 Football match	19	20	21	22	23	24
25	26	27	28 Exams	29	30 Lunch at Grandma's	31

3 *Student's own answers*

4 **1** February
2 25th
3 1st
4 October
5 March
6 4th

5 *Student's own answers*

6 **1** aren't/are not; are/'re
2 is; isn't/is not
3 are; aren't/are not
4 am/'m; 'm not/am not
5 isn't/is not; is/'s
6 isn't/is not; is/'s; is/'s

7 *Student's own answers*

8 *Student's own answers*

Remind students to do all the exercises in their notebook

LESSON FOCUS

Grammar Present simple *be*: negative, *yes/no* questions
Vocabulary Dates
Listening Important dates on a calendar
Speaking Short personal questions and questions about dates
Project task 4 Carry out a survey

Resources
Teacher's i-solutions, Student's Book audio

Preparation A big calendar

Flipped Learning

GEORGE'S VLOG: School timetable

- Make sure to set up the **Flipped Learning** work with the students beforehand. **See pages 22-23 for complete Flipped Learning guidelines.**
- Ask students to put the **Flipped Learning worksheets** on their desks and walk around to check how many have completed the Flipped task.
- In pairs or small groups, ask students to compare and check the *Before you watch...* and *While you watch...* exercises on the worksheet.
- Show students **George's vlog** and ask volunteers to provide correct answers and clarify any doubts other students may have.
- Choose three or four students to read aloud their answers to the *After you watch...* exercises on the worksheet and encourage some class discussion.
- Move straight to exercise 1 on page 18.

Warmer

Watch George's vlog and discuss the questions with the whole class. If you don't have video facilities, simply discuss the questions.

1 1.15 (See page 170 for transcripts) After completing the exercise, test students by pointing at random dates on the calendar.

2 1.16 (See page 170 for transcripts) Alternatively, just get students to write down the dates and what they refer to as they hear them. As you check the answers, elicit the dates as ordinal numbers.

Pronunciation

3 1.17 (See page 170 for transcripts) After the exercise, test students on the calendar from exercise 3 using full sentence answers for extra practice: *When's the girl's birthday? The girl's birthday is on Tuesday, the 12th of October.*

4 Encourage students to check the answers in pairs and listen to check they're pronouncing the 'th' sounds correctly.

5 Get one student to close their book and the other to test him/her; then they can swap roles.

FAST FINISHERS Students can complete this exercise alone or in pairs.

Flipped Learning

PRESENT SIMPLE *BE*: NEGATIVE

Draw students' attention to the **Grammar table**. Remind students that they can use this as a quick reference while completing the exercises.
Show students the **Grammar animation** and/or refer students to the **Grammar reference** on page 108 for further information on form and use.

→ See page 23 for how to flip the **grammar lesson**

6 Point to the photo and ask them what it shows: a volleyball team in the gym. Do the first item as an example and tell them that the sentences are a mix of affirmative and negative sentences. Students complete the exercise. Get the students to write extra sentences about the picture using their imagination if there's time.

Flipped Learning

PRESENT SIMPLE *BE*: *YES/NO* QUESTIONS

Draw students' attention to the **Grammar table**. Remind students that they can use this as a quick reference while completing the exercises.
Show students the **Grammar animation** and/or refer students to the **Grammar reference** on page 108 for further information on form and use.

→ See page 23 for how to flip the **grammar lesson**

7 Model the exercise by answering the questions for yourself before students complete the exercise.

8 **NOW YOU!** Put prompts on the board: *... from...?; ... years old?; ... happy/tired/excited?; ... your birthday soon?; ... good at sport/English/drawing?* Elicit full questions using the prompts and ask students the questions. Then get students to do the exercise in pairs or small groups.

PROJECT TASK 4 Survey

Put the class into their survey teams and get them to take out their survey forms. Students choose the people they want to survey or you choose for them to make sure everyone is surveyed by at least one group. Remind students that they need to keep their project notes together in their **Workbook** (page 20) or in their own notebook.

→ See pages 24-27 **Projects**

FURTHER PRACTICE

Workbook pages 12-13
- **Grammar reference and practice** pages 85 and 93
- **Wordlist and exercises** pages 98 and 102

Remind students to do all the exercises in their notebook

CONTINUOUS ASSESSMENT Students can talk about dates and use the present simple *be* negative and *yes/no* questions.

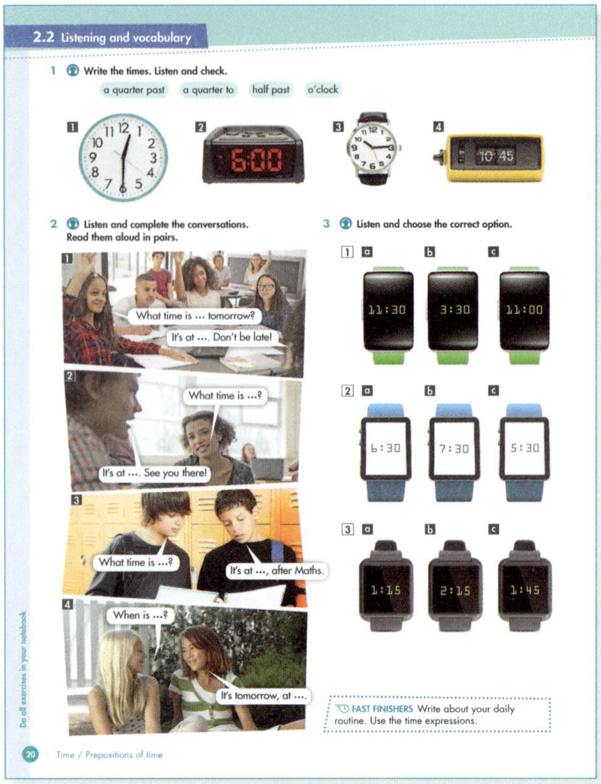

2.2 Listening and vocabulary

1 Write the times. Listen and check.

a quarter past | a quarter to | half past | o'clock

2 Listen and complete the conversations. Read them aloud in pairs.

3 Listen and choose the correct option.

FAST FINISHERS Write about your daily routine. Use the time expressions.

Do all exercises in your notebook

20 Time / Prepositions of time

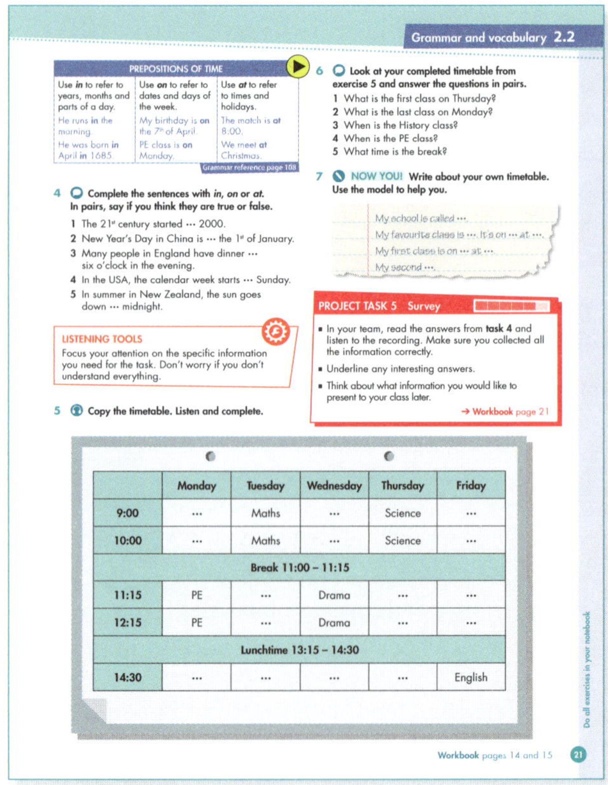

Grammar and vocabulary 2.2

PREPOSITIONS OF TIME

Use *in* to refer to years, months and parts of a day.	Use *on* to refer to dates and days of the week.	Use *at* to refer to times and holidays.
He runs in the morning. He was born in April in 1685.	My birthday is on the 7th of April. PE class is on Monday.	The match is at 8:00. We meet at Christmas.

Grammar reference page 108

4 Complete the sentences with *in*, *on* or *at*. In pairs, say if you think they are true or false.

1 The 21st century started ··· 2000.
2 New Year's Day in China is ··· the 1st of January.
3 Many people in England have dinner ··· six o'clock in the evening.
4 In the USA, the calendar week starts ··· Sunday.
5 In summer in New Zealand, the sun goes down ··· midnight.

LISTENING TOOLS
Focus your attention on the specific information you need for the task. Don't worry if you don't understand everything.

5 Copy the timetable. Listen and complete.

	Monday	Tuesday	Wednesday	Thursday	Friday
9:00	···	Maths	···	Science	···
10:00	···	Maths	···	Science	···
Break 11:00 – 11:15					
11:15	PE	···	Drama	···	···
12:15	PE	···	Drama	···	···
Lunchtime 13:15 – 14:30					
14:30	···	···	···	···	English

6 Look at your completed timetable from exercise 5 and answer the questions in pairs.
1 What is the first class on Thursday?
2 What is the last class on Monday?
3 When is the History class?
4 When is the PE class?
5 What time is the break?

7 NOW YOU! Write about your own timetable. Use the model to help you.

My school is called ···
My favourite class is ··· . It's on ··· at ··· .
My first class is on ··· at ··· .
My second ···

PROJECT TASK 5 Survey
- In your team, read the answers from task 4 and listen to the recording. Make sure you collected all the information correctly.
- Underline any interesting answers.
- Think about what information you would like to present to your class later.

→ Workbook page 21

Workbook pages 14 and 15 21

Do all exercises in your notebook

ANSWER KEY

Pages 20-21

1 **1** half past twelve **2** six o'clock **3** a quarter past ten **4** a quarter to eleven

2 **1** the exam; half past one
2 the basketball match; seven o'clock
3 Geography class; a quarter past eleven
4 the party; a quarter to nine

3 **1** a **2** a **3** b

4 **1** in; false (It started in 2001.)
2 on; false (It's at the end of January or the beginning of February.)
3 at; true
4 on; true
5 at; false (In the far south, the latest it goes down is at around eleven o'clock.)

5

	Monday	Tuesday	Wednesday	Thursday	Friday
9:00	History	Maths	English	Science	PE
10:00	History	Maths	English	Science	PE
11:15	PE	Music	Drama	History	Geography
12:15	PE	Music	Drama	History	Geography
14:30	Art	Science	Art	Science	English

6 **1** Science
2 Art
3 On Monday at nine o'clock and on Thursday at a quarter past eleven
4 On Monday at a quarter past eleven and on Friday at nine o'clock
5 At eleven o'clock

7 *Student's own answers*

Remind students to do all the exercises in their notebook

LESSON FOCUS

Grammar Prepositions of time
Vocabulary Time
Listening Conversations about time
Speaking Comparing information about dates and timetables
Project task 5 Check and review the information from the survey

Resources

Teacher's i-solutions, Student's Book audio

Preparation Two clocks you can move the hands of, or draw two clock faces

Warmer

Put the clocks up on the board and get two students to come to the board. Say a time and see who can make the clocks tell the right time first. If using drawing clock faces, get them to draw both hands. Write the expressions from exercise 1 on the board, and get the winner of one pair to say the time for the next pair to show or draw. You could also whisper a time for the pair to draw and have the rest of the class say the correct time. This could be done in teams.

1 1.18 (See page 170 for transcripts) This could be done all together as a class, stopping after each item to repeat and give the students time to write the answer.

2 1.19 (See page 170 for transcripts) Give students a context by asking where the children in the photos are (in and around school). Give the students time to write the answers, pausing if necessary. Get the students to repeat the conversations after playing the audio and before they practise reading them aloud.

3 1.20 (See page 170 for transcripts) Help students by eliciting the times shown in all options before they complete the exercise.

FAST FINISHERS Students can complete this exercise alone or in pairs.

PREPOSITIONS OF TIME

Flipped Learning

Draw students' attention to the **Grammar table**. Remind students that they can use this as a quick reference while completing the exercises.

Show students the **Grammar animation** and/or refer students to the **Grammar reference** on page 108 for further information on form and use.

→ See page 23 for how to flip the **grammar lesson**

4 Refer students to the **Grammar table** to complete the sentences and encourage them to discuss what they think the correct answer is for each of the sentences they think are false before you go through the answers.

LISTENING TOOLS

Remind students that in exercise 3 they were listening specifically for times. Draw their attention to exercise 5 and ask what they'll be listening for (school subjects). Get them to read the **Listening tool.**

5 1.21 (See page 170 for transcripts) Tell students that the answers are not all in chronological order and that you will let them hear the conversation a second and third time if they need it, pausing after each answer if necessary.

6 Extend this activity: get one student to close his/her notebook and another to ask more questions, then swap.

7 **NOW YOU!** After completing the exercise, get students to compare favourite subjects.

PROJECT TASK 5 Survey

Put the students into their teams and emphasise that the information they will present should be accurate and truthful, as well as interesting for the whole class to hear. Remind students that they need to keep their project notes together in their **Workbook** (page 21) or in their own notebook.

→ See pages 24-27 **Projects**

FURTHER PRACTICE

Workbook pages 14-15
- **Grammar reference and practice** pages 85 and 93
- **Wordlist and exercises** pages 98 and 102

Vocabulary and Grammar worksheets available to download and edit from the **Richmond***Learning***Platform**

→ See pages 38-39 **Mixed-ability classes**

Remind students to do all the exercises in their notebook

CONTINUOUS ASSESSMENT Students can tell the time and use prepositions of time.

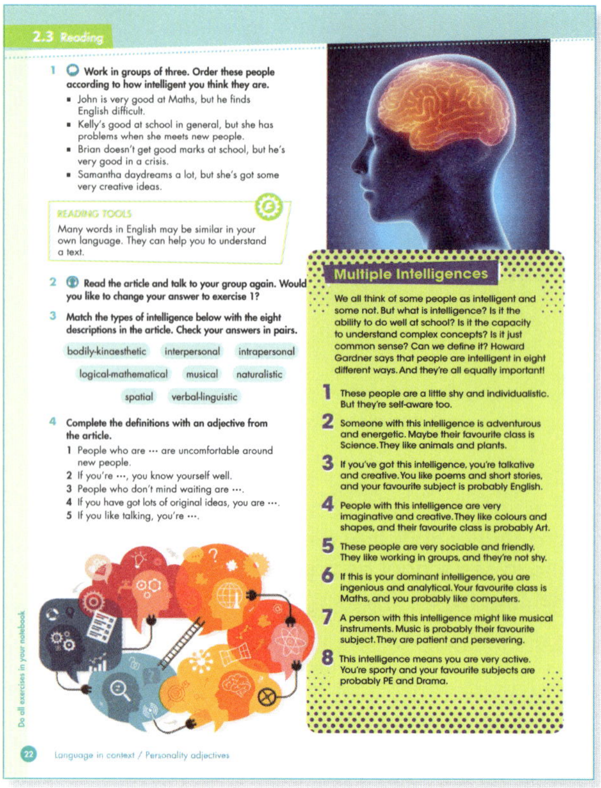

1 Work in groups of three. Order these people according to how intelligent you think they are.
- John is very good at Maths, but he finds English difficult.
- Kelly's good at school in general, but she has problems when she meets new people.
- Brian doesn't get good marks at school, but he's very good in a crisis.
- Samantha daydreams a lot, but she's got some very creative ideas.

READING TOOLS
Many words in English may be similar in your own language. They can help you to understand a text.

2 Read the article and talk to your group again. Would you like to change your answer to exercise 1?

3 Match the types of intelligence below with the eight descriptions in the article. Check your answers in pairs.

bodily-kinaesthetic · interpersonal · intrapersonal · logical-mathematical · musical · naturalistic · spatial · verbal-linguistic

4 Complete the definitions with an adjective from the article.
1 People who are ··· are uncomfortable around new people.
2 If you're ···, you know yourself well.
3 People who don't mind waiting are ···.
4 If you have got lots of original ideas, you are ···.
5 If you like talking, you're ···.

Multiple Intelligences

We all think of some people as intelligent and some not. But what is intelligence? Is it the ability to do well at school? Is it the capacity to understand complex concepts? Is it just common sense? Can we define it? Howard Gardner says that people are intelligent in eight different ways. And they're all equally important!

1 These people are a little shy and individualistic. But they're self-aware too.
2 Someone with this intelligence is adventurous and energetic. Maybe their favourite class is Science. They like animals and plants.
3 If you've got this intelligence, you're talkative and creative. You like poems and short stories, and your favourite subject is probably English.
4 People with this intelligence are very imaginative and creative. They like colours and shapes, and their favourite class is probably Art.
5 These people are very sociable and friendly. They like working in groups, and they're not shy.
6 If this is your dominant intelligence, you are ingenious and analytical. Your favourite class is Maths, and you probably like computers.
7 A person with this intelligence might like musical instruments. Music is probably their favourite subject. They are patient and persevering.
8 This intelligence means you are very active. You're sporty and your favourite subjects are probably PE and Drama.

Do all exercises in your notebook

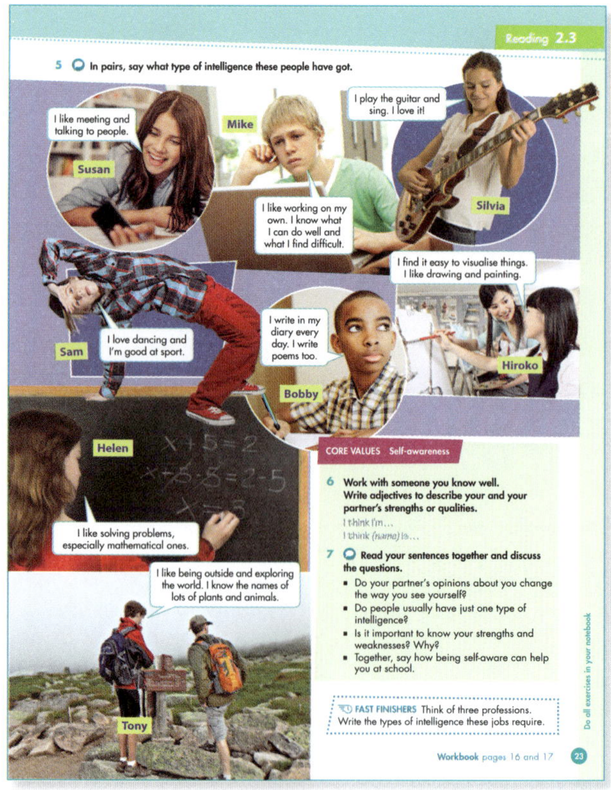

5 In pairs, say what type of intelligence these people have got.

CORE VALUES Self-awareness

6 Work with someone you know well. Write adjectives to describe your and your partner's strengths or qualities.
I think I'm ...
I think (name) is ...

7 Read your sentences together and discuss the questions.
- Do your partner's opinions about you change the way you see yourself?
- Do people usually have just one type of intelligence?
- Is it important to know your strengths and weaknesses? Why?
- Together, say how being self-aware can help you at school.

FAST FINISHERS Think of three professions. Write the types of intelligence these jobs require.

Do all exercises in your notebook

ANSWER KEY

Pages 22-23

1 *Student's own answers*

2 *Student's own answers*

3
1 Intrapersonal
2 Naturalistic
3 Verbal-linguistic
4 Spatial
5 Interpersonal
6 Logical-mathematical
7 Musical
8 Bodily-kinaesthetic

4
1 shy
2 self-aware
3 patient
4 creative
5 sociable

5
Susan – Interpersonal
Mike – Intrapersonal
Silvia – Musical
Sam – Bodily-kinaesthetic
Bobby – Verbal-linguistic
Hiroko – Spatial
Helen – Logical-mathematical
Tony – Naturalistic

6 *Student's own answers*

7 *Student's own answers*

Remind students to do all the exercises in their notebook

LESSON FOCUS

Language in context Personality adjectives

Core values Self-awareness

Resources

Teacher's i-solutions, Student's Book audio

→ See pages 36-37 **Literature**

Warmer

Elicit a list of school subjects to write on the board. Then ask students in pairs or small groups to name a student they think is really good at that subject and discuss why. Ask them to look beyond test results for their answers.

1 Elicit possible definitions of intelligence and challenge students to justify their definitions, but don't confirm or give a clear definition. These definitions may affect their answers to this exercise; for example, if you think intelligence is the ability to deal with unfamiliar problems effectively, you might rank Brian as number 1.

READING TOOLS

Ask students how many school subjects they can think of that are similar in English to their language and which are completely different. Then get them to read the **Reading tool**. Point out that similar words are often the words we say and write incorrectly because of their similarity.

2 1.22 (See page 170 for transcripts) Get students to read the first paragraph of the article and compare the definitions offered with theirs. Ask what they think Howard Gardner might say (each of the people would have an intelligence described in the article, so he might well say they're all equally intelligent).

3 Remind students of the **Reading tool** and elicit some possible definitions for the types of intelligence. Students then complete the exercise to check their answers. Extend this exercise by asking them which types of intelligence they think the people in exercise 1 would be strong and weak in.

4 Get students to find all the personality adjectives in the article and check if they know what they mean. Some may be cognates and easy to guess. Elicit or give definitions or explanations for any they ask you about. Students then complete the exercise. Extend the exercise by getting them to give definitions for other adjectives from the text for others to guess.

5 Extend this exercise by applying it to the students themselves and their friends.

CORE VALUES Self-awareness

6 Ask which intelligence is supposed to be associated with self-awareness (intrapersonal) and tell them that they are going to do a quick self-awareness test. Read through the exercise with them. You could also add another sentence stem: *I think (name) thinks I'm...* . Get them to write two strengths and two weaknesses, and tell them they don't have to be related to intelligence.

7 Encourage them to see self-awareness as something important that everyone develops over time and that others can help you achieve, but that ultimately it depends on yourself. Self-awareness at school can help students find courses of study and study habits that are most effective for them and to see school as part of the bigger picture of life in general.

FAST FINISHERS Students can complete this exercise alone or in pairs.

FURTHER PRACTICE

Workbook pages 16-17

Remind students to do all the exercises in their notebook

CONTINUOUS ASSESSMENT Students can understand personality adjectives in a text about multiple intelligences.

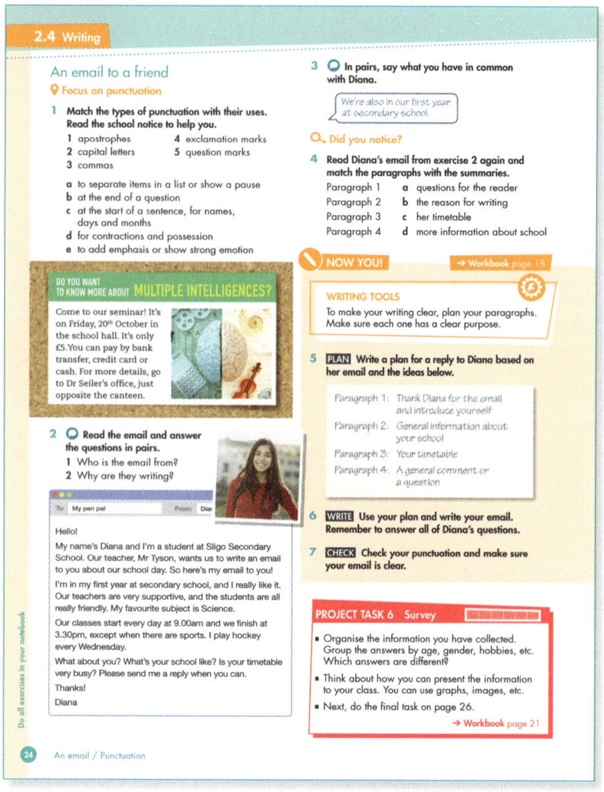

2.4 Writing

An email to a friend

Focus on punctuation

1 **Match the types of punctuation with their uses. Read the school notice to help you.**

1 apostrophes
2 capital letters
3 commas
4 exclamation marks
5 question marks

a to separate items in a list or show a pause
b at the end of a question
c at the start of a sentence, for names, days and months
d for contractions and possession
e to add emphasis or show strong emotion

DO YOU WANT TO KNOW MORE ABOUT MULTIPLE INTELLIGENCES?

Come to our seminar! It's on Friday, 20th October in the school hall. It's only £5.You can pay by bank transfer, credit card or cash. For more details, go to Dr Seiler's office, just opposite the canteen.

2 **Read the email and answer the questions in pairs.**

1 Who is the email from?
2 Why are they writing?

To: My pen pal From: Dia

Hello!

My name's Diana and I'm a student at Sligo Secondary School. Our teacher, Mr Tyson, wants us to write an email to you about our school day. So here's my email to you!

I'm in my first year at secondary school, and I really like it. Our teachers are very supportive, and the students are all really friendly. My favourite subject is Science.

Our classes start every day at 9.00am and we finish at 3.30pm, except when there are sports. I play hockey every Wednesday.

What about you? What's your school like? Is your timetable very busy? Please send me a reply when you can.

Thanks!

Diana

3 **In pairs, say what you have in common with Diana.**

We're also in our first year at secondary school.

Did you notice?

4 **Read Diana's email from exercise 2 again and match the paragraphs with the summaries.**

Paragraph 1 a questions for the reader
Paragraph 2 b the reason for writing
Paragraph 3 c her timetable
Paragraph 4 d more information about school

NOW YOU! → Workbook page 18

WRITING TOOLS

To make your writing clear, plan your paragraphs. Make sure each one has a clear purpose.

5 PLAN **Write a plan for a reply to Diana based on her email and the ideas below.**

Paragraph 1: Thank Diana for the email and introduce yourself
Paragraph 2: General information about your school
Paragraph 3: Your timetable
Paragraph 4: A general comment or a question

6 WRITE **Use your plan and write your email. Remember to answer all of Diana's questions.**

7 CHECK **Check your punctuation and make sure your email is clear.**

PROJECT TASK 6 Survey

- Organise the information you have collected. Group the answers by age, gender, hobbies, etc. Which answers are different?
- Think about how you can present the information to your class. You can use graphs, images, etc.
- Next, do the final task on page 26.

→ Workbook page 21

Do all exercises in your notebook

24 An email / Punctuation

ANSWER KEY

Page 24

1 **1** d
2 c
3 a
4 e
5 b

2 **1** Diana, a student at Sligo Secondary School
2 Their teacher wants them to write an email to their pen pals about their school day.

3 *Student's own answers*

4 Paragraph 1 – b
Paragraph 2 – d
Paragraph 3 – c
Paragraph 4 – a

5 *Student's own answers*

6 *Student's own answers*

7 *Student's own answers*

FURTHER PRACTICE

Workbook page 18

LESSON FOCUS

Focus on Punctuation: apostrophes, capital letters, commas, exclamation marks, question marks

Writing An email to a friend

Project task 6 Organise and analyse the information from the survey

Resources

Teacher's i-solutions

Warmer

Write this sentence on the board, but without punctuation: *What is this thing called love?* Tell them it's a song title and ask them how they think it's punctuated. Change the punctuation to this: *What is this thing called, love?* Ask them what it means now. Then put them in pairs or small groups to think of as many different ways of punctuating it as they can with different meanings.

Focus on punctuation

1 Draw the punctuation symbols on the board and ask students to name them using the terms in the exercise. Students then complete the exercise.

2 Do this exercise quickly as a class and give them more reading time before doing exercise 3.

3 Tell them that one thing they have in common is that their teacher is also going to ask them to write a similar email.

Did you notice?

4 Ask the class how many paragraphs there are in the main part of the email and ask what Diana's doing in the first paragraph (introducing herself and giving her reason for writing). Students then complete the exercise.

WRITING TOOLS

Remind students of the purposes of each paragraph in the model and have them read the **Writing tool**.

5 PLAN Have students discuss in pairs what they might write in answer to Diana's questions before starting to write their plans, and to find any vocabulary from the model they could use.

6 WRITE Before students start writing, make a checklist on the board of any elements related to content, structure, language and style that they should bear in mind.

7 CHECK When they have finished, get them to check their work against the checklist.

PROJECT TASK 6 Survey

Put students in their teams again to organise and plan the presentation. Tell students that they need to keep their project notes together in their **Workbook** (page 21) or in their own notebook.

→ See pages 24-27 **Projects**

Remind students to do all the exercises in their notebook

 CONTINUOUS ASSESSMENT Students can use appropriate punctuation to write an email to a friend.

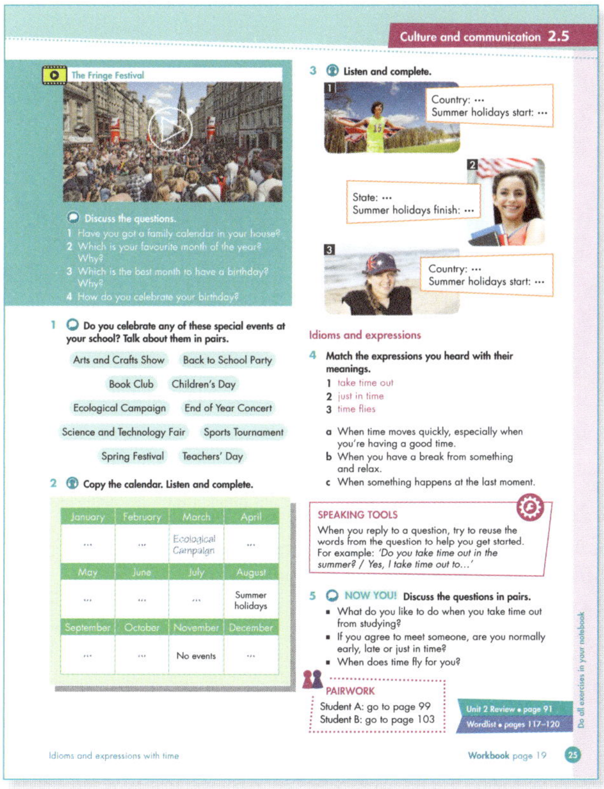
Culture and communication 2.5

The Fringe Festival

Discuss the questions.
1 Have you got a family calendar in your house?
2 Which is your favourite month of the year? Why?
3 Which is the best month to have a birthday? Why?
4 How do you celebrate your birthday?

1 Do you celebrate any of these special events at your school? Talk about them in pairs.

Arts and Crafts Show · Back to School Party · Book Club · Children's Day · Ecological Campaign · End of Year Concert · Science and Technology Fair · Sports Tournament · Spring Festival · Teachers' Day

2 Copy the calendar. Listen and complete.

January	February	March	April
...	...	Ecological Campaign	...
May	**June**	**July**	**August**
...	...	...	Summer holidays
September	**October**	**November**	**December**
...	...	No events	...

3 Listen and complete.
1 Country: ··· Summer holidays start: ···
2 State: ··· Summer holidays finish: ···
3 Country: ··· Summer holidays start: ···

Idioms and expressions

4 Match the expressions you heard with their meanings.
1 take time out
2 just in time
3 time flies

a When time moves quickly, especially when you're having a good time.
b When you have a break from something and relax.
c When something happens at the last moment.

SPEAKING TOOLS
When you reply to a question, try to reuse the words from the question to help you get started. For example: *'Do you take time out in the summer? / Yes, I take time out to...'*

5 NOW YOU! Discuss the questions in pairs.
- What do you like to do when you take time out from studying?
- If you agree to meet someone, are you normally early, late or just in time?
- When does time fly for you?

PAIRWORK
Student A: go to page 99
Student B: go to page 103

Unit 2 Review • page 91
Wordlist • pages 117–120

Do all exercises in your notebook

Idioms and expressions with time

Workbook page 19

25

ANSWER KEY

Page 25

1 *Student's own answers*

2

January Back to School Party	**February** Sports Tournament	**March** Ecological Campaign	**April** Spring Festival
May Teachers' Day	**June** Children's Day	**July** Arts and Crafts Show	**August** Summer holidays
September Book Club	**October** Science and Technology Fair	**November** No events	**December** End of Year Concert

3 1 **Country:** England
Summer holidays start: the 24th of July
2 **State:** Texas
Summer holidays finish: the 20th of August
3 **Country:** Australia
Summer holidays start: the 15th of December

4 **1** b **2** c **3** a

5 *Student's own answers*

FURTHER PRACTICE AND UNIT ASSESSSMENT

Unit 2 Review **Student's Book** page 91
Workbook page 19
- Reflect on your learning page 19
- Grammar reference and practice pages 85 and 93
- Wordlist and exercises pages 98 and 102

Tests available to download and edit from the **Richmond***Learning***Platform**

→ See pages 40-41 **Assessment**

LESSON FOCUS

Idioms and expressions Time
Listening Completing a calendar of annual events, taking notes on summer holidays
Speaking Discussing personal habits

Resources
Teacher's i-solutions, Student's Book audio, Culture video and worksheet

The Fringe Festival

Video and worksheet available on the Richmond*Learning***Platform**

- In pairs, ask students to complete the *What I know…* exercises on the **Culture video worksheet**.
- Show students the **Culture video** and ask them to complete the *What I learned…* exercises on the worksheet.
- In pairs, students compare answers.
- In small groups, tell students to complete the *What I wonder…* exercises on the worksheet.

Warmer

Watch the Culture video and discuss the questions with the whole class. If you don't have video facilities, simply discuss the questions.

1 Ask the class the question and get students to tell you about an event the school celebrates or an event they know something about. Get students to discuss the rest in pairs.

2 1.23 (See page 171 for transcripts) Make sure students know they will only hear the event and the month, not the complete date.

3 1.24 (See page 171 for transcripts) Ask the class if they know the starting and finishing dates for their summer holidays. Then tell them they will hear three people from different countries talking briefly about theirs. Get them to guess the countries from the flags beforehand if you want.

Idioms and expressions

4 Ask students if they remember how the expressions were used in the listening exercise. This should help them to guess the meaning. Write the sentences on the board for reference.

SPEAKING TOOLS

Get students to look at the **Speaking tool** and ask if they can think of other advantages to this (for example, it can help them consolidate new language and shows the speaker that they're listening properly).

5 NOW YOU! Ask a student the first question to check that they use the strategy from the Speaking tool and remind them of it if not. Students complete the activity in pairs.

PAIRWORK **Student's Book** pages 99 and 103
See **Teacher's Book** page 74 for more information.

→ See pages 30-33 **Mediation**

Remind students to do all the exercises in their notebook

CONTINUOUS ASSESSMENT Students can use idioms and expressions with time.

Unit 2 Review

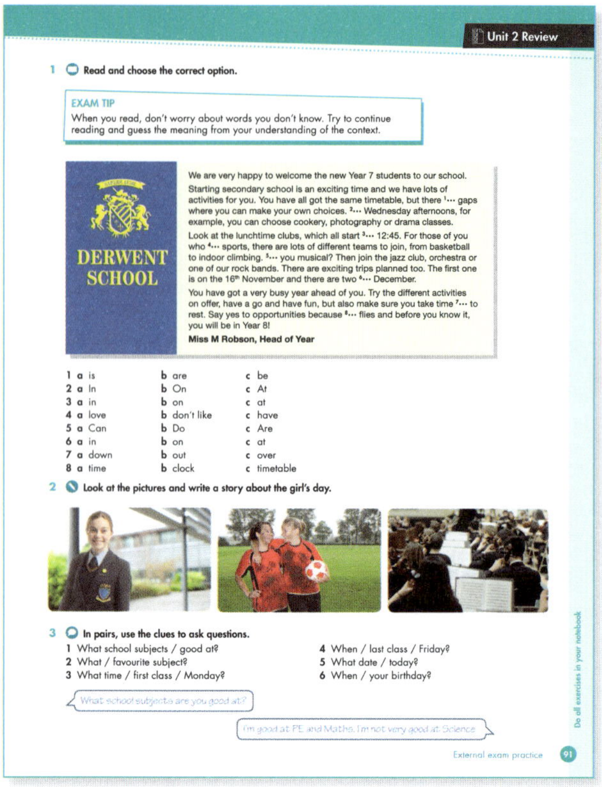

Unit 2 Review

1 Read and choose the correct option.

EXAM TIP
When you read, don't worry about words you don't know. Try to continue reading and guess the meaning from your understanding of the context.

DERWENT SCHOOL

We are very happy to welcome the new Year 7 students to our school.

Starting secondary school is an exciting time and we have lots of activities for you. You have all got the same timetable, but there [1]··· gaps where you can make your own choices. [2]··· Wednesday afternoons, for example, you can choose cookery, photography or drama classes.

Look at the lunchtime clubs, which all start [3]··· 12:45. For those of you who [4]··· sports, there are lots of different teams to join, from basketball to indoor climbing. [5]··· you musical? Then join the jazz club, orchestra or one of our rock bands. There are exciting trips planned too. The first one is on the 16th November and there are two [6]··· December.

You have got a very busy year ahead of you. Try the different activities on offer, have a go and have fun, but also make sure you take time [7]··· to rest. Say yes to opportunities because [8]··· flies and before you know it, you will be in Year 8!

Miss M Robson, Head of Year

1 a is b are c be
2 a In b On c At
3 a in b on c at
4 a love b don't like c have
5 a Can b Do c Are
6 a in b on c at
7 a down b out c over
8 a time b clock c timetable

2 Look at the pictures and write a story about the girl's day.

3 In pairs, use the clues to ask questions.
1 What school subjects / good at?
2 What / favourite subject?
3 What time / first class / Monday?
4 When / last class / Friday?
5 What date / today?
6 When / your birthday?

What school subjects are you good at?

I'm good at PE and Maths. I'm not very good at Science

Do all exercises in your notebook

External exam practice 91

Student's Book page 91

ANSWER KEY

1 **1** b
2 b
3 c
4 a
5 c
6 a
7 b
8 a

2 *Student's own answers*

3 *Suggested questions:*
1 What school subjects are you good at?
2 What's your favourite subject?
3 What time is your first class on Monday?
4 When's your last class on Friday?
5 What's the date today? / What date is it today?
6 When's your birthday?
Student's own answers

Pairwork

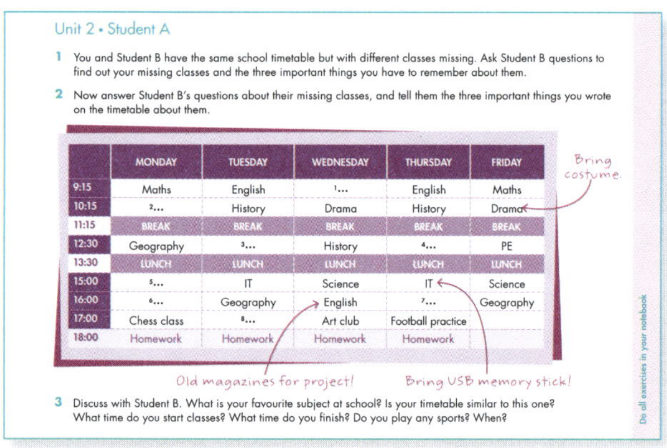

Unit 2 • Student A

1 You and Student B have the same school timetable but with different classes missing. Ask Student B questions to find out your missing classes and the three important things you have to remember about them.

2 Now answer Student B's questions about their missing classes, and tell them the three important things you wrote on the timetable about them.

	MONDAY	TUESDAY	WEDNESDAY	THURSDAY	FRIDAY
9:15	Maths	English	1···	English	Maths
10:15	2···	History	Drama	History	Drama
11:15	BREAK	BREAK	BREAK	BREAK	BREAK
12:30	Geography	3···	History	4···	PE
13:30	LUNCH	LUNCH	LUNCH	LUNCH	LUNCH
15:00	5···	IT	Science	IT	Science
16:00	6···	Geography	English	7···	Geography
17:00	Chess class	8···	Art club	Football practice	
18:00	Homework	Homework	Homework	Homework	

3 Discuss with Student B. What is your favourite subject at school? Is your timetable similar to this one? What time do you start classes? What time do you finish? Do you play any sports? When?

Do all exercises in your notebook

Student's Book page 99

CEFR MEDIATION DESCRIPTOR

- **Relaying specific information in speech**

Students can relay simple, predictable information about times and places given in short, simple statements.

- **Interpreting a timetable**

Tell students they each have the same school timetable, but with different classes missing. They should ask each other questions in order to fill in the gaps. They also need to provide each other with extra information about certain classes.

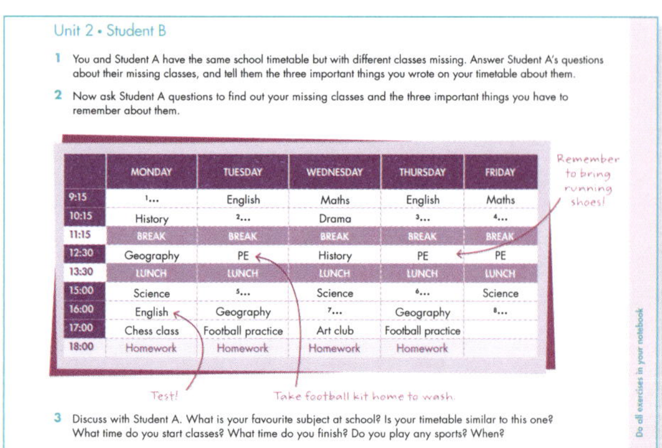

Unit 2 • Student B

1 You and Student A have the same school timetable but with different classes missing. Answer Student A's questions about their missing classes, and tell them the three important things you wrote on your timetable about them.

2 Now ask Student A questions to find out your missing classes and the three important things you have to remember about them.

	MONDAY	TUESDAY	WEDNESDAY	THURSDAY	FRIDAY
9:15	1···	English	Maths	English	Maths
10:15	History	2···	Drama	3···	4···
11:15	BREAK	BREAK	BREAK	BREAK	BREAK
12:30	Geography	PE	History	PE	PE
13:30	LUNCH	LUNCH	LUNCH	LUNCH	LUNCH
15:00	Science	5···	Science	6···	Science
16:00	English	Geography	7···	Geography	8···
17:00	Chess class	Football practice	Art club	Football practice	
18:00	Homework	Homework	Homework	Homework	

3 Discuss with Student A. What is your favourite subject at school? Is your timetable similar to this one? What time do you start classes? What time do you finish? Do you play any sports? When?

Do all exercises in your notebook

Student's Book page 103

Grammar reference

Unit 2 Grammar reference

Present simple *be*: negative

I	am not ('m not)	in Maths class.
He She It	is not (isn't)	German. in my school. Saturday today.
You We They	are not (aren't)	16 years old. from Japan. German.

We always put ***not*** after the verb ***be*** in the negative. We generally use the contracted forms of the negative.
I'**m not** very tall.
She **isn't** the oldest in the family.
They **aren't** English, they're Irish.

Present simple *be*: *yes/no* questions

Am I third in the competition?	Yes, I am.	No, I'm not.
Is he Chinese? **Is she** called Karen? **Is it** Tuesday?	Yes, he is. Yes, she is. Yes, it is.	No, he isn't. No, she isn't. No, it isn't.
Are you in the same class? **Are we** finished? **Are they** free on Thursday?	Yes, you are. Yes, we are. Yes, they are.	No, you aren't. No, we aren't. No, they aren't.

We use *yes/no* questions when the answer is *yes* or *no*.
Are Paola and Giovanni in your class?
Is your sister in the swimming pool?
Am I invited to the party?

We always invert the position of the verb and the subject to create *yes/no* questions with ***be***.
Are you happy today?
NOT ~~You are happy today?~~

Prepositions of time: *in, on, at*

Use ***in*** to refer to years and months. He runs **in** the morning. He was born **in** April **in** 1685.	Use ***on*** to refer to dates and days of the week. My birthday is **on** the 7th of April. PE class is **on** Monday.	Use ***at*** to refer to times. The match is **at** 8:00. We meet **at** Christmas.

We use prepositions with time expressions in the following ways:

in + years, months and parts of a day
in 2016
in December
in the morning

on + dates and days of the week
on the 19th of July
on your birthday
on Saturday

at + times and holidays
at three o'clock
at midnight
at Easter

However, there are common exceptions, for example:
at night
at the weekend

Do all exercises in your notebook

108 **Workbook** pages 93–96

Student's Book page 108

Wordlist

Wordlist

UNIT 2

Dates

Days
Monday
Tuesday
Wednesday
Thursday
Friday
Saturday
Sunday

Months
January
February
March
April
May
June
July
August
September
October
November
December

Time

a quarter past
a quarter to
break
half past
It's at …
late
lunchtime
midnight
o'clock
timetable
What time is …?
What time is it?

Personality adjectives

active
adventurous
analytical
creative
energetic
friendly
imaginative
ingenious
intelligent
patient
persevering
self-aware
shy
sociable
sporty
talkative

Do all exercises in your notebook

Workbook pages 102–104 117

Student's Book page 117

2.50 2.51 2.52

Remind students to do all the exercises in their notebook

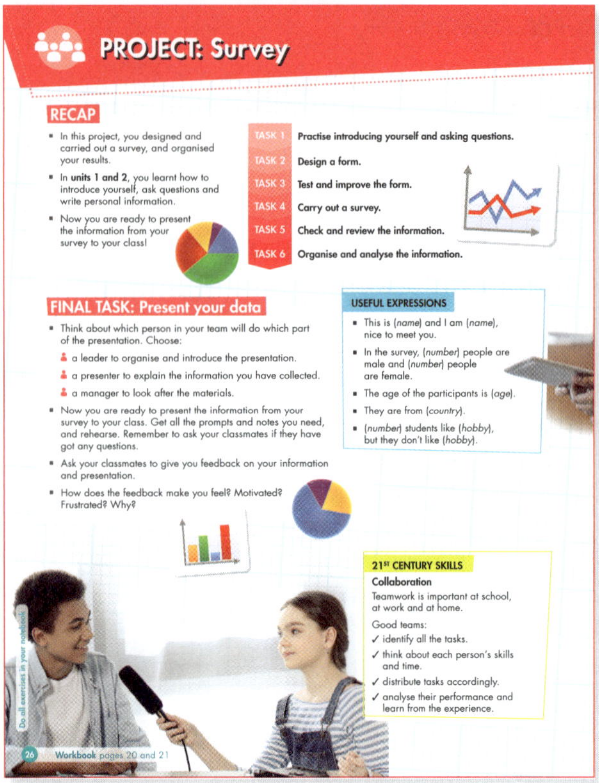

PROJECT: Survey

RECAP

- In this project, you designed and carried out a survey, and organised your results.
- In **units 1 and 2**, you learnt how to introduce yourself, ask questions and write personal information.
- Now you are ready to present the information from your survey to your class!

TASK 1 Practise introducing yourself and asking questions.
TASK 2 Design a form.
TASK 3 Test and improve the form.
TASK 4 Carry out a survey.
TASK 5 Check and review the information.
TASK 6 Organise and analyse the information.

FINAL TASK: Present your data

- Think about which person in your team will do which part of the presentation. Choose:
  - a leader to organise and introduce the presentation.
  - a presenter to explain the information you have collected.
  - a manager to look after the materials.
- Now you are ready to present the information from your survey to your class. Get all the prompts and notes you need, and rehearse. Remember to ask your classmates if they have got any questions.
- Ask your classmates to give you feedback on your information and presentation.
- How does the feedback make you feel? Motivated? Frustrated? Why?

USEFUL EXPRESSIONS
- This is (*name*) and I am (*name*), nice to meet you.
- In the survey, (*number*) people are male and (*number*) people are female.
- The age of the participants is (*age*).
- They are from (*country*).
- (*number*) students like (*hobby*), but they don't like (*hobby*).

21ST CENTURY SKILLS
Collaboration
Teamwork is important at school, at work and at home.
Good teams:
✓ identify all the tasks.
✓ think about each person's skills and time.
✓ distribute tasks accordingly.
✓ analyse their performance and learn from the experience.

Do all exercises in your notebook.

26 Workbook pages 20 and 21

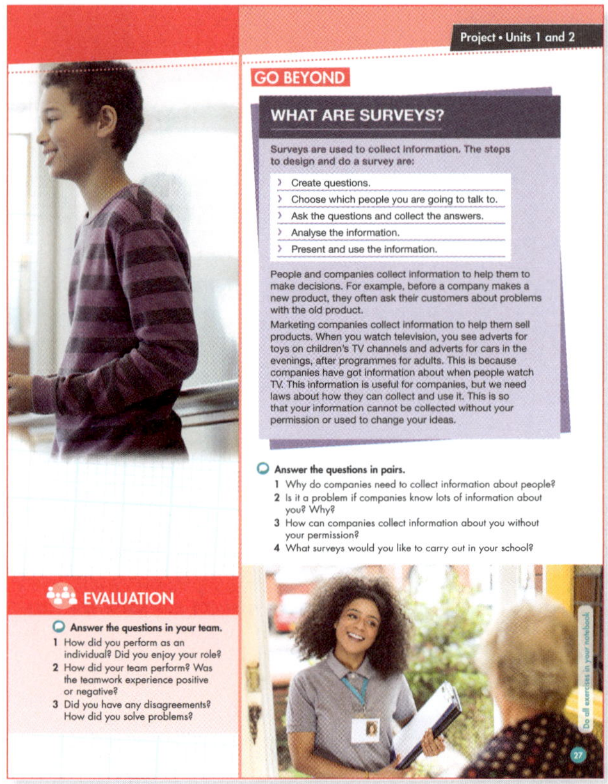

Project • Units 1 and 2

GO BEYOND

WHAT ARE SURVEYS?

Surveys are used to collect information. The steps to design and do a survey are:

- Create questions.
- Choose which people you are going to talk to.
- Ask the questions and collect the answers.
- Analyse the information.
- Present and use the information.

People and companies collect information to help them to make decisions. For example, before a company makes a new product, they often ask their customers about problems with the old product.

Marketing companies collect information to help them sell products. When you watch television, you see adverts for toys on children's TV channels and adverts for cars in the evenings, after programmes for adults. This is because companies have got information about when people watch TV. This information is useful for companies, but we need laws about how they can collect and use it. This is so that your information cannot be collected without your permission or used to change your ideas.

Answer the questions in pairs.
1 Why do companies need to collect information about people?
2 Is it a problem if companies know lots of information about you? Why?
3 How can companies collect information about you without your permission?
4 What surveys would you like to carry out in your school?

EVALUATION

Answer the questions in your team.
1 How did you perform as an individual? Did you enjoy your role?
2 How did your team perform? Was the teamwork experience positive or negative?
3 Did you have any disagreements? How did you solve problems?

Do all exercises in your notebook.

27

Workbook project task notes

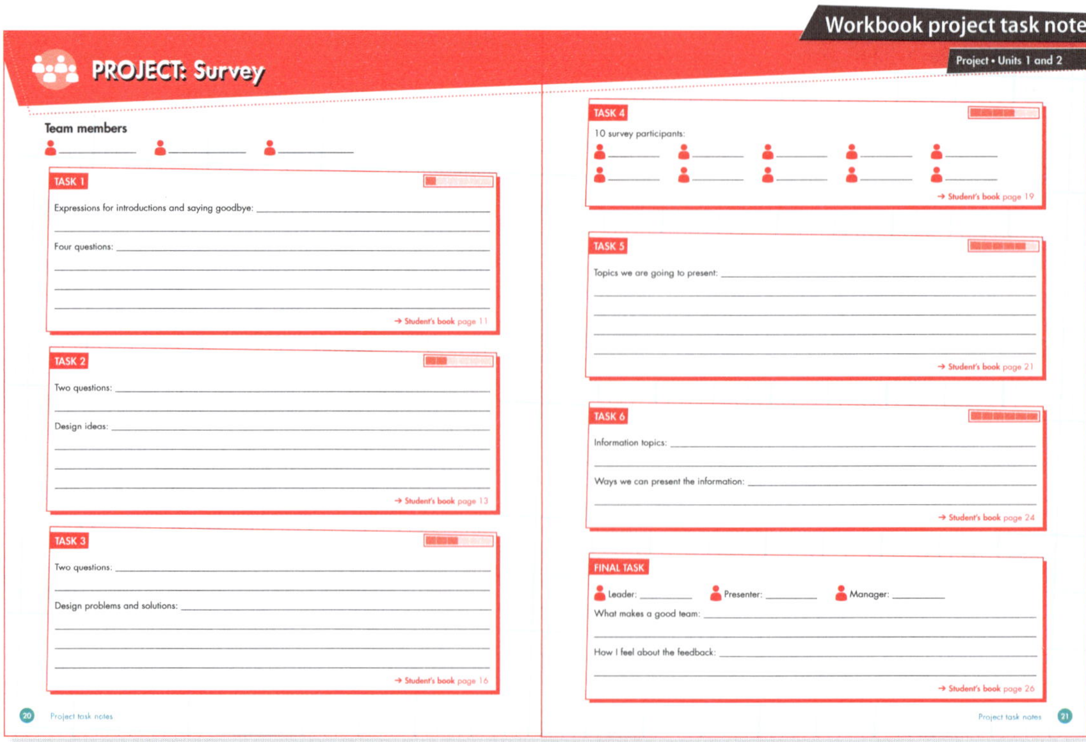

PROJECT: Survey

Project • Units 1 and 2

Team members
______ ______ ______

TASK 1
Expressions for introductions and saying goodbye: ______
Four questions: ______
→ Student's book page 11

TASK 2
Two questions: ______
Design ideas: ______
→ Student's book page 13

TASK 3
Two questions: ______
Design problems and solutions: ______
→ Student's book page 16

TASK 4
10 survey participants:
______ ______ ______ ______ ______
______ ______ ______ ______ ______
→ Student's book page 19

TASK 5
Topics we are going to present: ______
→ Student's book page 21

TASK 6
Information topics: ______
Ways we can present the information: ______
→ Student's book page 24

FINAL TASK
Leader: ______ Presenter: ______ Manager: ______
What makes a good team: ______
How I feel about the feedback: ______
→ Student's book page 26

20 Project task notes

Project task notes 21

Remind students to do all the exercises in their notebook

PROJECT FOCUS

→ See pages 24-27 **Projects**

Skills

- Write questions and carry out a survey
- Use polite introductions
- Listen and note down answers to check against recordings
- Collate interesting information in note form
- Discuss and assign roles within teams
- Discuss collated information and present it to the class
- Discuss and evaluate the project
- Read and discuss a text related to the project

CEFR mediation

Explaining data in speech

Can interpret and describe simple visuals on familiar topics.

→ See pages 30-33 **Mediation**

Preparation Remind students to bring their work from tasks 1-6 and their notes from the **Workbook** project task notes (pages 20-21) or their own notebook. Bring cue cards if needed for the presentation. Have students bring in their self-assessment diaries if you decided that you wanted them to keep one.

Recap

Put students in their teams and read through the **Recap** as a class. Draw their attention to the project tasks and the unit objectives and ask which tasks helped achieve which objectives. Make sure they have all the materials and notes that they need (see **Preparation**) for the **Final task**.

Final Task: Present your data

Tell students they are now going to present the data from their surveys. Before starting the task, direct their attention to the **21st Century skill** (see next column).

Read through the first step of the task and ask which tip from the **21st Century skill** has already been done (the first). Monitor them as they distribute tasks, helping them to do it respectfully and according to the skills of each team member. Remind them that, although they have different roles, are equally ressponsible for the presentation and should help each other wherever possible, by suggesting ideas and giving constructive feedback.

Read through the second step of the task and monitor students as they carry it out, but only offer support if students are really stuck or are having problems collaborating. Then get them to do the presentations, eliciting questions and feedback after each one. Consider asking each group to respond to the feedback immediately and say how they feel, as this may help subsequent groups to give more confident and effective presentations, as well as building class unity through empathy. Add constructive feedback of your own.

21ST CENTURY SKILLS

Read through the **21st Century skill** with the students and tell them that they are going to apply the first three tips at the beginning of the task.

→ See pages 28-29 **21st Century skills**

Evaluation

Before students discuss the questions as a group, give them time to prepare notes about their experience in the project. Remind students to be supportive and give constructive criticism, if necessary, with ideas on how to do things better next time. Monitor discussions, adding your own feedback where appropriate and noting common observations to convey to the class. Open up to a class discussion about what students have learnt from the project, reminding them of the unit objectives, the **Core values** and the **Learning tools** in units 1 and 2, as well as the **21st Century skills** section of the **Project** pages.

As suggested in the introductory notes on **assessment**, the **evaluation** section of the project could be an opportunity for students to write a diary of self-assessment, with short comments on the knowledge and skills they have acquired and developed, as well as those which they want to work on and their feelings about their learning and progress. Encourage them to use the **Evaluation** discussion as a base and to refer to the **Reflect on your learning** section of the **Workbook** if they have one.

→ See pages 40-41 **Assessment**

Go Beyond

Before students read the text, ask them what other kinds of surveys they know of, who does them and why. Have students volunteer their answers and make a list on the board. You can then compare the list on the board with the text.

The questions can be discussed in pairs or the students' project groups.

Remind students to do all the exercises in their notebook

3 DIFFERENT PEOPLE

At the start of each unit and lesson, explain to the students what the objectives are.

Language objectives

Grammar

Plural nouns: spelling

- Students focus on different spelling changes in plural nouns.

Subject pronouns and possessive adjectives

- Students learn the forms of pronouns with corresponding possesive adjectives and practise using them.

Vocabulary

Body parts: *arm, cheek, chest, ear, elbow, eye, eyebrow, eyelash, foot, head, heel, hip, knee, leg, mouth, neck, nose, shoulder, stomach, tooth, toe, tongue, waist*

- Students use vocabulary for different parts of the body.

Body actions: *bend, pull, scratch, stand on tiptoes, stick out your tongue, stretch, swing, touch, wiggle, wink*

- Students use vocabulary for actions related to the body.

Physical appearance: Body: *athletic, fat, little, medium height, plump, short, skinny, slim, tall, thin;* Face: *beautiful, cute, freckled, handsome, pretty;* Hair: *bald, blonde, curly, grey, red, straight, wavy*

- Students practise vocabulary for describing physical appearance.

Idioms and expressions

Body parts: *be all heart, be all ears, give someone a hand*

- Students look at idioms with body parts in the context of short monologues.

Recycled language

Present simple in all forms; Subject pronouns

Skills objectives

Speaking

- Students give each other simple physical instructions to follow.
- Students practise describing people physically.
- Students discuss prejudices and the importance of keeping an open mind.
- Students perform conversations using new expressions.

Pronunciation: Students focus on differences in pronunciation in *-s* endings.

Pairwork: Students use various mediation techniques in order to guess the identity of a person.

Listening

- Students listen for specific vocabulary.
- Students listen for specific information.
- Students listen to identify people from descriptions.
- Students listen to idioms and expressions in context.

Reading

- Students read to compare their ideas with those in a text.
- Students read in detail to decide between statements that paraphrase the content of a text.
- Students read to notice different forms of words.

Core values: Students discuss the importance of **keeping an open mind**.

Writing

- Students develop their ability to write detailed descriptions of people.
- Students plan, write and check a description of someone they admire.

Focus on adverbs of degree: *a bit, a little, absolutely, exceptionally, extremely, quite, rather, really, totally, very*

Remind students to do all the exercises in their notebook

Learning to learn tools

SPEAKING TOOLS Students practise subvocalising language to help them sound more natural.	LISTENING TOOLS Students practise predicting content based on task.
READING TOOLS Students learn the value of activating their schemata before engaging with a text.	WRITING TOOLS Students develop their ability to elaborate on descriptions.

Project objectives: Scrapbook

Task 1 Students create a scrapbook and label a photo of themselves.

Task 2 Students describe themselves and plan the scrapbook design.

Task 3 Students describe and express their personalities.

Audiovisual objectives

Vlog: Students watch and listen to Emma talk about her parents and her dream job.

Culture: Students watch and listen to Emma talk about school uniforms.

Grammar animations: Students are presented with visual presentations of the unit grammar.

Key competences

Linguistic
pages 28-35

Mathematical and Science and Technology
pages 28-29, 32-33

Digital
pages 28, 35

Social and Civic
pages 29, 32-33, 35

Cultural awareness and expression
pages 28-29, 31, 34, 35

Learning to learn
pages 30-32, 34

Sense of initiative and entrepreneurship
pages 29, 31, 34

→ See pages 42-43 **Key competences**

CEFR Mediation

3.1 Relaying information in speech
Can relay short, simple instructions

3.2 Relaying information in writing
Can list specific information contained in simple texts on everyday subjects.

3.3 Encouraging conceptual talk
Can ask what somebody thinks of a certain idea.

3.4 Processing text in speech
Can convey the main points in short, simple written texts.

3.5 Facilitating pluricultural space
Can ask for clarification and express agreement and interest.

Project Encouraging conceptual talk
Can ask questions to invite people to clarify their reasoning.

Unit review Relaying information in writing
Can relay specific information in short, simple texts.

Pairwork Adapting language
Can repeat the main point of a simple message using different words to help someone else understand it.

→ See pages 30-33 **Mediation**

Remind students to do all the exercises in their notebook

3 DIFFERENT PEOPLE

In unit 3 you will:
- talk about people and what they look like.
- say when something belongs to a person.
- give and follow simple instructions.
- write a description of a person.

3.1 Vocabulary and listening

EMMA'S VLOG: Visit to the gym

Discuss the questions.
1 What's your dream job?
2 Would you prefer a job that pays a lot of money or one that you enjoy?
3 Do you have a role model? Who is it?

Flipped Learning

1 Match the words with the body parts. Use a dictionary if you need to.

The body
arm chest elbow foot heel hip knee leg mouth neck shoulder stomach toe waist

The head
cheek ear eye eyebrow eyelash hair nose tongue tooth

2 Listen and check your answers. Repeat the words as you listen.

3 Copy and complete the table in pairs.

Singular	Plural
ear	...
...	feet
tooth	...
...	arms
eye	...

FAST FINISHERS Draw a superhero and label the body parts.

Do all exercises in your notebook

28 Body parts / Body actions / Plural nouns: spelling

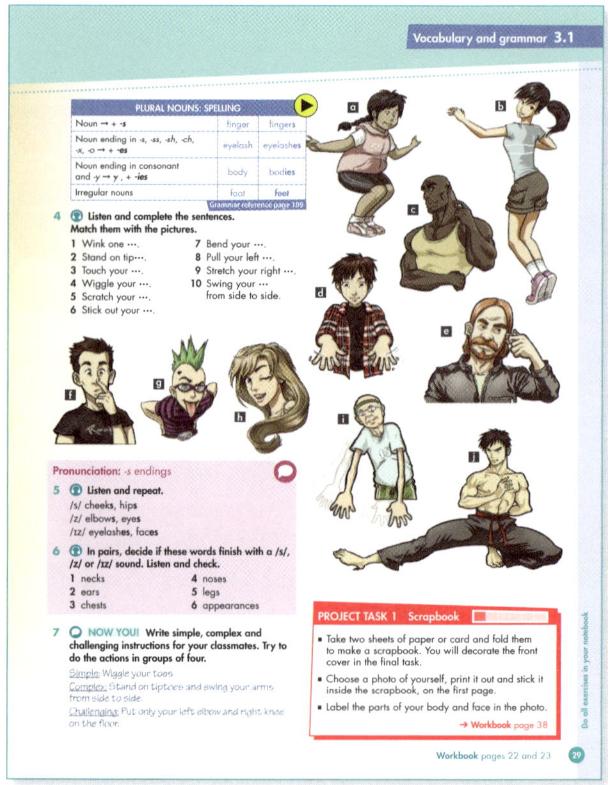

Vocabulary and grammar 3.1

PLURAL NOUNS: SPELLING

Noun → + -s	finger	fingers
Noun ending in -s, -ss, -sh, -ch, -x, -o → + -es	eyelash	eyelashes
Noun ending in consonant and -y → y + -ies	body	bodies
Irregular nouns	foot	feet

Grammar reference page 109

4 Listen and complete the sentences. Match them with the pictures.
1 Wink one ….
2 Stand on tip….
3 Touch your ….
4 Wiggle your ….
5 Scratch your ….
6 Stick out your ….
7 Bend your ….
8 Pull your left ….
9 Stretch your right ….
10 Swing your … from side to side.

Pronunciation: -s endings

5 Listen and repeat.
/s/ cheeks, hips
/z/ elbows, eyes
/ɪz/ eyelashes, faces

6 In pairs, decide if these words finish with a /s/, /z/ or /ɪz/ sound. Listen and check.
1 necks 2 ears 3 chests 4 noses 5 legs 6 appearances

7 NOW YOU! Write simple, complex and challenging instructions for your classmates. Try to do the actions in groups of four.
Simple: Wiggle your toes.
Complex: Stand on tiptoe and swing your arms from side to side.
Challenging: Put only your left elbow and right knee on the floor.

PROJECT TASK 1 Scrapbook
- Take two sheets of paper or card and fold them to make a scrapbook. You will decorate the front cover in the final task.
- Choose a photo of yourself, print it out and stick it inside the scrapbook, on the first page.
- Label the parts of your body and face in the photo.

→ Workbook page 38

Workbook pages 22 and 23 29

Do all exercises in your notebook

ANSWER KEY

Pages 28-29

1
1 arm
2 elbow
3 shoulder
4 mouth
5 neck
6 chest
7 stomach
8 waist
9 hip
10 leg
11 knee
12 heel
13 foot
14 toe
15 tongue
16 tooth
17 eye
18 hair
19 eyebrow
20 eyelash
21 ear
22 nose
23 cheek

2 *Student's own answers*

3

Singular	Plural
ear	ears
foot	feet
tooth	teeth
arm	arms
eye	eyes

4
1 eye; h
2 toes; b
3 nose; f
4 fingers; d
5 neck; c
6 tongue; g
7 knees; a
8 ear; e
9 leg; j
10 arms; i

5 *Student's own answers*

6
1 /s/
2 /z/
3 /s/
4 /ɪz/
5 /z/
6 /ɪz/

7 *Student's own answers*

Remind students to do all the exercises in their notebook

LESSON FOCUS

Grammar Plural nouns: spelling
Vocabulary Body parts; Body actions
Listening Body vocabulary
Speaking Giving physical instructions
Project task 1 Create a scrapbook and label a photo

Resources

Teacher's i-solutions, Student's Book audio, Vlog and worksheets

Preparation Ask students to bring in photos of themselves for their scrapbook, a sheet of card for every student to use as a scrapbook cover, an example scrapbook if possible.

Flipped Learning

EMMA'S VLOG: Visit to the gym

- Make sure to set up the **Flipped Learning** work with the students beforehand. **See pages 20-23 for complete Flipped Learning guidelines.**
- Ask students to put the **Flipped Learning worksheets** on their desks and walk around to check how many have completed the Flipped task.
- In pairs or small groups, ask students to compare and check the *Before you watch...* and *While you watch...* exercises on the worksheet.
- Show students **Emma's vlog** and ask volunteers to provide correct answers and clarify any doubts other students may have.
- Choose three or four students to read aloud their answers to the *After you watch...* exercises on the worksheet and encourage some class discussion.
- Move straight to exercise 1 on page 28.

Warmer

Watch Emma's vlog and discuss the questions with the whole class. If you don't have video facilities, simply discuss the questions.

1 Make sure students can see which body parts are numbered in the photos.

2 1.25 (See page 171 for transcripts) Show students on your own body which part each word refers to. Then test students by pointing to parts of your body and asking them to name them. Students can continue this exercise respectfully in pairs.

3 Ask students to name body parts we have two of and check their pronunciation. Add other words to the table if you think it will benefit the students.

FAST FINISHERS Students can complete this exercise alone or in pairs.

Flipped Learning

PLURAL NOUNS: SPELLING

Draw students' attention to the **Grammar table**. Remind students that they can use this as a quick reference while completing the exercises.

Show students the **Grammar animation** and/or refer students to the **Grammar reference** on page 109 for further information on form and use.

→ See page 23 for how to flip the **grammar lesson**

4 1.26 (See page 171 for transcripts) Give students time to complete as many sentences as they can. Then play the audio and model the instructions as you elicit answers.

Pronunciation

5 1.27 (See page 171 for transcripts) Play the audio and point out that the determining factor is the final sound of the singular noun; if it's an unvoiced consonant (remind them of the difference between voiced and unvoiced *-th* sounds), then the *-s* is also unvoiced; if voiced then a voiced *-s*; and if it's a sibilant sound (s/z/ʃ/ʒ/ʧ/ʤ), we add a syllable and a voiced -s. Give more examples of each category.

6 1.28 (See page 171 for transcripts) Encourage students to say the singular and plural of each noun to help decide the endings.

7 **NOW YOU!** Make sure that students give instructions that are realistic with respect to their abilities and the space available.

PROJECT TASK 1 Scrapbook

Tell students that this project will be an individual one to make a personal scrapbook. Show them an example if you have one and ask them what you might find in one. Give students the card and show how they can make the cover. Then get them to do the rest of the task. Remind students that they need to keep their project notes together in their **Workbook** (page 38) or in their own notebook.

→ See pages 24-27 **Projects**

FURTHER PRACTICE

Workbook pages 22-23
- **Grammar reference and practice** pages 86 and 93-94
- **Wordlist and exercises** pages 99 and 102-103

Remind students to do all the exercises in their notebook

CONTINUOUS ASSESSMENT Students can talk about body parts and actions and spell plural nouns.

ANSWER KEY

Page 30-31

1

1 little
2 plump
3 blonde
4 short
5 cute
6 skinny
7 height
8 slim
9 wavy
10 handsome
11 He's
12 elderly
13 slim
14 grey

2

Name	Height	Age	Opinion	Body	Hair	Eyes
Melissa	short	8	funny	slim	wavy, blonde	brown
David	tall	32	friendly	thin	brown	brown
Barbara	medium height	40	happy	slim	short, curly (dyed orange)	brown

3 **1** Jenny **2** Maria **3** Anita **4** Sarah **5** Paula **6** David

4 **1** your **2** Their **3** They **4** My **5** His **6** He **7** She **8** Her **9** it

5 **a** Dana **b** David **c** Sam and Tom

6 *Student's own answers*

Remind students to do all the exercises in their notebook

LESSON FOCUS

Grammar Subject pronouns and possessive adjectives
Vocabulary Physical appearance
Listening Physical descriptions
Speaking Physical descriptions to identify individuals
Project task 2 Students describe themselves and plan the scrapbook design

Resources

Teacher's i-solutions, Student's Book audio

Preparation Photos of various famous people the students will probably know

Warmer

Put the photos where the students can see them. Describe one of the people and get the students to guess who it is. Whoever guesses correctly first then describes someone else. Students continue in pairs or small groups.

1 1.29 (See page 171 for transcripts) Tell students they will hear two children describing the people in the order they appear in the photos. As you play the audio, also ask what relationship the people are to the speakers (Maggie – speaker's cousin, Paul – speaker's brother, Amy – speaker's friend, Steve – speaker's guitar teacher, Sue – speaker's grandma).

LISTENING TOOLS

Draw students' attention to the **Listening tool** and encourage them to look over the table of information before playing the audio for exercise 2.

2 1.30 (See page 171 for transcripts) Tell students they will hear the people described in order from the top of the table to the bottom and elicit a guess for Melissa's height and age. Stop and check before continuing.

FAST FINISHERS Students can complete this exercise alone or in pairs.

3 1.31 (See page 172 for transcripts) Get students to describe the numbered people to each other. Then play the audio and have the students write names for the numbered people.

SUBJECT PRONOUNS AND POSSESSIVE ADJECTIVES

Flipped Learning

Draw students' attention to the **Grammar table**. Remind students that they can use this as a quick reference while completing the exercises.

Show students the **Grammar animation** and/or refer students to the **Grammar reference** on page 109 for further information on form and use.

→ See page 23 for how to flip the **grammar lesson**

4 Tell students that the conversation is about the people in the photos in exercise 5. Get them to check each other's answers to exercise 4 in pairs and then discuss their answers to exercise 5.

5 Ask them to give the reasons for their answers from the text in exercise 4 and check their pronunciation.

SPEAKING TOOLS

Write some longer or more problematic expressions from the unit thus far on the board (e.g. *medium height, an elderly woman, identical twins,* etc.) and drill them with students. Then tell them they have a minute to repeat the expressions in their minds. Then erase the expressions from the board and test students on them and see how naturally they can remember and say them. Get them to read the **Speaking tool.**

6 NOW YOU! Tell the class you will listen to the conversations and choose people to read their descriptions to the whole class. This will help make sure descriptions are respectful.

PROJECT TASK 2 Scrapbook

Make sure the students understand the task and write drafts first. Remind students that they need to keep their project notes together in their **Workbook** (page 38) or in their own notebook.

→ See pages 24-27 **Projects**

FURTHER PRACTICE

Workbook pages 24-25
- **Grammar reference and practice** pages 86 and 93-94
- **Wordlist and exercises** pages 99 and 102-103

Vocabulary and Grammar worksheets available to download from the **Richmond** *Learning* **Platform**

→ See pages 39-39 **Mixed-ability classes**

CONTINUOUS ASSESSMENT Students can talk about physical appearance and use subject pronouns and possessive adjectives.

Remind students to do all the exercises in their notebook

1 In pairs, describe the three people in the photos. What do you think they are like?

READING TOOLS
Before you start reading a text, look at the title and think quickly about your own opinions on the topic. This will help you to understand and read the text critically.

2 Read the article. Compare your ideas from exercise 1 with the text.

3 Read the text again and choose the best answers.
1 Why are the photographs included in the article?
a To show that sometimes appearance and reality are different.
b Because they are famous people.
2 What are the consequences of judging people by their appearance?
a Sometimes we believe things that are not true about people.
b Not everyone is successful.
3 According to the article, what kind of people are more successful in business?
a Attractive people.
b People with dominant facial features.
4 Why do we judge people by their appearance?
a It helps us to stay safe.
b It helps us understand what people are really like.

4 Copy the table and complete it with words from the text.

Noun	Adjective
comfort	···
complexity	···
···	judgemental
success	···
shyness	···
···	trustworthy

5 Complete the sentences with words from exercise 4.
1 If you aren't feeling ···, tell me and I'll get a different chair for you.
2 If you don't like talking to people, you are ···.
3 Can you keep a secret? Are you ···?
4 People who are too critical of others are ···.

CAN YOU JUDGE A BOOK BY ITS COVER?

Look at the photos of these people. What do you see? An elderly woman with a shy smile, a man who probably isn't very interested in appearance, and a man with a face that inspires trust.

Who are they really? The woman is Rita Levi-Montalcini, 1986 winner of the Nobel Prize in Physiology or Medicine. The man with the beard is Austrian artist Gustav Klimt, famous for his beautiful gold leaf paintings. The man with the white hair is ex-criminal Frank Abagnale. His story is the basis of the Leonardo DiCaprio film *Catch Me If You Can*.

We often make judgements about people based on their appearance. An attractive politician has more chances of winning an election. People with dominant facial features are usually more successful in business and we prefer nurses with soft facial features, because it makes us feel more comfortable. But obviously not all attractive people make good politicians and not all soft-featured people are kind and caring. Sometimes our initial judgements are very wrong.

Do all exercises in your notebook

So, why do we make them? Well, it's an evolutionary advantage to make quick judgements. It helps us to recognise people who may be dangerous.

But this doesn't mean that it's a good idea to believe your first impressions. People are usually much more complex than you first think.

6 Complete this sentence for you and read it for your partner. Do they agree?
When people first meet me, they sometimes think I'm ···, but really I'm ···.

CORE VALUES Keeping an open mind

7 Discuss the questions in pairs.
- According to the article, why is it important to keep an open mind about people?
- Do you ever change your opinion about people? Can you think of examples?
- 'Prejudice' means judging someone too quickly in a negative way. What different kinds of prejudice can you think of?
- Do you think it's good to keep an open mind about other cultures? Why?
- Look at the pictures below. What judgements do you think people might make about these people?

a

b

c

FAST FINISHERS Write about someone you know whose personality doesn't match their appearance.

Do all exercises in your notebook

ANSWER KEY

Pages 32-33

1 *Student's own answers*

2 *Student's own answers*

3 **1** a
2 a
3 b
4 a

4

Noun	Adjective
comfort	comfortable
complexity	complex
judgement	judgemental
success	successful
shyness	shy
trust	trustworthy

5 **1** comfortable
2 shy
3 trustworthy
4 judgemental

6 *Student's own answers*

7 *Student's own answers*

Remind students to do all the exercises in their notebook

LESSON FOCUS

Language in context Nouns and adjectives

Core values Keeping an open mind

Resources

Teacher's i-solutions, Student's Book audio

Preparation The same photos of famous people used in the previous lesson

→ See pages 36-37 **Literature**

Warmer

Put the photos up on the board again. Ask students in pairs to discuss what they can say about the personalities of the people. Do they agree with each other?

1 Draw students' attention to the three photos within the text and ask them to answer the questions in pairs. Tell them they will read about the people in the text.

READING TOOLS

Get students to look at the title of the text and tell you what it means. Ask how many people think the answer is 'yes', how many 'no' and how many 'sometimes'. Get them to read the **Reading tool**.

2 1.32 (See page 172 for transcripts) Ask students to read the text to see what the answer given to the title is (no). If there's time, get them back in pairs to compare their ideas with those of the text.

3 Answer the first question together, and then give them more reading time to answer the remaining questions.

4 Tell students that the words missing from the table are all in the text and check that they understand the meaning, using the text to help them guess meanings of unfamiliar words.

5 After students complete the exercise, get them to write more sentences with gaps for other words from exercise 4 for his/her partner to guess.

6 Try to put students with different classmates from those they worked with in the last **Core values** lesson on page 23 and remind them of their answers from that lesson to help prompt them here.

CORE VALUES Keeping an open mind

7 This topic can be difficult in a classroom. The message of the article is simply that our initial judgements can be wrong, and that people are usually more complex than we first think. Other types of prejudice that could be brought up are racism, sexism, ageism and classism, for example. Remind students of the value of diversity as discussed in unit 1, and that prejudices are best combatted with an open mind and factual information.

After they look at the photos, you could share the following information:

- That Chinese and Singaporean students usually score the highest in PISA tests.
- There are many reasons people become homeless and many organisations that provide very useful support.
- In the US, cheerleading is taken very seriously and cheerleaders dedicate a lot of time to perfecting their routines.

FAST FINISHERS Students can complete this exercise alone or in pairs.

FURTHER PRACTICE
Workbook pages 26-27

Remind students to do all the exercises in their notebook

CONTINUOUS ASSESSMENT Students can understand abstract nouns and adjectives in a text about judging people by appearances.

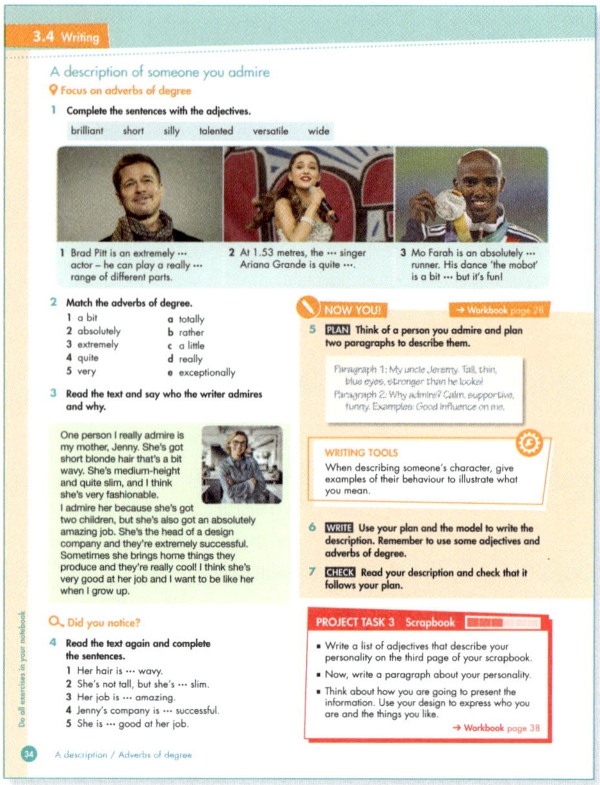

3.4 Writing

A description of someone you admire

Focus on adverbs of degree

1 Complete the sentences with the adjectives.

brilliant short silly talented versatile wide

1 Brad Pitt is an extremely ··· actor – he can play a really ··· range of different parts.
2 At 1.53 metres, the ··· singer Ariana Grande is quite ···.
3 Mo Farah is an absolutely ··· runner. His dance 'the mobot' is a bit ··· but it's fun!

2 Match the adverbs of degree.

1 a bit a totally
2 absolutely b rather
3 extremely c a little
4 quite d really
5 very e exceptionally

3 Read the text and say who the writer admires and why.

One person I really admire is my mother, Jenny. She's got short blonde hair that's a bit wavy. She's medium-height and quite slim, and I think she's very fashionable.
I admire her because she's got two children, but she's also got an absolutely amazing job. She's the head of a design company and they're extremely successful. Sometimes she brings home things they produce and they're really cool! I think she's very good at her job and I want to be like her when I grow up.

Did you notice?

4 Read the text again and complete the sentences.

1 Her hair is ··· wavy.
2 She's not tall, but she's ··· slim.
3 Her job is ··· amazing.
4 Jenny's company is ··· successful.
5 She is ··· good at her job.

NOW YOU! → Workbook page 28

5 PLAN Think of a person you admire and plan two paragraphs to describe them.

Paragraph 1: My uncle Jeremy. Tall, thin, blue eyes, stronger than he looks!
Paragraph 2: Why admire? Calm, supportive, funny. Examples: Good influence on me.

WRITING TOOLS
When describing someone's character, give examples of their behaviour to illustrate what you mean.

6 WRITE Use your plan and the model to write the description. Remember to use some adjectives and adverbs of degree.

7 CHECK Read your description and check that it follows your plan.

PROJECT TASK 3 Scrapbook

- Write a list of adjectives that describe your personality on the third page of your scrapbook.
- Now, write a paragraph about your personality.
- Think about how you are going to present the information. Use your design to express who you are and the things you like.

→ Workbook page 38

Do all exercises in your notebook

34 A description / Adverbs of degree

ANSWER KEY

Page 34

1 **1** versatile; wide
2 talented; short
3 brilliant; silly

2 **1** c **2** a **3** e **4** b **5** d

3 *Suggested answer:*
Her mother Jenny, because she's got two children and is very good at her job as head of a design company.

4 **1** a bit
2 quite
3 absolutely
4 extremely
5 very

5 *Student's own answers*

6 *Student's own answers*

7 *Student's own answers*

FURTHER PRACTICE

Workbook page 28

LESSON FOCUS

Focus on Adverbs of degree

Writing A description of someone you admire

Project task 3 Describing and expressing personalities

Resources

Teacher's i-solutions

Warmer

Ask students in pairs to write a short description of a famous person: one sentence about their appearance and one about their personality. Students read out their descriptions for the rest of the class to guess the person and say how much they agree with the descriptions.

Focus on adverbs of degree

1 Draw student's attention to the photos and ask what they know about the people. Students then complete the exercise.

2 Point out that the adverbs come from the sentences in exercise 1 and get students to complete the exercise. Tell them that *absolutely* and *totally* are used with ungradable adjectives, like *brilliant, amazing* or *terrible*.

3 Give students just enough time to complete the exercise by scan reading.

Did you notice?

4 Give students a bit more time with the text and deal with any vocabulary issues.

5 **PLAN** Put students in pairs or small groups to discuss who they think they will choose. Get them to look at the example plan and the model before making a plan for their own description.

WRITING TOOLS

Get students to read the **Writing tool** and find an example in the model text: *Sometimes she brings home things they produce and they're really cool.*

6 **WRITE** Before students start writing, make a checklist on the board of any elements related to content, structure, language and style that they should bear in mind.

7 **CHECK** Once they have checked their own descriptions, they can swap with a partner and check theirs.

PROJECT TASK 3 Scrapbook

Go over the task with the class. Students will come up with a paragraph to describe themselves and decide how to present the information in their scrapbook. Tell students that they need to keep their project notes together in their **Workbook** (page 38) or in their own notebook.

→ See pages 24-27 **Projects**

Remind students to do all the exercises in their notebook

CONTINUOUS ASSESSMENT Students can use adverbs of degree to write a description of someone they admire.

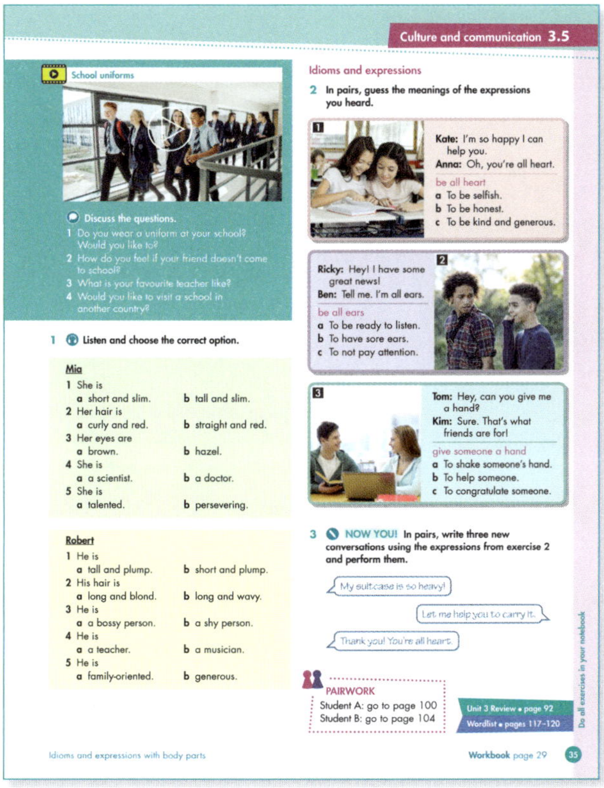

Culture and communication 3.5

School uniforms

Discuss the questions.

1 Do you wear a uniform at your school? Would you like to?
2 How do you feel if your friend doesn't come to school?
3 What is your favourite teacher like?
4 Would you like to visit a school in another country?

1 Listen and choose the correct option.

Mia

1 She is
 a short and slim. b tall and slim.
2 Her hair is
 a curly and red. b straight and red.
3 Her eyes are
 a brown. b hazel.
4 She is
 a a scientist. b a doctor.
5 She is
 a talented. b persevering.

Robert

1 He is
 a tall and plump. b short and plump.
2 His hair is
 a long and blond. b long and wavy.
3 He is
 a a bossy person. b a shy person.
4 He is
 a a teacher. b a musician.
5 He is
 a family-oriented. b generous.

Idioms and expressions

2 In pairs, guess the meanings of the expressions you heard.

1
Kate: I'm so happy I can help you.
Anna: Oh, you're all heart.
be all heart
a To be selfish.
b To be honest.
c To be kind and generous.

2
Ricky: Hey! I have some great news!
Ben: Tell me. I'm all ears.
be all ears
a To be ready to listen.
b To have sore ears.
c To not pay attention.

3
Tom: Hey, can you give me a hand?
Kim: Sure. That's what friends are for!
give someone a hand
a To shake someone's hand.
b To help someone.
c To congratulate someone.

3 NOW YOU! In pairs, write three new conversations using the expressions from exercise 2 and perform them.

My suitcase is so heavy!
Let me help you to carry it.
Thank you! You're all heart.

PAIRWORK
Student A: go to page 100
Student B: go to page 104

Unit 3 Review • page 92
Wordlist • pages 117-120

Do all exercises in your notebook

Idioms and expressions with body parts

Workbook page 29

35

LESSON FOCUS

Idioms and expressions Body parts

Listening Answering multiple-choice questions from a conversation

Speaking Practising written conversations using new expressions

Resources

Teacher's i-solutions, Student's Book audio, Culture video and worksheets

School uniforms

Video and worksheet available on the Richmond*Learning*Platform

- In pairs, ask students to complete the *What I know...* exercises on the **Culture video worksheet.**
- Show students the **Culture video** and ask them to complete the *What I learned...* exercises on the worksheet.
- In pairs, students compare answers.
- In small groups, tell students to complete the *What I wonder...* exercises on the worksheet.

Warmer

Watch the Culture video and discuss the questions with the whole class. If you don't have video facilities, simply discuss the questions.

1 1.33 (See page 172 for transcripts) Tell students they will hear a boy and a girl describe people who are important to them. Give them time to read the sentence stems and options before playing the audio. After they have listened once, ask them if they heard what relationships the speakers had to the people they're describing (Mia is the boy's mum and Robert is the girl's dad) and let them listen one more time to the audio if they need it before going through the answers.

Idioms and expressions

2 Ask students if they remember any idioms from the audio related to body parts and draw attention to the context to see if students can guess their meanings. Then show them the new contexts in this exercise and see if they were right about the meanings.

3 NOW YOU! To extend this exercise, get pairs to perform their conversations for other pairs and have the other pairs try and interrupt the conversation to predict the expression the first pair put in the conversation before they reach it.

ANSWER KEY

Page 35

1

Mia	Robert
1 b	1 b
2 a	2 b
3 a	3 b
4 a	4 b
5 a	5 a

2 1 c 2 a 3 b

3 *Student's own answers*

FURTHER PRACTICE AND UNIT ASSESSSMENT

Unit 3 Review **Student's Book** page 92

Workbook page 29

- **Reflect on your learning** page 29
- **Grammar reference and practice** pages 86 and 93-94
- **Wordlist and exercises** pages 99 and 102-103

Tests available to download and edit from the **Richmond*Learning*Platform**

→ See pages 40-41 **Assessment**

PAIRWORK **Student's Book** pages 100 and 104

See **Teacher's Book** page 88 for more information.

→ See pages 30-33 **Mediation**

Remind students to do all the exercises in their notebook

Unit 3 Review

Unit 3 Review

1 Listen and match the person with the adjective. There are three adjectives you don't need.

EXAM TIP
Write an answer for every question. You do not lose points for wrong answers.

1 Amina	a adventurous	e plump
2 Scott	b cute	f shy
3 Jessica	c extrovert	g slim
4 Dale	d friendly	h tall
5 Yasmin		

2 Read and choose the correct option.

Jo

My aunt Ellie is my favourite relative. She's got hazel eyes and long, straight brown hair. She comes to our house on Sundays. She's a brilliant guitar player and a successful businesswoman. She has her own online company selling handmade guitars all over the world. She's really patient and she's teaching me to play.

Polly

My favourite relative is my cousin Molly. She's 19 and goes to university. She's tall and slim. Her eyes are brown and her hair is long and black. She's a talented artist and always gives me a hand with my school projects. Her work is really cool. I'm very proud of her. She's really adventurous and travels to other countries on her own.

Alison

I really love my grandfather Roger. He's quite old now, but he's still very active. He's not bald; he's got long, grey hair. He's extremely family-oriented and loves spending time with us. He's always at our house when I get home from school. He's an absolutely fantastic cook and makes the most delicious cakes and biscuits!

	Jo	Polly	Alison
1 Whose relative is focused on family?	a	b	c
2 Whose relative is a student?	a	b	c
3 Whose relative has her own business?	a	b	c
4 Whose relative travels alone?	a	b	c
5 Whose relative visits their house once a week?	a	b	c

Do all exercises in your notebook

92 External exam practice

Student's Book page 92

ANSWER KEY

See page 180 for transcripts

1 2.42
1 f
2 g
3 d
4 a
5 c

2 **1** c
2 b
3 a
4 b
5 a

Pairwork

Unit 3 • Student A

1 Look at the people in the pictures. Student B has chosen one of them. Ask questions about their appearance to try and guess which person Student B chose.

2 In your notebook, create a personality for that person. Imagine what their likes and dislikes are. Think about their job and their hobbies. Now compare your answers with Student B's answers. Are your ideas similar?

3 Now you choose a person. Student B will ask you questions about their appearance to try and guess which person you chose.

4 Repeat exercise 2 for the person you chose.

Student's Book page 100

Unit 3 • Student B

1 Look at the people in the pictures. Choose one person. Student A will ask you questions about their appearance to try and guess which person you chose.

2 In your notebook, create a personality for that person. Imagine what their likes and dislikes are. Think about their job and their hobbies. Now compare your answers with Student A's answers. Are your ideas similar?

3 Student A will now choose a person. Ask questions about their appearance to try and guess which person Student A chose.

4 Repeat exercise 2 for the person Student A chose.

Student's Book page 104

CEFR MEDIATION DESCRIPTOR

- **Collaborating to construct meaning**

Students can express an idea with very simple words and ask what others think.

- **Describing people**

Tell Student A and B they both have photos of the same people and that they will take it in turns to describe the appearance of a person for the other to guess. Then each student will imagine and write a personality to compare with their partner's.

Remind students to do all the exercises in their notebook

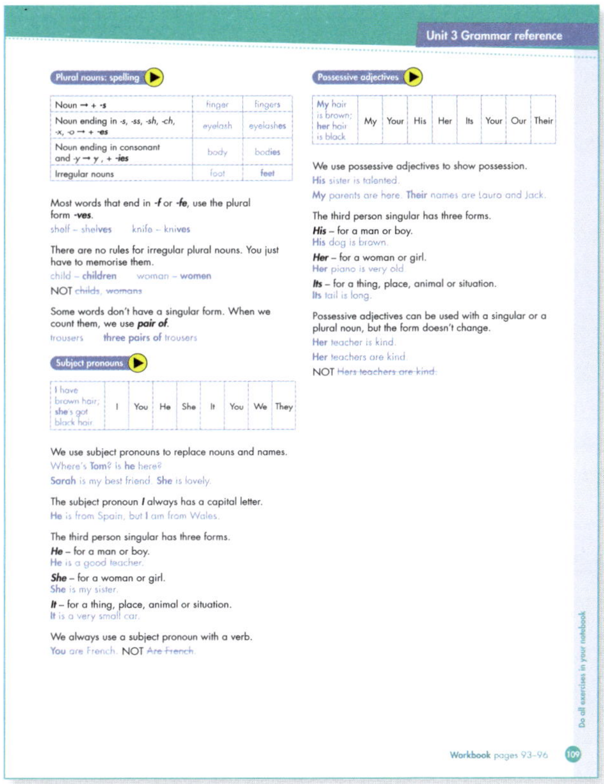

Plural nouns: spelling

Noun → + -s	finger	fingers
Noun ending in -s, -ss, -sh, -ch, -x, -o → + -es	eyelash	eyelashes
Noun ending in consonant and -y → y, + -ies	body	bodies
Irregular nouns	foot	feet

Most words that end in *-f* or *-fe*, use the plural form ***-ves***.
shelf – shelves   knife – knives

There are no rules for irregular plural nouns. You just have to memorise them.
child – **children**   woman – **women**
NOT ~~childs, womans~~

Some words don't have a singular form. When we count them, we use ***pair of***.
trousers   **three pairs of** trousers

Subject pronouns

I have brown hair; **she**'s got black hair	I	You	He	She	It	You	We	They

We use subject pronouns to replace nouns and names.
Where's **Tom**? Is **he** here?
Sarah is my best friend. **She** is lovely.

The subject pronoun ***I*** always has a capital letter.
He is from Spain, but **I** am from Wales.

The third person singular has three forms.
He – for a man or boy.
He is a good teacher.
She – for a woman or girl.
She is my sister.
It – for a thing, place, animal or situation.
It is a very small car.

We always use a subject pronoun with a verb.
You are French. NOT ~~Are French.~~

Possessive adjectives

My hair is brown; **her** hair is black	My	Your	His	Her	Its	Your	Our	Their

We use possessive adjectives to show possession.
His sister is talented.
My parents are here. **Their** names are Laura and Jack.

The third person singular has three forms.
His – for a man or boy.
His dog is brown.
Her – for a woman or girl.
Her piano is very old.
Its – for a thing, place, animal or situation.
Its tail is long.

Possessive adjectives can be used with a singular or a plural noun, but the form doesn't change.
Her teacher is kind.
Her teachers are kind.
NOT ~~Hers teachers are kind.~~

Do all exercises in your notebook

Student's Book page 109

Wordlist

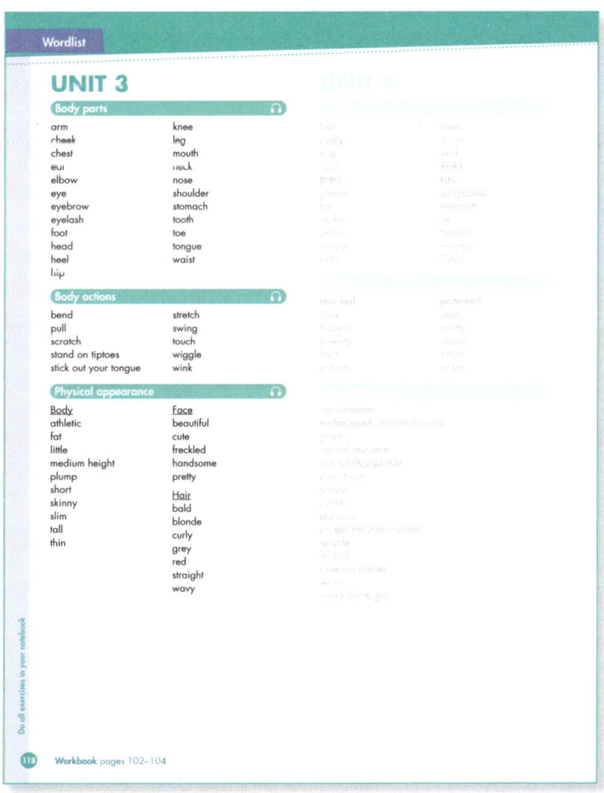

UNIT 3

Body parts

arm
cheek
chest
ear
elbow
eye
eyebrow
eyelash
foot
head
heel
hip
knee
leg
mouth
neck
nose
shoulder
stomach
tooth
toe
tongue
waist

Body actions

bend
pull
scratch
stand on tiptoes
stick out your tongue
stretch
swing
touch
wiggle
wink

Physical appearance

Body
athletic
fat
little
medium height
plump
short
skinny
slim
tall
thin

Face
beautiful
cute
freckled
handsome
pretty

Hair
bald
blonde
curly
grey
red
straight
wavy

Do all exercises in your notebook

Student's Book page 118
2.53 2.54 2.55

Remind students to do all the exercises in their notebook

4 LIFESTYLE

At the start of each unit and lesson, explain to the students what the objectives are.

Language objectives

Grammar

Demonstrative pronouns
- Students learn the differences between *this, that, these* and *those*.

Present continuous
- Students learn the present continuous in affirmative, negative and question forms.

Vocabulary

Clothes: *belt, boots, cap, coat, dress, gloves, hat, jacket, jeans, jumper, shirt, shoes, shorts, skirt, socks, suit, sunglasses, swimsuit, tie, trainers, trousers, T-shirt*
- Students learn vocabulary for clothes and accessories.

Patterns: *checked, dark, flowers, flowery, light, pattern, patterned, spots, spotty, stripes, stripy, tartan*
- Students practise vocabulary for patterns used in clothing.

The environment: *conservation, endangered animals/species, green, natural resource, non-biodegradable, plant trees, plastic, pollute, pollution, protect the environment, recycle, rubbish, save our planet, waste, water shortages*
- Students use vocabulary related to the environment.

Idioms and expressions

Clothes: *pull your socks up; put yourself in my shoes; I take my hat off to you*
- Students look at idioms and expressions related to clothes in the context of short conversations.

Recycled language

The verb *be*; Question words; Pronouns and possessive adjectives

Skills objectives

Speaking

- Students describe the clothes people are wearing.
- Students ask and answer questions about a family.
- Students ask and answer questions about environmental awareness.
- Students write and perform conversations using idioms and expressions.

Pronunciation: Students practise using the /ŋ/ sound in *-ing* endings.

Pairwork: Students use various mediation techniques to find out more about body language.

Listening

- Students listen to complete sentences with new vocabulary.
- Students listen to check verb forms in a short conversation.
- Students listen to idioms and expressions in context.

Reading

- Students read a text to compare its content with their own ideas.
- Students read a text about different people to match sentences with the people that they describe.
- Students read a text to find vocabulary to match with definitions.

Core values: Students use their own knowledge to assess the effectiveness of different **conservation** measures.

Writing

- Students focus on language for cause and effect in context.
- Students plan, write and check a blog entry about an organisation they know or will invent.

Focus on linking language: *by, so, so that, in order to*

Remind students to do all the exercises in their notebook

Learning to learn tools

SPEAKING TOOLS Students focus on asking and answering questions in pairs to develop their confidence and competence in speaking.	LISTENING TOOLS Students practise subvocalising new vocabulary to aid their pronunciation.
READING TOOLS Students practise finding information that's paraphrased and summarised.	WRITING TOOLS Students consolidate their skills in using models to help develop and structure their writing.

VOCABULARY TOOLS Students practise keeping lists of categorised vocabulary.

Project objectives: Scrapbook

Task 4 Students write about their clothes.

Task 5 Students present their families and draw a family tree.

Task 6 Students describe their family members.

Audiovisual objectives

Vlog: Students watch and listen to Sarah unbox a collection of clothes she ordered.

Culture: Students watch and listen to Sarah talk about aspects of life in Australia.

Grammar animations: Students are presented with visual presentations of the unit grammar.

Key competences

LC **Linguistic**
pages 36-43

MST **Mathematical and Science and Technology**
pages 40-42

DC **Digital**
pages 36, 38, 43

SCC **Social and Civic**
pages 39-43

CAE **Cultural awareness and expression**
pages 36-37, 40-41

LL **Learning to learn**
pages 36-37, 39, 40, 42

IE **Sense of initiative and entrepreneurship**
pages 37, 39, 42

→ See pages 42-43 **Key competences**

CEFR Mediation

4.1 Relaying information in writing
Can relay in writing specific information in short, simple texts.

4.2 Relaying information in writing
Can list specific information in simple texts.

4.3 Processing text in writing
Can pick out and reproduce key words and phrases from a short text.

4.4 Processing text in writing
Can render short texts on familiar themes.

4.5 Facilitating communication in delicate situations and disagreements
Can recognise when speakers disagree and adapt phrases to seek a compromise.

Project Encouraging conceptual talk
Can ask questions to invite people to clarify their reasoning.

Unit review Encouraging conceptual talk
Can ask what somebody thinks of a certain idea.

Pairwork Processing text in speech
Can report information in short, simple texts with illustrations or tables.

→ See pages 30-33 **Mediation**

Remind students to do all the exercises in their notebook

4.1 Vocabulary and grammar

4 LIFESTYLE

In unit 4 you will:
- talk about families and clothes.
- say if things are close to you or far away.
- talk about what people are doing.
- write a blog entry.

4.1 Vocabulary and grammar

SARAH'S VLOG: Unboxing

Discuss the questions.
1 Do you like shopping for clothes?
2 What is your favourite outfit? Why?
3 What kinds of clothes don't you like?

Flipped Learning

1 **Categorise the words into *Clothes, Footwear* or *Accessories*. Identify the items in the picture.**

belt boots cap coat dress gloves hat jacket jeans jumper shirt shoes shorts skirt socks suit sunglasses swimsuit tie trainers trousers T-shirt

DEMONSTRATIVE PRONOUNS		
Singular	Use ***this*** for a thing that is close to you. This is my jacket.	Use ***that*** for a thing that is far from you. That is Dad's hat.
Plural	Use ***these*** for things that are close to you. These are Mum's gloves.	Use ***those*** for things that are far from you. Those are Julia's shoes.

Grammar reference page 110

2 **Complete the dialogue with *this, that, these* or *those*.**

Dad: Julia, can you come here and help me with the laundry? Whose things are [1]…?
Julia: I can see from here. [2]… white T-shirt is Mum's, and [3]… blue trousers are Billy's.
Dad: And what about [4]… green skirt?
Julia: [5]…'s Mum's too. And [6]… socks are Billy's. Dad, bring [7]… laundry basket over here and we can put everything on [8]… table and identify it all.

VOCABULARY TOOLS
Keep different types of wordlists in a notebook and categorise new words when you learn them. This will help you to remember the vocabulary.

FAST FINISHERS Write a paragraph about your and your friends' clothes.

Do all exercises in your notebook

36 Clothes / Demonstrative pronouns / Patterns

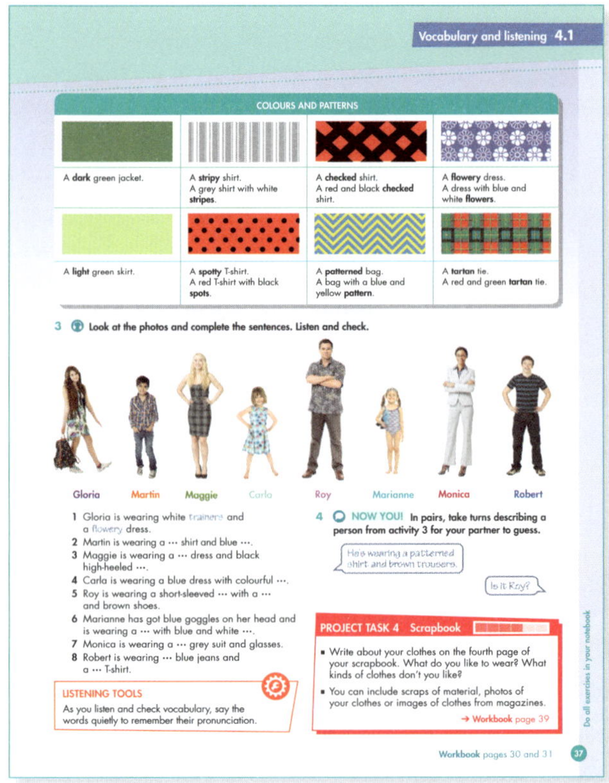

Vocabulary and listening 4.1

COLOURS AND PATTERNS			
A **dark** green jacket.	A **stripy** shirt. A grey shirt with white **stripes**.	A **checked** shirt. A red and black **checked** shirt.	A **flowery** dress. A dress with blue and white **flowers**.
A **light** green skirt.	A **spotty** T-shirt. A red T-shirt with black **spots**.	A **patterned** bag. A bag with a blue and yellow **pattern**.	A **tartan** tie. A red and green **tartan** tie.

3 **Look at the photos and complete the sentences. Listen and check.**

Gloria Martin Maggie Carla Roy Marianne Monica Robert

1 Gloria is wearing white trainers and a flowery dress.
2 Martin is wearing a … shirt and blue ….
3 Maggie is wearing a … dress and black high-heeled ….
4 Carla is wearing a blue dress with colourful ….
5 Roy is wearing a short-sleeved … with a … and brown shoes.
6 Marianne has got blue goggles on her head and is wearing a … with blue and white ….
7 Monica is wearing a … grey suit and glasses.
8 Robert is wearing … blue jeans and a … T-shirt.

LISTENING TOOLS
As you listen and check vocabulary, say the words quietly to remember their pronunciation.

4 NOW YOU! **In pairs, take turns describing a person from activity 3 for your partner to guess.**

He's wearing a patterned shirt and brown trousers.

Is it Roy?

PROJECT TASK 4 Scrapbook
- Write about your clothes on the fourth page of your scrapbook. What do you like to wear? What kinds of clothes don't you like?
- You can include scraps of material, photos of your clothes or images of clothes from magazines.

→ Workbook page 39

Do all exercises in your notebook

Workbook pages 30 and 31 37

ANSWER KEY

Pages 36-37

1 **Clothes:** coat, dress, jacket, jeans, jumper, shirt, shorts, skirt, socks, suit, swimsuit, trousers, T-shirt
Footwear: boots, shoes, trainers
Accessories: belt, cap, gloves, hat, sunglasses, tie

1 belt
2 coat
3 T-shirt
4 cap
5 jumper
6 socks
7 shirt
8 boots
9 gloves
10 trousers
11 tie
12 skirt
13 trainers
14 swimsuit

2
1 these
2 That
3 those
4 this
5 That
6 those
7 that
8 this

3
1 trainers; flowery
2 checked; jeans
3 tartan; shoes
4 spots
5 shirt; pattern
6 swimsuit; stripes
7 light
8 dark; stripy

4 *Student's own answers*

Remind students to do all the exercises in their notebook

LESSON FOCUS

Grammar Demonstrative pronouns
Vocabulary Clothes; Patterns
Listening Completing descriptions
Speaking Describing what people are wearing
Project task 4 Talk about your clothes

Resources

Teacher's i-solutions, Student's Book audio, Vlog and worksheet

Preparation The students' photos of themselves from their scrapbooks if possible

Flipped Learning

SARAH'S VLOG: Unboxing

- Make sure to set up the **Flipped Learning** work with the students beforehand. **See page 20-23 for complete Flipped Learning guidelines.**
- Ask students to put the **Flipped Learning worksheets** on their desks and walk around to check how many have completed the Flipped task.
- In pairs or small groups, ask students to compare and check the *Before you watch...* and *While you watch...* exercises on the worksheet.
- Show students **Sarah's vlog** and ask volunteers to provide correct answers and clarify any doubts other students may have.
- Choose three or four students to read aloud their answers to the *After you watch...* exercises on the worksheet and encourage some class discussion.
- Move straight to exercise 1 on page 36.

Warmer

Watch Sarah's vlog and discuss the questions with the whole class. If you don't have video facilities, simply discuss the questions.

1 Put the categories on the board and put in any words you used in the Warmer. Tell students there are more words than pictures, elicit item 1 to name and categorise and let them continue. For items not in the picture, let them use dictionaries, draw pictures for them or point to the clothes if you're wearing them.

Flipped Learning

DEMONSTRATIVE PRONOUNS

Draw students' attention to the **Grammar table**. Remind students that they can use this as a quick reference while completing the exercises.

Show students the **Grammar animation** and/or refer students to the **Grammar reference** on page 110 for further information on form and use.

→ See page 23 for how to flip the **grammar lesson**

2 Ask students to look at the dialogue and the picture and ask who the person in the picture is (Julia's dad). Elicit the first answer, asking if the clothes are near him or far away. To help them refer to the **Grammar table**. Students complete the exercise.

VOCABULARY TOOLS

Refer students to what they wrote in exercise 1 and get them to read the **Vocabulary tool**. Ask why keeping categorised lists might help remember new vocabulary (it's easier to find to revise, easier to make connections between items, easier to practise together to help consolidate, etc.).

FAST FINISHERS Students can complete this exercise alone or in pairs.

3 1.34 (See page 172 for transcripts) Draw students' attention to the colours and patterns table. Then ask them to find examples of the patterns in the people in exercise 3. Students then complete the exercise before you play the audio for them to check.

LISTENING TOOLS

Draw students' attention to the **Listening tool**. Remind them that as they are listening to an audio, repeating words to themselves will help with pronunciation.

4 **NOW YOU!** Make sure that students give instructions that are realistic with respect to their abilities and the space available.

PROJECT TASK 4 Scrapbook

Get students to do this on their own. Help them with any clothes vocabulary they need that is not featured in the lesson. Remind students that they need to keep their project notes together in their **Workbook** (page 39) or in their own notebook.

→ See pages 24-27 **Projects**

FURTHER PRACTICE

Workbook pages 31-31
- **Grammar reference and practice** pages 87 and 94
- **Wordlist and exercises** pages 99 and 103

Remind students to do all the exercises in their notebook

CONTINUOUS ASSESSMENT Students can talk about clothes and patterns and use demonstrative pronouns.

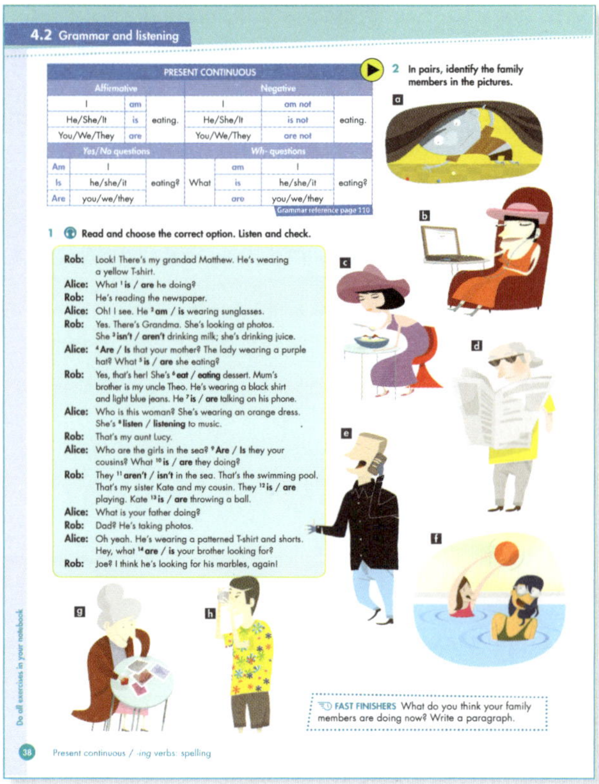

4.2 Grammar and listening

PRESENT CONTINUOUS					
Affirmative			Negative		
I	am	eating.	I	am not	eating.
He/She/It	is		He/She/It	is not	
You/We/They	are		You/We/They	are not	

Yes/No questions			Wh- questions			
Am	I	eating?	What	am	I	eating?
Is	he/she/it			is	he/she/it	
Are	you/we/they			are	you/we/they	

Grammar reference page 110

1 Read and choose the correct option. Listen and check.

Rob: Look! There's my grandad Matthew. He's wearing a yellow T-shirt.
Alice: What [1] **is / are** he doing?
Rob: He's reading the newspaper.
Alice: Oh! I see. He [2] **am / is** wearing sunglasses.
Rob: Yes. There's Grandma. She's looking at photos. She [3] **isn't / aren't** drinking milk; she's drinking juice.
Alice: [4] **Are / Is** that your mother? The lady wearing a purple hat? What [5] **is / are** she eating?
Rob: Yes, that's her! She's [6] **eat / eating** dessert. Mum's brother is my uncle Theo. He's wearing a black shirt and light blue jeans. He [7] **is / are** talking on his phone.
Alice: Who is this woman? She's wearing an orange dress. She's [8] **listen / listening** to music.
Rob: That's my aunt Lucy.
Alice: Who are the girls in the sea? [9] **Are / Is** they your cousins? What [10] **is / are** they doing?
Rob: They [11] **aren't / isn't** in the sea. That's the swimming pool. That's my sister Kate and my cousin. They [12] **is / are** playing. Kate [13] **is / are** throwing a ball.
Alice: What is your father doing?
Rob: Dad? He's taking photos.
Alice: Oh yeah. He's wearing a patterned T-shirt and shorts. Hey, what [14] **are / is** your brother looking for?
Rob: Joe? I think he's looking for his marbles, again!

2 In pairs, identify the family members in the pictures.

a b c d e f g h

FAST FINISHERS What do you think your family members are doing now? Write a paragraph.

Do all exercises in your notebook

38 Present continuous / -ing verbs: spelling

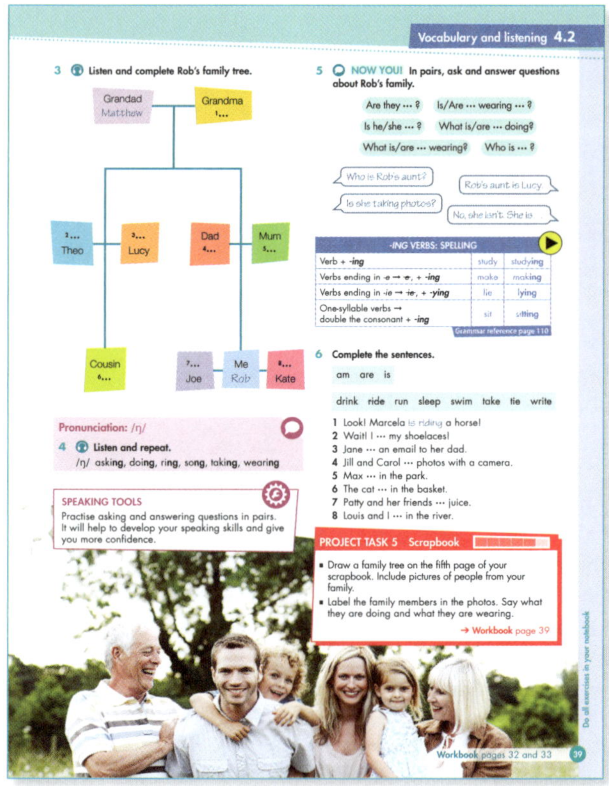

Vocabulary and listening 4.2

3 Listen and complete Rob's family tree.

Pronunciation: /ŋ/

4 Listen and repeat.

/ŋ/ asking, doing, ring, song, taking, wearing

SPEAKING TOOLS
Practise asking and answering questions in pairs. It will help to develop your speaking skills and give you more confidence.

5 NOW YOU! In pairs, ask and answer questions about Rob's family.

Are they … ? Is/Are … wearing … ? Is he/she … ? What is/are … doing? What is/are … wearing? Who is … ?

-ING VERBS: SPELLING		
Verb + -ing	study	studying
Verbs ending in -e → ~~e~~, + -ing	make	making
Verbs ending in -ie → ~~ie~~, + -ying	lie	lying
One-syllable verbs → double the consonant + -ing	sit	sitting

Grammar reference page 110

6 Complete the sentences.

am are is

drink ride run sleep swim take tie write

1 Look! Marcela is riding a horse!
2 Wait! I … my shoelaces!
3 Jane … an email to her dad.
4 Jill and Carol … photos with a camera.
5 Max … in the park.
6 The cat … in the basket.
7 Patty and her friends … juice.
8 Louis and I … in the river.

PROJECT TASK 5 Scrapbook

- Draw a family tree on the fifth page of your scrapbook. Include pictures of people from your family.
- Label the family members in the photos. Say what they are doing and what they are wearing.

→ Workbook page 39

Workbook pages 32 and 33 39

Do all exercises in your notebook

ANSWER KEY

Pages 38-39

1
1 is
2 is
3 isn't
4 Is
5 is
6 eating
7 is
8 listening
9 Are
10 are
11 aren't
12 are
13 is
14 is

2
a Brother Joe
b Aunt Lucy
c Mum
d Grandad Matthew
e Uncle Theo
f Sister Kate and cousin
g Grandma
h Dad

3
1 Rose
2 Uncle
3 Aunt
4 Michael
5 Isabel
6 Petra
7 Brother
8 Sister

4 *Student's own answers*

5 *Student's own answers*

6
1 is riding
2 am tying
3 is writing
4 are taking
5 is running
6 is sleeping
7 are drinking
8 are swimming

Remind students to do all the exercises in their notebook

LESSON FOCUS

Grammar Present continuous; *-ing* verbs: spelling
Listening A description of a family and of a family tree
Speaking Asking and answering questions about a family
Project task 5 Present your family and draw a family tree

Resources
Teacher's i-solutions, Student's Book audio

Warmer

Mime a verb you think students know and ask them what you're doing. Get the student who guesses right to mime their own verb. Students can continue in small groups. Put a list of actions on the board for them to choose from if you think that it will help.

PRESENT CONTINUOUS

Flipped Learning

Draw students' attention to the **Grammar table**. Remind students that they can use this as a quick reference while completing the exercises.
Show students the **Grammar animation** and/or refer students to the **Grammar reference** on page 110 for further information on form and use.

→ See page 23 for how to flip the **grammar lesson**

1 1.35 (See page 172 for transcripts) Tell the students that exercise 1 goes together with the pictures in exercise 2. Ask them to guess what the people in the pictures are doing. Then get them to do exercise 1 before you play the audio.

2 To extend this exercise, get students in pairs to ask who is doing what in the pictures. Note that in exercise 5 on the next page they will develop this activity, so don't spend too long on it here.

FAST FINISHERS Students can complete this exercise alone or in pairs.

3 1.36 (See page 172 for transcripts) Tell the students they are going to hear Rob talking more about his family, and get them to fill in what they can from the previous page before they listen. Tell them the information is not given in order in the audio.

SPEAKING TOOLS

Put students into pairs and get them to ask each other questions about their family tree. Explain that asking and responding to questions in this way builds confidence and helps speech to flow more naturally.

Pronunciation

4 1.37 (See page 172 for transcripts) Show students the correct position of the tongue for the sounds /n/ and /ŋ/ or draw a diagram (front of the mouth for /n/ and against the back of the throat for /ŋ/.

5 NOW YOU! Get one student to ask the questions with their book open and the other to close their book and answer from memory if possible. Then swap.

-ING VERBS: SPELLING

Flipped Learning

Draw students' attention to the **Grammar table**. Remind students that they can use this as a quick reference while completing the exercises.
Show students the **Grammar animation** and/or refer students to the **Grammar reference** on page 110 for further information on form and use.

→ See page 23 for how to flip the **grammar lesson**

6 Remind students to refer to the **Grammar tables** if they need help with exercise and that they should pay special attention to spelling.

PROJECT TASK 5 Scrapbook

Make sure students are realistic about how many family members will fit on their page. Remind students that they need to keep their project notes together in their **Workbook** (page 39) or in their own notebook.

→ See pages 24-27 **Projects**

FURTHER PRACTICE

Workbook pages 32-33
- **Grammar reference and practice** pages 87 and 94
- **Wordlist and exercises** pages 99 and 103

Vocabulary and Grammar worksheets available to download from the **Richmond***Learning***Platform**

→ See pages 38-39 **Mixed-ability classes**

Remind students to do all the exercises in their notebook

CONTINUOUS ASSESSMENT Students can spell *-ing* verbs and use the present continuous.

4.3 Reading

1 Match the words with the photos.

endangered animals plastic pollution rubbish water shortages

2 In pairs, think of solutions to the problems in exercise 1.

3 Read the article on page 41 and check if your solutions are mentioned.

READING TOOLS
Reading tasks often ask you to find information that's written in a different way in the text. Practise finding phrases that mean the same thing.

4 Read the article again and say who these sentences are about.
1 Her family is very big.
2 He doesn't mention his family.
3 They are involved in the Go Green project.
4 She is showing her neighbours how to help save the planet.
5 They are doing outdoor activities to help the environment.

5 Find words in the text that match the definitions.
1 lifting (something) off the ground
2 contaminate
3 very big
4 not able to decay naturally
5 a useful natural material such as water or minerals
6 use too much

6 Complete the questions using the words you found in exercise 5. Answer the questions in pairs.
1 What do you do to try not to ··· water?
2 Do you know anyone from a ··· family? How big is it?
3 Apart from water, what other ··· can you name?
4 Apart from plastic, what ··· materials can you name?
5 How do we ··· the air, water and land?
6 Can ··· ··· rubbish on the streets save animals from danger? What can happen if we don't do this?

Do all exercises in your notebook

40 Language in context / The environment

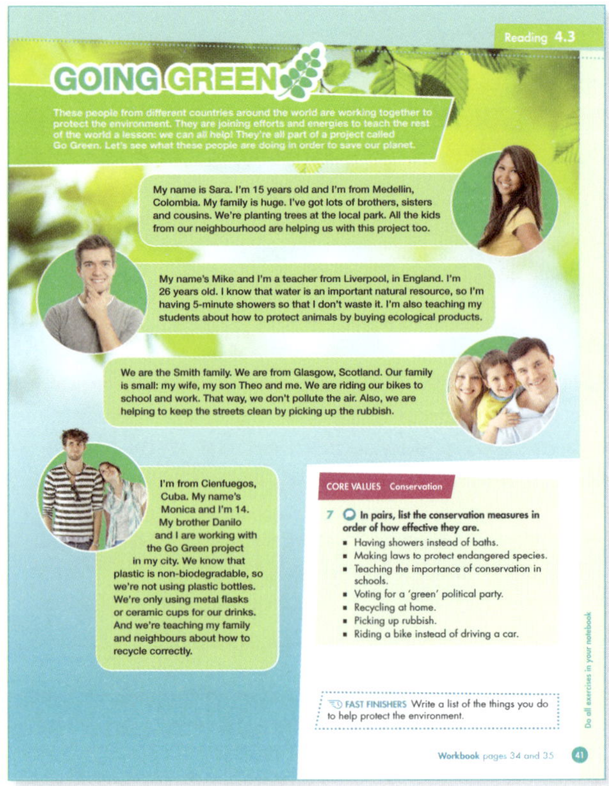
Reading 4.3

GOING GREEN

These people from different countries around the world are working together to protect the environment. They are joining efforts and energies to teach the rest of the world a lesson: we can all help! They're all part of a project called Go Green. Let's see what these people are doing in order to save our planet.

My name is Sara. I'm 15 years old and I'm from Medellin, Colombia. My family is huge. I've got lots of brothers, sisters and cousins. We're planting trees at the local park. All the kids from our neighbourhood are helping us with this project too.

My name's Mike and I'm a teacher from Liverpool, in England. I'm 26 years old. I know that water is an important natural resource, so I'm having 5-minute showers so that I don't waste it. I'm also teaching my students about how to protect animals by buying ecological products.

We are the Smith family. We are from Glasgow, Scotland. Our family is small: my wife, my son Theo and me. We are riding our bikes to school and work. That way, we don't pollute the air. Also, we are helping to keep the streets clean by picking up the rubbish.

I'm from Cienfuegos, Cuba. My name's Monica and I'm 14. My brother Danilo and I are working with the Go Green project in my city. We know that plastic is non-biodegradable, so we're not using plastic bottles. We're only using metal flasks or ceramic cups for our drinks. And we're teaching my family and neighbours about how to recycle correctly.

CORE VALUES Conservation

7 In pairs, list the conservation measures in order of how effective they are.
- Having showers instead of baths.
- Making laws to protect endangered species.
- Teaching the importance of conservation in schools.
- Voting for a 'green' political party.
- Recycling at home.
- Picking up rubbish.
- Riding a bike instead of driving a car.

FAST FINISHERS Write a list of the things you do to help protect the environment.

Workbook pages 34 and 35 41

Do all exercises in your notebook

ANSWER KEY

Pages 40-41

1
1 rubbish
2 water shortages
3 endangered animals
4 plastic
5 pollution

2 *Student's own answers*

3 *Student's own answers*

4
1 Sara
2 Mike
3 All of them
4 Monica
5 Sara; the Smith family

5
1 picking up
2 pollute
3 huge
4 non-biodegradable
5 natural resource
6 waste

6
1 waste; *Student's own answers*
2 huge; *Student's own answers*
3 natural resource; *Student's own answers*
4 non-biodegradable; *Student's own answers*
5 pollute; *Student's own answers*
6 picking up; *Student's own answers*

7 *Student's own answers*

Remind students to do all the exercises in their notebook

LESSON FOCUS

Language in context The environment

Core values Conservation

Resources

Teacher's i-solutions, Student's Book audio

Preparation Photos of people doing different things related to the environment (see **Warmer**)

→ See pages 36-37 **Literature**

Warmer

If you can find photos of people doing different activities related to the environment (e.g. throwing litter on the ground, putting things into bins, catching a bus or train, cutting down trees, etc.), put them where the students can see them and get them to describe what's happening in the photos. Then ask what topics the pictures have in common.

1 Tell students that the photos are all related to the environment and explain any terms that are not clearly explained by the photos.

2 Encourage students to come up with at least one solution for each problem and tell them that they'll discuss solutions in more depth at the end of the lesson. Write some on the board for reference in the next exercise.

3 1.38 (See page 173 for transcripts) After students have checked their own, compare with the solutions you collected and wrote on the board in exercise 2.

READING TOOLS

Get students to read the **Reading tool** and tell them that the next exercise is practice of this.

4 Give students enough time to do this, then they should check their answers in pairs or small groups and give reasons for their answers. Encourage them to quote the text when justifying their answers.

5 Tell students that the words and phrases they are looking for are not in the same order in the text, but they are in the same grammatical form and illustrate by finding the first item together (picking up).

6 Check that students have used the words and phrases in exercise 5 correctly before they start the speaking part of the exercise.

CORE VALUES Conservation

7 As they rank them, encourage students to think of how the measures listed can help us look after the environment. Get the most popular answer for the most effective 3 measures and see if the class can come up with other measures that are not mentioned.

FAST FINISHERS Students can complete this exercise alone or in pairs.

FURTHER PRACTICE

Workbook pages 34-35

Remind students to do all the exercises in their notebook

CONTINUOUS ASSESSMENT Students can understand language related to the environment and conservation.

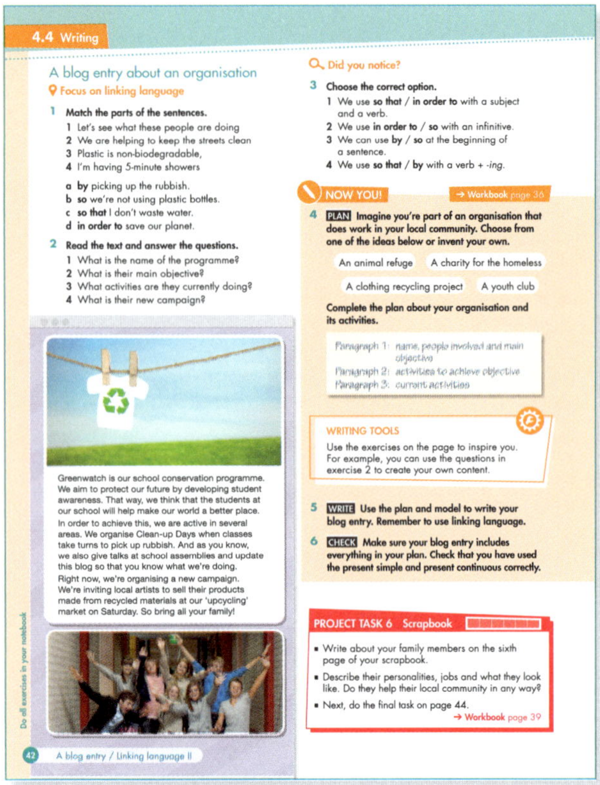

4.4 Writing

A blog entry about an organisation

Focus on linking language

1 **Match the parts of the sentences.**

1 Let's see what these people are doing
2 We are helping to keep the streets clean
3 Plastic is non-biodegradable,
4 I'm having 5-minute showers

a **by** picking up the rubbish.
b **so** we're not using plastic bottles.
c **so that** I don't waste water.
d **in order to** save our planet.

2 **Read the text and answer the questions.**

1 What is the name of the programme?
2 What is their main objective?
3 What activities are they currently doing?
4 What is their new campaign?

Greenwatch is our school conservation programme. We aim to protect our future by developing student awareness. That way, we think that the students at our school will help make our world a better place.

In order to achieve this, we are active in several areas. We organise Clean-up Days when classes take turns to pick up rubbish. And as you know, we also give talks at school assemblies and update this blog so that you know what we're doing.

Right now, we're organising a new campaign. We're inviting local artists to sell their products made from recycled materials at our 'upcycling' market on Saturday. So bring all your family!

Did you notice?

3 **Choose the correct option.**

1 We use **so that** / **in order to** with a subject and a verb.
2 We use **in order to** / **so** with an infinitive.
3 We can use **by** / **so** at the beginning of a sentence.
4 We use **so that** / **by** with a verb + *-ing*.

NOW YOU! → Workbook page 36

4 PLAN **Imagine you're part of an organisation that does work in your local community. Choose from one of the ideas below or invent your own.**

An animal refuge | A charity for the homeless | A clothing recycling project | A youth club

Complete the plan about your organisation and its activities.

Paragraph 1: name, people involved and main objective
Paragraph 2: activities to achieve objective
Paragraph 3: current activities

WRITING TOOLS

Use the exercises on the page to inspire you. For example, you can use the questions in exercise 2 to create your own content.

5 WRITE **Use the plan and model to write your blog entry. Remember to use linking language.**

6 CHECK **Make sure your blog entry includes everything in your plan. Check that you have used the present simple and present continuous correctly.**

PROJECT TASK 6 Scrapbook

- Write about your family members on the sixth page of your scrapbook.
- Describe their personalities, jobs and what they look like. Do they help their local community in any way?
- Next, do the final task on page 44.

→ Workbook page 39

Do all exercises in your notebook

42 A blog entry / Linking language II

LESSON FOCUS

Focus on Linking language II

Writing A blog entry about an organisation

Project task 6 Describe your family members

Resources

Teacher's i-solutions

Warmer

Write the names of various conservation organisations (e.g. Greenpeace, World Wildlife Fund, Royal Society for the Protection of Birds) on the board and ask students what they think they do.

Focus on linking language

1 Ask the students if they recognise the sentences (they are slightly paraphrased versions of sentences from the previous lesson). Let them check against the original sentences before you go through the answers.

2 Answer the first question together and then give students time to complete the exercise. Let them check in pairs and discuss what they think of the organisation and its activities.

Did you notice?

3 Tell students that there are examples in exercise 1 and in the text in exercise 2 for them to use in order to complete the exercise.

4 PLAN Let students discuss possible plans in pairs or small groups so they can share ideas. Then get them to start the plan on their own.

WRITING TOOLS

Get students to read the **Writing tool** and point out that the structure of the plan in exercise 4 comes from the answers to the questions in exercise 2. Encourage them to borrow ideas from the model if they like, but make sure that they somehow make them their own.

5 WRITE Ask if students also noticed what tenses are used in the model for general activities and for current activities (the former are in present simple and the latter present continuous). Make a checklist of this and other important points of content and language for them to consider as they write.

6 CHECK Once students have checked their own blog entries, they can swap within the group they discussed the plans with to see how their entries turned out.

PROJECT TASK 6 Scrapbook

Encourage students to review and use all the vocabulary they have learnt over the past two units to do this task. Tell students that they need to keep their project notes together in their **Workbook** (page 39) or in their own notebook.

→ See pages 24-27 **Projects**

ANSWER KEY

Page 42

1 **1** d
2 a
3 b
4 c

2 **1** Greenwatch
2 To protect their future by developing student awareness of conservation
3 Clean-up Days, talks at school assemblies and a blog
4 They are inviting local artists to sell their products made from recycled materials at an upcycling market.

3 **1** so that
2 in order to
3 so
4 by

4 *Student's own answers*

5 *Student's own answers*

6 *Student's own answers*

FURTHER PRACTICE

Workbook page 36

Remind students to do all the exercises in their notebook

CONTINUOUS ASSESSMENT Students can use appropriate linking language to write a blog entry about an organisation.

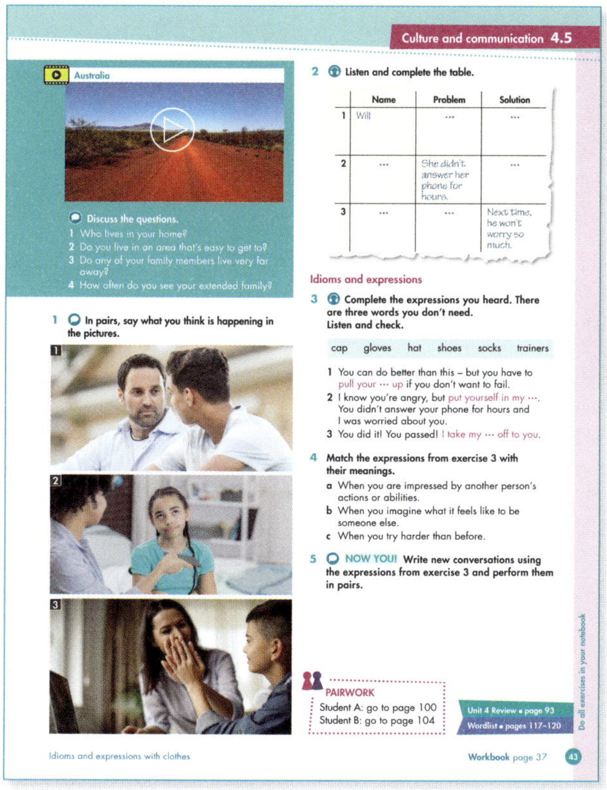

ANSWER KEY

Page 43

1 *Student's own answers*

2

	Name	Problem	Solution
1	Will	His exam results were bad.	He'll study hard for the real one.
2	Jennifer	She didn't answer her phone for hours.	She'll be more sensible next time.
3	Harry	He worries too much.	Next time he won't worry so much.

3 **1** socks **2** shoes **3** hat

4 **a** I take my hat off to you.
b Put yourself in my shoes.
c Pull your socks up.

5 *Student's own answers*

FURTHER PRACTICE AND UNIT ASSESSSMENT

Unit 4 Review Student's Book page 93
Workbook page 37
- **Reflect on your learning** page 37
- **Grammar reference and practice** pages 87 and 94
- **Wordlist and exercises** pages 99 and 103

Tests available to download and edit from the **Richmond***Learning***Platform**

→ See pages 40-41 **Assessment**

LESSON FOCUS

Idioms and expressions Clothes
Listening Taking notes on short conversations
Speaking Writing and performing short conversations with new idioms and expressions

Resources

Teacher's i-solutions, Student's Book audio, Culture video and worksheet

Australia

Video and worksheet available on the Richmond*Learning***Platform**

- In pairs, ask students to complete the *What I know…* exercises on the **Culture video worksheet**.
- Show students the **Culture video** and ask them to complete the *What I learned…* exercises on the worksheet.
- In pairs, students compare answers.
- In small groups, tell students to complete the *What I wonder…* exercises on the worksheet.

Warmer

Watch the Culture video and discuss the questions with the whole class. If you don't have video facilities, simply discuss the questions.

1 Ask for students' suggestions but don't confirm or dismiss any of their answers at this point.

2 1.39 (See page 173 for transcripts) Tell the students that they're going to hear three conversations between the people in the pictures. Ask them to check whether their guesses in exercise 1 were right and to complete the table.

Idioms and expressions

3 1.40 (See page 173 for transcripts) Check if students remember the idioms and expressions from the audio in exercise 2 before they do this exercise.

4 Elicit the expressions in the forms in which they're found in dictionaries for them to write in their notebooks: *pull your socks up, put yourself in someone's shoes, take your hat off to someone.* Point out that the first two are commonly used in the imperative and that the last one is usually in the first person.

5 **NOW YOU!** Give students time to write the conversations. To extend the activity, have them perform the convesations in front of the class, but pausing when they get to the expressions, for the class to shout out. 'beeped' out for others to say what the expression was.

PAIRWORK Student's Book pages 100 and 104
See **Teacher's Book** page 100 for more information.

→ See pages 30-33 **Mediation**

Remind students to do all the exercises in their notebook

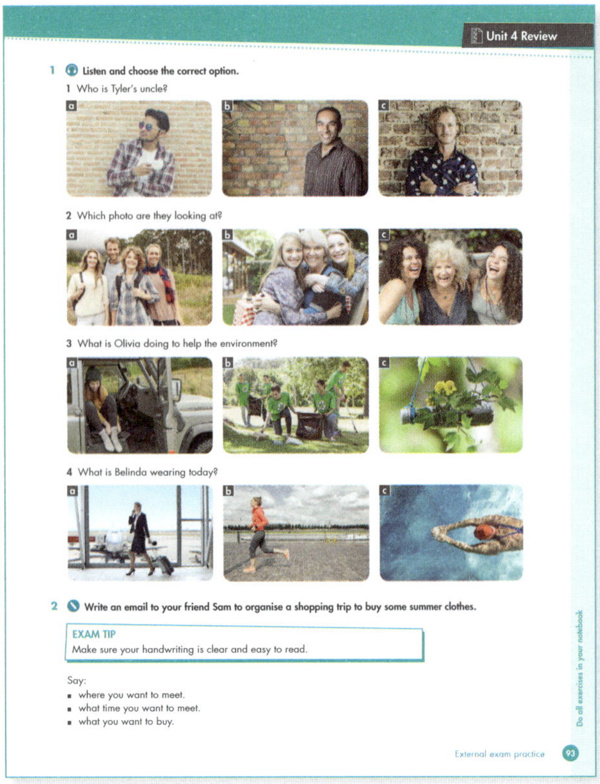
Unit 4 Review

1 Listen and choose the correct option.

1 Who is Tyler's uncle?

a b c

2 Which photo are they looking at?

a b c

3 What is Olivia doing to help the environment?

a b c

4 What is Belinda wearing today?

a b c

2 Write an email to your friend Sam to organise a shopping trip to buy some summer clothes.

EXAM TIP
Make sure your handwriting is clear and easy to read.

Say:
- where you want to meet.
- what time you want to meet.
- what you want to buy.

Do all exercises in your notebook

External exam practice 93

Student's Book page 93

ANSWER KEY

See page 180 for transcripts

1 2.43

1 b
2 c
3 b
4 b

2 *Student's own answers*

Pairwork

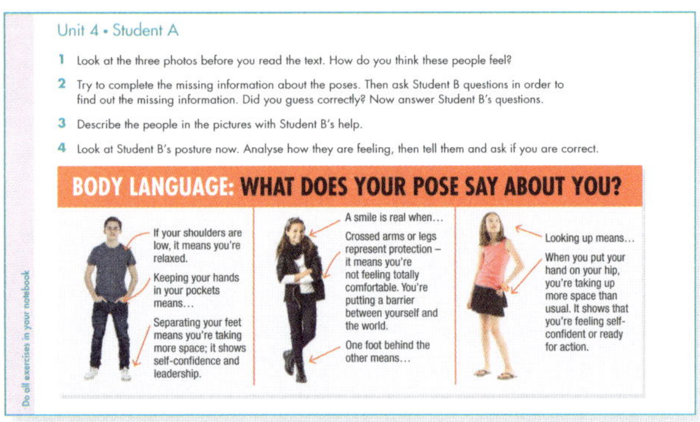
Unit 4 • Student A

1 Look at the three photos before you read the text. How do you think these people feel?

2 Try to complete the missing information about the poses. Then ask Student B questions in order to find out the missing information. Did you guess correctly? Now answer Student B's questions.

3 Describe the people in the pictures with Student B's help.

4 Look at Student B's posture now. Analyse how they are feeling, then tell them and ask if you are correct.

BODY LANGUAGE: WHAT DOES YOUR POSE SAY ABOUT YOU?

If your shoulders are low, it means you're relaxed.

Keeping your hands in your pockets means…

Separating your feet means you're taking more space; it shows self-confidence and leadership.

A smile is real when…

Crossed arms or legs represent protection – it means you're not feeling totally comfortable. You're putting a barrier between yourself and the world.

One foot behind the other means…

Looking up means…

When you put your hand on your hip, you're taking up more space than usual. It shows that you're feeling self-confident or ready for action.

Do all exercises in your notebook

Student's Book page 100

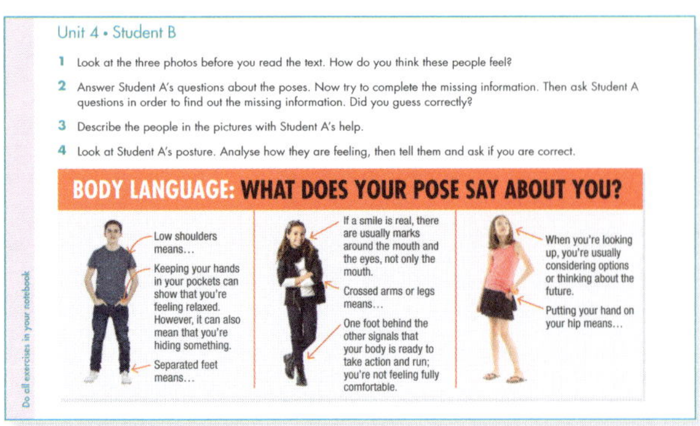
Unit 4 • Student B

1 Look at the three photos before you read the text. How do you think these people feel?

2 Answer Student A's questions about the poses. Now try to complete the missing information. Then ask Student A questions in order to find out the missing information. Did you guess correctly?

3 Describe the people in the pictures with Student A's help.

4 Look at Student A's posture. Analyse how they are feeling, then tell them and ask if you are correct.

BODY LANGUAGE: WHAT DOES YOUR POSE SAY ABOUT YOU?

Low shoulders means…

Keeping your hands in your pockets can show that you're feeling relaxed. However, it can also mean that you're hiding something.

Separated feet means…

If a smile is real, there are usually marks around the mouth and the eyes, not only the mouth.

Crossed arms or legs means…

One foot behind the other signals that your body is ready to take action and run; you're not feeling fully comfortable.

When you're looking up, you're usually considering options or thinking about the future.

Putting your hand on your hip means…

Do all exercises in your notebook

Student's Book page 104

CEFR MEDIATION DESCRIPTOR

- **Processing text in speech**

Students can report in simple sentences the information contained in clearly-structured, short, simple texts that have illustrations or tables.

- **Requesting information**

Tell Student A and B that they have the same photos and elicit descriptions of one or all of the children. Then tell them their partner has the missing information from their text and that they should try and guess what it is.

Remind students to do all the exercises in their notebook

Unit 4 Grammar reference

Demonstrative pronouns

Singular	Use ***this*** for a thing that is close to you. **This is** my jacket.	Use ***that*** for a thing that is far from you. **That is** Dad's hat.
Plural	Use ***these*** for things that are close to you. **These are** Mum's gloves.	Use ***those*** for things that are far from you. **Those are** Julia's shoes.

We use ***this*** and ***these*** to refer to people or things close to us when we are speaking.

We use ***this*** before a singular noun.
This is my brother, Steve.
This is my house. Come in!
This is the best restaurant in the city.

We use ***these*** before a plural noun.
These are my parents, Julie and Rick.
These are my favourite shoes.
These are the best shops in the city.

We don't use the contracted forms ***'s*** or ***'re*** after ***this*** and ***these***.
This is my brother. NOT ~~This's my brother.~~
These are my parents. NOT ~~These're my parents.~~

We use ***that*** and ***those*** to refer to people or things that are not close to us or present when we are speaking.

We use ***that*** before a singular noun.
That is our school over there.
That is my best friend, Frank.
That is the best museum in the city.

We use ***those*** before a plural noun.
Those are my socks. Give them to me!
Those are my cousins over there.
Those are the best parks in the city.

We can use the contracted form ***'s*** after ***that***. However, we can't use the contracted form ***'re*** after ***those***.
That's our school.
Those are my CDs. NOT ~~Those're my CDs.~~

Present continuous

Affirmative			Negative		
I	am	eating.	I	am not	eating.
He/She/It	is		He/She/It	is not	
You/We/They	are		You/We/They	are not	

Yes/No questions			Wh- questions			
Am	I	eating?	What	am	I	eating?
Is	he/she/it			is	he/she/it	
Are	you/we/they			are	you/we/they	

We use the present continuous to talk about activities in progress at the time of speaking and temporary situations.
I'm having breakfast now.
They **aren't listening** to music.
Are you **doing** your homework?

In short answers, we don't repeat the *-ing* form.
Are you **reading** a comic?
Yes, I am. NOT ~~Yes, I'm reading.~~

We can also use *wh-* question words with the present continuous.
Who's he **talking** to?
Why are they **running**?

We often use time expressions such as ***now*** and ***at the moment*** in present continuous sentences.
I'm doing my homework **at the moment**.
What **are** you **doing now**?

***-ing* verbs: spelling**

Verb + ***-ing***	study	studying
Verbs ending in *-e* → ~~-e~~, + ***-ing***	make	making
Verbs ending in *-ie* → ~~-ie~~, + ***-ying***	lie	lying
One-syllable verbs → double the consonant + ***-ing***	sit	sitting

Do all exercises in your notebook

110 **Workbook** pages 93–96

Student's Book page 110

Wordlist

Wordlist

UNIT 4

Clothes

belt	shoes
boots	shorts
cap	skirt
coat	socks
dress	suit
gloves	sunglasses
hat	swimsuit
jacket	tie
jeans	trainers
jumper	trousers
shirt	T-shirt

Patterns

checked	patterned
dark	spots
flowers	spotty
flowery	stripes
light	stripy
pattern	tartan

The environment

conservation
endangered animals/species
green
natural resource
non-biodegradable
plant trees
plastic
pollute
pollution
protect the environment
recycle
rubbish
save our planet
waste
water shortages

Do all exercises in your notebook

118 **Workbook** pages 102–104

Student's Book page 118

2.56 2.57 2.58

Remind students to do all the exercises in their notebook

Project • Units 3 and 4

PROJECT: Scrapbook

RECAP

- In this project you created a scrapbook about yourself.
- In **units 3 and 4**, you learnt how to describe people: their physical features, personalities, jobs, body parts, clothes and what they are doing. You also learnt how to talk about your family tree.
- Now you are ready to present your scrapbook!

TASK 1	**Create your scrapbook, label a photo of yourself.**
TASK 2	**Describe yourself, plan your scrapbook design.**
TASK 3	**Describe and express your personality.**
TASK 4	**Talk about your clothes.**
TASK 5	**Present your family, draw a family tree.**
TASK 6	**Describe your family members.**

FINAL TASK: Present your scrapbook

- Make sure that your scrapbook is complete and make final improvements.
- Decorate the front cover. Think about how it can show your personality.
- You are going to present your scrapbooks in groups of four. Think about which features of your scrapbook you would like to highlight.
- You are going to give your teammates feedback on their scrapbooks. Remember to make constructive comments that can help your teammates improve their work in the future.

USEFUL EXPRESSIONS

- Section number (*one/two/three*) is about…
- He/She is (*height/age/etc.*).
- This/That is my (*mother, brother, sister, etc.*).
- In this picture, he/she is wearing…
- We/They are (*verb + -ing*) in this photo.

21ST CENTURY SKILLS

Feedback

When you give someone feedback, avoid judgemental comments. Focus on how they can improve. Don't forget to give positive feedback, too.

It's also important to learn to receive feedback. Try to listen without feeling negative. You can use the feedback to develop your skills and correct mistakes.

Do all exercises in your notebook

GO BEYOND

SCRAPBOOKING

A scrapbook is an album where you keep memories of important moments and people in your life: a special holiday, family history, to celebrate a new baby in the family, etc.

In the past, people couldn't easily print lots of photographs like we can today, so they collected items and glued them into a book instead. Nowadays, scrapbooking is a popular hobby again. There are lots of websites where people share ideas of their scrapbooks. Journals are similar to scrapbooks. They are also a visual way to express memories, feelings and ideas. Journals are like diaries where people write their daily thoughts, but they include mind maps, bullet lists and sketches.

EVALUATION

Answer the questions in your team.

1. Which were your favourite sections to make? Which were difficult?
2. Is it difficult to show your personality on a page?
3. Are you happy with the English you used in your presentation?
4. Did you receive any useful feedback for the future?
5. Evaluate your presentation performance. Then ask a classmate to evaluate you. Are your evaluations similar?

Answer the questions in pairs.

1. What is a scrapbook?
2. Why do people keep scrapbooks?
3. What is the difference between a diary, a journal and a scrapbook?
4. Do you know anyone who keeps a scrapbook? Would you like to have one?

Do all exercises in your notebook

Workbook project task notes

PROJECT: Scrapbook

TASK 1

How to make your scrapbook.

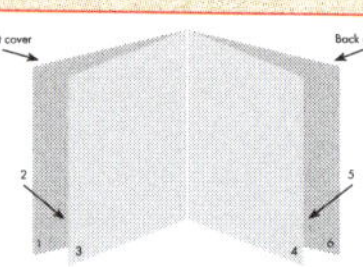

→ Student's book page 29

TASK 2

What I look like: ______

Presentation ideas: ______

→ Student's book page 31

TASK 3

My personality: ______

Presentation ideas: ______

→ Student's book page 34

TASK 4

My clothes: ______

Presentation ideas: ______

→ Student's book page 37

TASK 5

People to include on my family tree: ______

Comments for the photos: ______

→ Student's book page 39

TASK 6

My family members: ______

→ Student's book page 42

FINAL TASK

Team members: ______ ______ ______ ______

Things I want to highlight: ______

→ Student's book page 44

Remind students to do all the exercises in their notebook

PROJECT FOCUS

➔ See pages 24-27 **Projects**

Skills

- Label parts of their body and face on a photo
- Write paragraphs about appearance, personality and clothes
- Write about family members in photos: what they are doing and wearing, their personalities, jobs and appearance
- Present scrapbooks to the class
- Give feedback on scrapbooks
- Discuss evaluations of the project
- Read and discuss a text related to the project

CEFR mediation

Encouraging conceptual talk

Can ask questions to invite people to clarify their reasoning.

➔ See pages 30-33 **Mediation**

Preparation Remind students to bring the elements they create in tasks 1-6 and their notes from **Workbook** project task notes pages 38-39 or their own notebook. Have students bring in their self-assessment diaries if they are writing them.

RECAP

Put students in their teams and read through the **Recap** as a class. Draw their attention to the project tasks and the unit objectives and ask which task helped achieve which objectives. Make sure they have all the materials and notes that they need (see **Preparation**) for the **Final task**.

FINAL TASK: Present your scrapbook

Tell students they are now going to present their scrapbooks in groups of four. Before starting the task, direct their attention to the **21st Century skill** (see next column).

Read through the first two steps of the task and agree on a time limit for these steps that will allow the class to complete the presentations and evaluation. Students waiting for others to finish can choose useful expressions to include in their presentations and practise them.

Put students in groups of four that you think will feel comfortable sharing the information in their scrapbooks. Give them a time limit for each presentation and get them to decide on an order. Remind them the presentation is quite informal and encourage students to ask questions after or even during the presentations; make sure it's clear that the feedback for now is on the scrapbooks, not the presentation. Monitor them to check that everyone has an equal chance to give their presentations and that feedback is respectful and constructive. You could elicit a brief summary from each group of what they particularly liked about any of the scrapbooks.

21ST CENTURY SKILLS

Read through the **21st Century skill** with the students and tell them they are going to apply the advice for giving and receiving feedback effectively during the task and in the evaluation.

➔ See pages 28-29 **21st Century skills**

EVALUATION

Before students discuss the questions as a group, give them time to prepare notes about their experience in the project. Remind students to be supportive and give constructive criticism if necessary, with ideas on how to do things better next time. Monitor discussions, adding your own feedback where appropriate and noting common observations to then convey to the class as a whole. Have a class discussion about what students have learnt from the project, reminding them of the unit objectives, the **Core values** and the **Learning tools** sections of units 3 and 4, as well as the **21st Century skills** section of the **Project** pages.

If you have decided to use the **evaluation** exercise as a springboard for a student self-assessment diary (see **Evaluation notes** page 77), give them time to do this now and remind them to refer to the **Reflect on your learning** section of the **Workbook** if they have one.

➔ See pages 40-41 **Assessment**

GO BEYOND

First ask students to discuss their answers to the questions at the bottom of the page. Comment on their answers without giving away the answers given in the text and then get them to compare their ideas with those of the text. Ask them which of the ideas of what scrapbooks can include were included in the presentations in their group and which they could have included. Ask if any students are considering making a scrapbook of their own and what they might include.

Remind students to do all the exercises in their notebook

CONTINUOUS ASSESSMENT Students can prepare and present a scrapbook and give effective feedback.

5 THE GREAT OUTDOORS

At the start of each unit and lesson, explain to the students what the objectives are.

Language objectives

Grammar

Present simple
- Students practise all forms of the present simple.

Adverbs of frequency I
- Students learn and practise *always, sometimes* and *never.*

Vocabulary

Weather and seasons: Weather: *chilly, cloudy, cold, foggy, freezing, hot, raining, snowing, sunny, windy;* Seasons: *spring, summer, autumn, winter*
- Students use vocabulary to describe the weather and seasons in context.

Outdoor adventure and sports: Outdoor adventure: *cabin, campsite, canoeing, cave, countryside, hiking, light a fire, natural habitat, nature, put up a tent, tent, waterfall;* Sports: *climbing wall, court, equipment, facilities, fencing, field, hockey, Olympic-size pool, rugby, scuba dive, squash, tennis*
- Students encounter vocabulary in context related to outdoor adventure and sports.

Idioms and expressions

Weather: *be on cloud nine, break the ice, be a breeze*
- Students look at the idioms and expressions in the context of a talk about a camp.

Recycled language

Present continuous; Question words; The verb *be*; vocabulary for hobbies and interests

Skills objectives

Speaking

- Students ask and answer questions about seasons and the weather.
- Students ask and answer questions about their free-time activities.
- Students ask and answer questions about camp activities.

Pronunciation: Students contrast and practise short /ɪ/ and long /iː/ sounds.

Pairwork: Students use various mediation techniques in order to compare summer camps.

Listening

- Students listen and match conversations about the weather to pictures.
- Students listen and take notes to complete a table.
- Students listen and complete conversations with correct vocabulary and grammar structures.
- Students listen to idioms and expressions in context.

Reading

- Students predict the content of a text to help their comprehension.
- Students find names for pictured items in a text.
- Students read in detail to correct false information.

Core values: Students complete a survey to assess their **sense of adventure** and contemplate a healthy balance between this and caution.

Writing

- Students focus on writing a postcard to a friend in an appropriate tone.
- Students plan, write and check a postcard to a friend about their time at a camp.

Focus on present tenses

Learning to learn tools

SPEAKING TOOLS Students practise giving extended answers to develop their speaking skills.	LISTENING TOOLS Students practise taking notes while listening.
READING TOOLS Students practise recording vocabulary from reading texts effectively.	WRITING TOOLS Students focus on considering the reader's interests to develop their writing skills.

Project objectives: Tourist leaflet

Task 1 Students choose a famous city, find pictures of it and describe the weather.

Task 2 Students describe the activities that people do in that city.

Task 3 Students write about five activities that tourists do in that city and find photos.

Audiovisual objectives

Vlog: Students watch and listen to George talk about the weather.

Culture: Students watch and listen to George talk about a road trip to the USA.

Grammar animations: Students are presented with visual presentations of the unit grammar.

Key competences

LC **Linguistic**
pages 46-53

MST **Mathematical and Science and Technology**
pages 47, 49, 52

DC **Digital**
pages 46, 48, 49, 53

SCC **Social and Civic**
pages 47, 49, 51-53

CAE **Cultural awareness and expression**
pages 46, 47, 50-53

LL **Learning to learn**
pages 47, 49, 50, 52

IE **Sense of initiative and entrepreneurship**
pages 47, 49, 52

→ See pages 42-43 **Key competences**

CEFR Mediation

5.1 Note-taking
Can make simple notes about familiar subject matter.

5.2 Explaining data in writing
Can present in writing trends in simple diagrams.

5.3 Processing text in writing
Can pick out and reproduce key words and phrases from a text.

5.4 Adapting language
Can use different words to help someone understand a message.

5.5 Facilitating cultural space
Can ask for clarification and express agreement and interest.

Project Relaying specific information in writing
Can relay in writing specific information contained in short, simple informational texts.

Unit review Collaborating to construct meaning
Can make simple remarks and pose occasional questions to indicate that he/she is following.

Pairwork Adapting language
Can repeat the main point of a simple message using different words to help someone else understand it.

→ See pages 30-33 **Mediation**

Remind students to do all the exercises in their notebook

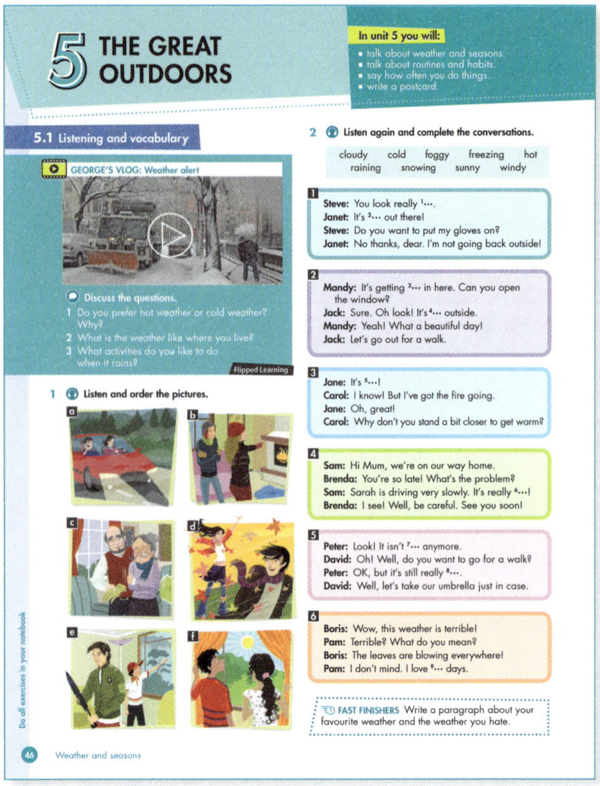

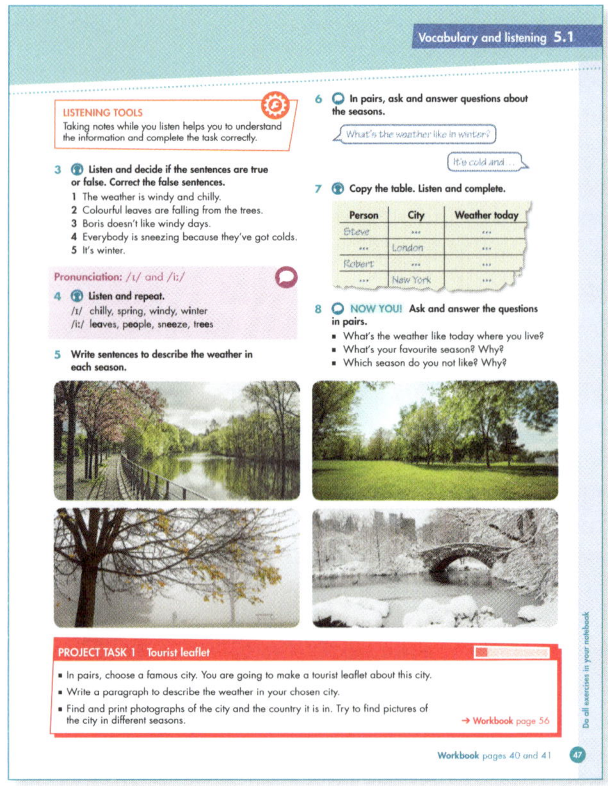

ANSWER KEY

Pages 46-47

1 c, f, b, a, e, d

2
1 cold
2 snowing
3 hot
4 sunny
5 freezing
6 foggy
7 raining
8 cloudy
9 windy

3
1 True
2 True
3 True
4 False. Boris is sneezing because he's got a cold.
5 False. It's autumn.

4 *Student's own answers*

5 *Student's own answers*

6 *Student's own answers*

7

Person	City	Weather today
Steve	Rio de Janeiro	hot and sunny
Amanda	London	freezing and cloudy
Robert	Buenos Aires	a nice day but a little windy
Sarah	New York	foggy and cold

8 *Student's own answers*

LESSON FOCUS

Vocabulary Weather and seasons
Listening Weather conversations
Speaking Comparing weather observations and personal preferences
Project task 1 Choose a famous city, find pictures of it and describe the weather

Resources

Teacher's i-solutions, Student's Book audio, Vlog and worksheets

Flipped Learning

GEORGE'S VLOG: Weather alert

- Make sure to set up the **Flipped Learning** work with the students beforehand. **See pages 20-23 for complete Flipped Learning guidelines.**
- Ask students to put the **Flipped Learning worksheets** on their desks and walk around to check how many have completed the Flipped task.
- In pairs or small groups, ask students to compare and check the *Before you watch...* and *While you watch...* exercises on the worksheet.
- Show students **George's vlog** and ask volunteers to provide correct answers and clarify any doubts other students may have.
- Choose three or four students to read aloud their answers to the *After you watch...* exercises on the worksheet and encourage some class discussion.
- Move straight to exercise 1 on page 46.

Warmer

Watch George's vlog and discuss the questions with the whole class. If you don't have video facilities, simply discuss the questions.

1 1.41 (See page 173 for transcripts) Ask the class what is happening in the pictures before you play the audio. The conversations are in the same order as in exercise 2, so you could do exercises 1 and 2 together, playing each short conversation once for exercise 1 and a second time for exercise 2 before moving on to the next conversation.

2 1.42 (See page 173 for transcripts) Give them time to read each conversation before playing the audio, and encourage them to guess the meanings of the weather vocabulary from context before checking their understanding.

FAST FINISHERS Students can complete this exercise alone or in pairs.

LISTENING TOOLS

Get them to read the **Listening tool** and tell them to practise their note taking in exercise 3.

3 1.43 (See page 173 for transcripts) Get them to close their books and tell them they must take notes on a longer conversation about the weather between Boris and Pam on page 46. Check their note-taking and play the audio a second time if they need it in order to take better notes. Students then try to do the exercise from memory before you play the audio again.

Pronunciation

4 1.44 (See page 174 for transcripts) Ask if students know the difference between the two sounds and point out that in the phonetic symbols, the two dots mean that the sound is longer. Point out that for the longer sound we also push our tongues further up in our mouths, like for the /j/ sound. For extra practice, get students to read aloud the true and corrected sentences from exercise 3.

5 Ask the students what the photos represent, check for pronunciation of the word 'season' and elicit and write on the board the four seasons (you could point them to the wordlist if they need help). Students then complete the exercise.

6 Make sure students don't just read their answers from exercise 5.

7 1.45 (See page 174 for transcripts) Tell students they will hear four people describe the weather in their cities and encourage them to only write short notes for the last column. Model notes for the first row if you think it will help.

8 **NOW YOU!** For extra practice, get them to time each other's responses and see who can give the longer answer for each question without much hesitation.

PROJECT TASK 1 Tourist leaflet

Put the students in their pairs for the project. Elicit some ideas for things to write about and things to look for photos of and let them continue in their pairs.
Remind students that they need to keep their project notes together in their **Workbook** (page 56) or in their own notebook.

→ See pages 24-27 **Projects**

FURTHER PRACTICE

Workbook pages 40-41
- **Grammar reference and practice** pages 88 and 94-95
- **Wordlist and exercises** pages 100 and 103

Remind students to do all the exercises in their notebook

CONTINUOUS ASSESSMENT Students can talk about weather and the seasons.

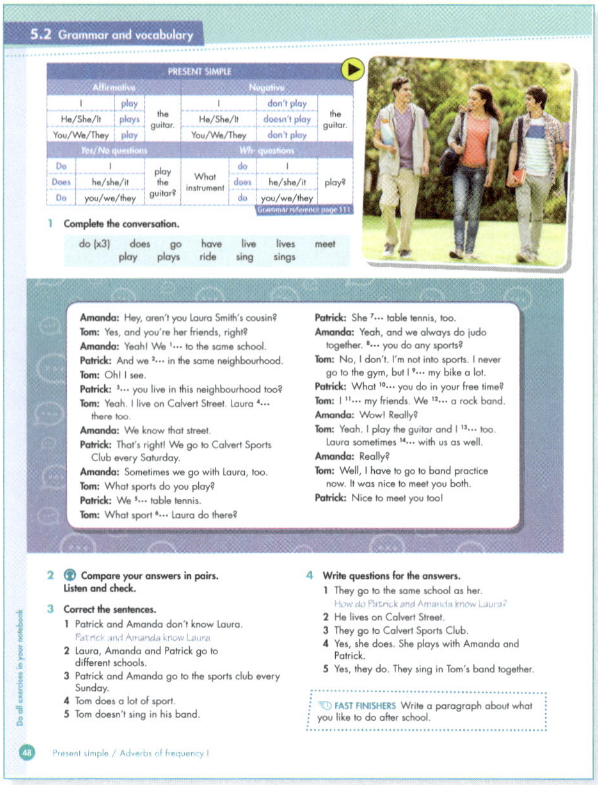
5.2 Grammar and vocabulary

PRESENT SIMPLE					
Affirmative			Negative		
I	play	the guitar.	I	don't play	the guitar.
He/She/It	plays		He/She/It	doesn't play	
You/We/They	play		You/We/They	don't play	
Yes/No questions			Wh- questions		
Do	I	play the guitar?	What instrument	do	I
Does	he/she/it			does	he/she/it
Do	you/we/they			do	you/we/they play?

Grammar reference page 111

1 Complete the conversation.

do (x3) does go have live lives meet play plays ride sing sings

Amanda: Hey, aren't you Laura Smith's cousin?
Tom: Yes, and you're her friends, right?
Amanda: Yeah! We [1]... to the same school.
Patrick: And we [2]... in the same neighbourhood.
Tom: Oh! I see.
Patrick: [3]... you live in this neighbourhood too?
Tom: Yeah. I live on Calvert Street. Laura [4]... there too.
Amanda: We know that street.
Patrick: That's right! We go to Calvert Sports Club every Saturday.
Amanda: Sometimes we go with Laura, too.
Tom: What sports do you play?
Patrick: We [5]... table tennis.
Tom: What sport [6]... Laura do there?
Patrick: She [7]... table tennis, too.
Amanda: Yeah, and we always do judo together. [8]... you do any sports?
Tom: No, I don't. I'm not into sports. I never go to the gym, but I [9]... my bike a lot.
Patrick: What [10]... you do in your free time?
Tom: I [11]... my friends. We [12]... a rock band.
Amanda: Wow! Really?
Tom: Yeah. I play the guitar and I [13]... too. Laura sometimes [14]... with us as well.
Amanda: Really?
Tom: Well, I have to go to band practice now. It was nice to meet you both.
Patrick: Nice to meet you too!

2 Compare your answers in pairs. Listen and check.

3 Correct the sentences.
1 Patrick and Amanda don't know Laura.
Patrick and Amanda know Laura.
2 Laura, Amanda and Patrick go to different schools.
3 Patrick and Amanda go to the sports club every Sunday.
4 Tom does a lot of sport.
5 Tom doesn't sing in his band.

4 Write questions for the answers.
1 They go to the same school as her.
How do Patrick and Amanda know Laura?
2 He lives on Calvert Street.
3 They go to Calvert Sports Club.
4 Yes, she does. She plays with Amanda and Patrick.
5 Yes, they do. They sing in Tom's band together.

FAST FINISHERS Write a paragraph about what you like to do after school.

Do all exercises in your notebook

48 Present simple / Adverbs of frequency I

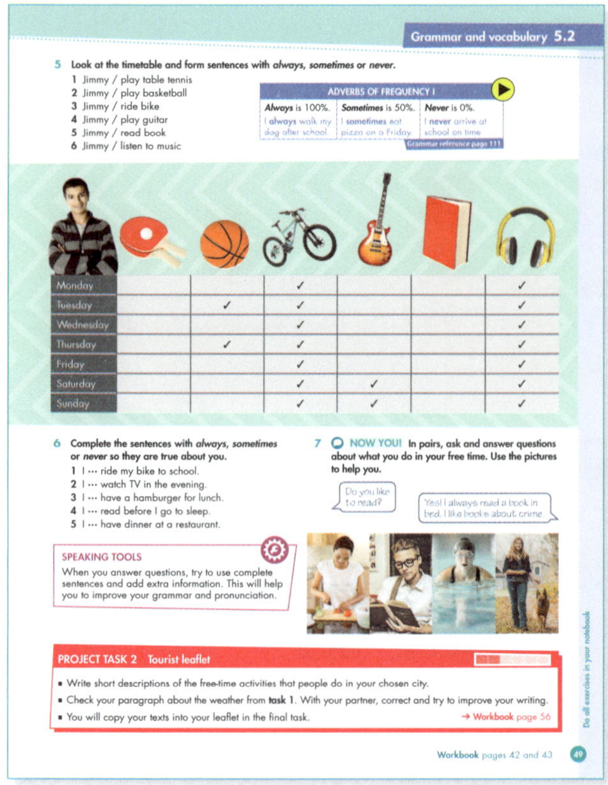
Grammar and vocabulary 5.2

5 Look at the timetable and form sentences with *always*, *sometimes* or *never*.
1 Jimmy / play table tennis
2 Jimmy / play basketball
3 Jimmy / ride bike
4 Jimmy / play guitar
5 Jimmy / read book
6 Jimmy / listen to music

ADVERBS OF FREQUENCY I		
Always is 100%.	**Sometimes** is 50%.	**Never** is 0%.
I **always** walk my dog after school.	I **sometimes** eat pizza on a Friday.	I **never** arrive at school on time.

Grammar reference page 111

	table tennis	basketball	bike	guitar	book	music
Monday			✓			✓
Tuesday		✓	✓			✓
Wednesday			✓			✓
Thursday		✓	✓			✓
Friday			✓			✓
Saturday			✓	✓		✓
Sunday			✓	✓		✓

6 Complete the sentences with *always*, *sometimes* or *never* so they are true about you.
1 I ... ride my bike to school.
2 I ... watch TV in the evening.
3 I ... have a hamburger for lunch.
4 I ... read before I go to sleep.
5 I ... have dinner at a restaurant.

7 NOW YOU! In pairs, ask and answer questions about what you do in your free time. Use the pictures to help you.

Do you like to read?
Yes! I always read a book in bed. I like books about crime.

SPEAKING TOOLS
When you answer questions, try to use complete sentences and add extra information. This will help you to improve your grammar and pronunciation.

PROJECT TASK 2 Tourist leaflet
- Write short descriptions of the free-time activities that people do in your chosen city.
- Check your paragraph about the weather from task 1. With your partner, correct and try to improve your writing.
- You will copy your texts into your leaflet in the final task. → Workbook page 56

Do all exercises in your notebook

Workbook pages 42 and 43 49

ANSWER KEY

Pages 48-49

1
1 go
2 live
3 Do
4 lives
5 play
6 does
7 plays
8 Do
9 ride
10 do
11 meet
12 have
13 sing
14 sings

2 *Student's own answers*

3
1 Patrick and Amanda know Laura.
2 Laura, Amanda and Patrick go to the same school./ Laura, Amanda and Patrick don't go to different schools.
3 Patrick and Amanda go to the sports club every Saturday.
4 Tom doesn't do any sport. / Tom doesn't do a lot of sport.
5 Tom sings in his band.

4 *Suggested answers:*
1 How do Patrick and Amanda know Laura?
2 Where does Tom live?
3 Where do Patrick and Amanda go every Saturday?
4 Does Laura play table tennis?
5 Do Laura and Tom sing together?

5
1 Jimmy never plays table tennis.
2 Jimmy sometimes plays basketball.
3 Jimmy always rides his bike.
4 Jimmy sometimes plays the guitar.
5 Jimmy never reads a book.
6 Jimmy always listens to music.

6 *Student's own answers*

7 *Student's own answers*

Remind students to do all the exercises in their notebook

LESSON FOCUS

Grammar Present simple; Adverbs of frequency I
Listening A conversation about free time
Speaking Comparing free-time activities
Project task 2 Describe the activities that people do in a city

Resources

Teacher's i-solutions, Student's Book audio, Grammar animation

Warmer

Put the class in pairs. Write *I like…* on the board and ask students to complete the sentence in their notebooks with as many things as they can. Draw their attention to the Unit 1 **Wordlist** Hobbies and interests section if they need help. Tell them not to show their partner. Then write *Do you like…?* on the board and get them to ask and answer questions with their partners to see how many of the items on each other's lists they can guess. You could put them in groups of two pairs to compete against each other, too.

PRESENT SIMPLE

Flipped Learning

Draw students' attention to the **Grammar table**. Remind students that they can use this as a quick reference while completing the exercises.

Show students the **Grammar animation** and/or refer students to the **Grammar reference** on page 111 for further information on form and use.

→ See page 23 for how to flip the **grammar lesson**

1 Refer students to the Grammar table to help them complete the conversation. Tell them they don't change the forms of the verbs.

2 1.46 (See page 174 for transcripts) You could remind them of the *-es* pronunciation endings for plurals on page 29, tell them the same rules apply and elicit and drill the pronunciation of the *-es* endings in the verbs in this exercise.

3 For extra speaking practice, get students to check each other's answers by saying their corrected sentences.

4 Point out that this exercise contains three *wh-* questions and two *yes/no* questions and draw their attention the bottom part of the **Grammar table.**

FAST FINISHERS Students can complete this exercise alone or in pairs.

ADVERBS OF FREQUENCY I

Flipped Learning

Draw students' attention to the **Grammar table**. Remind students that they can use this as a quick reference while completing the exercises.

Show students the **Grammar animation** and/or refer students to the **Grammar reference** on page 111 for further information on form and use.

→ See page 23 for how to flip the **grammar lesson**

5 Refer students to the Grammar table as they do the exercise. Extend the exercise by getting students to ask each other *When* questions about Jimmy's timetable.

6 To make this exercise more communicative, ask students to write one incorrect sentence and then read each other's sentences to try to guess the lie.

SPEAKING TOOLS

Get students to read the **Speaking tool** and tell them to put it into practice in exercise 7.

7 **NOW YOU!** Write question stems on the board to help prompt the students: *Where do you…?, When do you…?, What type of…?, How long do you…?*, etc. Tell students you will ask some of them to report things their partners said at the end of the exercise, so they should listen carefully and take notes if they think they won't remember.

PROJECT TASK 2 Tourist leaflet

Put the students in their pairs again to write the descriptions and check their work together.
Remind students that they need to keep their project notes together in their **Workbook** (page 56) or in their own notebook.

→ See pages 24-27 **Projects**

FURTHER PRACTICE

Workbook pages 42-43
- **Grammar reference and practice** pages 88 and 94-95
- **Wordlist and exercises** pages 100 and 103

Vocabulary and Grammar worksheets available to download from the **Richmond*Learning*Platform**

→ See pages 38-39 **Mixed-ability classes**

CONTINUOUS ASSESSMENT Students can use present simple and adverbs of frequency.

Remind students to do all the exercises in their notebook

5.3 Reading

1 Match the words with the pictures.

campsite climbing wall deer fencing hiking rugby field

2 Read the introduction and the two paragraph headings. Predict which paragraph contains the words from exercise 1.

READING TOOLS
Note the new vocabulary you learn from readings together with the title. If you connect the word with the context, it is easier to remember.

3 Read the text and check your answers to exercise 2.

MAKE THE MOST OF
YOUR EASTER!

Spring is here and the Easter holidays are coming. More and more students are staying in camps over the Easter holidays, so if you want to do something fun this spring, here are a couple of great ideas.

OUTDOOR ADVENTURE

This camp is all about enjoying the countryside and appreciating nature.
On the first morning, we go canoeing and then explore the area in the afternoon. We spend the first night in a comfortable cabin. On the second day, we wake up early, pack our bags and walk through the beautiful countryside. We stop for a picnic lunch and then put up our tents in the late afternoon. We stay for the rest of the week and go hiking in the area. We stop at caves and waterfalls, and we usually see lots of deer in their natural habitat. You also learn how to find a good campsite and light a fire. You'll love it!

SPORTS CAMP

At sports camp you can try lots of different sports. Our sports facilities include rugby fields, squash and tennis courts, an Olympic-size swimming pool and even a climbing wall. We've got all the equipment you need. We start your week with a general introduction.
On the first day, we play squash and tennis, and then go outside for games of rugby and hockey. The next day, we do fencing – you wear protective clothing and it's perfectly safe. Then, in the afternoon we take you to the pool to scuba dive. After that, you choose the sports you want to play for the rest of the week. Stay with us and discover your new hobby!

Do you like the sound of one of these camps? Why not sign up now?

Do all exercises in your notebook

50 Language in context / Outdoor adventure and sports

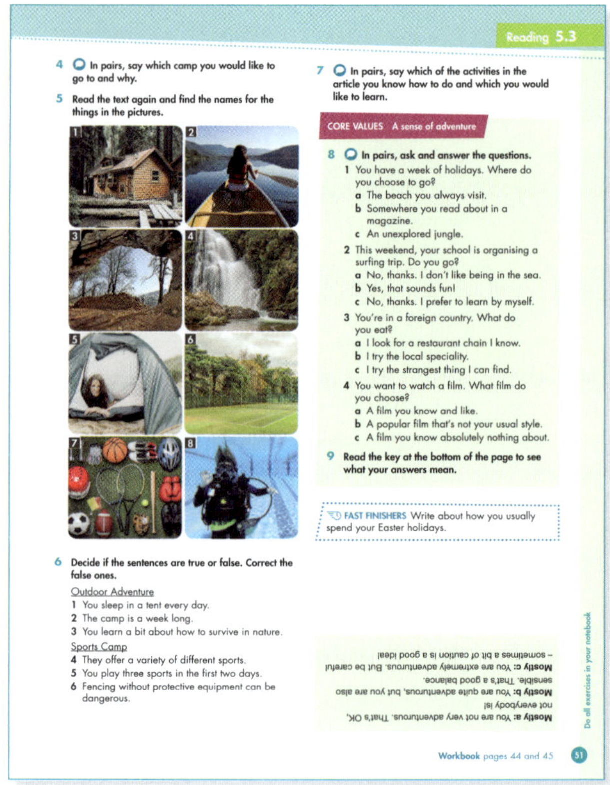

Reading 5.3

4 In pairs, say which camp you would like to go to and why.

5 Read the text again and find the names for the things in the pictures.

6 Decide if the sentences are true or false. Correct the false ones.

Outdoor Adventure
1 You sleep in a tent every day.
2 The camp is a week long.
3 You learn a bit about how to survive in nature.

Sports Camp
4 They offer a variety of different sports.
5 You play three sports in the first two days.
6 Fencing without protective equipment can be dangerous.

7 In pairs, say which of the activities in the article you know how to do and which you would like to learn.

CORE VALUES A sense of adventure

8 In pairs, ask and answer the questions.
1 You have a week of holidays. Where do you choose to go?
a The beach you always visit.
b Somewhere you read about in a magazine.
c An unexplored jungle.
2 This weekend, your school is organising a surfing trip. Do you go?
a No, thanks. I don't like being in the sea.
b Yes, that sounds fun!
c No, thanks. I prefer to learn by myself.
3 You're in a foreign country. What do you eat?
a I look for a restaurant chain I know.
b I try the local speciality.
c I try the strangest thing I can find.
4 You want to watch a film. What film do you choose?
a A film you know and like.
b A popular film that's not your usual style.
c A film you know absolutely nothing about.

9 Read the key at the bottom of the page to see what your answers mean.

FAST FINISHERS Write about how you usually spend your Easter holidays.

Mostly a: You are not very adventurous. That's OK, not everybody is!
Mostly b: You are quite adventurous, but you are also sensible. That's a good balance.
Mostly c: You are extremely adventurous. But be careful – sometimes a bit of caution is a good idea!

Do all exercises in your notebook

Workbook pages 44 and 45 51

ANSWER KEY

Pages 50-51

1
1 rugby field
2 climbing wall
3 hiking
4 fencing
5 deer
6 campsite

2 *Student's own answers*

3 *Student's own answers*

4 *Student's own answers*

5
1 cabin
2 canoeing
3 cave
4 waterfall
5 tent
6 tennis court
7 equipment
8 scuba dive

6 **Outdoor Adventure**
1 False. You sleep in a cabin for the first night.
2 True
3 True
Sports Camp
4 True
5 False. You play six sports in the first two days.
6 True

7 *Student's own answers*

8 *Student's own answers*

9 *Student's own answers*

Remind students to do all the exercises in their notebook

LESSON FOCUS

Language in context Outdoor adventure and sports

Core values A sense of adventure

Resources

Teacher's i-solutions, Student's Book audio

➔ See pages 36-37 **Literature**

Warmer

Write *Holidays* on the board and tell students what you do on holiday, using the adverbs of frequency from the previous lesson. Then get students in pairs or small groups to do the same. Afterwards, ask what holiday activities they have in common.

1 Ask the students to skim the text to find out what it's about (Easter camps). Tell the students that the words are all in the text and do this exercise together as a class.

2 Read the introduction together and do this exercise together as a class too, in order to prevent students reading ahead to check their predictions.

READING TOOLS

Get students to read the **Reading tool** and tell them they will have time after the reading exercises to note down more vocabulary. Remind them that putting vocabulary in lexical groups is also helpful (e.g. camp activities, facilities, things to see, etc.).

3 1.47 (See page 174 for transcripts) Get the students to check their answers to this exercise in pairs and then do exercise 4 before you check their answers.

4 Make sure students know they don't have to agree and that they should give reasons for their choices, but the idea here is for students to note their personal responses to the text, not to give them long speaking practice. There is another speaking activity in exercise 7, after the vocabulary focus.

5 Give students time to do this exercise and answer any vocabulary questions they have. Give them time to note the vocabulary in their notebooks.

6 Give them time for this exercise too and let them do it in pairs if you think it will help.

7 Elicit a list of the activities mentioned to write on the board, checking students' pronunciation.

CORE VALUES A sense of adventure

8 Tell students that you will ask some of them to report their partner's answers at the end of the two exercises.

9 Ask students about their and their partners' evaluations and if they agree. Discuss advantages and disadvantages of being adventurous and whether they think they should be more or less adventurous.

FAST FINISHERS Students can complete this exercise alone or in pairs.

FURTHER PRACTICE
Workbook pages 44-45

Remind students to do all the exercises in their notebook

CONTINUOUS ASSESSMENT Students can understand vocabulary for outdoor adventure and sports in a text about Easter camps.

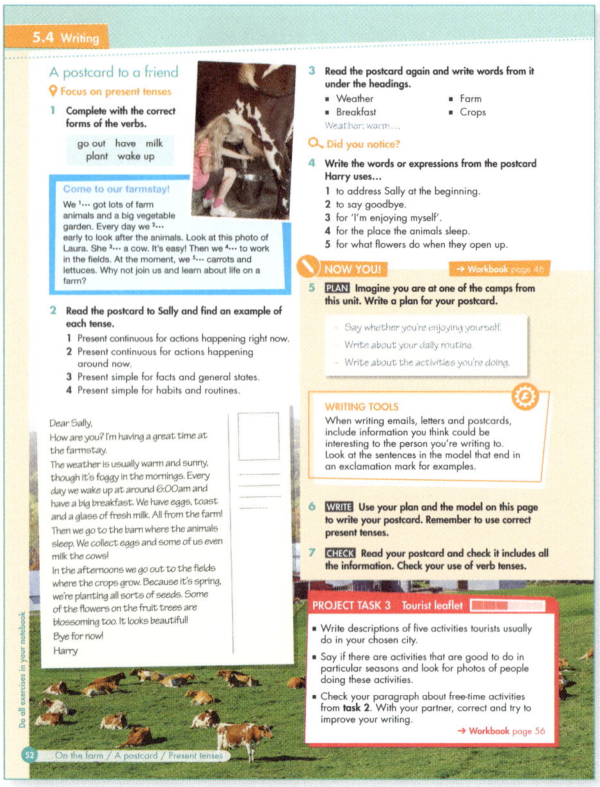

5.4 Writing

A postcard to a friend

Focus on present tenses

1 Complete with the correct forms of the verbs.

go out have milk plant wake up

Come to our farmstay!

We [1]··· got lots of farm animals and a big vegetable garden. Every day we [2]··· early to look after the animals. Look at this photo of Laura. She [3]··· a cow. It's easy! Then we [4]··· to work in the fields. At the moment, we [5]··· carrots and lettuces. Why not join us and learn about life on a farm?

2 Read the postcard to Sally and find an example of each tense.

1 Present continuous for actions happening right now.
2 Present continuous for actions happening around now.
3 Present simple for facts and general states.
4 Present simple for habits and routines.

Dear Sally,
How are you? I'm having a great time at the farmstay.
The weather is usually warm and sunny, though it's foggy in the mornings. Every day we wake up at around 6:00am and have a big breakfast. We have eggs, toast and a glass of fresh milk. All from the farm!
Then we go to the barn where the animals sleep. We collect eggs and some of us even milk the cows!
In the afternoons we go out to the fields where the crops grow. Because it's spring, we're planting all sorts of seeds. Some of the flowers on the fruit trees are blossoming too. It looks beautiful!
Bye for now!
Harry

3 Read the postcard again and write words from it under the headings.

- Weather
- Breakfast
- Farm
- Crops

Weather: warm…

Did you notice?

4 Write the words or expressions from the postcard Harry uses…

1 to address Sally at the beginning.
2 to say goodbye.
3 for 'I'm enjoying myself'.
4 for the place the animals sleep.
5 for what flowers do when they open up.

NOW YOU! → Workbook page 46

5 PLAN Imagine you are at one of the camps from this unit. Write a plan for your postcard.

- Say whether you're enjoying yourself.
- Write about your daily routine.
- Write about the activities you're doing.

WRITING TOOLS

When writing emails, letters and postcards, include information you think could be interesting to the person you're writing to. Look at the sentences in the model that end in an exclamation mark for examples.

6 WRITE Use your plan and the model on this page to write your postcard. Remember to use correct present tenses.

7 CHECK Read your postcard and check it includes all the information. Check your use of verb tenses.

PROJECT TASK 3 Tourist leaflet

- Write descriptions of five activities tourists usually do in your chosen city.
- Say if there are activities that are good to do in particular seasons and look for photos of people doing these activities.
- Check your paragraph about free-time activities from **task 2**. With your partner, correct and try to improve your writing.

→ Workbook page 56

Do all exercises in your notebook

52 On the farm / A postcard / Present tenses

ANSWER KEY

Page 52

1 **1** have **2** wake up **3** is milking **4** go out **5** are planting

2 *Suggested answers:*
1 I'm having (a great time)
2 (the fruit trees) are blossoming
3 (the weather) is warm
4 (every day) we wake up around 6:00am

3 **Weather:** warm, sunny, foggy
Breakfast: eggs, toast, fresh milk
Farm: farmstay, barn, animals, cows
Crops: fields, seeds, fruit trees

4 **1** Dear Sally,
2 Bye for now!
3 I'm having a great time.
4 barn
5 blossom

5 *Student's own answers*

6 *Student's own answers*

7 *Student's own answers*

FURTHER PRACTICE

Workbook page 46

LESSON FOCUS

Focus on Present tenses
Writing A postcard to a friend
Project task 3 Write about five activities that tourists do in the city and find photos

Resources

Teacher's i-solutions

Warmer

Draw a picture of someone doing one of the activities mentioned in the unit and have students guess the activity. Students continue in pairs or small groups.

Focus on present tenses

1 Remind students of the present tenses they have learnt (simple and continuous) and their different uses (see exercise 2). Tell them they will need to decide between these two tenses for this exercise.

2 Ask students to skim read the text to answer who is writing to whom and why (Harry to Sally to tell her about his time at the farmstay). Give students time to complete the exercise and answer any vocabulary questions.

3 Remind students of the importance of grouping lists of new vocabulary and check they know how to spell and pronounce the words they're writing.

Did you notice?

4 Give students more options for the first three expressions: *Hi (Sally), See you later!, I'm having lots of fun!*, etc.

5 PLAN Put students in pairs or small groups to share ideas on what they could write about before they write their plans on their own.

WRITING TOOLS

Get students to read the **Writing tool** and find the sentences in the text that have exclamation marks. Remind them not to use too many or it can feel a bit like they're shouting at the reader.

6 WRITE Before students start writing, make a checklist on the board of any elements related to content, structure, language and style that they should bear in mind.

7 CHECK Once students have checked their own postcards, they can swap with a partner and check theirs.

PROJECT TASK 3 Tourist leaflet

Tell students that they need to keep their project notes together in their **Workbook** (page 56) or in their own notebook.

→ See pages 24-27 **Projects**

Remind students to do all the exercises in their notebook

 CONTINUOUS ASSESSMENT Students can use appropriate present tenses to write a postcard to a friend.

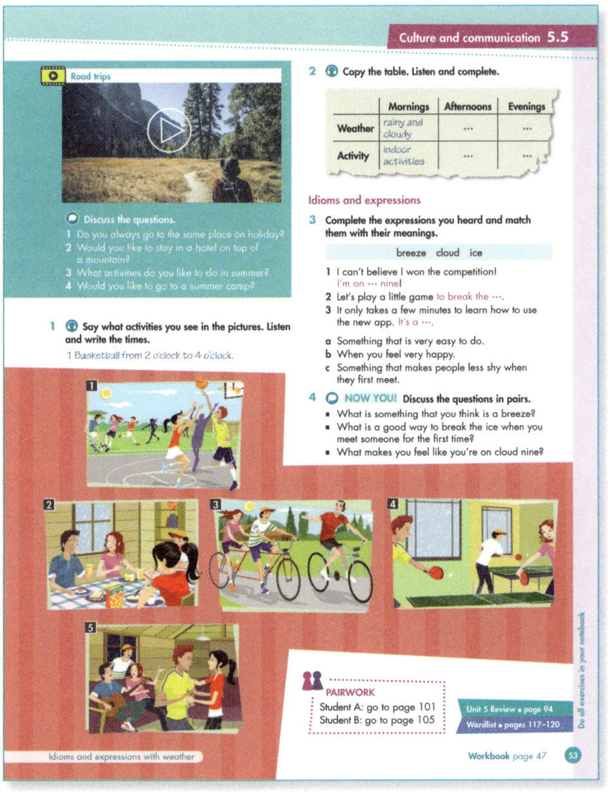

Culture and communication 5.5

Road trips

Discuss the questions.

1 Do you always go to the same place on holiday?
2 Would you like to stay in a hotel on top of a mountain?
3 What activities do you like to do in summer?
4 Would you like to go to a summer camp?

1 Say what activities you see in the pictures. Listen and write the times.

1 Basketball from 2 o'clock to 4 o'clock.

2 Copy the table. Listen and complete.

	Mornings	Afternoons	Evenings
Weather	rainy and cloudy	···	···
Activity	indoor activities	···	···

Idioms and expressions

3 Complete the expressions you heard and match them with their meanings.

breeze cloud ice

1 I can't believe I won the competition! I'm on ··· nine!
2 Let's play a little game to break the ···.
3 It only takes a few minutes to learn how to use the new app. It's a ···.

a Something that is very easy to do.
b When you feel very happy.
c Something that makes people less shy when they first meet.

4 NOW YOU! Discuss the questions in pairs.

- What is something that you think is a breeze?
- What is a good way to break the ice when you meet someone for the first time?
- What makes you feel like you're on cloud nine?

PAIRWORK
Student A: go to page 101
Student B: go to page 105

Unit 5 Review • page 94
Wordlist • pages 117-120

Do all exercises in your notebook

Idioms and expressions with weather

Workbook page 47

53

ANSWER KEY

Page 53

1 **1** Basketball from two o'clock to four o'clock.
2 Breakfast from nine o'clock to half past nine.
3 Ride bikes from five o'clock to six o'clock.
4 Table tennis from half past five to half past seven.
5 Dance and sing from half past seven to half past nine.

2

	Mornings	Afternoons	Evenings
Weather	rainy and cloudy	sunny and hot	foggy and cold
Activity	indoor activities, painting or watching TV	sports like cycling on tandem bikes	play music and dance or sing

3 **1** cloud; b **2** ice; c **3** breeze; a

4 *Student's own answers*

FURTHER PRACTICE AND UNIT ASSESSMENT

Unit 5 Review Student's Book page 94
Workbook page 47
- **Reflect on your learning** page 47
- **Grammar reference and practice** pages 88 and 94-95
- **Wordlist and exercises** pages 100 and 103

Tests available to download and edit from the **Richmond***Learning***Platform**

→ See pages 40-41 **Assessment**

LESSON FOCUS

Idioms and expressions Weather
Listening A conversation and a talk about camps
Speaking Asking and answering questions using idioms and expressions

Resources

Teacher's i-solutions, Student's Book audio, Culture video and worksheet

Road trips

Video and worksheet available on the Richmond*Learning***Platform**

- In pairs, ask students to complete the *What I know...* exercises on the **Culture video worksheet**.
- Show students the **Culture video** and ask them to complete the *What I learned...* exercises on the worksheet.
- In pairs, students compare answers.
- In small groups, tell students to complete the *What I wonder...* exercises on the worksheet.

Warmer

Watch the Culture video and discuss the questions with the whole class. If you don't have video facilities, simply discuss the questions.

1 1.48 (See page 174 for transcripts) Ask students what is happening in each picture and elicit answers. Before you play the audio, tell students that the pictures are not in the same order in which the activities are mentioned in the audio.

2 1.49 (See page 174 for transcripts) Tell students they are going to listen to a woman welcoming people to a summer camp and ask them to take notes in their copied tables.

Idioms and expressions

3 See if students remember where they heard the expressions and write or replay the sentences with them to remind them of their contexts. Students then complete the exercise.

4 NOW YOU! To extend the activity, put students in pairs to write questions to which the answer is one of the idioms or expressions: *Is it easy to put up a tent? (It's a breeze!), Why do people sometimes put name tags on at camps? (To help break the ice.), How do you feel when you watch your team win an important match? (I'm on cloud nine!).*

PAIRWORK Student's Book pages 101 and 105
See **Teacher's Book** page 114 for more information.

→ See pages 30-33 **Mediation**

Remind students to do all the exercises in their notebook

CONTINUOUS ASSESSMENT Students can use idioms and expressions with weather.

Unit 5 Review

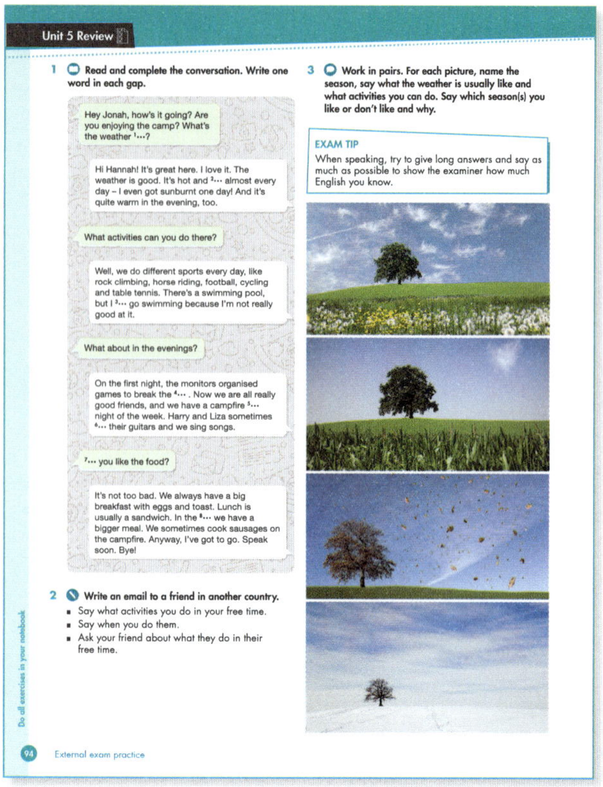
Unit 5 Review

1 Read and complete the conversation. Write one word in each gap.

Hey Jonah, how's it going? Are you enjoying the camp? What's the weather [1]…?

Hi Hannah! It's great here. I love it. The weather is good. It's hot and [2]… almost every day – I even got sunburnt one day! And it's quite warm in the evening, too.

What activities can you do there?

Well, we do different sports every day, like rock climbing, horse riding, football, cycling and table tennis. There's a swimming pool, but I [3]… go swimming because I'm not really good at it.

What about in the evenings?

On the first night, the monitors organised games to break the [4]… . Now we are all really good friends, and we have a campfire [5]… night of the week. Harry and Liza sometimes [6]… their guitars and we sing songs.

[7]… you like the food?

It's not too bad. We always have a big breakfast with eggs and toast. Lunch is usually a sandwich. In the [8]… we have a bigger meal. We sometimes cook sausages on the campfire. Anyway, I've got to go. Speak soon. Bye!

2 Write an email to a friend in another country.

- Say what activities you do in your free time.
- Say when you do them.
- Ask your friend about what they do in their free time.

3 Work in pairs. For each picture, name the season, say what the weather is usually like and what activities you can do. Say which season(s) you like or don't like and why.

EXAM TIP
When speaking, try to give long answers and say as much as possible to show the examiner how much English you know.

Do all exercises in your notebook

94 External exam practice

Student's Book page 94

ANSWER KEY

1 **1** like **2** sunny **3** don't **4** ice **5** every **6** play **7** Do **8** evening

2 *Student's own answers*

3 *Student's own answers*

Pairwork

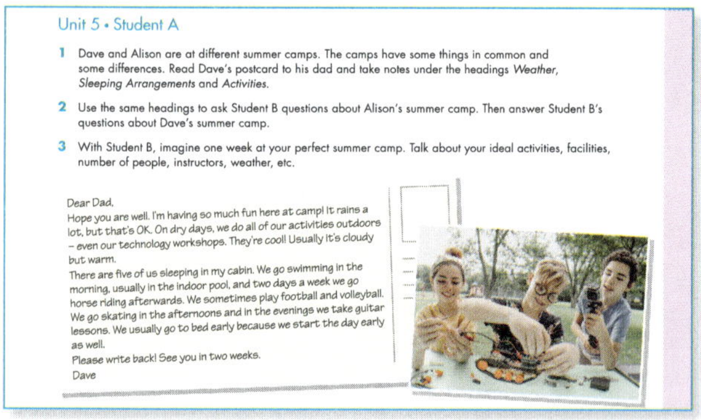
Unit 5 • Student A

1 Dave and Alison are at different summer camps. The camps have some things in common and some differences. Read Dave's postcard to his dad and take notes under the headings *Weather, Sleeping Arrangements* and *Activities*.

2 Use the same headings to ask Student B questions about Alison's summer camp. Then answer Student B's questions about Dave's summer camp.

3 With Student B, imagine one week at your perfect summer camp. Talk about your ideal activities, facilities, number of people, instructors, weather, etc.

Dear Dad,
Hope you are well. I'm having so much fun here at camp! It rains a lot, but that's OK. On dry days, we do all of our activities outdoors – even our technology workshops. They're cool! Usually it's cloudy but warm.
There are five of us sleeping in my cabin. We go swimming in the morning, usually in the indoor pool, and two days a week we go horse riding afterwards. We sometimes play football and volleyball. We go skating in the afternoons and in the evenings we take guitar lessons. We usually go to bed early because we start the day early as well.
Please write back! See you in two weeks.
Dave

Student's Book page 101

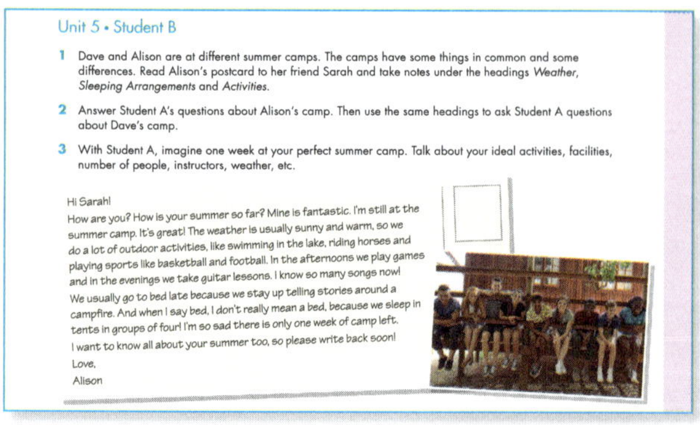
Unit 5 • Student B

1 Dave and Alison are at different summer camps. The camps have some things in common and some differences. Read Alison's postcard to her friend Sarah and take notes under the headings *Weather, Sleeping Arrangements* and *Activities*.

2 Answer Student A's questions about Alison's camp. Then use the same headings to ask Student A questions about Dave's camp.

3 With Student A, imagine one week at your perfect summer camp. Talk about your ideal activities, facilities, number of people, instructors, weather, etc.

Hi Sarah!
How are you? How is your summer so far? Mine is fantastic. I'm still at the summer camp. It's great! The weather is usually sunny and warm, so we do a lot of outdoor activities, like swimming in the lake, riding horses and playing sports like basketball and football. In the afternoons we play games and in the evenings we take guitar lessons. I know so many songs now!
We usually go to bed late because we stay up telling stories around a campfire. And when I say bed, I don't really mean a bed, because we sleep in tents in groups of four! I'm so sad there is only one week of camp left.
I want to know all about your summer too, so please write back soon!
Love,
Alison

Student's Book page 105

CEFR MEDIATION DESCRIPTOR

- **Adapting language**

Students can repeat the main point of a simple message on an everyday subject, using different words to help someone else understand it.

- **Comparing hobbies and interests**

Tell Student A and B they're going to compare two different summer camp experiences based on two different postcards and then together imagine a perfect summer camp.

Remind students to do all the exercises in their notebook

Present simple

Affirmative		
I	play	the guitar.
He/She/It	plays	
You/We/They	play	

We use the present simple to talk about regular actions such as habits and routines. We also use it to describe permanent situations and facts.

I **get** home from school at four o'clock.
We **live** in Manchester.

We add **-s** to the third person singular form in the affirmative.

She **plays** the piano. NOT ~~She play the piano.~~

Negative		
I	don't play	the guitar.
He/She/It	doesn't play	
You/We/They	don't play	

We use ***don't*** for all negative forms except the third person singular. For ***he***, ***she*** and ***it*** we always use ***doesn't***.

I **don't** like mushrooms.
He **doesn't** like cats. NOT ~~He don't like cats.~~

Yes/No questions		
Do	I	play the guitar?
Does	he/she/it	
Do	you/we/they	

We use ***do*** or ***does*** + **subject** + **infinitive** to form present simple questions. We always use the form ***does*** for the third person singular.

Do you have a pet?
Does Maria live here? NOT ~~Do Maria live here?~~

Wh- questions			
What instrument	do	I	play?
	does	he/she/it	
	do	you/we/they	

We can use question words before ***do*** or ***does*** when we want more information.

Where does your brother go to school?
When does the school year start?

Adverbs of frequency 1

Always is 100%	***Sometimes*** is 50%	***Never*** is 0%
I **always** walk my dog after school.	I **sometimes** eat pizza on a Friday.	I **never** arrive at school on time.

We use adverbs of frequency to talk about how often we do things.

We put adverbs of frequency before the verb.

I **always brush** my teeth at bedtime.
The teacher **sometimes gives** us extra work.
He **never comes** to school by bus.

However, we put the adverb of frequency after the verb ***be***.

Our teacher **is never** late.
NOT ~~Our teacher never is late.~~

We can also put ***sometimes*** at the start of a sentence.

Sometimes the teacher gives us extra work.

We cannot start a sentence with ***always*** or ***never***.

They **always** go to the gym on Mondays.
NOT ~~Always they go to the gym on Mondays.~~
She **never** goes to the pool at the weekend.
NOT ~~Never she goes to the pool at the weekend.~~

Do all exercises in your notebook

Student's Book page 111

UNIT 5

Weather and seasons

Weather	Seasons
chilly	spring
cloudy	summer
cold	autumn
foggy	winter
freezing	
hot	
raining	
snowing	
sunny	
windy	

Outdoor adventure and sports

Outdoor adventure	Sports
cabin	climbing wall
campsite	court
canoeing	equipment
cave	facilities
countryside	fencing
hiking	field
light a fire	hockey
natural habitat	Olympic-size pool
nature	rugby
put up a tent	scuba dive
tent	squash
waterfall	tennis

On the farm

barn
blossom (verb)
carrots
crops
eggs
farm animals
farmstay
field
fresh milk
fruit trees
grow
lettuces
look after the animals
milk (verb)
plant (verb)
seeds
vegetable garden
wake up early

Do all exercises in your notebook

Student's Book page 119

2.59 2.60 2.61

Remind students to do all the exercises in their notebook

6 OUT AND ABOUT

At the start of each unit and lesson, explain to the students what the objectives are.

Language objectives

Grammar

There is* and *There are

- Students practise the structures to talk about the presence and location of things.

Third person *-s*: spelling

- Students practise spelling verbs with different -*s* endings in the third person singular.

Adverbs of frequency II

- Students learn some more frequency adverbs and practise all of them together.

Vocabulary

Places in a city: *bakery, bookshop, bus station, butcher's, car park, clothes shop, gym, hairdresser's, hospital, hotel, museum, music shop, police station, post office, school, shopping centre, stadium*

- Students use the vocabulary to talk about places on a map.

Directions: *across from, behind, between, Excuse me, where's the ...?, go past, go straight ahead, How do I get to the ...?, Is this the way to ...?, near here, next to, on the corner of ... and ..., on your left, on your right, take the first/second/third left, take the first/second/third right, turn left, turn right, walk across*

- Students give each other directions around a town.

Historical monuments: *all over the world, ancient, artefact, city, civilisations, construction, design, history, palace, pyramid, repairs, research, rock, statue, tour guide, tourists, travel, visitors*

- Students focus on the vocabulary in an article.

Idioms and expressions

Travel: *when in Rome, do as the Romans do, few and far between, fits the bill*

- Students look at the idioms and expressions in the context of monologues based on photos.

Recycled language

Always; sometimes and *never;* Present simple

Skills objectives

Speaking

- Students ask for and give directions.
- Students ask and answer questions about someone's timetable.
- Students discuss jobs they might like to have.
- Students interview each other and report the answers using new idioms and expressions.

Pronunciation: Students encounter different letter combinations with the sound /e/ and practise saying them.

Pairwork: Students use various mediation techniques to guess professions.

Listening

- Students listen to and follow directions.
- Students listen to complete dialogues.
- Students listen to complete notes about a day in the working life of someone.
- Students listen to idioms and expressions in the context of three short monologues about photos.

Reading

- Students read short texts to find the names of important monuments.
- Students read in detail to choose answers in multiple choice questions.
- Students read to match words with their meanings.

Core values: Students discuss and write about the importance of **heritage** with reference to an important monument in their country.

Writing

- Students focus on writing in appropriate tone in an informal note.
- Students plan, write and check a note for a visitor to their town.

Focus on adverbs of frequency II

Remind students to do all the exercises in their notebook

Learning to learn tools

SPEAKING TOOLS Students practise saying word combinations in a linked way to sound more natural.	**LISTENING TOOLS** Students practise preparing for a listening by reading the questions beforehand.
READING TOOLS Students practise answering multiple-choice questions effectively through careful examination of both/all options.	**WRITING TOOLS** Students develop their ability to write effectively by considering the reader.

Project objectives: Vlog

Task 4 Students find the top two tourist attractions, add maps and write directions.

Task 5 Students write about a person who works at one of the tourist attractions.

Task 6 Students write about the two attractions and find photos.

Audiovisual objectives

Vlog: Students watch and listen to Emma talk about a weekend away in a quiet fishing village.

Culture: Students watch and listen to Emma talk about the Shetland Islands.

Grammar animations: Students are presented with visual presentations of the unit grammar.

Key competences

LC **Linguistic**
pages 54 - 61

MST **Mathematical and Science and Technology**
pages 54, 56, 58, 59, 61

DC **Digital**
pages 54, 55, 56, 61

SCC **Social and Civic**
pages 54-61

CAE **Cultural awareness and expression**
pages 54-61

LL **Learning to learn**
pages 55, 56, 59, 60

IE **Sense of initiative and entrepreneurship**
pages 55, 57, 60

→ See pages 42-43 **Key competences**

CEFR Mediation

6.1 Explaining data in speech
Can describe simple visuals on familiar topics.

6.2 Note-taking
Can make simple notes with familiar subject matter.

6.3 Facilitating communication in delicate situations and disagreements
Can recognise when speakers disagree and seek compromise and agreement.

6.4 Adapting language
Can use different words to help someone understand a message.

6.5 Acting as intermediary in informal situations
Can communicate the main point of what is said, conveying personal information back and forth.

Project Relaying specific information in writing
Can relay in writing specific information contained in short, simple informative texts.

Unit review Collaborating to construct meaning
Can make simple remarks and pose occasional questions to indicate that he/she is following.

Pairwork Relaying specific information in speech
Can relay specific, relevant information contained in short, simple texts.

→ See pages 30-33 **Mediation**

Remind students to do all the exercises in their notebook

6 OUT AND ABOUT

In unit 6 you will:
- give and ask for directions.
- say where things are.
- talk about routines and how often people do things.
- write a note for a visitor.

6.1 Vocabulary and listening

EMMA'S VLOG: Weekend away

Discuss the questions.
1 Do you like your town? Why?
2 Are there activities for teenagers?
3 Where would you like to live?

Flipped Learning

1 Listen and follow the route. Say where John, Alison, Vicky and Matt are going.

2 Write the names of the places.
This is where people...
1 buy clothes.
2 do exercise.
3 buy bread.
4 take the bus.
5 buy meat.
6 park their cars.
7 buy books.
8 go to study.
9 send letters and parcels.
10 go shopping.
11 get medical treatment.
12 attend sporting events.
13 get help from the police.
14 buy CDs and DVDs.
15 get their hair cut.
16 see exhibitions.

FAST FINISHERS Write a paragraph giving directions from your house to your school.

Do all exercises in your notebook

54 Places in a city / Directions / There is and There are

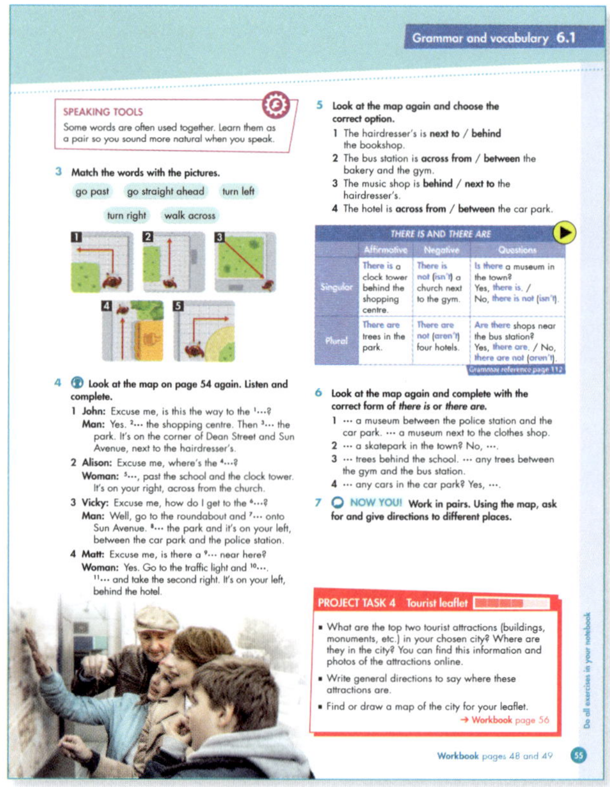
Grammar and vocabulary 6.1

SPEAKING TOOLS
Some words are often used together. Learn them as a pair so you sound more natural when you speak.

3 Match the words with the pictures.
go past | go straight ahead | turn left | turn right | walk across

4 Look at the map on page 54 again. Listen and complete.
1 **John:** Excuse me, is this the way to the [1]…?
Man: Yes. [2]… the shopping centre. Then [3]… the park. It's on the corner of Dean Street and Sun Avenue, next to the hairdresser's.
2 **Alison:** Excuse me, where's the [4]…?
Woman: [5]…, past the school and the clock tower. It's on your right, across from the church.
3 **Vicky:** Excuse me, how do I get to the [6]…?
Man: Well, go to the roundabout and [7]… onto Sun Avenue. [8]… the park and it's on your left, between the car park and the police station.
4 **Matt:** Excuse me, is there a [9]… near here?
Woman: Yes. Go to the traffic light and [10]…. [11]… and take the second right. It's on your left, behind the hotel.

5 Look at the map again and choose the correct option.
1 The hairdresser's is **next to / behind** the bookshop.
2 The bus station is **across from / between** the bakery and the gym.
3 The music shop is **behind / next to** the hairdresser's.
4 The hotel is **across from / between** the car park.

THERE IS AND THERE ARE

	Affirmative	Negative	Questions
Singular	There is a clock tower behind the shopping centre.	There is not (isn't) a church next to the gym.	Is there a museum in the town? Yes, there is. / No, there is not (isn't).
Plural	There are trees in the park.	There are not (aren't) four hotels.	Are there shops near the bus station? Yes, there are. / No, there are not (aren't).

Grammar reference page 112

6 Look at the map again and complete with the correct form of *there is* or *there are*.
1 … a museum between the police station and the car park. … a museum next to the clothes shop.
2 … a skatepark in the town? No, ….
3 … trees behind the school. … any trees between the gym and the bus station.
4 … any cars in the car park? Yes, ….

7 NOW YOU! Work in pairs. Using the map, ask for and give directions to different places.

PROJECT TASK 4 Tourist leaflet
- What are the top two tourist attractions (buildings, monuments, etc.) in your chosen city? Where are they in the city? You can find this information and photos of the attractions online.
- Write general directions to say where these attractions are.
- Find or draw a map of the city for your leaflet.

→ Workbook page 56

Workbook pages 48 and 49 55

Do all exercises in your notebook

ANSWER KEY

Pages 54-55

1 John is going to the shopping centre.
Alison is going to the police station.
Vicky is going to the hotel.
Matt is going to the clothes shop.

2
1 clothes shop
2 gym
3 bakery
4 bus station
5 butcher's
6 car park
7 bookshop
8 school
9 post office
10 shopping centre
11 hospital
12 stadium
13 police station
14 music shop
15 hairdresser's
16 museum

3
1 turn left
2 go straight ahead
3 walk across
4 go past
5 turn right

4
1 music shop
2 Go past
3 walk across
4 post office
5 Go straight ahead
6 museum
7 turn right
8 Go past
9 church
10 turn left
11 Go straight ahead

5
1 next to
2 between
3 behind
4 across from

6
1 There is; There isn't
2 Is there; there isn't
3 There are; There aren't
4 Are there; there are

7 *Student's own answers*

Remind students to do all the exercises in their notebook

LESSON FOCUS

Grammar *There is* and *There are*
Vocabulary Places in a city; Directions
Listening People asking for and giving directions
Speaking Asking for and giving directions
Project task 4 Find the top two tourist attractions, add maps and write directions

Resources

Teacher's i-solutions, Student's Book audio, Vlog and worksheet

Flipped Learning

EMMA'S VLOG: Weekend away

- Make sure to set up the **Flipped Learning** work with the students beforehand. **See pages 20-23 for complete Flipped Learning guidelines.**
- Ask students to put the **Flipped Learning worksheets** on their desks and walk around to check how many have completed the Flipped task.
- In pairs or small groups, ask students to compare and check the *Before you watch...* and *While you watch...* exercises on the worksheet.
- Show students **Emma's vlog** and ask volunteers to provide correct answers and clarify any doubts other students may have.
- Choose three or four students to read aloud their answers to the *After you watch...* exercises on the worksheet and encourage some class discussion.
- Move straight to exercise 1 on page 54

Warmer

Watch Emma's vlog and discuss the questions with the whole class. If you don't have video facilities, simply discuss the questions.

1 2.1 (See page 174 for transcripts) Draw students' attention to the map and explain any vocabulary they don't know. Tell them they will hear people giving directions to the people on the map and they should follow them to find out the destinations. Replay as many times as necessary.

2 Students consolidate their knowledge of the vocabulary from the map.

SPEAKING TOOLS

Get students to read the **Speaking tool** and ask them which places on page 54 have words in common (police station and bus station, clothes shop, bookshop and music shop). Drill the places.

3 Elicit and drill the answers to help them pronounce them naturally.

4 2.2 (See page 175 for transcripts) Tell students that they are listening for places and directions. After completing the exercise, get them to practise the conversations.

5 Tell students that the options are all prepositions of place. Give them time to answer using the map, and then drill the sentences again, paying attention to making the prepositions sounding linked and natural.

Flipped Learning

THERE IS AND THERE ARE

Draw students' attention to the **Grammar table**. Remind students that they can use this as a quick reference while completing the exercises.

Show students the **Grammar animation** and/or refer students to the **Grammar reference** on page 112 for further information on form and use.

→ See page 23 for how to flip the **grammar lesson**

6 Before doing this exercise, ask a couple of questions about the town in the map on page 54 using *Is there...?* and *Are there...?* and get students to ask each other questions in pairs or small groups to help consolidate the structure.

7 NOW YOU! To extend this activity, ask students to do the same with *There are* from memory.

PROJECT TASK 4 Tourist leaflet

Put students in their pairs again to discuss what information to include in this part of the leaflet. Remind students that they need to keep their project notes together in their **Workbook** (page 56) or in their own notebook.

→ See pages 24-27 **Projects**

FURTHER PRACTICE

Workbook pages 48-49
- **Grammar reference and practice** pages 89 and 95
- **Wordlist and exercises** pages 100 and 103

Remind students to do all the exercises in their notebook

CONTINUOUS ASSESSMENT Students can talk about places in a city, understand and give directions and use *There is* and *There are.*

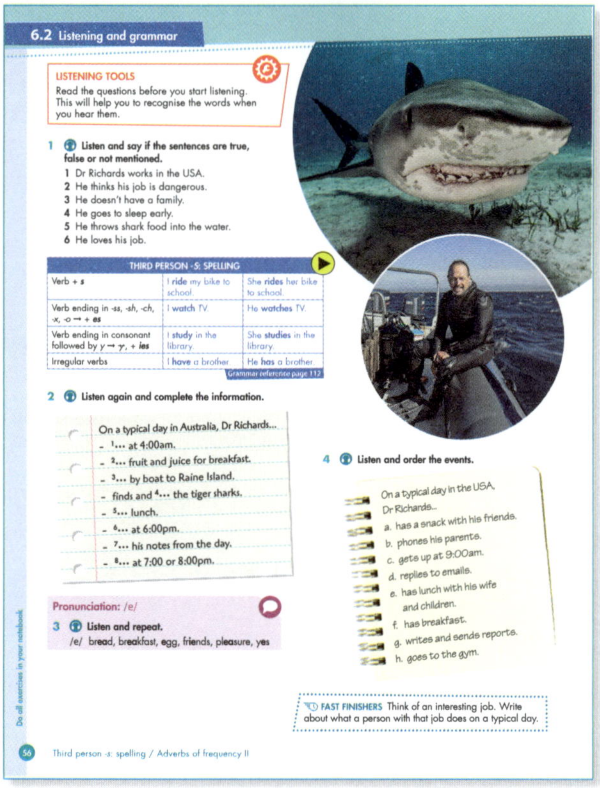

6.2 Listening and grammar

LISTENING TOOLS
Read the questions before you start listening. This will help you to recognise the words when you hear them.

1 Listen and say if the sentences are true, false or not mentioned.
1 Dr Richards works in the USA.
2 He thinks his job is dangerous.
3 He doesn't have a family.
4 He goes to sleep early.
5 He throws shark food into the water.
6 He loves his job.

THIRD PERSON -S: SPELLING		
Verb + s	I **ride** my bike to school.	She **rides** her bike to school.
Verb ending in -ss, -sh, -ch, -x, -o → + es	I **watch** TV.	He **watches** TV.
Verb ending in consonant followed by y → ~~y~~, + ies	I **study** in the library.	She **studies** in the library.
Irregular verbs	I **have** a brother.	He **has** a brother.

Grammar reference page 112

2 Listen again and complete the information.

On a typical day in Australia, Dr Richards...
- [1]... at 4:00am.
- [2]... fruit and juice for breakfast.
- [3]... by boat to Raine Island.
- finds and [4]... the tiger sharks.
- [5]... lunch.
- [6]... at 6:00pm.
- [7]... his notes from the day.
- [8]... at 7:00 or 8:00pm.

Pronunciation: /e/
3 Listen and repeat.
/e/ bread, breakfast, egg, friends, pleasure, yes

4 Listen and order the events.

On a typical day in the USA, Dr Richards...
a. has a snack with his friends.
b. phones his parents.
c. gets up at 9:00am.
d. replies to emails.
e. has lunch with his wife and children.
f. has breakfast.
g. writes and sends reports.
h. goes to the gym.

FAST FINISHERS Think of an interesting job. Write about what a person with that job does on a typical day.

Do all exercises in your notebook

56 Third person -s: spelling / Adverbs of frequency II

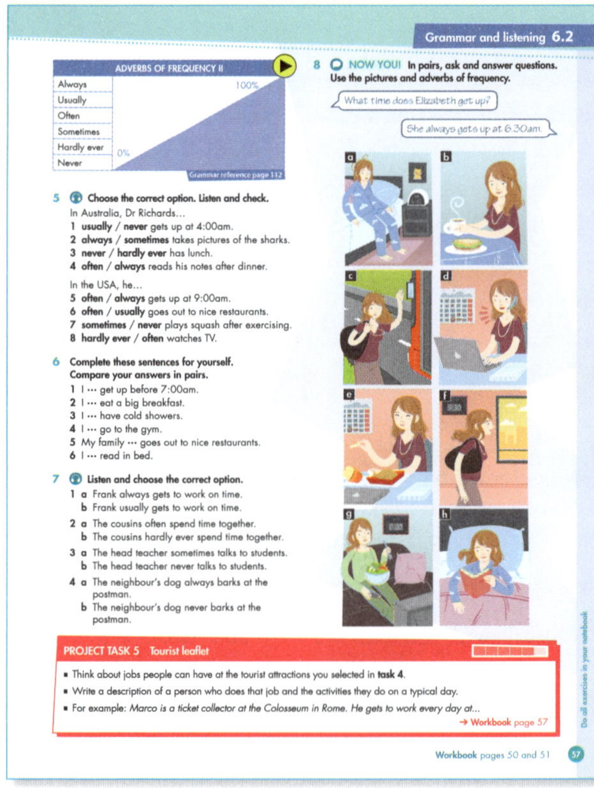

Grammar and listening 6.2

ADVERBS OF FREQUENCY II	
Always	100%
Usually	
Often	
Sometimes	
Hardly ever	
Never	0%

Grammar reference page 112

5 Choose the correct option. Listen and check.
In Australia, Dr Richards...
1 **usually** / **never** gets up at 4:00am.
2 **always** / **sometimes** takes pictures of the sharks.
3 **never** / **hardly ever** has lunch.
4 **often** / **always** reads his notes after dinner.
In the USA, he...
5 **often** / **always** gets up at 9:00am.
6 **often** / **usually** goes out to nice restaurants.
7 **sometimes** / **never** plays squash after exercising.
8 **hardly ever** / **often** watches TV.

6 Complete these sentences for yourself. Compare your answers in pairs.
1 I ··· get up before 7:00am.
2 I ··· eat a big breakfast.
3 I ··· have cold showers.
4 I ··· go to the gym.
5 My family ··· goes out to nice restaurants.
6 I ··· read in bed.

7 Listen and choose the correct option.
1 a Frank always gets to work on time.
b Frank usually gets to work on time.
2 a The cousins often spend time together.
b The cousins hardly ever spend time together.
3 a The head teacher sometimes talks to students.
b The head teacher never talks to students.
4 a The neighbour's dog always barks at the postman.
b The neighbour's dog never barks at the postman.

8 NOW YOU! In pairs, ask and answer questions. Use the pictures and adverbs of frequency.

What time does Elizabeth get up?

She always gets up at 6.30am.

a b c d e f g h

PROJECT TASK 5 Tourist leaflet
- Think about jobs people can have at the tourist attractions you selected in **task 4**.
- Write a description of a person who does that job and the activities they do on a typical day.
- For example: *Marco is a ticket collector at the Colosseum in Rome. He gets to work every day at...*

→ Workbook page 57

Workbook pages 50 and 51 57

Do all exercises in your notebook

ANSWER KEY

Pages 56-57

1
1 False
2 False
3 False
4 True
5 Not mentioned
6 True

2
1 gets up
2 has
3 goes
4 captures
5 never has / doesn't have
6 has/eats dinner
7 reads
8 goes to bed

3 *Student's own answers*

4 c, f, d, e, g, a, h, b

5
1 usually
2 sometimes
3 never
4 always
5 often
6 usually
7 sometimes
8 hardly ever

6 *Student's own answers*

7
1 a
2 b
3 a
4 a

8 *Student's own answers*

Remind students to do all the exercises in their notebook

LESSON FOCUS

Grammar Third person -s: spelling; Adverbs of frequency II
Listening Typical days in the lives of different people
Speaking Questions about a routine
Project task 5 Write about a person who works at a tourist attraction

Resources
Teacher's i-solutions, Student's Book audio

Warmer

Write verb phrases for daily routines on the board: *wake up, get up, have breakfast, have a shower, get to school, have lunch, get home, have a snack, have dinner, brush your teeth, go to bed* and *go to sleep*. Put students in pairs or small groups to ask each other when they do these things.

LISTENING TOOLS

Get students to read the **Listening tool** and tell them to apply it in the next exercise.

1 2.3 (See page 175 for transcripts) Tell students they're going to listen to a man talking about a day in his working life. Give them time to look at the photos and read the questions. Check they have done so by asking what job they think the man in the picture has. When students have completed the activity, you could also elicit corrected versions of the false sentences.

THIRD PERSON -S: SPELLING Flipped Learning

Draw students' attention to the **Grammar table**. Remind students that they can use this as a quick reference while completing the exercises.

Show students the **Grammar animation** and/or refer students to the **Grammar reference** on page 112 for further information on form and use.

→ See page 23 for how to flip the **grammar lesson**

2 2.4 (See page 175 for transcripts) Get students to complete what they can from memory before playing the audio again. Check pronunciation of the final -s as they read the answers out.

Pronunciation

3 2.5 (See page 175 for transcripts) Point out that the spelling combinations in bold are all pronounced identically; the 'a' and the 'i' are not pronounced.

4 2.6 (See page 175 for transcripts) Tell students they will now hear about a day in his life in the USA, for the second half of the year. Elicit the first answer, (c), and let them do the rest from the audio. You could put them in pairs to test each other's memories of both routines, one student doing the Australian routine and the other doing the US routine.

FAST FINISHERS Students can complete this exercise alone or in pairs.

ADVERBS OF FREQUENCY II Flipped Learning

Draw students' attention to the **Grammar table**. Remind students that they can use this as a quick reference while completing the exercises.

Show students the **Grammar animation** and/or refer students to the **Grammar reference** on page 112 for further information on form and use.

→ See page 23 for how to flip the **grammar lesson**

5 2.7 (See page 175 for transcripts) Let the students read the sentences and try to answer from memory. Tell them the audio is a short summary of the routines and play it for them to check.

6 To extend the exercise, write *How often* on the board and elicit the full question for the first sentence. Get them to swap pairs and ask and answer each other's *How often* questions.

7 2.8 (See page 175 for transcripts) Tell students they will hear four short monologues about people. Let them read each item before playing the conversation. Ask them what the speaker said that made them decide on their answer.

8 NOW YOU! Elicit questions for the exercise: *What does she have for breakfast?, How does she get to work?, What does she do at work?, Where does she have her lunch?, When does she finish work?, What does she do for dinner?, What does she do after dinner?* You could write the questions on the board and leave them there or rub out auxiliary (and even main) verbs and subjects. Tell them they should use the pictures and their imaginations to answer.

PROJECT TASK 5 Tourist Leaflet

Put them in their pairs again. Ask different pairs what tourist attractions they chose and elicit jobs people could do there. Then let them do the rest in their pairs. Remind students that they need to keep their project notes together in their **Workbook** (page 57) or in their own notebook.

→ See pages 24-27 **Projects**

FURTHER PRACTICE

Workbook pages 50-51
- **Grammar reference and practice** pages 89 and 95
- **Wordlist and exercises** pages 100 and 103

Vocabulary and Grammar worksheets available to download from the **Richmond***Learning***Platform**

→ See pages 38-39 **Mixed-ability classes**

Remind students to do all the exercises in their notebook

CONTINUOUS ASSESSMENT Students can spell third person forms of the present simple and use more adverbs of frequency.

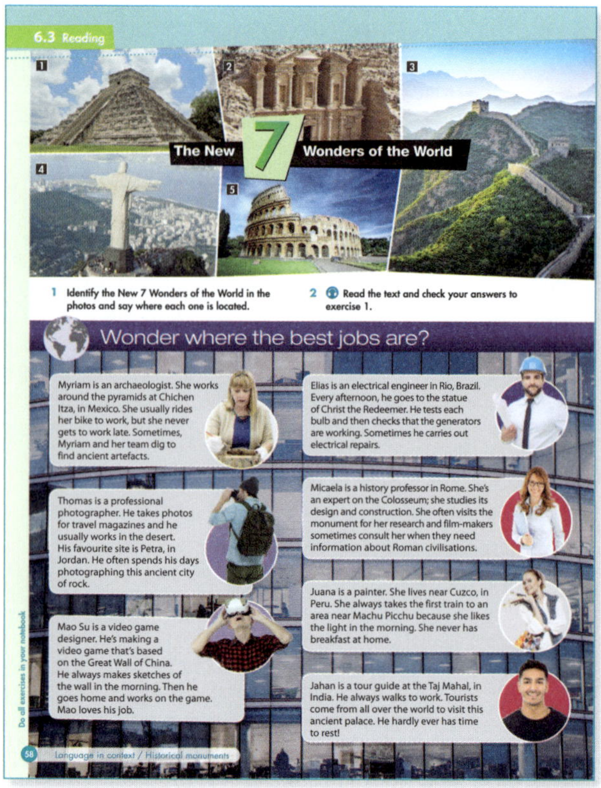

6.3 Reading

The New 7 Wonders of the World

1 Identify the New 7 Wonders of the World in the photos and say where each one is located.

2 Read the text and check your answers to exercise 1.

Wonder where the best jobs are?

Myriam is an archaeologist. She works around the pyramids at Chichen Itza, in Mexico. She usually rides her bike to work, but she never gets to work late. Sometimes, Myriam and her team dig to find ancient artefacts.

Thomas is a professional photographer. He takes photos for travel magazines and he usually works in the desert. His favourite site is Petra, in Jordan. He often spends his days photographing this ancient city of rock.

Mao Su is a video game designer. He's making a video game that's based on the Great Wall of China. He always makes sketches of the wall in the morning. Then he goes home and works on the game. Mao loves his job.

Elias is an electrical engineer in Rio, Brazil. Every afternoon, he goes to the statue of Christ the Redeemer. He tests each bulb and then checks that the generators are working. Sometimes he carries out electrical repairs.

Micaela is a history professor in Rome. She's an expert on the Colosseum; she studies its design and construction. She often visits the monument for her research and film-makers sometimes consult her when they need information about Roman civilisations.

Juana is a painter. She lives near Cuzco, in Peru. She always takes the first train to an area near Machu Picchu because she likes the light in the morning. She never has breakfast at home.

Jahan is a tour guide at the Taj Mahal, in India. He always walks to work. Tourists come from all over the world to visit this ancient palace. He hardly ever has time to rest!

Do all exercises in your notebook

58 Language in context / Historical monuments

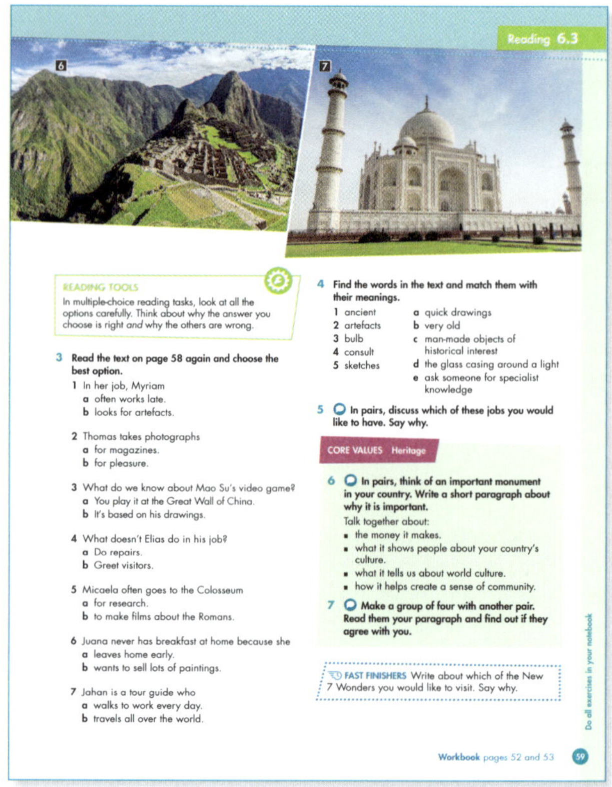

Reading 6.3

READING TOOLS
In multiple-choice reading tasks, look at all the options carefully. Think about why the answer you choose is right *and* why the others are wrong.

3 Read the text on page 58 again and choose the best option.
1 In her job, Myriam
a often works late.
b looks for artefacts.
2 Thomas takes photographs
a for magazines.
b for pleasure.
3 What do we know about Mao Su's video game?
a You play it at the Great Wall of China.
b It's based on his drawings.
4 What doesn't Elias do in his job?
a Do repairs.
b Greet visitors.
5 Micaela often goes to the Colosseum
a for research.
b to make films about the Romans.
6 Juana never has breakfast at home because she
a leaves home early.
b wants to sell lots of paintings.
7 Jahan is a tour guide who
a walks to work every day.
b travels all over the world.

4 Find the words in the text and match them with their meanings.

1 ancient	a quick drawings
2 artefacts	b very old
3 bulb	c man-made objects of historical interest
4 consult	d the glass casing around a light
5 sketches	e ask someone for specialist knowledge

5 In pairs, discuss which of these jobs you would like to have. Say why.

CORE VALUES Heritage

6 In pairs, think of an important monument in your country. Write a short paragraph about why it is important.
Talk together about:
- the money it makes.
- what it shows people about your country's culture.
- what it tells us about world culture.
- how it helps create a sense of community.

7 Make a group of four with another pair. Read them your paragraph and find out if they agree with you.

FAST FINISHERS Write about which of the New 7 Wonders you would like to visit. Say why.

Do all exercises in your notebook

Workbook pages 52 and 53 59

ANSWER KEY

Pages 58-59

1
1 Chichen Itza, Mexico
2 Petra, Jordan
3 The Great Wall of China, China
4 Christ the Redeemer, Brazil
5 The Colosseum, Italy
6 Machu Picchu, Peru
7 Taj Mahal, India

2 *Student's own answers*

3
1 b **3** b **5** a **7** a
2 a **4** b **6** a

4
1 b
2 c
3 d
4 e
5 a

5 *Student's own answers*

6 *Student's own answers*

7 *Student's own answers*

Remind students to do all the exercises in their notebook

LESSON FOCUS

Language in context Historical monuments

Core values Heritage

Resources

Teacher's i-solutions, Student's Book audio

→ See pages 36-37 **Literature**

Warmer

Write a list of common jobs on the board and tell students you're thinking of one and they have to ask yes/no questions to find out which. Give them ideas for questions if they need help: *Do you work in an office?, Do you wear a uniform? Is your job well paid?*, etc. Get them to continue in pairs or small groups.

1 Tell students they are going to read a text about people with jobs in special places. Draw their attention to the photos and see how many they can name, but don't tell them the ones they don't know.

2 2.9 (See page 176 for transcripts) Tell them that the texts are in the order of the pictures and see how quickly they can check their answers. Tell them they will have more time to read in exercise 3.

READING TOOLS

Get students to read the **Reading tool** before they do exercise 3. Once they have finished exercise 3 suggest that they go back over the questions and consider why the different options are correct or incorrect.

3 Put students in pairs and tell them to compare their answers and to correct the incorrect options aloud.

4 For extra practice, get students in pairs to write sentences with gaps that elicit the key words in the exercise. Then they will ask another pair to complete the sentences.

5 You could give students time to prepare an answer that includes one or more words from the text that they didn't know before. They can then read their answers aloud and their partner can try to guess which words were the new ones.

CORE VALUES Heritage

6 Get students to discuss before they write and encourage them not to use the monuments they chose for their projects.

7 Open up a class discussion about the importance of heritage.

FAST FINISHERS Students can complete this exercise alone or in pairs.

FURTHER PRACTICE

Workbook pages 52-53

Remind students to do all the exercises in their notebook

CONTINUOUS ASSESSMENT Students can understand vocabulary for historical monuments in a text about people who work at World Heritage sites.

6.4 Writing

A note for a visitor

Focus on adverbs of frequency

1 Choose the best option for you.

1 My relatives **often** / **sometimes** / **never** come to visit me.
2 There are **usually** / **sometimes** / **hardly ever** a lot of people in my town on Saturdays.
3 You can **always** / **usually** / **never** find a taxi in my town.

2 Look at the position of the adverbs in exercise 1 and choose the best option.

1 Adverbs of frequency usually come **before** / **after** verbs.
2 Adverbs of frequency come **before** / **after** the verb *be*.
3 Adverbs of frequency come **before** / **after** auxiliary verbs like *can*.

3 Read the notes and answer the questions.

1 Who is writing?
2 Who are they writing to?
3 Why are they writing?

Kylie,

I can't believe you're finally here! Welcome to Edinburgh! I hope you're OK waiting with Mum till I get back. I have volleyball practice, but I'm always back at 6pm. We can get the bus into town tomorrow morning. The festival's on this weekend, so there are loads of music, theatre and comedy shows.

Samantha

Kylie,

I forgot! There's also the castle, Holyrood Palace and all of the old town. On Sunday we can do the spooky underground walking tour! There's often a queue, but we can get there early. We'll go sightseeing in the morning, then go to the festival in the afternoon. It'll be awesome!

Samantha

Did you notice?

4 Look at the notes again and find informal ways of saying...

1 until
2 return
3 lots of
4 scary

NOW YOU! → Workbook page 54

5 PLAN Order the parts and use them to plan a note to a friend. Imagine they are coming to visit you and will arrive before you get home.

a Sign off.
b Say why you're not there and when you will get home.
c Welcome your guest.
d Say what there is to do in your town and suggest a plan.

WRITING TOOLS

When writing a text, think about your reader. Who are they? What do they know? What do you think they want to know? Should you use formal or informal language?

6 WRITE Use your plan and the model to write your note. Remember to use adverbs of frequency and some informal expressions.

7 CHECK Read your note and check it follows your plan. Make sure you have used informal expressions and the adverbs are in the right position.

PROJECT TASK 6 Tourist leaflet

- Write descriptions of the activities visitors usually do when they visit the tourist attractions you selected in **task 4**. For example, at the Eiffel Tower, tourists usually take the lift to the top floor.
- Choose photos to show the attractions.
- Check your paragraph about the person in **task 5**. With your partner, correct and try to improve your writing.
- Next, do the final task on page 62.

→ Workbook page 57

Do all exercises in your notebook

60 A note / Adverbs of frequency

ANSWER KEY

Page 60

1 *Student's own answers*

2 **1** before
2 after
3 after

3 **1** Samantha
2 Kylie
3 To welcome Kylie to Edinburgh

4 **1** till
2 get back
3 loads of
4 spooky

5 c, b, d, a; *Student's own answers*

6 *Student's own answers*

7 *Student's own answers*

FURTHER PRACTICE

Workbook page 54

LESSON FOCUS

Focus on Adverbs of frequency

Writing A note for a visitor

Project task 6 Write about the two attractions and find photos

Resources

Teacher's i-solutions

Preparation A sheet of lined paper big enough to write five sentences on for every student

Warmer

Write all the adverbs of frequency on the board. Put students in groups of four or more. Hand out the sheets of paper and get them to write one true sentence about themselves for each of the adverbs. They then turn them face down and put them all in the middle to redistribute in their groups. Each person reads out the sentences they now have and the group guesses who wrote them.

Focus on linking language

1 Get students to compare their answers in pairs and see if they agree about the last two.

2 Give them time to be sure of their answers before you confirm.

3 Get them to skim read the notes to answer the questions quickly.

Did you notice?

4 Give them more time to read to check any other vocabulary they don't understand. Ask them if they think Kylie's suggestions sound like fun to them.

5 PLAN Once students have finished their plan, encourage them to talk it though with a partner.

WRITING TOOLS

Get students to read the **Writing tool**. Ask them to think of a real friend or imagine one and write answers to the questions and then see if that changes their plan.

6 WRITE Before students start writing, make a checklist on the board of any elements related to content, structure, language and style that they should bear in mind.

7 CHECK Once students have checked their own notes, they can swap with a partner and check theirs.

PROJECT TASK 6 Tourist Leaflet

Put students in their pairs and make sure they discuss and plan before they write and check afterwards. Tell students that they need to keep their projects notes together in their **Workbook** (page 57) or in their own notebook.

→ See pages 24-27 **Projects**

Remind students to do all the exercises in their notebook

 CONTINUOUS ASSESSMENT Students can use adverbs of frequency to write a note for a visitor.

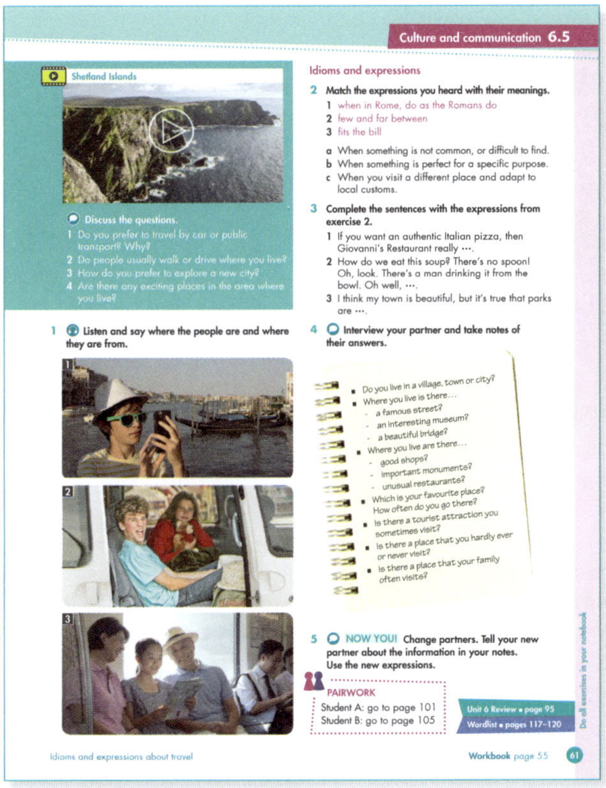
Culture and communication 6.5

Shetland Islands

Discuss the questions.
1 Do you prefer to travel by car or public transport? Why?
2 Do people usually walk or drive where you live?
3 How do you prefer to explore a new city?
4 Are there any exciting places in the area where you live?

1 Listen and say where the people are and where they are from.

Idioms and expressions
2 Match the expressions you heard with their meanings.
1 when in Rome, do as the Romans do
2 few and far between
3 fits the bill
a When something is not common, or difficult to find.
b When something is perfect for a specific purpose.
c When you visit a different place and adapt to local customs.

3 Complete the sentences with the expressions from exercise 2.
1 If you want an authentic Italian pizza, then Giovanni's Restaurant really ….
2 How do we eat this soup? There's no spoon! Oh, look. There's a man drinking it from the bowl. Oh well, ….
3 I think my town is beautiful, but it's true that parks are ….

4 Interview your partner and take notes of their answers.
- Do you live in a village, town or city?
- Where you live is there…
  - a famous street?
  - an interesting museum?
  - a beautiful bridge?
- Where you live are there…
  - good shops?
  - important monuments?
  - unusual restaurants?
- Which is your favourite place? How often do you go there?
- Is there a tourist attraction you sometimes visit?
- Is there a place that you hardly ever or never visit?
- Is there a place that your family often visits?

5 NOW YOU! Change partners. Tell your new partner about the information in your notes. Use the new expressions.

PAIRWORK
Student A: go to page 101
Student B: go to page 105

Unit 6 Review • page 95
Wordlist • pages 117–120

Do all exercises in your notebook

Idioms and expressions about travel
Workbook page 55 61

ANSWER KEY

Page 61

1 **1** Venice; South Africa
2 Scotland; England
3 China; USA

2 **1** c **2** a **3** b

3 **1** fits the bill
2 when in Rome, do as the Romans do
3 few and far between

4 *Student's own answers*

5 *Student's own answers*

FURTHER PRACTICE AND UNIT ASSESSMENT

Unit 6 Review **Student's Book** page 95
Workbook page 55
- **Reflect on your learning** page 55
- **Grammar reference and practice** pages 88 and 95
- **Wordlist and exercises** pages 100 and 103

Tests available to download and edit from the **Richmond***Learning***Platform**

➔ See pages 40-41 **Assessment**

LESSON FOCUS
Idioms and expressions Travel
Listening Short monologues about travel photos
Speaking An interview and interview report

Resources
Teacher's i-solutions, Student's Book audio, Culture video and worksheet

Shetland Islands

Video and worksheet available on the Richmond*Learning***Platform**

- In pairs, ask students to complete the *What I know…* exercises on the **Culture video worksheet**.
- Show students the **Culture video** and ask them to complete the *What I learned…* exercises on the worksheet.
- In pairs, students compare answers.
- In small groups, tell students to complete the *What I wonder…* exercises on the worksheet.

Warmer

Watch the Culture video and discuss the questions with the whole class. If you don't have video facilities, simply discuss the questions.

1 2.10 (See page 176 for transcripts) Let students look at the photos and guess the answers before you play the audio.

Idioms and expressions

2 Ask if students remember the contexts of the idioms and expressions and write the sentences with them on the board to help them guess the meanings.

3 Ask students questions to find other contexts for the expressions: *When you're really hungry, what kind of food really fits the bill? What other things do people in other countries do that's different from in our country? Would you do those things? What things are few and far between in our town?*

4 Ask students to read the questions and write an answer to one of them using one of the expressions. Before students do the interview, get them to read their answers and guess what the questions were. Make sure they take notes so they can do the next exercise.

5 **NOW YOU!** Ask individual students to tell you answers they had in common and any other interesting things that came up during the interviews.

PAIRWORK **Student's Book** pages 101 and 105
See **Teacher's Book** page 126 for more information.
➔ See pages 30-33 **Mediation**

Remind students to do all the exercises in their notebook

CONTINUOUS ASSESSMENT Students can use idioms and expressions for travel.

Unit 6 Review

Unit 6 Review

1 Listen and choose the correct option.

1 You will hear two people talking about their town. Where is the gym?
  a It's behind the shopping centre.
  b It's next to the shopping centre.
  c It's next to the bookshop.

2 You will hear a girl talking about her routine. What time does she get up on Saturday?
  a 7:15
  b 8:15
  c 9:15

3 You will hear a man talking about his travels. Where does he go?
  a He usually goes somewhere new.
  b He never goes back to the same place.
  c He always goes to the same place.

4 You will hear a man talking. Which country is he in?
  a Egypt
  b England
  c Italy

5 You will hear two people talking. Where is Patricia going?
  a To the hairdresser's.
  b To the stadium.
  c To the butcher's.

6 You will hear a woman talking about her town. Who is she?
  a A grandmother.
  b A taxi driver.
  c A tour guide.

2 Look at the pictures. In pairs, say which of the activities you like or don't like and why. Say how often you do them.

EXAM TIP
When speaking, remember to keep talking. If you forget a word, try to find another way to say the same thing. Don't get stuck!

3 Write a note to your uncle, who is picking you up from school. Give him instructions about how to get from the school gate to your classroom.
Say:
- where you want him to meet you.
- what time to arrive.
- how to get there.

Do all exercises in your notebook

External exam practice 95

Student's Book page 95

ANSWER KEY

See page 181 for transcripts

1 2.44

1 a
2 b
3 a
4 b
5 c
6 b

2 *Student's own answers*

3 *Student's own answers*

Pairwork

Unit 6 • Student A

1 Tell Student B about Richard's daily routine. Can they guess his job?

A day in the life of Richard Brown

11am	get up; usually do some gardening
1pm	have a light lunch
2pm	get the train to work
3pm – 11pm	work: consult hospital staff, decide menu and prepare meals
Midnight	have dinner at home
2am	go to bed

(Job: Richard is a chef in a hospital.)

2 Now listen to Student B tell you about Isabel's daily routine. Ask questions to guess her job.

Do all exercises in your notebook

Student's Book page 101

Unit 6 • Student B

1 Listen to Student A tell you about Richard's daily routine. Ask questions to guess his job.

2 Now tell Student A about Isabel's daily routine. Can they guess her job?

A day in the life of Isabel Green

5:30am	get up
5:45am	have breakfast, go to work
6:30am – 2pm	work: help clients with their businesses
3pm	have big lunch, relax
4pm – 9pm	do yoga, read travel magazines
9pm	have healthy dinner, go to bed

(Job: Isabel is a business consultant.)

Do all exercises in your notebook

Student's Book page 105

CEFR MEDIATION DESCRIPTOR

- **Relaying specific information in speech**

Students can relay specific, relevant information contained in short, simple texts, labels and notices on familiar subjects.

- **Describing daily routines**

Tell Student A and B they each have information about a person's job for their partner to guess and four job options to help them guess their partner's person's job. Encourage them to ask questions before they guess.

Remind students to do all the exercises in their notebook

Grammar reference

Unit 6 Grammar reference

There is and There are

	Affirmative	Negative	Questions
Singular	**There is** a clock tower behind the shopping centre.	**There is not (isn't)** a church next to the gym.	**Is there** a museum in the town? Yes, **there is.** No, **there is not (isn't).**
Plural	**There are** trees in the park.	**There are not (aren't)** four hotels.	**Are there** shops near the bus station? Yes, **there are.** No, **there are not (aren't).**

We use ***there is*** and ***there are*** to describe scenes in the present.

Countable nouns

With singular countable nouns in the affirmative, we can use the full form ***there is*** or the contracted form ***there's***.

There's a dog under the table.

There is an apple in my bag.

With plural countable nouns in the affirmative, we use the full form ***there are***.

There are people in the restaurant.

NOT ~~There're people in the restaurant.~~

In the negative, we generally use the contracted forms ***there isn't*** and ***there aren't*** for singular and plural countable nouns.

There isn't an orange in the bowl.

There aren't any pyramids in England.

Uncountable nouns

With uncountable nouns in the affirmative, we can use the full form ***there is + some*** or the contracted form ***there's + some***.

There's some money on the floor.

There is some ice in the freezer.

In the negative, we generally use the contracted form ***there isn't + any*** with uncountable nouns.

There isn't any bread in the cupboard.

Third person -s: spelling

Verb + **s**	I **ride** my bike to school.	She **rides** her bike to school.
Verb ending in -ss, -sh, -ch, -x, -o = + **-es**	I **watch** TV.	He **watches** TV.
Verb ending in consonant followed by y = ~~y~~, + **-ies**	I **study** in the library.	She **studies** in the library.
Irregular verbs	I **have** a brother.	He **has** a brother.

We add **-s** to the third person singular form of regular verbs in the affirmative.

John **lives** in the city centre.

NOT ~~John live in the city centre.~~

We do not add **-s** to the third person singular form of regular verbs in the negative.

Mary doesn't **play** the guitar.

NOT ~~Mary doesn't plays the guitar.~~

Adverbs of frequency II

Always
Usually
Often
Sometimes
Hardly ever
Never

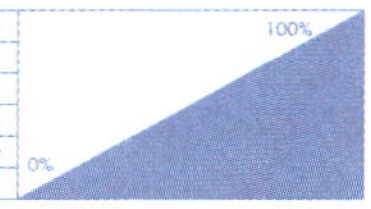

We use adverbs of frequency to talk about how often we do things.

I **always** have a cup of tea for breakfast.

It does**n't often** rain in summer.

Remember that we usually put adverbs of frequency before the main verb in the present simple. But with ***be***, we put them after the verb.

We **never go** to bed early on Fridays.

Lucy **is usually** the last person to arrive.

Usually, ***often*** and ***sometimes*** can start a sentence, but ***never*** and ***always*** cannot.

I **sometimes** walk to school.

BUT **Sometimes** I walk to school.

I **always** eat my vegetables.

NOT ~~Always I eat my vegetables.~~

Do all exercises in your notebook

112 **Workbook** pages 93–96

Student's Book page 112

Wordlist

UNIT 6

Places in a city

bakery
bookshop
bus station
butcher's
car park
clothes shop
gym
hairdresser's
hospital
hotel
museum
music shop
police station
post office
school
shopping centre
stadium

Directions

across from
behind
between
Excuse me, where's the …?
go past
go straight ahead
How do I get to the …?
Is this the way to …?
near here
next to
on the corner of … and …
on your left
on your right
take the first/second/third left
take the first/second/third right
turn left
turn right
walk across

Historical monuments

all over the world
ancient
artefact
city
civilisations
construction
design
history
palace
pyramid
repairs
research
rock
statue
tour guide
tourists
travel
visitors

Do all exercises in your notebook

Workbook pages 102–104 119

Student's Book page 119

2.62 2.63 2.64

Remind students to do all the exercises in their notebook

PROJECT: Tourist leaflet

RECAP

- In this project, you collected material for a tourist leaflet.
- In **units 5 and 6**, you learnt how to talk about the seasons and weather, routines and habits, and how to give and ask for directions.
- Now you are ready to complete and display your tourist leaflet.

TASK 1 Choose a famous city, find pictures of it and describe the weather.
TASK 2 Describe the activities that people do in that city.
TASK 3 Write about five activities that tourists do in that city and find photos.
TASK 4 Find the top two tourist attractions, add maps and write directions.
TASK 5 Write about a person who works at one of the tourist attractions.
TASK 6 Write about the two attractions and find photos.

FINAL TASK: Present your data

- In your pairs, fold a sheet of paper in two or three. This is your leaflet.
- Think of a good title. Your goal is to persuade readers to visit the city.
- For each part, decide if you are going to use your text, your partner's or a combination. Also decide where you are going to put your photos.
- Copy the texts you have written onto coloured paper and stick them into your leaflet.
- You are going to display your tourist leaflets around the classroom and walk around and read the other leaflets.
- Choose your two favourites. Why do you like them? Which places would you like to visit?

USEFUL EXPRESSIONS

- This is our tourist leaflet.
- The weather in (*city*) is…
- In this town there are two top attractions. They are…
- This is (*name*). He/She works at…
- At this attraction, tourists usually…

21ST CENTURY SKILLS

Cultural awareness

How can you be more culturally aware when you travel?

You can learn how to say hello, thank you, etc. in the local language before you visit.

You can also talk to local people at the places you visit and try to understand how they see the world.

It's important to understand and respect differences between people, so that we can learn about ourselves and others, and grow.

Do all exercises in your notebook

EVALUATION

Answer the questions in your team.

1 Is it easy to correct and improve your work?
2 What is the difference between working in pairs and working in groups?
3 Look at the list below and choose the three things that you think are most important for successful collaboration.
- Actively participating
- Completing all the tasks
- Listening to teammates
- Helping others to learn
- Being creative
- Sharing ideas openly
- Having a leader
- Being respectful

GO BEYOND

Tourist information

Tourist leaflets contain promotional information about a town or city. They often describe the weather, the activities people can do there and the most important places to visit. They usually include maps with directions on how to get to those places and attractive photographs to catch the reader's attention. Sometimes, they talk about important traditions or customs, like how to greet people or how to eat the local food.

A tourist leaflet sometimes includes vouchers or tickets so that the reader can save money when they visit attractions, restaurants or shops. This is good for the tourists, and also helps businesses to attract customers.

Nowadays, the same content is often presented in different ways, on websites and apps, for example. This means that the information is easy to find and available to everyone.

Answer the questions in pairs.

1 Do you use tourist leaflets on holiday?
2 What elements make a good tourist leaflet?
3 What are alternatives to a tourist leaflet? Which do you prefer to use?
4 How is a tourist leaflet different from a holiday brochure or a travel guide?

Do all exercises in your notebook

Workbook project task notes

PROJECT: Tourist leaflet

TASK 1

My partner: ______

Famous city: ______

The weather in our chosen city: ______

→ Student's book page 47

TASK 2

Free time activities in our chosen city: ______

→ Student's book page 49

TASK 3

Tourist activities in our chosen city: ______

→ Student's book page 52

TASK 4

Top two tourist attractions: ______

Directions: ______

→ Student's book page 55

TASK 5

Jobs at the tourist attractions: ______

One person's day: ______

→ Student's book page 57

TASK 6

Activities at the tourist attractions: ______

→ Student's book page 60

FINAL TASK

Title: ______

About my two favourite leaflets: ______

Different ways to make your leaflet.

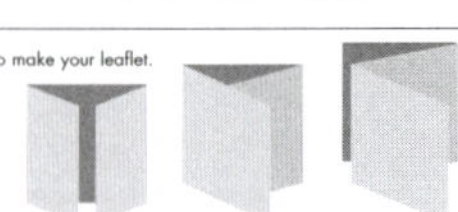

→ Student's book page 62

Remind students to do all the exercises in their notebook

PROJECT FOCUS

➔ See pages 24-27 **Projects**

Skills

- Plan and check texts in pairs
- Write paragraphs about a city, including weather and popular activities done by locals and tourists
- Describe and write directions to tourist attractions in the city
- Write a description of the daily lives of people who work around the tourist attractions
- Discuss and decide on the leaflet layout
- Present leaflets
- Read leaflets and discuss favourite tourist destinations
- Discuss evaluations of the project
- Read and discuss a text related to the project

CEFR mediation

Relaying specific information in writing

Can relay in writing specific information contained in short simple informational texts.

➔ See pages 30-33 **Mediation**

Preparation Remind students to bring the elements they create in tasks 1-6 and their notes from **Workbook** project task notes pages 56-57 or their own notebook. Bring a piece of card for students to put their prepared texts and photos on and have thumbtacks, adhesive putty or something for students to display their leaflets in the classroom. Have students bring in their self-assessment diaries if they are writing them.

RECAP

Put students in their pairs and read through the **Recap** as a class. Draw their attention to the project tasks and the unit objectives and ask which task helped achieve which objectives. Make sure they have all the materials and notes that they need (see **Preparation**) for the **Final task**.

FINAL TASK: Present your leaflet

Tell students they are now going to complete and display their leaflets. Put them in their pairs, hand out the pieces of card to each pair and get them to fold them in whichever way they think appropriate (see **Workbook** page 57 for two options). Give them a time limit to prepare their leaflets for display and read through the first four steps with them. Encourage them to make their leaflets eye-catching, attractive and easy to read.

Read through the last two steps of the task, get them to display their leaflets and tell them to discuss them in their original pairs so they can compare them with their own. Tell them to discuss their favourites but point out that they don't have to agree. After everyone has finished reading and discussing favourites, elicit answers and comments from volunteers. Have a class discussion about students' travel experiences and interests and ask them about the benefits of travel. Then direct their attention to the 21st Century skill.

21ST CENTURY SKILLS

Read through the **21st Century skill** with them and ask them how they think learning about other cultures can help us grow as human beings.

➔ See pages 28-29 **21st century skills**

EVALUATION

Before students discuss the questions in pairs, give them time to prepare notes about their experience in the project. Point out that question 2 asks them to compare their experience in this project with that of the first, and ask them to discuss question 3 for pairs and for groups. Remind students to be supportive and give constructive feedback to each other and say which things they thought they did well and which they found most difficult. Monitor discussions, adding your own feedback where appropriate and noting common observations to then convey to the class as a whole.

Have a class discussion about what students have learnt from the project, reminding them of the unit objectives, the **Core values** and the **Learning tools** sections of units 5 and 6, as well as the **21st Century skills** section of the **Project** pages.

If you have decided to use the **evaluation** exercise as a springboard for a student self-assessment diary (see **Evaluation notes** page 77), give them time to do this now and remind them to refer to the **Reflect on your learning** section of the **Workbook** if they have one.

➔ See pages 40-41 **Assessment**

GO BEYOND

Ask students which of the leaflets that they saw they liked most (irrespective of whether they liked the destination) and why. Ask what goes into a good tourist leaflet and tell them to read the text to compare ideas and answer the questions.

End with a class discussion. Elicit all the alternatives they came up with and discuss the differences, advantages and disadvantages. Point out that holiday brochures are advertisements for private companies – hotels, resorts, package tours, etc. – and that travel guides give more detailed information. Ask them what different online options they know of and prefer and let them share recommendations.

Remind students to do all the exercises in their notebook

CONTINUOUS ASSESSMENT Students can prepare and present a leaflet and show some cultural awareness.

7 A SPIRIT OF ADVENTURE

At the start of each unit and lesson, explain to the students what the objectives are.

Language objectives

Grammar

Adjectives: *-ing* and *-ed*
- Students focus on the differences in meaning and use of adjectives ending in *-ing* and *-ed*.

Past simple *be*
- Students practise affirmative and negative forms of *be* in the past simple.

Past simple *be*: questions
- Students practise *wh-* and *yes/no* question forms of *be* in the past simple.

Vocabulary

Adjectives *-ing* and *-ed*: *bored, boring, excited, exciting, fascinated, fascinating, frightened, frightening, interested, interesting, surprised, surprising, terrified, terrifying*
- Students focus on adjectives to describe emotions and situations.

Travelling: *countries, culture, dangerous, history, maps, places, return home, travel, traveller, trips, visit*
- Students use vocabulary related to travelling in context.

Famous explorers: *brave, conquer, courageous, daring, discover, early life, expedition, explorer, first person, Mount Everest, philanthropy, pioneer, tribute, trip*
- Students use vocabulary related to famous explorers in context.

Idioms and expressions

Experiences: *be face to face with something, be over the moon, it beats me*
- Students look at idioms and expressions related to experiences in the context of a story.

Recycled language

Present simple; Present continuous; *There is/are*

Skills objectives

Speaking

- Students talk about an interesting member of their family.
- Students ask and answer questions about famous explorers.
- Students discuss and order achievements of famous people.
- Students tell a story from their childhood or from the childhood of someone they know.

Pronunciation: Students practise strong and weak forms of *was* and *were*.

Pairwork: Students use various mediation techniques in order to answer questions on a famous historical discovery.

Listening

- Students listen and take notes on a famous explorer.
- Students listen for specific biographical information.
- Students listen to idioms and expressions in context.

Reading

- Students skim a text to understand the gist.
- Students read a text in order to match vocabulary and definitions.
- Students read a biographical text in order to find out the subject's background and achievements.

Core values: Students learn about and discuss the **achievements** of some well-known people.

Writing

- Students focus on paragraph order in the context of a biography.
- Students plan, write and check a biography focusing on achievements and successes of a well-known person.

Focus on linking language III: *after, as, but, later, so*

Remind students to do all the exercises in their notebook

Learning to learn tools

SPEAKING TOOLS Students practise using visual images to remember new expressions.	LISTENING TOOLS Students take notes on new vocabulary and make notes on the context.
READING TOOLS Students focus on images included in a text in order to help with understanding.	WRITING TOOLS Students look at ways to avoid repetition of subjects (*he/she*, etc.) when writing a biography.

Project objectives: Memorabilia chest

Task 1 Students make an information card with a summary of a famous explorer.

Task 2 Students make a map and collect information about an explorer.

Task 3 Students write a letter from an explorer.

Audiovisual objectives

Vlog: Students watch and listen to Sarah talk about how her grandma inspires her.

Culture: Students watch and listen to Sarah talk about an African safari her friend has been on.

Grammar animations: Students watch a visual presentation of the unit grammar.

Key competences

Linguistic
pages 64-67, 70-71

Mathematical and Science and Technology
pages 66-69

Digital
pages 64-66, 71

Social and Civic
pages 65, 67, 69, 70-71

Cultural awareness and expression
pages 64, 69, 71

Learning to learn
pages 65, 68, 70-71

Sense of initiative and entrepreneurship
pages 65, 67, 70

→ See pages 42-43 **Key competences**

CEFR Mediation

7.1 Note-taking
Can make simple notes with familiar subject matter.

7.2 Relaying specific information in speech
Can relay specific relevant information in short texts on familiar subjects.

7.3 Facilitating collaborative interaction with peers
Can collaborate in simple, shared tasks.

7.4 Processing text in writing
Can pick out and reproduce key words and phrases from a text.

7.5 Processing text in speech
Can convey the main points in short spoken texts.

Project Facilitating collaborative interaction with peers
Can invite others to contribute to very simple tasks using short, simple phrases.

Unit review Relaying specific information in writing
Can relay in writing specific information in short texts.

Pairwork Collaborating to construct meaning
Can express an idea with very simple words and ask what others think.

→ See pages 30-33 **Mediation**

Remind students to do all the exercises in their notebook

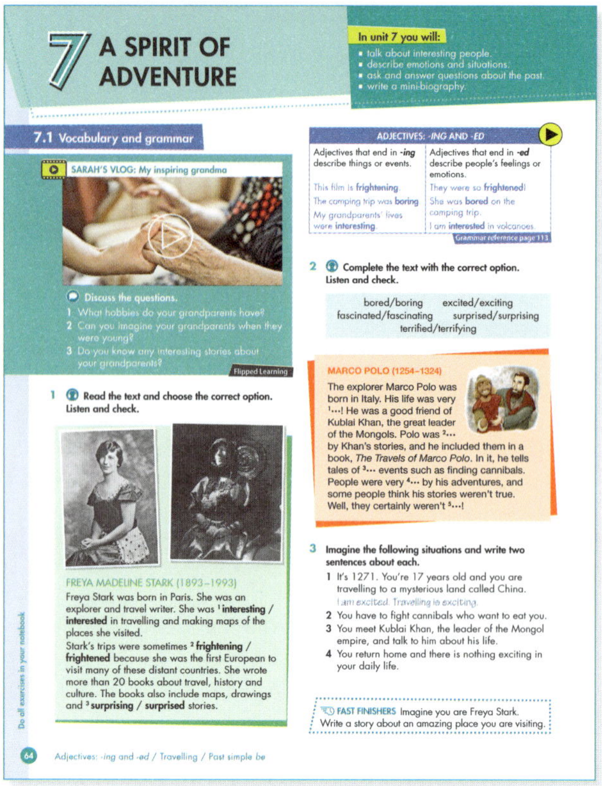

7 A SPIRIT OF ADVENTURE

In unit 7 you will:
- talk about interesting people.
- describe emotions and situations.
- ask and answer questions about the past.
- write a mini-biography.

7.1 Vocabulary and grammar

SARAH'S VLOG: My inspiring grandma

Discuss the questions.
1 What hobbies do your grandparents have?
2 Can you imagine your grandparents when they were young?
3 Do you know any interesting stories about your grandparents?

Flipped Learning

1 Read the text and choose the correct option. Listen and check.

FREYA MADELINE STARK (1893–1993)
Freya Stark was born in Paris. She was an explorer and travel writer. She was [1] **interesting** / **interested** in travelling and making maps of the places she visited.
Stark's trips were sometimes [2] **frightening** / **frightened** because she was the first European to visit many of these distant countries. She wrote more than 20 books about travel, history and culture. The books also include maps, drawings and [3] **surprising** / **surprised** stories.

ADJECTIVES: -ING AND -ED	
Adjectives that end in **-ing** describe things or events.	Adjectives that end in **-ed** describe people's feelings or emotions.
This film is **frightening**.	They were so **frightened**!
The camping trip was **boring**	She was **bored** on the camping trip.
My grandparents' lives were **interesting**.	I am **interested** in volcanoes.

Grammar reference page 113

2 Complete the text with the correct option. Listen and check.

bored/boring excited/exciting fascinated/fascinating surprised/surprising terrified/terrifying

MARCO POLO (1254–1324)
The explorer Marco Polo was born in Italy. His life was very [1]…! He was a good friend of Kublai Khan, the great leader of the Mongols. Polo was [2]… by Khan's stories, and he included them in a book, *The Travels of Marco Polo*. In it, he tells tales of [3]… events such as finding cannibals. People were very [4]… by his adventures, and some people think his stories weren't true. Well, they certainly weren't [5]…!

3 Imagine the following situations and write two sentences about each.
1 It's 1271. You're 17 years old and you are travelling to a mysterious land called China.
I am excited. Travelling is exciting.
2 You have to fight cannibals who want to eat you.
3 You meet Kublai Khan, the leader of the Mongol empire, and talk to him about his life.
4 You return home and there is nothing exciting in your daily life.

FAST FINISHERS Imagine you are Freya Stark. Write a story about an amazing place you are visiting.

Do all exercises in your notebook

64 Adjectives: -ing and -ed / Travelling / Past simple *be*

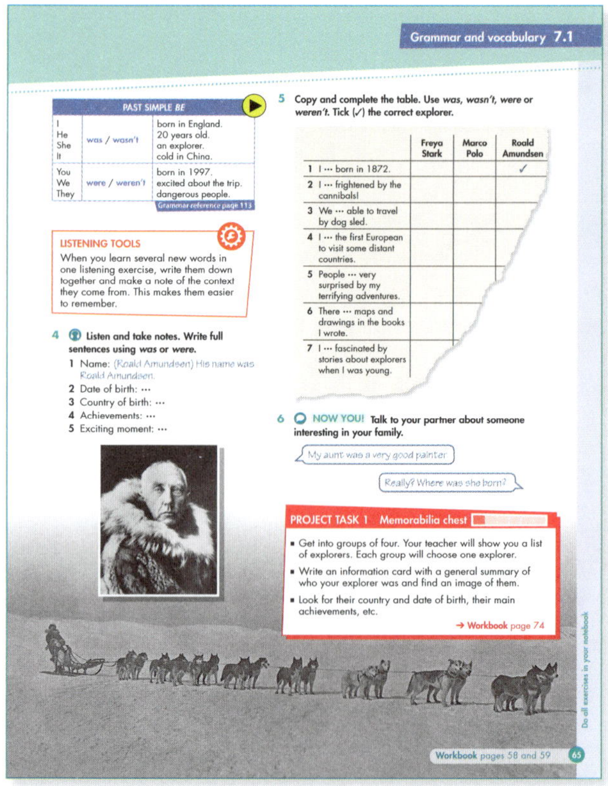

Grammar and vocabulary 7.1

PAST SIMPLE *BE*		
I He She It	was / wasn't	born in England. 20 years old. an explorer. cold in China.
You We They	were / weren't	born in 1997. excited about the trip. dangerous people.

Grammar reference page 113

LISTENING TOOLS
When you learn several new words in one listening exercise, write them down together and make a note of the context they come from. This makes them easier to remember.

4 Listen and take notes. Write full sentences using *was* or *were*.
1 Name: (Roald Amundsen) His name was Roald Amundsen.
2 Date of birth: …
3 Country of birth: …
4 Achievements: …
5 Exciting moment: …

5 Copy and complete the table. Use *was, wasn't, were* or *weren't*. Tick (✓) the correct explorer.

	Freya Stark	Marco Polo	Roald Amundsen
1 I … born in 1872.			✓
2 I … frightened by the cannibals!			
3 We … able to travel by dog sled.			
4 I … the first European to visit some distant countries.			
5 People … very surprised by my terrifying adventures.			
6 There … maps and drawings in the books I wrote.			
7 I … fascinated by stories about explorers when I was young.			

6 NOW YOU! Talk to your partner about someone interesting in your family.

My aunt was a very good painter

Really? Where was she born?

PROJECT TASK 1 Memorabilia chest
- Get into groups of four. Your teacher will show you a list of explorers. Each group will choose one explorer.
- Write an information card with a general summary of who your explorer was and find an image of them.
- Look for their country and date of birth, their main achievements, etc.

→ Workbook page 74

Do all exercises in your notebook

Workbook pages 58 and 59 65

ANSWER KEY

Pages 64-65

1
1 interested
2 frightening
3 surprising

2
1 exciting
2 fascinated
3 terrifying
4 surprised
5 boring

3 Suggested answers:
1 I am excited. Travelling is exciting.
2 I am terrified. Fighting cannibals is terrifying.
3 I am fascinated. Kublai Khan's life is fascinating.
4 I am bored. My daily life is boring.

4
1 His name was Roald Amundsen.
2 He was born on July 16th, 1872.
3 He was born in Norway.
4 He was the first person to travel to both the North Pole and the South Pole.
5 One of his most exciting moments was when the Inuit people taught him how to use dog sleds to travel faster.

5

	Freya Stark	Marco Polo	Roald Amundsen
1 I **was** born in 1872.			✓
2 I **was** frightened by the cannibals!		✓	
3 We **were** able to travel by dog sled.			✓
4 I **was** the first European to visit some distant countries.	✓		
5 People **were** very surprised by my terrifying adventures.		✓	
6 There **were** maps and drawings in the books I wrote.	✓		
7 I **was** fascinated by stories about explorers when I was young.			✓

6 *Student's own answers*

Remind students to do all the exercises in their notebook

LESSON FOCUS

Grammar Adjectives: *-ing* and *-ed*; Past simple *be*
Vocabulary Travelling
Listening Biographical information
Speaking Share biographical information about family members
Project task 1 Make an information card with a summary of a famous explorer

Resources

Teacher's i-solutions, Student's Book audio, Vlog and worksheet

Flipped Learning

SARAH'S VLOG: My inspiring grandma

- Make sure to set up the **Flipped Learning** work with the students beforehand. **See pages 20-23 for complete Flipped Learning guidelines.**
- Ask students to put the **Flipped Learning worksheets** on their desks and walk around to check how many have completed the Flipped task.
- In pairs or small groups, ask students to compare and check the *Before you watch…* and *While you watch…* exercises on the worksheet.
- Show students **Sarah's vlog** and ask volunteers to provide correct answers and clarify any doubts other students may have.
- Choose three or four students to read aloud their answers to the *After you watch…* exercises on the worksheet and encourage some class discussion.
- Move straight to exercise 1 on page 64.

Warmer

Watch Sarah's vlog and discuss the questions with the whole class. If you don't have video facilities, simply discuss the questions.

1 2.11 (See page 176 for transcripts) Before doing the exercise, ask students to cover the text and look at the photos. In pairs, students guess who Freya Stark was, where and when she lived, and what she did. Students then complete the exercise.

Flipped Learning

ADJECTIVES: *-ING* AND *-ED*

Draw students' attention to the **Grammar table**. Remind students that they can use this as a quick reference while completing the exercises.

Show students the **Grammar animation** and/or refer students to the **Grammar reference** on page 113 for further information on form and use.

→ See page 23 for how to flip the **grammar lesson**

2 2.12 (See page 176 for transcripts) Ask students to tell you everything they know about Marco Polo; write key words/phrases on the board. Students then complete the exercise.

3 Ask students to quickly tell you the difference between adjectives ending in *-ed* and *-ing*. Students then complete the exercise.

FAST FINISHERS Students can complete this exercise alone or in pairs.

Flipped Learning

PAST SIMPLE *BE*

Draw students' attention to the **Grammar table**. Remind students that they can use this as a quick reference while completing the exercises.

Show students the **Grammar animation** and/or refer students to the **Grammar reference** on page 113 for further information on form and use.

→ See page 23 for how to flip the **grammar lesson**

LISTENING TOOLS

In the centre of the board write the word *Explorers*. Tell students to call out associated words and write them on the board. Tell students to read the **Listening tool** and discuss why this would be helpful.

4 2.13 (See page 176 for transcripts) In pairs tell students to look at the picture of Roald Amundsen and guess the rest of the answers before listening. Once students have listened, tell them to make sure their answers are full sentences.

5 Divide the class into groups of three. Give each student in the group the name of one of the explorers to quickly review. Groups can then complete the table together.

6 **NOW YOU!** Ask students to think back to Sarah's vlog about her inspiring grandma (show the video again if needed). Tell students to make notes about an interesting member of their family to discuss with their partner.

PROJECT TASK 1
Memorabilia chest

Organise students into groups of four. Tell students that during this project they will be putting together a memorabilia chest and presenting it to the rest of the class. Tell students that they need to keep their project notes together in their **Workbook** (page 74) or in their own notebook.

→ See pages 24-27 **Projects**

FURTHER PRACTICE

Workbook pages 58-59
- **Grammar reference and practice** pages 90 and 95
- **Wordlist and exercises** pages 101 and 104

Remind students to do all the exercises in their notebook

CONTINUOUS ASSESSMENT Students can talk about travelling and use *-ing* and *-ed* adjectives and the past simple *be*.

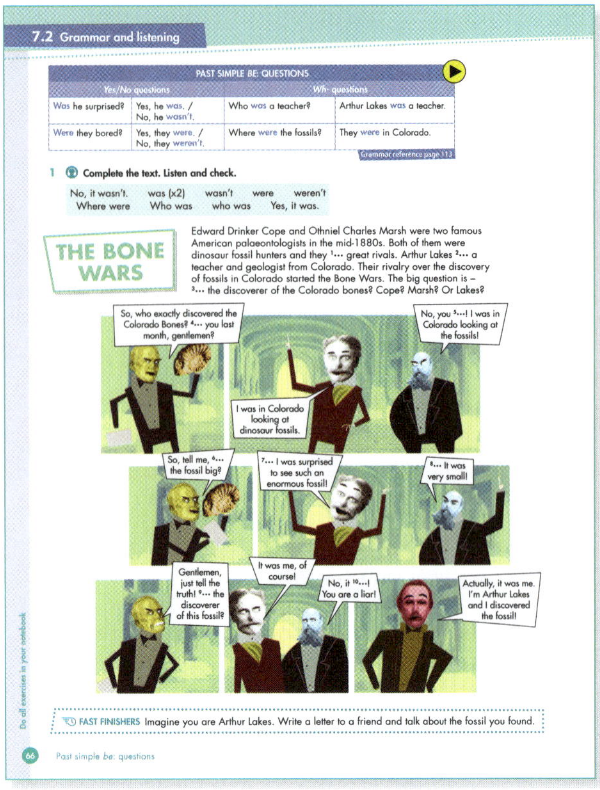

7.2 Grammar and listening

PAST SIMPLE BE: QUESTIONS			
Yes/No questions		Wh- questions	
Was he surprised?	Yes, he was. / No, he wasn't.	Who was a teacher?	Arthur Lakes was a teacher.
Were they bored?	Yes, they were. / No, they weren't.	Where were the fossils?	They were in Colorado.

Grammar reference page 113

1 Complete the text. Listen and check.

No, it wasn't. was (x2) wasn't were weren't Where were Who was who was Yes, it was.

THE BONE WARS

Edward Drinker Cope and Othniel Charles Marsh were two famous American palaeontologists in the mid-1880s. Both of them were dinosaur fossil hunters and they [1]··· great rivals. Arthur Lakes [2]··· a teacher and geologist from Colorado. Their rivalry over the discovery of fossils in Colorado started the Bone Wars. The big question is – [3]··· the discoverer of the Colorado bones? Cope? Marsh? Or Lakes?

FAST FINISHERS Imagine you are Arthur Lakes. Write a letter to a friend and talk about the fossil you found.

Do all exercises in your notebook

66 Past simple be: questions

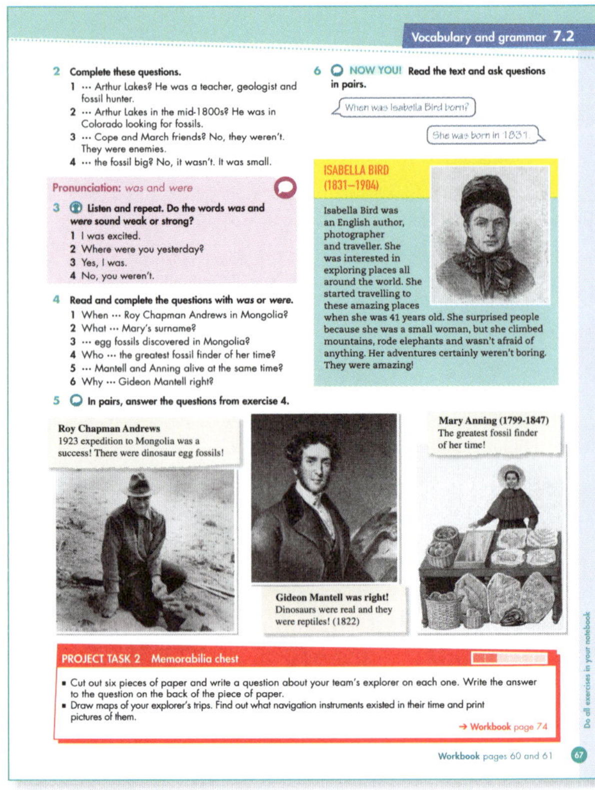

Vocabulary and grammar 7.2

2 Complete these questions.
1 ··· Arthur Lakes? He was a teacher, geologist and fossil hunter.
2 ··· Arthur Lakes in the mid-1800s? He was in Colorado looking for fossils.
3 ··· Cope and March friends? No, they weren't. They were enemies.
4 ··· the fossil big? No, it wasn't. It was small.

Pronunciation: *was* and *were*

3 Listen and repeat. Do the words *was* and *were* sound weak or strong?
1 I was excited.
2 Where were you yesterday?
3 Yes, I was.
4 No, you weren't.

4 Read and complete the questions with *was* or *were*.
1 When ··· Roy Chapman Andrews in Mongolia?
2 What ··· Mary's surname?
3 ··· egg fossils discovered in Mongolia?
4 Who ··· the greatest fossil finder of her time?
5 ··· Mantell and Anning alive at the same time?
6 Why ··· Gideon Mantell right?

5 In pairs, answer the questions from exercise 4.

6 NOW YOU! Read the text and ask questions in pairs.

ISABELLA BIRD (1831–1904)

Isabella Bird was an English author, photographer and traveller. She was interested in exploring places all around the world. She started travelling to these amazing places when she was 41 years old. She surprised people because she was a small woman, but she climbed mountains, rode elephants and wasn't afraid of anything. Her adventures certainly weren't boring. They were amazing!

Roy Chapman Andrews
1923 expedition to Mongolia was a success! There were dinosaur egg fossils!

Gideon Mantell was right!
Dinosaurs were real and they were reptiles! (1822)

Mary Anning (1799-1847)
The greatest fossil finder of her time!

PROJECT TASK 2 Memorabilia chest

- Cut out six pieces of paper and write a question about your team's explorer on each one. Write the answer to the question on the back of the piece of paper.
- Draw maps of your explorer's trips. Find out what navigation instruments existed in their time and print pictures of them.

→ Workbook page 74

Workbook pages 60 and 61 67

Do all exercises in your notebook

ANSWER KEY

Pages 66-67

1
1 were
2 was
3 who was
4 Where were
5 weren't
6 was
7 Yes, it was.
8 No, it wasn't.
9 Who was
10 wasn't

2
1 Who was
2 Where was
3 Were
4 Was

3
1 weak
2 weak
3 strong
4 strong

4
1 was
2 was
3 Were
4 was
5 Were
6 was

5
1 He was in Mongolia in 1923.
2 Her surname was 'Anning'.
3 Yes, they were.
4 Mary Anning was.
5 Yes, they were.
6 Dinosaurs were real and they were reptiles.

6 *Student's own answers*

LESSON FOCUS

Grammar Past simple *be*: questions
Vocabulary Famous explorers
Listening Biographical information
Speaking Sharing biographical information about famous explorers
Project task 2 Draw a map and collect information about an explorer

Resources
Teacher's i-solutions, Student's Book audio

Preparation Paper and scissors for each Project group

Warmer

Ask students if they know what a *palaeontologist* is (a person who studies forms of life from prehistoric times). In pairs, tell students the year is 3000 and that they are both palaeontologists. Students take turns to point out things around the classroom or their personal belongings and their partner must describe what the items were and what they were used for.

PAST SIMPLE *BE*: QUESTIONS

Flipped Learning

Draw students' attention to the **Grammar table**. Remind students that they can use this as a quick reference while completing the exercises.

Show students the **Grammar animation** and/or refer students to the **Grammar reference** on page 113 for further information on form and use.

→ See page 23 for how to flip the **grammar lesson**

1 2.14 (See page 176 for transcripts) Write *The Bone Wars* on the board and some key vocabulary from the text: *palaeontologists*, 1800s, *fossil hunters*, *rivals*, *Colorado*. In pairs, ask students to guess what the text is about. Students then complete the exercise.

FAST FINISHERS Students can complete this exercise alone or in pairs.

2 Ask students to look at the answers to the questions and decide if they are *wh-* or *yes/no* questions and if they refer to people, places or things. Students then complete the exercise.

Pronunciation

3 2.15 (See page 176 for transcripts) On the board write the strong and weak forms of *was* and *were* in phonetic script and drill.

	Strong	Weak
was	/wɒz/	/wəz/
were	/wɜː/	/wə/

4 Before completing the questions, refer students to the **Grammar table** on page 66. Students then complete the exercise.

5 In pairs, students look back at exercise 4 and decide what type of information they need to answer the questions. Students then complete the exercise.

6 **NOW YOU!** Tell students to read the text and prepare 5 questions about Isabella Bird. Students now close their books and test their partner's memory using their questions.

PROJECT TASK 2
Memorabilia chest

Tell students to get into their groups from Task 1. Remind students they are putting together a memorabilia chest and presenting it to the rest of the class. Tell students that they need to keep their project notes together in their **Workbook** (page 74) or in their own notebook.

→ See pages 24-27 **Projects**

FURTHER PRACTICE

Workbook pages 60-61
- **Grammar reference and practice** pages 90 and 95
- **Wordlist and exercises** pages 101 and 104

Vocabulary and Grammar worksheets available to download and edit from the **Richmond** *Learning* **Platform**

→ See pages 38-39 **Mixed-ability classes**

Remind students to do all the exercises in their notebook

CONTINUOUS ASSESSMENT Students can use *be* in past simple questions.

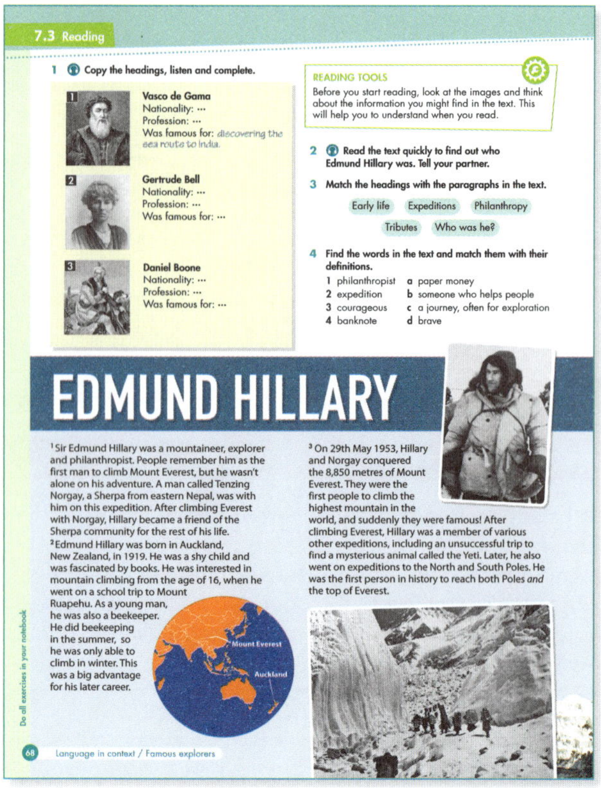

1 Copy the headings, listen and complete.

1 **Vasco de Gama**
Nationality: ···
Profession: ···
Was famous for: discovering the sea route to India.

2 **Gertrude Bell**
Nationality: ···
Profession: ···
Was famous for: ···

3 **Daniel Boone**
Nationality: ···
Profession: ···
Was famous for: ···

READING TOOLS
Before you start reading, look at the images and think about the information you might find in the text. This will help you to understand when you read.

2 Read the text quickly to find out who Edmund Hillary was. Tell your partner.

3 Match the headings with the paragraphs in the text.

Early life / Expeditions / Philanthropy / Tributes / Who was he?

4 Find the words in the text and match them with their definitions.

1 philanthropist — a paper money
2 expedition — b someone who helps people
3 courageous — c a journey, often for exploration
4 banknote — d brave

EDMUND HILLARY

[1] Sir Edmund Hillary was a mountaineer, explorer and philanthropist. People remember him as the first man to climb Mount Everest, but he wasn't alone on his adventure. A man called Tenzing Norgay, a Sherpa from eastern Nepal, was with him on this expedition. After climbing Everest with Norgay, Hillary became a friend of the Sherpa community for the rest of his life.

[2] Edmund Hillary was born in Auckland, New Zealand, in 1919. He was a shy child and was fascinated by books. He was interested in mountain climbing from the age of 16, when he went on a school trip to Mount Ruapehu. As a young man, he was also a beekeeper. He did beekeeping in the summer, so he was only able to climb in winter. This was a big advantage for his later career.

Mount Everest
Auckland

[3] On 29th May 1953, Hillary and Norgay conquered the 8,850 metres of Mount Everest. They were the first people to climb the highest mountain in the world, and suddenly they were famous! After climbing Everest, Hillary was a member of various other expeditions, including an unsuccessful trip to find a mysterious animal called the Yeti. Later, he also went on expeditions to the North and South Poles. He was the first person in history to reach both Poles *and* the top of Everest.

Do all exercises in your notebook

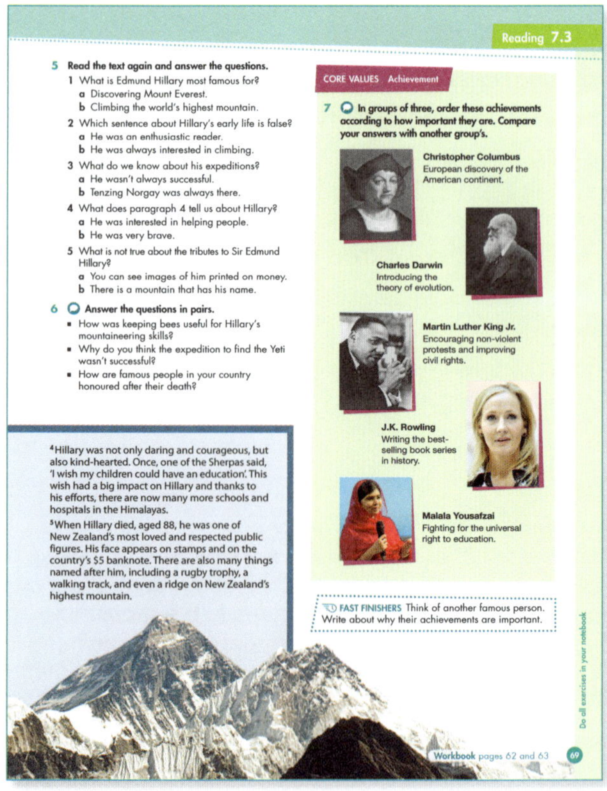

5 Read the text again and answer the questions.

1 What is Edmund Hillary most famous for?
a Discovering Mount Everest.
b Climbing the world's highest mountain.

2 Which sentence about Hillary's early life is false?
a He was an enthusiastic reader.
b He was always interested in climbing.

3 What do we know about his expeditions?
a He wasn't always successful.
b Tenzing Norgay was always there.

4 What does paragraph 4 tell us about Hillary?
a He was interested in helping people.
b He was very brave.

5 What is not true about the tributes to Sir Edmund Hillary?
a You can see images of him printed on money.
b There is a mountain that has his name.

6 Answer the questions in pairs.
- How was keeping bees useful for Hillary's mountaineering skills?
- Why do you think the expedition to find the Yeti wasn't successful?
- How are famous people in your country honoured after their death?

[4] Hillary was not only daring and courageous, but also kind-hearted. Once, one of the Sherpas said, 'I wish my children could have an education'. This wish had a big impact on Hillary and thanks to his efforts, there are now many more schools and hospitals in the Himalayas.

[5] When Hillary died, aged 88, he was one of New Zealand's most loved and respected public figures. His face appears on stamps and on the country's $5 banknote. There are also many things named after him, including a rugby trophy, a walking track, and even a ridge on New Zealand's highest mountain.

CORE VALUES Achievement

7 In groups of three, order these achievements according to how important they are. Compare your answers with another group's.

Christopher Columbus European discovery of the American continent.

Charles Darwin Introducing the theory of evolution.

Martin Luther King Jr. Encouraging non-violent protests and improving civil rights.

J.K. Rowling Writing the best-selling book series in history.

Malala Yousafzai Fighting for the universal right to education.

FAST FINISHERS Think of another famous person. Write about why their achievements are important.

Do all exercises in your notebook

ANSWER KEY

Pages 68-69

1
1 Nationality: Portuguese; Profession: ocean explorer; Was famous for: discovering the sea route to India
2 Nationality: English; Profession: archaeologist; Was famous for: her work in the Middle East
3 Nationality: American; Profession: explorer; Was famous for: establishing the first colony in Kentucky

2 *Student's own answers*

3
Early life: 2
Expeditions: 3
Philanthropy: 4
Tributes: 5
Who was he?: 1

4
1 b
2 c
3 d
4 a

5
1 b
2 b
3 a
4 b
5 b

6 *Student's own answers*

7 *Student's own answers*

Remind students to do all the exercises in their notebook

LESSON FOCUS

Language in context Famous explorers

Core values Achievement

Resources

Teacher's i-solutions, Student's Book audio

Preparation Large map of the continents

→ See pages 36-37 **Literature**

Warmer

Ask students to name the seven continents of the world: Asia, Africa, North America, South America, Antarctica, Europe, Australia. Put the continent map on the board. In small groups, ask students to list discoveries that were made on each continent.

1 2.16 (See page 176 for transcripts) In pairs, ask students to make notes about what they think they are going to hear and the context of each answer. Students then complete the exercise.

READING TOOLS

Tell students to read the **Reading tool** and discuss why this would be helpful. Tell students to look at the photos in the reading text and decide what they can deduce about the content.

2 2.17 (See page 177 for transcripts) Along with their **Reading tool** ideas, tell students to make short notes about the text.

3 Before reading the text again, ask students if they can match the notes they made in exercise 2 to the paragraph headings.

4 Tell students they have thirty seconds to scan the text for the words before matching with the definitions.

5 Tell students to discuss the questions in pairs, then read the text again and answer.

6 Before answering the questions, ask students to call out any facts they remember about Edmund Hillary.

CORE VALUES Achievement

7 Tell students to write notes on why they have chosen to order the achievements in that particular way before they compare with another group. You may want to make a definitive class order.

FAST FINISHERS Students can complete this exercise alone or in pairs.

Remind students to do all the exercises in their notebook

FURTHER PRACTICE
Workbook pages 62-63

CONTINUOUS ASSESSMENT Students can use vocabulary related to famous explorers to understand the biography of an explorer.

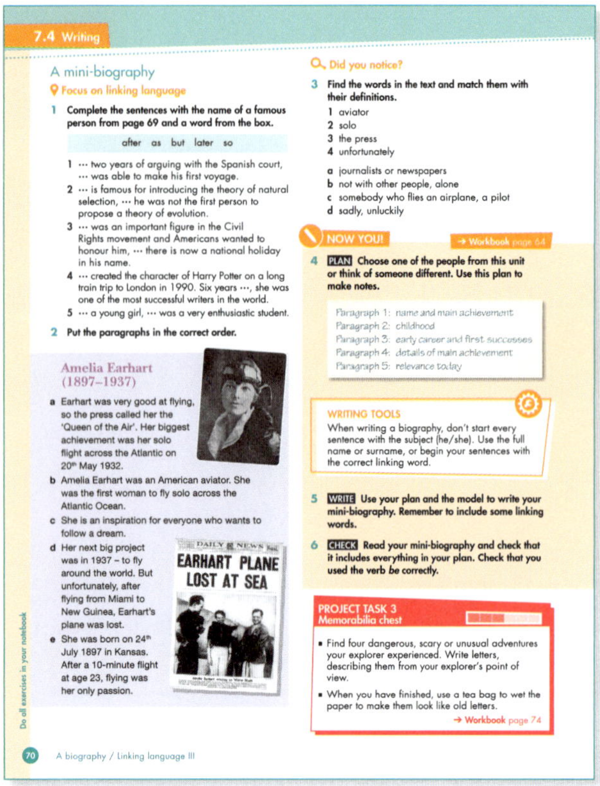
7.4 Writing

A mini-biography

Focus on linking language

1 **Complete the sentences with the name of a famous person from page 69 and a word from the box.**

after as but later so

1 ··· two years of arguing with the Spanish court, ··· was able to make his first voyage.
2 ··· is famous for introducing the theory of natural selection, ··· he was not the first person to propose a theory of evolution.
3 ··· was an important figure in the Civil Rights movement and Americans wanted to honour him, ··· there is now a national holiday in his name.
4 ··· created the character of Harry Potter on a long train trip to London in 1990. Six years ···, she was one of the most successful writers in the world.
5 ··· a young girl, ··· was a very enthusiastic student.

2 **Put the paragraphs in the correct order.**

Amelia Earhart (1897–1937)

a Earhart was very good at flying, so the press called her the 'Queen of the Air'. Her biggest achievement was her solo flight across the Atlantic on 20th May 1932.
b Amelia Earhart was an American aviator. She was the first woman to fly solo across the Atlantic Ocean.
c She is an inspiration for everyone who wants to follow a dream.
d Her next big project was in 1937 – to fly around the world. But unfortunately, after flying from Miami to New Guinea, Earhart's plane was lost.
e She was born on 24th July 1897 in Kansas. After a 10-minute flight at age 23, flying was her only passion.

Did you notice?

3 **Find the words in the text and match them with their definitions.**

1 aviator
2 solo
3 the press
4 unfortunately

a journalists or newspapers
b not with other people, alone
c somebody who flies an airplane, a pilot
d sadly, unluckily

NOW YOU! → Workbook page 64

4 PLAN **Choose one of the people from this unit or think of someone different. Use this plan to make notes.**

Paragraph 1: name and main achievement
Paragraph 2: childhood
Paragraph 3: early career and first successes
Paragraph 4: details of main achievement
Paragraph 5: relevance today

WRITING TOOLS
When writing a biography, don't start every sentence with the subject (he/she). Use the full name or surname, or begin your sentences with the correct linking word.

5 WRITE **Use your plan and the model to write your mini-biography. Remember to include some linking words.**

6 CHECK **Read your mini-biography and check that it includes everything in your plan. Check that you used the verb *be* correctly.**

PROJECT TASK 3
Memorabilia chest
- Find four dangerous, scary or unusual adventures your explorer experienced. Write letters, describing them from your explorer's point of view.
- When you have finished, use a tea bag to wet the paper to make them look like old letters.

→ Workbook page 74

Do all exercises in your notebook

70 A biography / Linking language III

ANSWER KEY

Page 70

1 **1** After; Christopher Columbus
2 Charles Darwin; but
3 Martin Luther King Jr.; so
4 J.K. Rowling; later
5 As; Malala Yousafzai

2 b, e, a, d, c

3 **1** c
2 b
3 a
4 d

4 *Student's own answers*

5 *Student's own answers*

6 *Student's own answers*

LESSON FOCUS

Focus on Linking language III: *after, as, but, later, so*
Writing Mini-biography

Resources
Teacher's i-solutions

Project task 3 Write a letter from an explorer

Warmer

On the board write the names of the famous people students looked at in the previous lesson. In pairs students discuss what they can remember.

Focus on linking language

1 Write the following on the board and ask students to match the words to the famous people in the previous lesson: *Spanish court, theory of natural selection, Civil Rights Movement, Harry Potter, enthusiastic student.* Students can then complete the exercise.

2 Ask students to look at the photo and what initial questions they would ask about her – name, date of birth, etc. Tell students to scan the text for the opening paragraph (b). Students can then order the rest.

Did you notice?

3 When students have finished the exercise, they can choose three more words from the text and write a single word definition.

4 **PLAN** Once students have finished their plan, encourage them to talk it through with a partner.

WRITING TOOLS

Tell students to read the **Writing tool** and discuss why this would be helpful. Tell students that this is something they should remember when they reach the 'check' stage.

5 **WRITE** Before students start writing, make a checklist on the board of any grammar, vocabulary, punctuation and any other language elements they should consider.

6 **CHECK** Once students have checked their own biographies, they can swap with a partner and check theirs.

PROJECT TASK 3
Memorabilia chest

Tell students to get into their groups from Tasks 1 and 2. Remind students they are putting together a memorabilia chest and presenting it to the rest of the class. Tell students that they need to keep their project notes together in their **Workbook** (page 74) or in their own notebook.

→ See pages 24-27 **Projects**

FURTHER PRACTICE

Workbook page 64

Remind students to do all the exercises in their notebook

CONTINUOUS ASSESSMENT Students can use appropriate linking language to write a mini-biography.

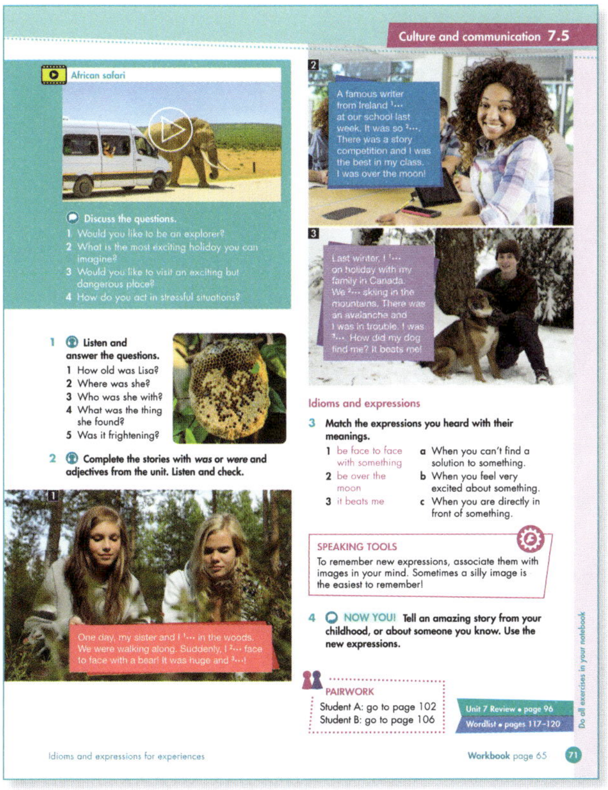

Culture and communication 7.5

African safari

Discuss the questions.
1 Would you like to be an explorer?
2 What is the most exciting holiday you can imagine?
3 Would you like to visit an exciting but dangerous place?
4 How do you act in stressful situations?

1 Listen and answer the questions.
1 How old was Lisa?
2 Where was she?
3 Who was she with?
4 What was the thing she found?
5 Was it frightening?

2 Complete the stories with *was* or *were* and adjectives from the unit. Listen and check.

1 One day, my sister and I [1]… in the woods. We were walking along. Suddenly, I [2]… face to face with a bear! It was huge and [3]…!

2 A famous writer from Ireland [1]… at our school last week. It was so [2]…. There was a story competition and I was the best in my class. I was over the moon!

3 Last winter, I [1]… on holiday with my family in Canada. We [2]… skiing in the mountains. There was an avalanche and I was in trouble. I was [3]…. How did my dog find me? It beats me!

Idioms and expressions

3 Match the expressions you heard with their meanings.
1 be face to face with something — a When you can't find a solution to something.
2 be over the moon — b When you feel very excited about something.
3 it beats me — c When you are directly in front of something.

SPEAKING TOOLS
To remember new expressions, associate them with images in your mind. Sometimes a silly image is the easiest to remember!

4 NOW YOU! Tell an amazing story from your childhood, or about someone you know. Use the new expressions.

PAIRWORK
Student A: go to page 102
Student B: go to page 106

Unit 7 Review • page 96
Wordlist • pages 117–120

Do all exercises in your notebook

Idioms and expressions for experiences

Workbook page 65

71

ANSWER KEY

Page 71

1 **1** She was eight years old.
2 She was in the garden.
3 She was with her cousin Rick.
4 It was a beehive.
5 Yes, it was.

2 **1** 1 were; 2 was; 3 terrifying
2 1 was; 2 interesting
3 1 was; 2 were; 3 terrified

3 **1** c **2** b **3** a

4 *Student's own answers*

FURTHER PRACTICE AND UNIT ASSESSMENT

Unit 7 Review **Student's Book** page 96
Workbook page 65
- Reflect on your learning page 65
- Grammar reference and practice pages 90 and 95
- Wordlist and exercises pages 101 and 104

Tests available to download and edit from the **Richmond** *Learning* **Platform**

➔ See pages 40-41 **Assessment**

LESSON FOCUS

Idioms and expressions Experiences
Listening Taking notes on a story
Speaking Telling stories about experiences

Resources

Teacher's i-solutions, Student's Book audio, Culture video and worksheet

African safari

- In pairs, ask students to complete the *What I know…* exercises on the **Culture video worksheet**.
- Show students the **Culture video** and ask them to complete the *What I learned…* exercises on the worksheet.
- In pairs, students compare answers.
- In small groups, tell students to complete the *What I wonder…* exercises on the worksheet.

Warmer

Watch the culture video and discuss the questions with the whole class. If you don't have video facilities, simply discuss the questions.

1 2.18 (See page 177 for transcripts) Ask students to quickly predict what information they need to listen out for, e.g. *How old was Lisa?* (A number).

2 2.19 (See page 177 for transcripts) Review the form and use of adjectives ending in *-ing* and *-ed* and past simple *be* (see **Grammar tables** on pages 64 and 65) with the students.

Idioms and expressions

3 Ask students to find expressions 1-3 in the texts in exercise 2. In pairs, students discuss what they think the expressions mean via the context.

SPEAKING TOOLS

Tell students to read the **Speaking tool** and discuss why this would be helpful. Ask students to draw something that represents the expressions in exercise 3.

4 NOW YOU! Ask students to think of a strange thing that happened to them and make some notes trying to include the expressions in exercise 3.

PAIRWORK **Student's Book** pages 102 and 106
See **Teacher's Book** page 140 for more information.
➔ See pages 30-33 **Mediation**

Remind students to do all the exercises in their notebook

Unit 7 Review

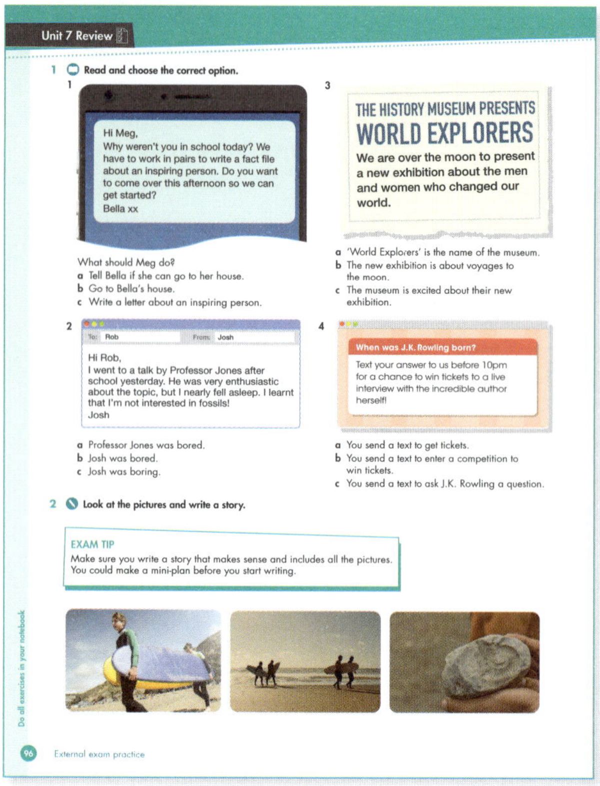

Unit 7 Review

1 Read and choose the correct option.

1

Hi Meg,
Why weren't you in school today? We have to work in pairs to write a fact file about an inspiring person. Do you want to come over this afternoon so we can get started?
Bella xx

What should Meg do?
a Tell Bella if she can go to her house.
b Go to Bella's house.
c Write a letter about an inspiring person.

2

To: Rob From: Josh

Hi Rob,
I went to a talk by Professor Jones after school yesterday. He was very enthusiastic about the topic, but I nearly fell asleep. I learnt that I'm not interested in fossils!
Josh

a Professor Jones was bored.
b Josh was bored.
c Josh was boring.

3

THE HISTORY MUSEUM PRESENTS
WORLD EXPLORERS
We are over the moon to present a new exhibition about the men and women who changed our world.

a 'World Explorers' is the name of the museum.
b The new exhibition is about voyages to the moon.
c The museum is excited about their new exhibition.

4

When was J.K. Rowling born?
Text your answer to us before 10pm for a chance to win tickets to a live interview with the incredible author herself!

a You send a text to get tickets.
b You send a text to enter a competition to win tickets.
c You send a text to ask J.K. Rowling a question.

2 Look at the pictures and write a story.

EXAM TIP
Make sure you write a story that makes sense and includes all the pictures. You could make a mini-plan before you start writing.

Do all exercises in your notebook

96 External exam practice

Student's Book page 96

ANSWER KEY

1 **1** a
2 b
3 c
4 b

2 *Student's own answers*

Pairwork

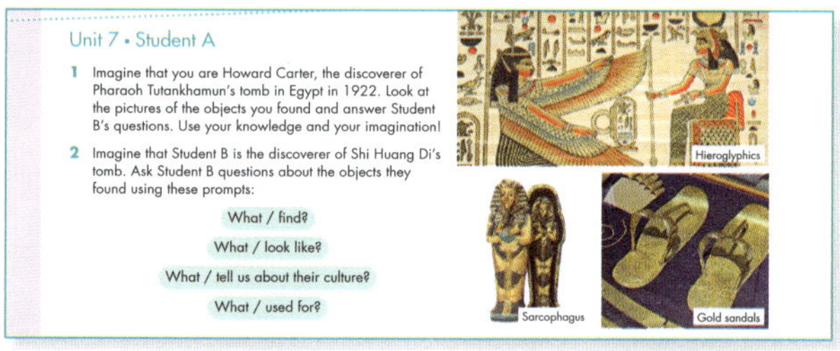

Unit 7 • Student A

1 Imagine that you are Howard Carter, the discoverer of Pharaoh Tutankhamun's tomb in Egypt in 1922. Look at the pictures of the objects you found and answer Student B's questions. Use your knowledge and your imagination!

2 Imagine that Student B is the discoverer of Shi Huang Di's tomb. Ask Student B questions about the objects they found using these prompts:

What / find?
What / look like?
What / tell us about their culture?
What / used for?

Hieroglyphics
Sarcophagus
Gold sandals

Student's Book page 102

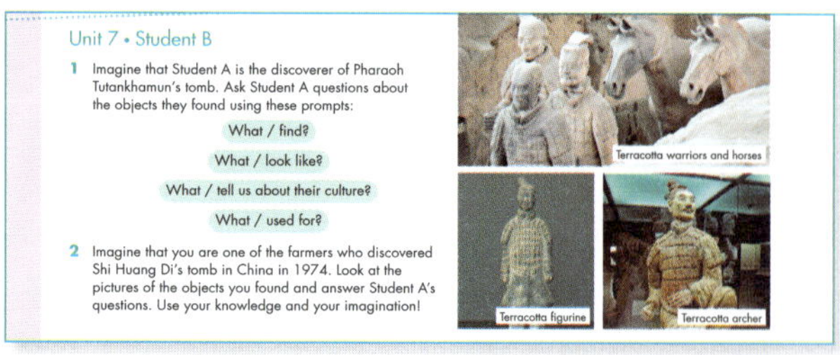

Unit 7 • Student B

1 Imagine that Student A is the discoverer of Pharaoh Tutankhamun's tomb. Ask Student A questions about the objects they found using these prompts:

What / find?
What / look like?
What / tell us about their culture?
What / used for?

2 Imagine that you are one of the farmers who discovered Shi Huang Di's tomb in China in 1974. Look at the pictures of the objects you found and answer Student A's questions. Use your knowledge and your imagination!

Terracotta warriors and horses
Terracotta figurine
Terracotta archer

Student's Book page 106

CEFR MEDIATION DESCRIPTOR

- **Collaborating to construct meaning**

Students can express an idea with very simple words and ask what others think.

- **Interpreting information**

Tell Student A and B that they need to convey as much information as possible to their partner. Draw students' attention to the question prompts that they can use to prepare their answers.

Remind students to do all the exercises in their notebook

Adjectives: -*ing* and -*ed*

Adjectives that end in **-*ing*** describe things or events.	Adjectives that end in **-*ed*** describe people's feelings or emotions.
This film is **frightening**.	They were so **frightened**.
The camping trip was **boring**.	She was **bored** on the camping trip.
My grandparents' lives were **interesting**.	I am **interested** in volcanoes.

Usually, adjectives ending in **-*ing*** describe a thing or a situation, and adjectives ending in **-*ed*** describe how a person is feeling.

It's an **exciting** book. The book makes me feel **excited**.

The story is **shocking**. The story makes me feel **shocked**.

Be careful!

I am feeling bored: I'm bor**ed**.

I have a boring personality: I'm bor**ing**.

Past simple *be*

I He She It	was / wasn't	born in England. 20 years old. an explorer. cold in China.
You We They	were / weren't	born in 1997. excited about the trip. dangerous people.

We use the past simple of the verb ***be*** to talk about situations or describe events in the past. ***Was*** and ***were*** do not have contracted forms in the affirmative.

It **was** a nice day.

They **were** in the classroom.

In the negative, ***not*** always comes after ***was*** and ***were***. We often use the contracted forms ***wasn't*** and ***weren't***.

He **wasn't** at school yesterday.

We **weren't** invited to your party.

We also use ***was*** and ***were*** to say when someone was born.

My sister **was** born in April.

They **were** born in the 1970s.

Past simple *be*: questions

Yes/No questions	
Was he surprised?	Yes, he was. No, he wasn't.
Were they bored?	Yes, they were. No, they weren't.

In questions, ***was*** and ***were*** come before the subject pronoun, not after.

Was she an explorer?

NOT ~~She was an explorer?~~

Were you at the museum yesterday?

NOT ~~You were at the museum yesterday?~~

Wh- questions	
Who was a teacher?	Arthur Lakes was a teacher.
Where were the fossils?	They were in Colorado.

In *wh-* questions, we add a question word before ***was*** and ***were***.

Why was she at the hospital last week?

Where were you yesterday?

Do all exercises in your notebook

Workbook pages 93–96

Student's Book page 113

Wordlist

UNIT 7

Adjectives: -*ing* and -*ed*

bored	fascinating	surprised
boring	frightened	surprising
excited	frightening	terrified
exciting	interested	terrifying
fascinated	interesting	

Travelling

countries	maps	traveller
culture	places	trips
dangerous	return home	visit
history	travel	

Famous explorers

brave	early life	philanthropy
conquer	expedition	pioneer
courageous	explorer	tribute
daring	first person	trip
discover	Mount Everest	

Do all exercises in your notebook

 Workbook pages 102–104

Student's Book page 120

2.65 2.66 2.67

Remind students to do all the exercises in their notebook

8 TELL ME A STORY

At the start of each unit and lesson, explain to the students what the objectives are.

Language objectives

Grammar

Past simple: regular and irregular verbs
- Students focus on regular and irregular forms of past simple verbs.

Past simple: questions
- Students practise *wh-* and *yes/no* question forms using regular and irregular verbs.

Vocabulary

Time expressions: *after some time, afterwards, as, before long, before that, finally, just after, just before, last weekend, last year, next, one Christmas, one day, one winter, one year, suddenly, then, when*
- Students use the time expressions in conjunction with the past simple to tell a story.

Ghost stories: *believe, blood, curious, ghost, haunted, hear, murdered, noise, plot, stain, story*
- Students use the vocabulary in context related to a ghost story.

Parts of a story: *characters, description, dialogue, drama, punctuate, setting, tension, title, twist*
- Students use the vocabulary to prepare and write a ghost story.

Idioms and expressions

Mysteries: *a shot in the dark, a skeleton in the closet, blood is thicker than water*
- Students look at the idioms and expressions related to telling a detective story.

Recycled language

Past simple *be*: affirmative, negative and questions

Skills objectives

Speaking

- Students compare endings to a story.
- Students deduce the perpetrator of a crime using evidence presented to them.
- Students discuss a ghost story.
- Students use notes in order to compare what they understood of a story.

Pronunciation: Students practise *-ed* endings /t/, /d/, /ɪd/

Pairwork: Students use various mediation techniques in order to provide information about a crime scene.

Listening

- Students listen and identify the main focus of a story, avoiding distractors.
- Students listen and take notes on a story.
- Students listen and complete notes.

Reading

- Students use a title and visuals in a text to predict the genre and content.
- Students read a text in detail in order to aid comprehension.
- Students analyse a text and deduce meaning.

Core values: Students discuss what **empathy** is and to what level they are empathetic.

Writing

- Students identify the parts of a story.
- Students plan, write and check a scary story.

Focus on the past simple

Remind students to do all the exercises in their notebook

Learning to learn tools

SPEAKING TOOLS Students look at how to take notes and use them while speaking.	LISTENING TOOLS Students look at the use of distractors and how to focus on the important content of a text. Students listen out for homophones and distinguishing words regarding context.
READING TOOLS Students focus on the main events and general idea of a story in order to follow the plot.	WRITING TOOLS Students look at the use of dialogue in a story to create interest.

Project objectives: Memorabilia chest

Task 4 Students write a role play about an explorer.

Task 5 Students write questions to ask about other explorers.

Task 6 Students make a memorabilia chest.

Audiovisual objectives

Vlog: Students watch and listen to George talk about urban myths and his experience.

Culture: Students watch and listen to George talk about Sherlock Holmes.

Grammar animations: Students are presented with visual presentations of the unit grammar.

Key competences

Linguistic
pages 72-75, 78, 79

Digital
pages 72, 79

Social and Civic
pages 73, 75, 76, 78, 79

Cultural awareness and expression
pages 76-77, 79

Learning to learn
pages 72, 75, 76, 78, 79

Sense of initiative and entrepreneurship
pages 73, 75, 78

→ See pages 42-43 **Key competences**

CEFR Mediation

8.1 Expressing a personal response to creative texts
Can express reactions to a work, reporting feelings and ideas in simple language.

8.2 Acting as intermediary in informal situations
Can communicate the main point of what is said, conveying back and forth personal information.

8.3 Analysis and criticism of creative texts
Can briefly describe the key themes and characters in short, simple narratives.

8.4 Analysis and criticism of creative texts
Can point out the most important events in a narrative and the connection between them.

8.5 Processing text in speech
Can convey the main points in short, simple spoken texts.

Project Facilitating collaborative interaction with peers
Can invite others' contributions to very simple tasks using short, simple phrases.

Unit review Processing text in speech
Can convey the main point in short, simple spoken texts.

Pairwork Generating conceptual talk
Can ask what somebody thinks of a certain idea.

→ See pages 30-33 **Mediation**

Remind students to do all the exercises in their notebook

8 TELL ME A STORY

In unit 8 you will:
- learn how to tell a story.
- talk about things that happened in the past.
- ask and answer questions about the past.
- write a scary story.

8.1 Listening and vocabulary

GEORGE'S VLOG: Urban myths

Discuss the questions.
1 What is an 'urban myth'?
2 What urban myths do you know?
3 Has something strange ever happened to you or someone you know?

Flipped Learning

LISTENING TOOLS
Remember that listening exercises sometimes include distractors; words which distract you from the correct answer.

1 **Listen and choose the best picture for each story.**

1 a b
2 a b
3 a b

2 **Choose the correct option. Listen again and check.**

1 [1] **Last weekend / Last year**, I went camping with some friends. We arrived [2] **just after / just before** lunch and we put up our tent. As we started to make lunch, we heard a strange noise. I thought it was a bear and I was really scared, so I climbed up a tree. [3] **But as / But when** I looked down, I saw it was only a goat! It walked towards the food, but it didn't eat any. Instead, it ate a sock from my backpack!

2 My grandma lives in a big old house in the country. [1] **One winter / One day**, when I was younger, I was at her house. We had dinner and told each other ghost stories. [2] **Finally / After some time**, I went to bed. As I sat in bed, I saw the curtain moving. It was strange because the window was shut. [3] **Afterwards / Suddenly**, it flew open! I shouted out to my grandma. But when she arrived, she didn't believe me. I still don't really know what happened.

3 My cousin and I like the same things. Right now, for example, we're both learning to play the guitar. [1] **One Christmas / One year**, I bought him a book. We started opening presents. [2] **Before that / Before long**, his turn came to open my present to him. [3] **Then / Next** he said, 'But this present is for you.' I showed him the label with his name on it. 'Oh,' he said. 'I think I got you the same present as you got me!'

FAST FINISHERS Write about something strange that happened to you or someone you know.

Do all exercises in your notebook

72 Time expressions / Past simple: regular and irregular

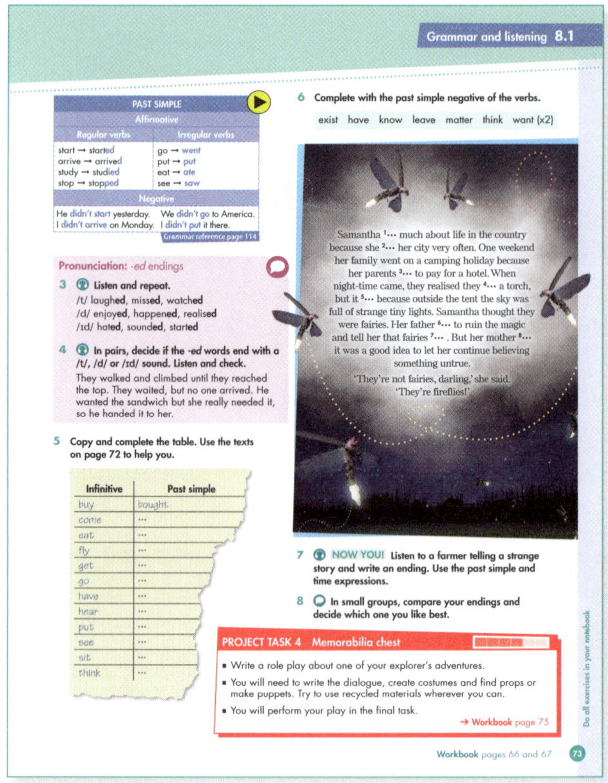

Grammar and listening 8.1

PAST SIMPLE	
Affirmative	
Regular verbs	Irregular verbs
start → started arrive → arrived study → studied stop → stopped	go → went put → put eat → ate see → saw
Negative	
He didn't start yesterday. I didn't arrive on Monday.	We didn't go to America. I didn't put it there.

Grammar reference page 114

Pronunciation: *-ed* endings

3 **Listen and repeat.**
/t/ laughed, missed, watched
/d/ enjoyed, happened, realised
/ɪd/ hated, sounded, started

4 **In pairs, decide if the *-ed* words end with a /t/, /d/ or /ɪd/ sound. Listen and check.**
They walked and climbed until they reached the top. They waited, but no one arrived. He wanted the sandwich but she really needed it, so he handed it to her.

5 **Copy and complete the table. Use the texts on page 72 to help you.**

Infinitive	Past simple
buy	bought
come	…
eat	…
fly	…
get	…
go	…
have	…
hear	…
put	…
see	…
sit	…
think	…

6 **Complete with the past simple negative of the verbs.**

exist have know leave matter think want (x2)

Samantha [1]… much about life in the country because she [2]… her city very often. One weekend her family went on a camping holiday because her parents [3]… to pay for a hotel. When night-time came, they realised they [4]… a torch, but it [5]… because outside the tent the sky was full of strange tiny lights. Samantha thought they were fairies. Her father [6]… to ruin the magic and tell her that fairies [7]… . But her mother [8]… it was a good idea to let her continue believing something untrue.
'They're not fairies, darling,' she said. 'They're fireflies!'

7 NOW YOU! **Listen to a farmer telling a strange story and write an ending. Use the past simple and time expressions.**

8 **In small groups, compare your endings and decide which one you like best.**

PROJECT TASK 4 Memorabilia chest
- Write a role play about one of your explorer's adventures.
- You will need to write the dialogue, create costumes and find props or make puppets. Try to use recycled materials wherever you can.
- You will perform your play in the final task.

→ Workbook page 75

Do all exercises in your notebook

Workbook pages 66 and 67 73

ANSWER KEY

Pages 72-73

1 1 b 2 a 3 b

2
1
1 Last weekend
2 Just before
3 But when

2
1 One day
2 After some time
3 Suddenly

3
1 One Christmas
2 Before long
3 Then

3 *Student's own answers*

4 /t/ - walked, reached
/d/ - climbed, arrived
/ɪd/ - waited, wanted, needed, handed

5

Infinitive	Past simple
buy	bought
come	came
eat	ate
fly	flew
get	got
go	went

Infinitive	Past simple
have	had
hear	heard
put	put
see	saw
sit	sat
think	thought

6
1 didn't know
2 didn't leave
3 didn't want
4 didn't have
5 didn't matter
6 didn't want
7 didn't exist
8 didn't think

7 *Student's own answers*

8 *Student's own answers*

Remind students to do all the exercises in their notebook

LESSON FOCUS

Grammar Past simple: regular and irregular verbs
Vocabulary Time expressions
Listening Telling stories
Speaking Complete a story using the target language
Project task 4 Write a role play about an explorer

Resources
Teacher's i-solutions, Student's Book audio, Vlog and worksheets

Flipped Learning

GEORGE'S VLOG: Urban myths

- Make sure to set up the **Flipped Learning** work with the students beforehand. **See pages 20-23 for complete Flipped Learning guidelines.**
- Ask students to put the **Flipped Learning worksheets** on their desks and walk around to check how many have completed the Flipped task.
- In pairs or small groups, ask students to compare and check the *Before you watch...* and *While you watch...* exercises on the worksheet.
- Show students **George's vlog** and ask volunteers to provide correct answers and clarify any doubts other students may have.
- Choose three or four students to read aloud their answers to the *After you watch...* exercises on the worksheet and encourage some class discussion.
- Move straight to exercise 1 on page 72.

Warmer

Watch George's vlog and discuss the questions with the whole class. If you don't have video facilities, simply discuss the questions.

LISTENING TOOLS

Remind students that when we tell stories we often include extra information to create interest, although that extra information might not be important. Ask students why people do this. Students then read the **Listening tool** and discuss why it's important to bear distractors in mind.

1 2.20 (See page 177 for transcripts) Before students listen to the stories, ask them to identify what they can see in each picture and what connection might be.

2 2.21 (See page 177 for transcripts) Ask students to quickly scan the texts for the words in bold and, with a partner, discuss the difference between the options.

FAST FINISHERS Students can complete this exercise alone or in pairs.

Flipped Learning

PAST SIMPLE

Draw students' attention to the **Grammar table**. Remind students that they can use this as a quick reference while completing the exercises.

Show students the **Grammar animation** and/or refer students to the **Grammar reference** on page 114 for further information on form and use.

→ See page 23 for how to flip the **grammar lesson**

Pronunciation

3 2.22 (See page 177 for transcripts) Before completing the exercise, ask students to repeat the three different *-ed* endings in isolation, /t/, /d/, /ɪd/. Remind students that /ed/ is not a past tense ending.

4 2.23 (See page 177 for transcripts) In pairs, tell students to take turns reciting the paragraph to each other.

5 Once students have completed the table correctly, they can test each other.

6 Tell students to look at the verbs in the box and decide if they are regular or irregular. Students can then complete the exercise.

7 2.24 **NOW YOU!** (See page 177 for transcripts) As students listen, encourage them to take notes in order to complete the story.

8 In groups, first ask students to compare the notes they took while listening to ensure they have understood the start of the story correctly. Students may wish to compile the endings they have written to make a definitive ending.

PROJECT TASK 4
Memorabilia chest

Tell students to get into their groups from Tasks 1-3 (Unit 7). Tell students that using the work they did in Tasks 1-3, they are going to prepare a role play. Remind students that they need to keep their project notes together in their **Workbook** (page 75) or in their own notebook.

→ See page 24-27 **Projects**

FURTHER PRACTICE

Workbook pages 66-67
- **Grammar reference and practice** pages 91 and 96
- **Wordlist and exercises** pages 101 and 104

Remind students to do all the exercises in their notebook

CONTINUOUS ASSESSMENT Students can use time expressions, and regular and irregular past simple verbs.

8.2 Listening and grammar

1 Complete the text with the correct form of the verb. Listen and check.

Dt Gregson: Did you wear your diamond necklace tonight, Mrs Templeton?
Mrs Templeton: No, I didn't. I [1]… (think) it would be too heavy, but I [2]… (show) it to everyone before dinner. Then, when we [3]… (finish) eating, the lights went out and it disappeared!
Dt Gregson: I see. Where did you go after dinner, Miss Olive?
Miss Olive: I [4]… (go) to my aunt's room to look for her medicine.
Dt Gregson: Mmm… and you, Mr Parker, why did you leave the room?
Mr Parker: Because I [5]… (want) to go to the kitchen to get another bottle of champagne for my aunt.
Dt Gregson: Is that true, Mrs Templeton? Did you ask Mr Parker for more champagne?
Mrs Templeton: Not exactly. I [6]… (ask) him to get more red wine, not champagne. But it's true that I [7]… (tell) him to go to the kitchen.
Dt Gregson: And you, Mr Davies. Mr Smith [8]… (see) you hiding something in your jacket after the lights [9]… (come) back on. What did you hide?
Mr Davies: Uh, well, it's glue for my wig. I didn't want Mrs Templeton to know that I wear one.
Mrs Templeton: Oh, Mr Davies my dear, I [10]… (know) about that!

2 In pairs, decide who stole the necklace and why.

3 Listen and complete the questions Detective Gregson asks. Did you guess the thief correctly?
1 So, Miss Scarlet, where … ?
2 Mr Davies, did … ?
3 Mr Smith, who … ?
4 Hmm! And did … ?
5 Well then, tell us, why … ?

FAST FINISHERS Write questions for Detective Gregson to ask the suspects.

Do all exercises in your notebook

74 Past simple: questions / Homophones

Grammar and listening 8.2

PAST SIMPLE: QUESTIONS

Yes/No questions	Wh- questions
Did you wear your diamond necklace tonight? Yes, I did. / No, I didn't.	Where did you go after dinner, Miss Olive? I went to my aunt's room.
Did she ask Mr Parker for more champagne? Yes, she did. / No, she didn't.	What did he hide? He hid his glue.

Grammar reference page 114

4 In pairs, use the prompts to ask each other questions. Switch partners and tell your new partner the answers you heard.
1 Where / go / yesterday afternoon?
2 see / an interesting film / last week?
3 What / buy / the last time you went to the shopping centre?
4 visit / your family / last summer?
5 What / do / last night?
6 have / Maths class / before English today?

5 Listen and answer the questions.
1 When did the man go to the supermarket?
2 What did he buy?
3 Did he run home? Why?
4 What did he eat?
5 Did he win something?
6 What did he win?

LISTENING TOOLS
Homophones have
- the same pronunciation.
- different spelling and meaning.

ate / eight *eye / I*
be / bee *meat / meet*
buy / bye *Wales / whales*

6 Say the words in bold out loud. Choose the correct option.
1 I put some **flower** / **flour** in the cake I **maid** / **made**.
2 She didn't comb her **hair** / **hare**.
3 He wore a Santa **Claws** / **Claus** costume.
4 Angie **flu** / **flew** to New York with her teddy **bare** / **bear**.

7 Match the pairs of homophones. Listen again and point to the pictures when you hear the words.

PROJECT TASK 5
Memorabilia chest
- Look at the list of explorers from project task 1.
- Write four questions for the other groups' explorers. These can be questions about their lives, their experiences, important dates, etc.

→ Workbook page 75

Do all exercises in your notebook

Workbook pages 68 and 69 75

ANSWER KEY

Pages 74-75

1 **1** thought
2 showed
3 finished
4 went
5 wanted
6 asked
7 told
8 saw
9 came
10 knew

2 *Student's own answers*

3 **1** did you go when the lights went off?
2 you see Miss Scarlet go to the bathroom?
3 did you talk to?
4 you buy an expensive flat in London last week?
5 did you steal Mrs Templeton's necklace?

4 **1** Where did you go yesterday afternoon?
Student's own answers
2 Did you see an interesting film last week?
Student's own answers
3 What did you buy the last time you went to the shopping centre?
Student's own answers
4 Did you visit your family last summer?
Student's own answers
5 What did you do last night?
Student's own answers
6 Did you have Maths class before English today?
Student's own answers

5 **1** He went to the supermarket last night.
2 He bought some flour and a meat pie.
3 Yes, he did. He ran home because he wanted to be on time to watch a show on TV.
4 He ate his dinner.
5 Yes, he did.
6 He won a trip to Wales.

6 **1** flour; made
2 hair
3 Claus
4 flew; bear

7 **1** (whales) c (Wales)
2 (flower) a (flour)
3 (knight) d (night)
4 (write) e (right)
5 (ate) b (eight)

Remind students to do all the exercises in their notebook

LESSON FOCUS

Grammar Past simple: questions
Listening Homphones, A detective story
Speaking Asking and answering questions
Project task 5 Write questions to ask about other explorers

Resources
Teacher's i-solutions, Student's Book audio

Warmer

Ask students if they have ever had anything stolen and how it made them feel.

1 2.25 (See page 178 for transcripts) Tell students that a robbery has been committed. Someone has stolen a diamond necklace. In pairs, tell students to look at the illustrations of the people involved in the investigation – who are they and what are they like? Ask students to tell you their ideas. Students can then listen and complete the exercise.

2 Again in pairs, ask students to look at each of the suspects and decide who they think stole the diamond and necklace and why.

3 2.26 (See page 178 for transcripts) In pairs, tell students to decide what other questions they would ask the suspects before listening to the second part of the investigation.

FAST FINISHERS Students can complete this exercise alone or in pairs.

PAST SIMPLE: QUESTIONS

Flipped Learning

Draw students' attention to the **Grammar table**. Remind students that they can use this as a quick reference while completing the exercises.

Show students the **Grammar animation** and/or refer students to the **Grammar reference** on page 114 for further information on form and use.

→ See page 23 for how to flip the **grammar lesson**

4 Give students a couple of minutes to prepare their answers before they speak to a partner.

5 2.27 (See page 178 for transcripts) Tell students write one word notes rather than complete answers while they are listening.

LISTENING TOOLS

Once students have read the **Listening tool**, drill the words and ask students if they know of any more examples.

6 Before students complete the exercise, ask them to look at the words in bold and guess their meaning.

7 2.28 (See page 178 for transcripts) Before completing the exercise, quickly call out the words and ask students to point to the correct picture.

PROJECT TASK 5
Memorabilia chest

Tell students to get into their groups from Tasks 1-4
Remind students they are putting together a memorabilia chest and presenting it to the rest of the class. Tell students to read through the **Grammar table** before preparing their questions.
Tell students that they need to keep their projects notes together in their **Workbook** (page 75) or in their own notebook.

→ See pages 24-27 **Projects**

FURTHER PRACTICE

Workbook pages 68-69
- **Grammar reference and practice** pages 91 and 96
- **Wordlist and exercises** pages 101 and 104

Vocabulary and Grammar worksheets available to download and edit from the
Richmond*Learning***Platform**

→ See pages 38-39 **Mixed-ability classes**

Remind students to do all the exercises in their notebook

CONTINUOUS ASSESSMENT Students can understand and use homophones, and ask and answer questions in the past simple.

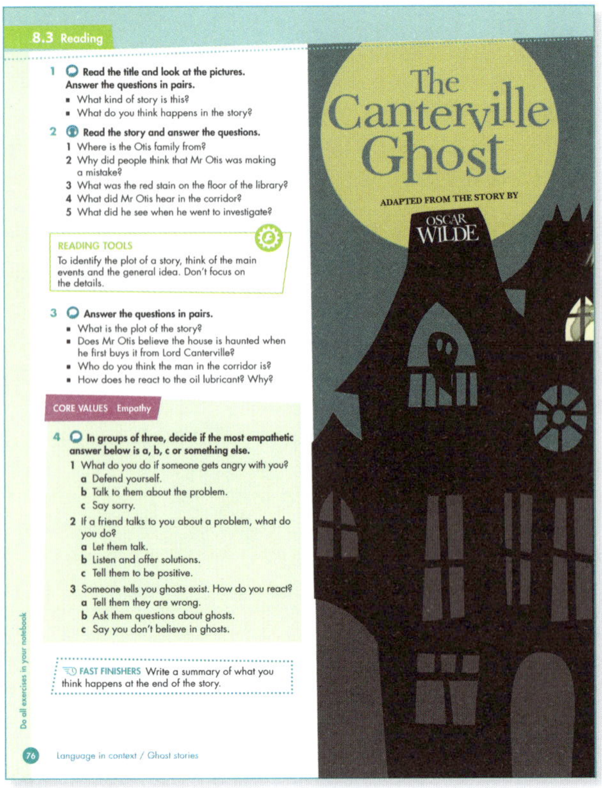

8.3 Reading

1 Read the title and look at the pictures. Answer the questions in pairs.
- What kind of story is this?
- What do you think happens in the story?

2 Read the story and answer the questions.
1 Where is the Otis family from?
2 Why did people think that Mr Otis was making a mistake?
3 What was the red stain on the floor of the library?
4 What did Mr Otis hear in the corridor?
5 What did he see when he went to investigate?

READING TOOLS
To identify the plot of a story, think of the main events and the general idea. Don't focus on the details.

3 Answer the questions in pairs.
- What is the plot of the story?
- Does Mr Otis believe the house is haunted when he first buys it from Lord Canterville?
- Who do you think the man in the corridor is?
- How does he react to the oil lubricant? Why?

CORE VALUES Empathy

4 In groups of three, decide if the most empathetic answer below is a, b, c or something else.
1 What do you do if someone gets angry with you?
a Defend yourself.
b Talk to them about the problem.
c Say sorry.
2 If a friend talks to you about a problem, what do you do?
a Let them talk.
b Listen and offer solutions.
c Tell them to be positive.
3 Someone tells you ghosts exist. How do you react?
a Tell them they are wrong.
b Ask them questions about ghosts.
c Say you don't believe in ghosts.

FAST FINISHERS Write a summary of what you think happens at the end of the story.

Do all exercises in your notebook

76 Language in context / Ghost stories

The Canterville Ghost

ADAPTED FROM THE STORY BY OSCAR WILDE

Reading 8.3

When Mr Otis moved to England from America and bought Canterville Chase, everyone told him he was making a mistake because it was haunted. In fact, when Lord Canterville sold the house to Mr Otis, he felt it was his duty to mention the ghost.

'My Lord,' answered Mr Otis, 'I will take the house with the furniture and the ghost. I come from a modern country, where we have everything that money can buy.'

So, Mr Otis moved to Canterville Chase with his family. When they arrived, Mrs Umney, the housekeeper, took them into the library. She pointed to a red stain on the floor. She said, 'This is the blood of Lady Eleanor of Canterville, who was murdered on that very spot by Sir Simon of Canterville, in 1575. The blood stain cannot be removed.'

'That is nonsense,' cried Washington Otis, Mr Otis's son. 'Pinkerton's Champion Stain Remover will clean it up in no time,' he said. Before the terrified housekeeper could stop him, he cleaned the stain.

'I knew Pinkerton would do it,' he exclaimed triumphantly, as he looked at his admiring family. Then, a terrible flash of lightning lit up the room and Mrs Umney fainted.

One night, Mr Otis heard a curious, metallic noise in the corridor outside his bedroom. He opened the door and right in front of him there was a terrifying old man. His eyes were red; long, grey hair fell over his shoulders; his clothes were dirty and ragged, and he had heavy, rusty chains hanging from his wrists.

'My dear sir,' said Mr Otis, 'I really must insist you oil those chains. Here, I have brought you some Rising Sun Lubricator!' Mr Otis put a bottle down in front of the ghost and returned to bed. For a moment the Canterville ghost remained motionless in anger. Then, knocking the lubricator over violently onto the floor, he flew down the corridor, crying noisily.

Do all exercises in your notebook

Workbook pages 70 and 71 77

ANSWER KEY

Pages 76-77

1 *Student's own answers*

2
1 The Otis family is from America.
2 Because the house was haunted.
3 It was the blood of Lady Eleanor or Canterville.
4 He heard a curious, metallic noise.
5 He saw a terrifying old man.

3 *Suggested answers:*
1 An American buys a haunted house and moves there with his family, but the family is not scared of the ghost. They suggest practical solutions to the problems and this upsets the ghost.
2 No
3 Sir Simon of Canterville
4 He is angry because Mr Otis is not scared of him.

4 *Student's own answers*

LESSON FOCUS

Language in context Ghost stories

Core values Empathy

Resources

Teacher's i-solutions, Student's Book audio

Preparation 1 minute of spooky, atmospheric music

→ See pages 36-37 **Literature**

Warmer

Tell students to close their eyes and listen to some music. After 20-30 seconds, ask students to open their eyes and write down any words they associate with the music. Students can then compare what they have written with a partner.

1 Before students answer the questions, ask them if they have heard of Oscar Wilde and if they know anything about him.

2 2.29 (See page 178 for transcripts) Once students have read the story with the accompanying audio and answered the questions, you could ask them to read it again, this time accompanied by the music used in the **Warmer**.

READING TOOLS

Tell students to read the **Reading tool** and discuss why this would be helpful. Tell students to discuss with a partner the main events and the general idea of this story.

3 Tell students to answer the questions alone before discussing them with a partner.

CORE VALUES Empathy

4 Ask students if they or anyone they know believe in ghosts and why or why not. As students discuss the topic, write the word *EMPATHY* on the board. Ask students if they were empathetic to others' opinions and beliefs. Students can then discuss the questions.

FAST FINISHERS Students can complete this exercise alone or in pairs.

FURTHER PRACTICE
Workbook pages 70-71

Remind students to do all the exercises in their notebook

CONTINUOUS ASSESSMENT Students can understand a ghost story.

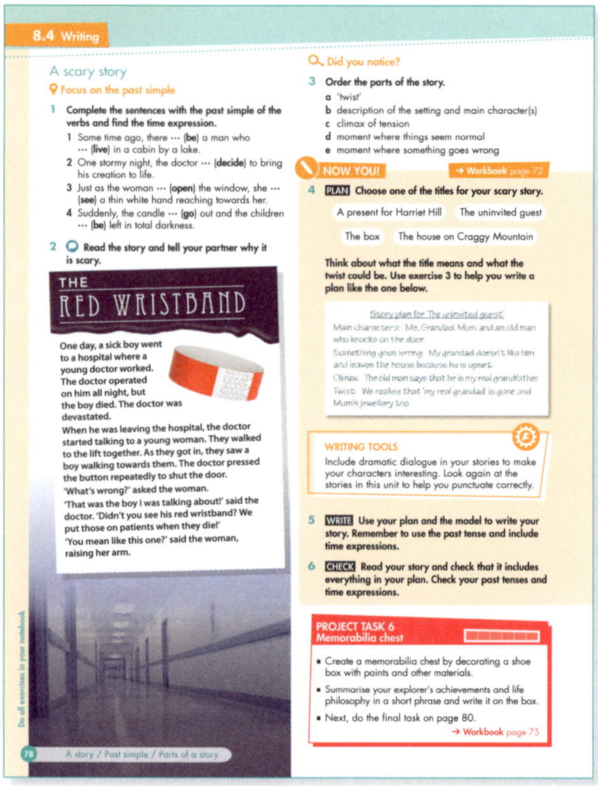

8.4 Writing

A scary story

Focus on the past simple

1 **Complete the sentences with the past simple of the verbs and find the time expression.**
1 Some time ago, there ··· (**be**) a man who ··· (**live**) in a cabin by a lake.
2 One stormy night, the doctor ··· (**decide**) to bring his creation to life.
3 Just as the woman ··· (**open**) the window, she ··· (**see**) a thin white hand reaching towards her.
4 Suddenly, the candle ··· (**go**) out and the children ··· (**be**) left in total darkness.

2 **Read the story and tell your partner why it is scary.**

THE RED WRISTBAND

One day, a sick boy went to a hospital where a young doctor worked. The doctor operated on him all night, but the boy died. The doctor was devastated.
When he was leaving the hospital, the doctor started talking to a young woman. They walked to the lift together. As they got in, they saw a boy walking towards them. The doctor pressed the button repeatedly to shut the door.
'What's wrong?' asked the woman.
'That was the boy I was talking about!' said the doctor. 'Didn't you see his red wristband? We put those on patients when they die!'
'You mean like this one?' said the woman, raising her arm.

Did you notice?

3 **Order the parts of the story.**
a 'twist'
b description of the setting and main character(s)
c climax of tension
d moment where things seem normal
e moment where something goes wrong

NOW YOU! → Workbook page 72

4 PLAN **Choose one of the titles for your scary story.**
A present for Harriet Hill | The uninvited guest | The box | The house on Craggy Mountain

Think about what the title means and what the twist could be. Use exercise 3 to help you write a plan like the one below.

Story plan for 'The uninvited guest'
Main characters: Me, Grandad, Mum and an old man who knocks on the door.
Something goes wrong: My grandad doesn't like him and leaves the house because he is upset.
Climax: The old man says that he is my real grandfather.
Twist: We realise that 'my real grandad' is gone and Mum's jewellery too.

WRITING TOOLS
Include dramatic dialogue in your stories to make your characters interesting. Look again at the stories in this unit to help you punctuate correctly.

5 WRITE **Use your plan and the model to write your story. Remember to use the past tense and include time expressions.**

6 CHECK **Read your story and check that it includes everything in your plan. Check your past tenses and time expressions.**

PROJECT TASK 6
Memorabilia chest
- Create a memorabilia chest by decorating a shoe box with paints and other materials.
- Summarise your explorer's achievements and life philosophy in a short phrase and write it on the box.
- Next, do the final task on page 80.

→ Workbook page 75

Do all exercises in your notebook

78 A story / Past simple / Parts of a story

ANSWER KEY

Page 78

1 **1** was; lived; some time ago
2 decided; One stormy night
3 opened; saw; Just as
4 went; were; Suddenly

2 *Student's own answers*

3 b, e, d, c, a

4 *Student's own answers*

5 *Student's own answers*

6 *Student's own answers*

LESSON FOCUS
Focus on The past simple
Writing A scary story; parts of a story
Project task 6 Make a memorabilia chest
Resources
Teacher's i-solutions

Warmer

Tell students to list all the elements of a scary story – characters, setting, atmosphere, etc. Ask students to call out their ideas and make a list on the board.

Focus on the past simple

1 When students have completed the sentences, ask them to think about what happened before and after each sentence.

2 Before students read the story, tell them to look at the images and decide what might happen. Ask students to give you their ideas.

Did you notice?

3 When students have matched the parts of the story to *The red wristband*, ask them to look at the sentences in exercise 1 again and see if they can identify which part of the story they could be.

4 **PLAN** This exercise could be done in groups according to story title. Students don't have to write the story as a group, but they can generate ideas together.

WRITING TOOLS

Tell students to read the **Writing tool** and discuss why this would be helpful. Tell students to look again at *The red wristband* for examples of dialogue.

5 **WRITE** Before students start to write, make a checklist on the board of any grammar, vocabulary, punctuation and any other language elements they should consider.

6 **CHECK** Once students have checked their own stories, they can swap with a partner and check theirs.

PROJECT TASK 6
Memorabilia chest

Tell students to get into their project groups.
As this part of the project is very practical, it may be better for students to work on this step outside the classroom, in their own time. Tell students that they need to keep their projects notes together in their **Workbook** (page 74) or in their own notebook.

→ See pages 24-27 **Projects**

FURTHER PRACTICE

Workbook page 72

Remind students to do all the exercises in their notebook

 CONTINUOUS ASSESSMENT Students can use the past simple to write a scary story.

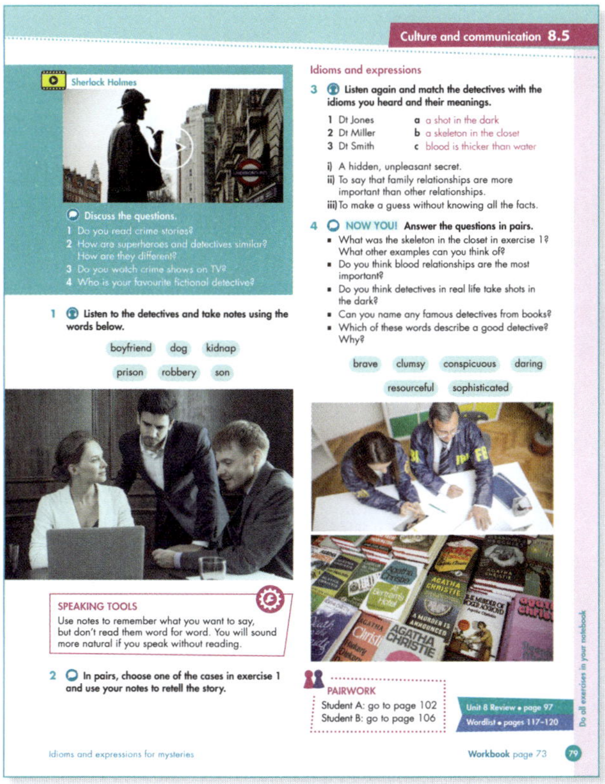

Culture and communication 8.5

Sherlock Holmes

Discuss the questions.
1 Do you read crime stories?
2 How are superheroes and detectives similar? How are they different?
3 Do you watch crime shows on TV?
4 Who is your favourite fictional detective?

1 Listen to the detectives and take notes using the words below.

boyfriend dog kidnap prison robbery son

Idioms and expressions

3 Listen again and match the detectives with the idioms you heard and their meanings.

1 Dt Jones a a shot in the dark
2 Dt Miller b a skeleton in the closet
3 Dt Smith c blood is thicker than water

i) A hidden, unpleasant secret.
ii) To say that family relationships are more important than other relationships.
iii) To make a guess without knowing all the facts.

4 NOW YOU! Answer the questions in pairs.
- What was the skeleton in the closet in exercise 1? What other examples can you think of?
- Do you think blood relationships are the most important?
- Do you think detectives in real life take shots in the dark?
- Can you name any famous detectives from books?
- Which of these words describe a good detective? Why?

brave clumsy conspicuous daring resourceful sophisticated

SPEAKING TOOLS
Use notes to remember what you want to say, but don't read them word for word. You will sound more natural if you speak without reading.

2 In pairs, choose one of the cases in exercise 1 and use your notes to retell the story.

PAIRWORK
Student A: go to page 102
Student B: go to page 106

Unit 8 Review • page 97
Wordlist • pages 117–120

Do all exercises in your notebook

Idioms and expressions for mysteries

Workbook page 73

79

ANSWER KEY

Page 79

1 *Student's own answers*

2 *Student's own answers*

3 **1** c; ii **2** a; iii **3** b; i

4 *Student's own answers*

LESSON FOCUS

Idioms and expressions Mysteries
Listening Taking notes on a detective story
Speaking Talking about mysteries

Resources

Teacher's i-solutions, Student's Book audio, Culture video and worksheet

Sherlock Holmes

- In pairs, ask students to compare/complete the *What I know...* exercises on the **Culture video worksheet.**
- Show students the **Culture video** and ask them to check/complete the *What I learned...* exercises on the worksheet. If students are completing the exercises for the first time, they will need to watch the video twice.
- In pairs, students compare answers.
- In small groups, tell students to complete/discuss the *What I wonder...* exercises on the worksheet.

Warmer

Watch the culture video and discuss the questions with the whole class. If you don't have video facilities, simply discuss the questions.

1 2.30 (See page 178 for transcripts) Before students listen, ask them how they think the words may be associated.

SPEAKING TOOLS

Tell students to read the **Speaking tool** and discuss why this would be helpful for communication to be more natural.

2 Students can first compare their notes in case they are missing any key information. You could ask for volunteers to retell their story to the class, the rest of the groups can check they have included everything.

Idioms and expressions

3 2.31 (See page 180 for transcripts) Before students complete the exercise, write the idioms on the board and ask students to tell you what each word means and guess the meaning of the idiom.

4 NOW YOU! Tell students to look back at the notes they have taken during this lesson before they complete the exercise and remind students of the speaking tool.

FURTHER PRACTICE AND UNIT ASSESSMENT

Unit 8 Review Student's Book page 97
Workbook page 73
- **Reflect on your learning** page 73
- **Grammar reference and practice** pages 91 and 96
- **Wordlist and exercises** pages 101 and 104

Tests available to download and edit from the **Richmond** *Learning* **Platform**

→ See pages 40-41 **Assessment**

PAIRWORK Student's Book pages 102 and 106
See **Teacher's Book** page 152 for more information.

→ See pages 30-33 **Mediation**

Remind students to do all the exercises in their notebook

CONTINUOUS ASSESSMENT Students can use idioms and expressions for mysteries.

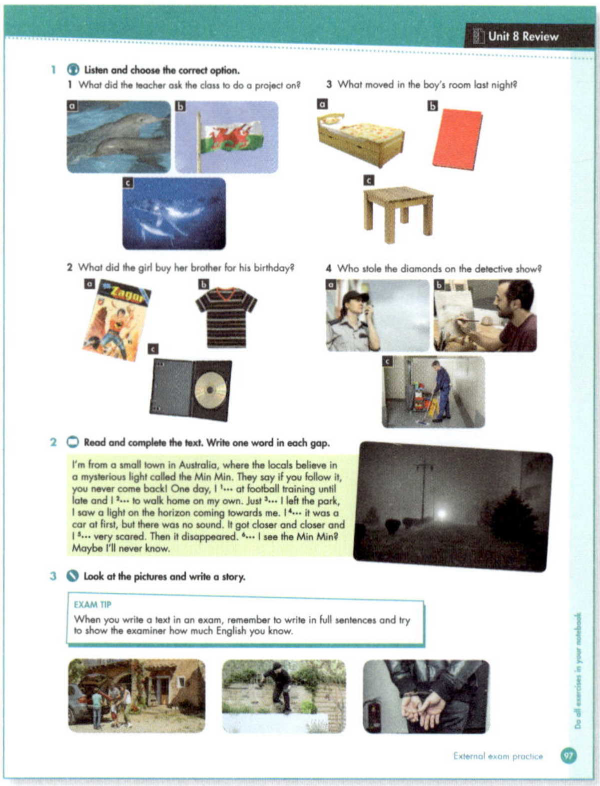

Unit 8 Review

1 Listen and choose the correct option.

1 What did the teacher ask the class to do a project on?

a b c

2 What did the girl buy her brother for his birthday?

a b c

3 What moved in the boy's room last night?

a b c

4 Who stole the diamonds on the detective show?

a b c

2 Read and complete the text. Write one word in each gap.

I'm from a small town in Australia, where the locals believe in a mysterious light called the Min Min. They say if you follow it, you never come back! One day, I [1]… at football training until late and I [2]… to walk home on my own. Just [3]… I left the park, I saw a light on the horizon coming towards me. I [4]… it was a car at first, but there was no sound. It got closer and closer and I [5]… very scared. Then it disappeared. [6]… I see the Min Min? Maybe I'll never know.

3 Look at the pictures and write a story.

EXAM TIP

When you write a text in an exam, remember to write in full sentences and try to show the examiner how much English you know.

Do all exercises in your notebook

External exam practice 97

Student's Book page 97

ANSWER KEY

See page 181 for transcripts

1 2.45

1 b
2 a
3 b
4 b

2 **1** was
2 decided
3 as
4 thought
5 was/got
6 Did

3 *Student's own answers*

Pairwork

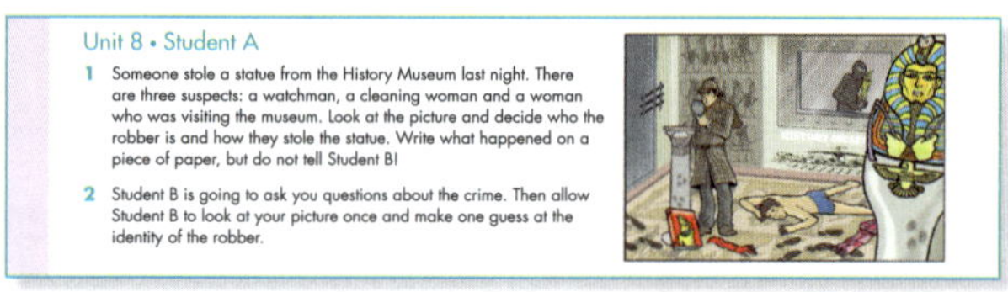

Unit 8 • Student A

1 Someone stole a statue from the History Museum last night. There are three suspects: a watchman, a cleaning woman and a woman who was visiting the museum. Look at the picture and decide who the robber is and how they stole the statue. Write what happened on a piece of paper, but do not tell Student B!

2 Student B is going to ask you questions about the crime. Then allow Student B to look at your picture once and make one guess at the identity of the robber.

Student's Book page 102

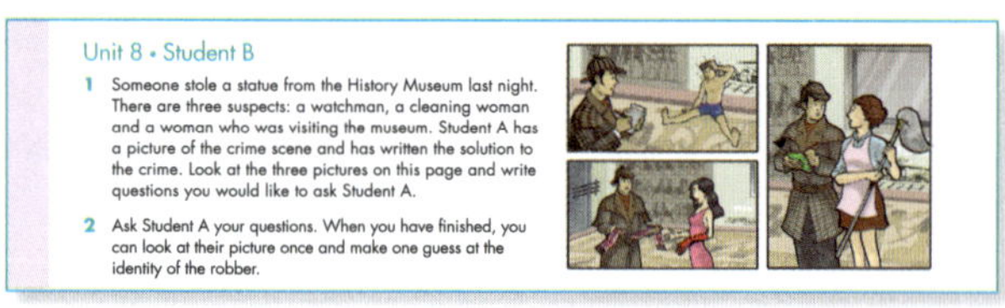

Unit 8 • Student B

1 Someone stole a statue from the History Museum last night. There are three suspects: a watchman, a cleaning woman and a woman who was visiting the museum. Student A has a picture of the crime scene and has written the solution to the crime. Look at the three pictures on this page and write questions you would like to ask Student A.

2 Ask Student A your questions. When you have finished, you can look at their picture once and make one guess at the identity of the robber.

Student's Book page 106

CEFR MEDIATION DESCRIPTOR

- **Generating conceptual talk**

Students can ask what somebody thinks of a certain idea.

- **Analysing clues**

Tell Student A and B that they need to convey as much information as possible to their partner. Once students have finished, they can compare their guesses with others.

Remind students to do all the exercises in their notebook

Grammar reference

Unit 8 Grammar reference

Past simple: regular and irregular

Affirmative	
Regular verbs	**Irregular verbs**
start → started arrive → arrived study → studied stop → stopped	go → went put → put eat → ate see → saw
Negative	
He didn't start yesterday. I didn't arrive on Monday. We didn't study hard. She didn't stop until the evening.	We didn't go to America. I didn't put it there. You didn't eat much. They didn't see the dog.

We use the past simple to talk about actions and events in the past.

She **climbed** all the way to the top.

We **got** really good marks in our exams.

They **didn't know** the answers.

With regular verbs, we usually form the past simple by adding ***-ed*** to the infinitive.

She **played** football yesterday.

We **visited** our grandparents last year.

Kyle **wanted** to go to the pool.

With regular and irregular verbs, the negative of the past simple is formed by putting ***did not*** or ***didn't*** before the verb. We usually use the contracted form ***didn't***.

She **did not work** today.

We **didn't buy** Laura a birthday present.

I'm sorry, I **didn't hear** you.

We use the infinitive form of the verb after ***didn't***.

We **didn't arrive** in time for the concert.

NOT ~~We didn't arrived in time for the concert.~~

We often use past time expressions with past simple verbs.

I **worked** really hard **last year**.

My sister **went** to the cinema **at the weekend**.

He **didn't play** volleyball **last month**.

Go to page 116 to see a list of irregular verbs in the past simple.

Past simple: questions

Yes/No questions	*Wh-* questions
Did you wear your diamond necklace tonight? Yes, I did. No, I didn't.	Where did you go after dinner, Miss Olive? I went to my aunt's room.
Did she ask Mr Parker for more champagne? Yes, she did. No, she didn't.	What did he hide? He hid his glue.

We use ***did*** + **pronoun** + **infinitive** to form *yes/no* questions in the past simple.

Did he go to the concert last night?

Did they know the answer?

Did you ask the teacher?

Questions in the past simple are formed in the same way with regular and irregular verbs.

Did you **talk** about it?

Did you **hear** the story?

When we give a short answer in the past simple, we do not use the verb.

Did she open the door?

Yes, she did. NOT ~~Yes, she did open.~~

To ask for more information about the past, we use *wh-* question words before ***did***. The question words include ***how***, ***how long***, ***how many***, ***how much***, ***what***, ***when***, ***where***, ***who*** and ***why***.

How did you travel to Greece?

When did they make the cake?

Why did they cancel the game?

We use the infinitive of the verb in all question forms.

Did they **leave** after the class?

NOT ~~Did they left after the class?~~

Where did you **go?**

NOT ~~Where did you went?~~

Do all exercises in your notebook

 Workbook pages 93–96

Student's Book page 114

Wordlist

Wordlist

UNIT 8

Time expressions

after some time
afterwards
as
before long
before that
finally
just after
just before
last weekend
last year
next
one Christmas
one day
one winter
one year
suddenly
then
when

Ghost stories

believe
blood
curious
ghost
haunted
hear
murdered
noise
plot
stain
story

Parts of a story

characters
description
dialogue
drama
punctuate
setting
tension
title
twist

Do all exercises in your notebook

 Workbook pages 102–104

Student's Book page 120

2.68 2.69 2.70

Remind students to do all the exercises in their notebook

PROJECT: Memorabilia chest

RECAP

- In this project, you have investigated a famous explorer and designed a memorabilia chest filled with information about their life.
- In **units 7 and 8**, you learnt how to tell stories, and how to use time expressions and the past tense. You also learnt interesting expressions such as *a skeleton in the closet* and adjectives like *frightening* and *frightened*.
- Now you are ready to show off your new skills!

TASK 1 You made an information card with a summary of your explorer.
TASK 2 You made maps and collected information about your explorer.
TASK 3 You wrote letters from your explorer about their adventures.
TASK 4 You wrote a role play about your explorer.
TASK 5 You wrote questions about the other explorers.
TASK 6 You made a memorabilia chest.

FINAL TASK: Give your presentation

- Use the elements you created in **tasks 1–6** to fill your memorabilia chest and prepare a presentation.
- Choose someone to:
  - organise the presentation.
  - explain the memorabilia chest and its contents.
  - read out the information card and the letters.
  - look after the props and direct the role play.
- Present your memorabilia chest to the class.
- Your classmates will ask you the questions they prepared in **task 5**.

USEFUL EXPRESSIONS

About the explorer's life experiences:
- He/She was a … person.
- His/Her experiences were amazing/daring/unbelievable.
- Among his/her achievements, we should mention…

About the memorabilia chests:
- This memorabilia collection shows…
- This photo represents…

21ST CENTURY SKILLS

Communication

We can tell stories in many different ways, in written and spoken language and also through videos and photos, art and dance, etc.

Learning to tell stories in another language helps us to communicate and connect with other people. Storytelling also helps you to develop skills such as creativity and memory.

Do all exercises in your notebook

GO BEYOND

WHY STUDY THE PAST?

Historians look for clues that help them to reconstruct and make sense of the past. Historical evidence can be a piece of pottery, a stone or a fragment of glass. Other evidence includes written material and archaeological data.

So why go to all this effort and study history? Why does studying life during ancient Greek, Roman or Medieval times matter, for example? Well, because what people from the past thought and did still influences our modern world. When we study history, we can understand how things have evolved or disappeared. For example, why were there fewer female explorers than male explorers in the 1800s? Questions like this make us think about our future and how we can make things better, by, for example, creating equal opportunities for all. History helps us see beyond our own horizons and understand that there are other ways of thinking and behaving.

Answer the questions in pairs.

1 Do you agree that studying history is useful?
2 Do you think that understanding history helps us to improve our future? How?
3 What can you learn from your explorer's experiences?
4 Do your explorer's experiences make you think differently about your own future?

EVALUATION

Answer the questions in your team.

1 Did your team work well together? Was everybody in the team happy with the presentation?
2 Did one person do more work than the other members? How could you solve this problem?
3 Did all the people in the team enjoy the tasks they had?
4 Did you have enough time to complete all the work? How can you avoid running out of time?

Do all exercises in your notebook

Workbook project task notes

PROJECT: Memorabilia chest

Team members

______ ______ ______

TASK 1

Our chosen explorer: ______

General information: ______

→ Student's book page 65

TASK 2

Information to include in the questions: ______

Ideas for maps: ______

→ Student's book page 67

TASK 3

Four special adventures: ______

Ideas for letter: ______

→ Student's book page 70

TASK 4

Ideas for play: ______

→ Student's book page 73

TASK 5

Questions for the other explorers: ______

→ Student's book page 75

TASK 6

Phrase to summarise our explorer's life: ______

→ Student's book page 78

FINAL TASK

Organiser: ______ Presenter: ______

Reader: ______ Director: ______

→ Student's book page 80

Remind students to do all the exercises in their notebook

PROJECT FOCUS

→ See pages 24-27 **Projects**

Skills

- Write an information card about an explorer
- Write questions and answers about the explorer
- Research navigational instruments
- Write letters about adventures
- Write and perform a roleplay
- Write interview questions for other explorers
- Write a short phrase to summarise an explorer's achievements and life philosophy

CEFR mediation

Facilitating collaborative interaction with peers

Can invite others' contributions to very simple tasks using short, simple phrases.

→ See pages 30-33 **Mediation**

Preparation Remind students to bring the elements they create in tasks 1-6 and their notes from **Workbook** project task notes pages 74-75 or their own notebook. Have students bring in their self-assessment diaries if they are writing them.

RECAP

Put students in their teams and read through the **Recap** as a class. Draw their attention to the project tasks and the unit objectives and ask which task helped achieve which objectives. Make sure they have all the materials and notes that they need (see **Preparation**) for the **Final task**.

FINAL TASK: Give your presentation

Tell students they are now going to present their memorabilia chests to the class. Put them in their groups and first direct their attention to the **21st Century skill** (see next page). Give them a time limit for preparation and for each presentation to ensure they all have enough time, including for the questions they have prepared for the others. Draw their attention to the useful phrases and encourage them to use them. In choosing roles for their team, encourage them this time to assign roles to team-members who might find them challenging, but remind them that it is everyone's role to support their team and to help carry out the presentation to the best of their abilities.

Get them to rehearse parts or all of their presentations if they have time and to try to convey a sense of drama and intrigue about the explorer and his/her stories.

21ST CENTURY SKILLS

Read through the **21st Century skill** with them and ask them to consider how effective the different ways they are telling the story of their explorer are.

→ See pages 28-29 **21st century skills**

EVALUATION

Before students discuss the questions in pairs, give them time to prepare notes about their experience in the project. Remind students to be supportive and give constructive feedback to each other and say which things they thought they did well and which they found most difficult. Monitor discussions, adding your own feedback where appropriate and noting common observations to then convey to the class as a whole.

Have a class discussion about what students have learnt from the project, reminding them of the unit objectives, the **Core values** and the **Learning tools** sections of units 7 and 8, as well as the **21st Century skills** section of the **Project** pages.

If you have decided to use the **evaluation** exercise as a springboard for a student self-assessment diary (see **Evaluation notes** page 77), give them time to do this now and remind them to refer to the **Reflect on your learning** section of the **Workbook** if they have one

→ See pages 40-41 **Assessment**

GO BEYOND

Before students read the text, ask them to answer the question in the title: *Why study the past?* Have students volunteer their answers and make a list on the board. You can then compare the list on the board with the text before students discuss their answers to the questions below the text.

Remind students to do all the exercises in their notebook

9 HEALTHY FOOD

At the start of each unit and lesson, explain to the students what the objectives are.

Language objectives

Grammar

Nouns: Countable and uncountable

- Students focus on the differences in use between these two types of noun.

Quantifiers

- Students practise using quantifiers with countable and uncountable nouns.

Vocabulary

Food: *beans, bread, broccoli, butter, cereals, dairy, eggs, fish, meat, milk, nuts, oil, onions, pasta, peas, plums, poultry, raisins, rice, seeds, spinach, tangerines, tomatoes, vegetables*

- Students use vocabulary for a range of foods.

Units of measurement: *a bag of …, a bottle of …, a bowl of …, a box of …, a jar of …, a kilo of …, a loaf of …, a packet of …, a slice of …, a spoonful of …, a tin of …*

- Students practise units of measurement with different foods.

Nutrition: *calcium, calories, carbohydrates, energy, fat, fibre, healthy, minerals, nutrients, protein, salt, unhealthy, vitamins*

- Students practise using vocabulary about nutrition.

Idioms and expressions

Food: *a bad egg, a smart cookie, a couch potato*

- Students look at idioms and expressions in the context of short monologues.

Recycled language

Present simple; *There is* and *There are*; Linking expressions; Questions

Skills objectives

Speaking

- Students ask and answer questions about their eating habits.
- Students ask and answer questions about sandwiches.
- Students share recipes.
- Students discuss personality traits using idioms and expressions.

Pronunciation: Students practise correct word stress in compound nouns.

Pairwork: Student use various mediation techniques in order to complete two recipes.

Listening

- Students listen to complete and order the preparation steps of a recipe.
- Students listen to complete a conversation about the contents of a fridge.
- Students listen to idioms and expressions in context.

Reading

- Students scan a text for specific information.
- Students read a text in detail to decide if sentences about it are true or false, or if it doesn't say.
- Students look for words in context to match them with definitions.

Core values: Students read World Health Organisation recommendations about **healthy eating** and discuss their diets.

Writing

- Students look at the language and structure of a report.
- Students plan, write and check a report on a school canteen.

Focus on quantifiers: *a few, a little, a lot of, no, not many, not much, plenty of*

Learning to learn tools

SPEAKING TOOLS Students practise circumlocution to improve their fluency.	**LISTENING TOOLS** Students practise thorough listening to improve accuracy of comprehension.
READING TOOLS Students practise targeted skim reading.	**WRITING TOOLS** Students practise making effective critical comments.

VOCABULARY TOOLS Students practise ways of distinguishing between countable and uncountable nouns.

Review task objectives: Mind maps

Review Task 1 Students start planning mind maps for revision.

Review Task 2 Students add vocabulary to their mind maps.

Review Task 3 Students complete their mind maps with example sentences and idioms and expressions.

Audiovisual objectives

Vlog: Students watch and listen to Emma talk about healthy pizza.

Culture: Students watch and listen to Emma talk about the US tradition of the 'cookout'.

Grammar animations: Students are presented with visual presentations of the unit grammar.

Key competences

LC **Linguistic**
pages 82-89

MST **Mathematical and Science and Technology**
pages 82-83, 86-87

DC **Digital**
pages 82, 89

SCC **Social and Civic**
pages 82-83, 86-89

CAE **Cultural awareness and expression**
pages 82, 89

LL **Learning to learn**
pages 85-86, 88-89

IE **Sense of initiative and entrepreneurship**
pages 83, 85, 88

→ See pages 42-43 **Key competences**

CEFR Mediation

9.1 Processing text in speech
Can convey the main points in short, simple spoken texts.

9.2 Processing text in writing
Can pick out and reproduce key words and phrases.

9.3 Encouraging conceptual talk
Can ask what somebody thinks of a certain idea.

9.4 Facilitating communication in delicate situations and disagreements
Can use memorised phrases to seek compromise.

9.5 Facilitating cultural space
Can show interest, understanding and agreement where appropriate.

Review Explaining data in speech
Can interpret and describe visuals on familiar topics.

Unit review Relaying specific information in writing
Can list numbers and other simple information from spoken texts.

Pairwork Facilitating collaborative interaction with peers
Can collaborate in simple, shared tasks if participants speak slowly and help contribute and express suggestions.

→ See pages 30-33 **Mediation**

Remind students to do all the exercises in their notebook

9 HEALTHY FOOD

In unit 9 you will:
- talk about food, quantities and recipes.
- identify countable and uncountable nouns.
- talk about measurements of food.
- write a report.

9.1 Vocabulary and grammar

EMMA'S VLOG: Healthy pizza!

Discuss the questions.
1 What's your favourite meal of the day?
2 How does the food you eat affect the way you feel?
3 What makes you feel good about yourself?

Flipped Learning

1 **Choose the correct option. Listen and check.**

Breakfast is important!

Breakfast gives you energy to start the day, and there are many options to choose from. You can have some [1] **cereal / orange** with [2] **butter / milk** or an [3] **egg / banana** and some [4] **biscuit / bread**. If you don't know what to eat for breakfast, open the fridge. Maybe there is some [5] **yogurt / plum**.

If there isn't any, look again. Is there any fruit? Have some! Cut an [6] **kiwi / apple**, a [7] **kiwi / apple** or a [8] **banana / grapes** into pieces and mix it with some [9] **muesli / sausage** and milk. Some [10] **coffee / peach**, some [11] **cheese / egg** and some [12] **toast / strawberry** can be a nice alternative too. The important thing is to have something nutritious to start the day!

2 **Copy and complete the table with your answers from exercise 1.**

	Breakfast ideas	
A	…	…
An	…	…
Some	cereal	…
	…	…
	…	…
	…	…

NOUNS	
Countable nouns	**Uncountable nouns**
You can count them. **A** lemon, **two** lemons. **An** apple, **two** apples.	To count them, you need to use a unit of measurement or a container. **Some** bread, **a slice of** bread. **Some** coffee, **a cup of** coffee.
They have a singular and a plural form. I eat **a banana** for breakfast. I ate two **bananas** yesterday!	They don't have a plural form. I drink **milk** at night. I drank two glasses of **milk** last night!
Use ***there is*** or ***there are***. **There is** a plum on the table. **There are** two plums on the table.	Use ***there is some***. **There is some** butter in the fridge.
Use ***there aren't any***. **There aren't any** mangoes in the fridge.	Use ***there isn't any***. **There isn't any** toast on the plate.

Grammar reference page 115

3 **Categorise the nouns as countable or uncountable.**

cake carrot egg jam juice meat pasta onion rice sausage tomato

FAST FINISHERS Write a paragraph about your favourite food.

Do all exercises in your notebook

82 Nouns: Countable and uncountable / Food / Quantifiers

Grammar and vocabulary 9.1

VOCABULARY TOOLS
To decide if a food is countable or uncountable, ask yourself: Is it a liquid? Is it a slice of something from a bigger piece?

4 **Look at the picture and complete the text with *is, isn't, are, aren't, some* and *any*. Listen and check.**

Eating well

1 The grain group includes bread, pasta, cereals and rice. There [1]… two kinds of grains: wholemeal and refined.

2 There [2]… meat in this group! Instead, there [3]… onions, tomatoes and peas. There [4]… also broccoli and spinach. Plums, raisins and tangerines are [5]… of the fruits you can eat in this group. Remember to drink [6]… fruit juice too!

3 All products made from milk are part of this group. So, there [7]… rice or pasta in this group.

4 Solid fats, like butter, come from animals. Liquid fats, like oil, usually come from plants and fish. [8]… oils are cholesterol-free. But there [9]… cholesterol-free solid fats.

5 There [10]… lots of different kinds of meat, poultry and fish here. Nuts, seeds, beans and eggs also go in this group.

QUANTIFIERS	
Countable nouns	**Uncountable nouns**
Use ***how many*** for countable nouns. **How many** apples do you eat a week?	Use ***how much*** for uncountable nouns. **How much** bread do you eat a day?
Use a number, ***a lot of*** or ***a few*** to answer the question. I eat **2** apples a week. I eat **a lot of** apples. I eat **a few** apples.	Use ***some, a lot of*** or ***a little*** to answer the question. I eat **some** bread every day. I eat **a lot of** bread. I eat **a little** bread.

Grammar reference page 115

5 **Answer the questions. Add two more and ask your partner.**

1 How much fruit do you eat a day?
 a I don't eat any.
 b I eat a few pieces of fruit every day.
 c I eat a lot of fruit – more than five pieces a day.

2 How many eggs do you eat a week?
 a I eat a few, maybe three.
 b I don't eat any. I don't like eggs.
 c I eat a lot of eggs.

3 How much white bread do you eat a day?
 a I don't eat any white bread.
 b I eat some white bread.
 c I eat a little, but I prefer wholemeal bread.

6 **In pairs, talk about how much food you eat for breakfast, lunch and dinner. Use the appropriate quantifiers.**

7 NOW YOU! **Listen and, in pairs, write and perform a similar conversation.**

REVIEW TASK 1 Mind maps
- You are going to make mind maps. Take nine pieces of paper and write a unit title from this book in the middle of each one. For example, *Unit 1 – Our World.*
- Write the vocabulary topics you learnt in each unit around the title. For example, *Unit 1 – Countries and nationalities* (etc).
- You can find this information on page 2.

Do all exercises in your notebook

Workbook pages 76 and 77 83

ANSWER KEY

Pages 82-83

1
1 cereal
2 milk
3 egg
4 bread
5 yogurt
6 apple
7 kiwi
8 banana
9 muesli
10 coffee
11 cheese
12 toast

2

	Breakfast ideas	
A	kiwi	banana
An	egg	apple
Some	cereal milk bread yoghurt	muesli coffee cheese toast

3 **Countable:** carrot, egg, pear, onion, sausage, tomato
Uncountable: cake, jam, juice, meat, pasta, rice

4
1 are
2 isn't any
3 are
4 is
5 some
6 some
7 isn't any
8 Some
9 aren't any
10 are

5 *Student's own answers*

6 *Student's own answers*

7 *Student's own answers*

Remind students to do all the exercises in their notebook

LESSON FOCUS

Grammar Nouns: Countable and uncountable; Quantifiers
Vocabulary Food
Listening Reports on breakfast and eating well
Speaking Discussions about eating habits
Review task 1 Start mind maps for revision of the whole Student's book

Resources

Teacher's i-solutions, Student's Book audio, Vlog and worksheets

Preparation Nine pieces of paper for each student (or pair) for the review task

Flipped Learning

EMMA'S VLOG: Healthy pizza!

- Make sure to set up the **Flipped Learning** work with the students beforehand. **See pages 20-23 for complete Flipped Learning guidelines.**
- Ask students to put the **Flipped Learning worksheets** on their desks and walk around to check how many have completed the Flipped task.
- In pairs or small groups, ask students to compare and check the *Before you watch...* and *While you watch...* exercises on the worksheet.
- Show students **Emma's vlog** and ask volunteers to provide correct answers and clarify any doubts other students may have.
- Choose three or four students to read aloud their answers to the *After you watch...* exercises on the worksheet and encourage some class discussion.
- Move straight to exercise 1 on page 82.

Warmer

Watch Emma's vlog and discuss the questions with the whole class. If you don't have video facilities, simply discuss the questions.

1 2.32 (See page 179 for transcripts) Ask students what they usually have for breakfast and find out what the most common breakfast is and if anyone has something more unusual. Then have students choose the options before you play the audio.

2 When students have completed the exercise, ask which items in the table you can count (the top four) and tell them that we call them countable nouns and nouns we can't count are called uncountable nouns.

Flipped Learning

NOUNS: COUNTABLE AND UNCOUNTABLE

Draw students' attention to the **Grammar table**. Remind students that they can use this as a quick reference while completing the exercises.

Show students the **Grammar animation** and/or refer students to the **Grammar reference** on page 115 for further information on form and use.

→ See page 23 for how to flip the **grammar lesson**

3 Get students to refer to the **Grammar table** for support. Tell them that many things we can count are considered uncountable if we're considering them as part of a whole, like cake (you can count cakes, but we normally eat pieces of cake).

FAST FINISHERS Students can complete this exercise alone or in pairs.

VOCABULARY TOOLS

Get students to read the **Vocabulary tool** and give examples of things that are parts of a bigger whole: *some cake, some chicken, some bread,* etc.

4 2.33 (See page 179 for transcripts) Ask if students have seen a healthy eating plate like this before. Explain that the text identifies the elements of it and get them to complete the exercise. Help with any new vocabulary.

Flipped Learning

QUANTIFIERS

Draw students' attention to the **Grammar table**. Remind students that they can use this as a quick reference while completing the exercises.

Show students the **Grammar animation** and/or refer students to the **Grammar reference** on page 115 for further information on form and use.

→ See page 23 for how to flip the **grammar lesson**

5 You could combine this and the next exercise. Check their sentences before they start the speaking practice.

6 Ask students to compare the quantities they eat with the recommended quantities on the plate in exercise 4.

7 2.34 **NOW YOU!** (See page 179 for transcripts) You could get students to plan a picnic by each writing a list of items they would take. Then they could take it in turns to ask about each other's picnic.

REVIEW TASK 1 Mind maps

Decide if you want them to do this exercise individually or in pairs and hand out the paper accordingly. Then demonstrate the activity by drawing up the start of a mind map for unit 1 on the board.

FURTHER PRACTICE

Workbook pages 76-77
- **Grammar reference and practice** pages 92 and 96
- **Wordlist and exercises** pages 101 and 104

Remind students to do all the exercises in their notebook

CONTINUOUS ASSESSMENT Students talk about food and use quantifiers with countable and uncountable nouns.

9.2 Listening and grammar

UNITS OF MEASUREMENT

Use units of measurement with uncountable nouns.	Use units of measurement or numbers with countable nouns.
a tin of tuna, a bottle of oil, a spoonful of mayonnaise, a loaf of bread, a slice of ham	a bowl of strawberries, a jar of pickles, a bag of oranges, a packet of biscuits, a box of eggs

1 Listen and complete the list of ingredients.

Snack Pizza

Ingredients
four ¹··· of bread
a ²··· of tomato sauce
³··· an onion and ⁴··· tomatoes
two ⁵··· of ham
a ⁶··· of cheese

2 Match the steps of the recipe with the pictures. Listen and check.

Preparation
a Put the onion and ham on top of the cheese.
b Spread the tomatoes and tomato sauce on the bread.
c Cook the pizzas in the microwave.
d Grate the cheese and add it.
e Chop the onion and tomatoes.

Pronunciation: compound noun stress

3 Listen and repeat. Is the first or the second word stressed?
1 animal fat
2 breakfast cereal
3 chocolate cake
4 dairy products
5 fruit juice
6 olive oil

4 Choose the correct option.

TUNA SANDWICH
Ingredients
1 two spoonfuls of / a bottle of mayonnaise
2 a kilo of / two spoonfuls of ketchup
3 a loaf of / two slices of wholemeal bread
4 a bag of / a tin of tuna
5 three slices of / two loaves of cheese

5 Answer the questions in pairs.
- Would you like to eat this sandwich?
- What are the ingredients of your favourite sandwich?
- Is this sandwich healthy?
- Do you prefer sweet or savoury sandwiches?

FAST FINISHERS Write about who cooks in your home and say what they make.

Do all exercises in your notebook

84 Units of measurement

Vocabulary and grammar 9.2

6 Complete the recipe in pairs.

Gourmet turkey sandwiches

Ingredients
¹··· of turkey
a ²··· of pineapple
half a ³··· of wholemeal bread
a ⁴··· of mustard
a ⁵··· of chopped apple

Preparation
1 First, spread ···.
2 Then, chop ···.
3 After that, put ···.
4 Finally, add ···.

7 Look at the fridge and complete the conversation. Listen and check.

Jane: What have we got for lunch?
Larry: Yeah! I'm hungry. ¹··· there ²··· bread?
Jane: Yes, there's a ³··· of bread.
Larry: What about jam. Is there any jam?
Jane: There's a ⁴··· of jam.
Larry: Are there any eggs?
Jane: No, there ⁵··· eggs.
Larry: Is there any cheese?
Jane: Yes, there's ⁶··· cheese. There are four ⁷···.
Larry: Is there any juice?
Jane: Yes, there are two ⁸··· of juice. There's also some spinach, ⁹··· mango, a ¹⁰··· of sweetcorn and a ¹¹··· of olive oil.
Larry: OK! What can we make with all that?
Jane: Well, we can use the bread and cheese to make ¹²···!

SPEAKING TOOLS
If you can't remember a word, try to find an alternative so you can continue speaking. For example, if you can't remember the word *tuna*, say *fish*.

8 NOW YOU! Tell your partner about the ingredients for your favourite recipe and how to prepare it.

REVIEW TASK 2 Mind maps
- Fill the mind maps you started in **task 1**. Add five to ten words for each vocabulary topic. Try to remember as many as you can before you look at your book.
- Colour-code, highlight or draw pictures of words that are difficult to remember, say or spell.

Do all exercises in your notebook

Workbook pages 78 and 79 85

ANSWER KEY

Pages 84-85

1
1 slices
2 jar
3 half
4 two
5 slices
6 block

2
1 e
2 b
3 d
4 a
5 c

3
1 animal
2 breakfast
3 chocolate
4 dairy
5 fruit
6 olive

4
1 two spoonfuls of
2 two spoonfuls of
3 two slices of
4 a tin of
5 three slices of

5 *Student's own answers*

6 **Ingredients**
1 slices
2 tin
3 loaf
4 bottle
5 cup

Preparation
1 the mustard on a slice of bread
2 the apple
3 the turkey and the apple on the bread
4 another slice of bread and the slice of pineapple

7
1 Is
2 any
3 loaf
4 jar
5 aren't any
6 some
7 slices
8 bottles
9 a
10 tin
11 bottle
12 sandwiches

8 *Student's own answers*

Remind students to do all the exercises in their notebook

LESSON FOCUS

Vocabulary Units of measurement

Listening A recipe and a conversation about the contents of a fridge

Speaking Sharing recipes

Review task 2 Add vocabulary to mind maps

Resources

Teacher's i-solutions, Student's Book audio

Warmer

Write *a slice of bread* on the board and draw it. Ask students to think of other things you can have a slice of (e.g. *toast, ham, cheese,* etc.). Give them a time limit and see who can come up with the most. Do the same with other units of measurement from page 84.

1 2.35 (See page 179 for transcripts) Ask students what ingredients there normally are in pizza and compare with the ingredients in the exercise. Play the audio for students to complete the exercise.

2 2.36 (See page 179 for transcripts) Give students time to do the exercise and encourage them to use the pictures to help them understand new vocabulary.

Pronunciation

3 2.37 (See page 179 for transcripts) You could play the audio first so students can answer the question and then get them to listen and repeat. Ask them if they know other types of cake, juice and oil and check their word stress.

4 Refer students to the units of measurement table at the top of the page as they do this exercise.

5 Tell the class your favourite sandwich by way of example and get them to do the exercise. You could leave this exercise until after exercise 6 so they can compare the sandwiches.

FAST FINISHERS Students can complete this exercise alone or in pairs.

6 Help them identify the items and make sure they understand the vocabulary.

7 2.38 (See page 179 for transcripts) Before they complete the conversation, ask what they can see in (and on) the fridge.

SPEAKING TOOLS

Get students to read the **Speaking tool**. Tell them they can use more generic words.

8 **NOW YOU!** Let them look up any vocabulary they need and tell them to be prepared to explain any unusual ingredients to their partners.

REVIEW TASK 2 Mind maps

Make sure students look at the wordlists and note any vocabulary they didn't remember as easily. Get them to discuss possible ways of adding information to the mind map for remembering difficult vocabulary so they can learn new techniques from each other.

FURTHER PRACTICE

Workbook pages 78-79

- **Grammar reference and practice** pages 92 and 96
- **Wordlist and exercises** pages 101 and 104

Vocabulary and Grammar worksheets available to download from the **Richmond***Learning***Platform**

→ See pages 38-39 **Mixed-ability classes**

Remind students to do all the exercises in their notebook

CONTINUOUS ASSESSMENT Students can use units of measurement.

1 Answer the questions in pairs.
- What information can you find on a nutrition fact label?
- Is this information useful? Why?
- Do you read food labels? Why?

READING TOOLS
If a reading task asks for specific information, try to find it without reading all of the text in detail. Tables, headings and key words may help you.

2 Read the text on page 87 and answer the questions.
1 What food is the label for?
2 How many calories does a quarter of a pot contain?
3 In what ways is this product good/bad for you?
4 Which mineral does the article mention?
5 What are the healthiest sources of carbohydrates?

3 Read the text again and decide if the sentences are true, false or if it doesn't say.
1 The colours give you a quick idea of how healthy a product is.
2 Men generally need fewer calories than women.
3 Most people get their protein from meat.
4 All types of fat are bad for you.
5 There are some vitamins we need to get from our food.

4 Find the words in the text and match them with their definitions.
1 amount
2 store
3 sources
4 key
5 wholemeal

a to keep something to use later
b made using all of the grain of a cereal
c the quantity of something
d the places things come from
e essential or very important

5 Complete the sentences with words from exercise 4.
1 Spinach and broccoli are good ··· of iron.
2 ··· pasta is better for you than white.
3 You only need a small ··· of toothpaste.
4 It's important to ··· eggs at a constant temperature.
5 Eating fruit and vegetables is a ··· habit for good health.

6 Discuss the questions in pairs.
- What foods do you know that are a good source of vitamins?
- What kinds of food do you have to store in the fridge?
- Do you prefer white or wholemeal bread? Why?

CORE VALUES Healthy eating

7 Complete the recommendations from the World Health Organisation.

calories fats fruit grains nuts salt sugars vegetables

1 Eat approximately as many [1]··· in a day as your body needs.
2 No more than 30% of your calories should come from [2]···, preferably unsaturated.
3 Eat some legumes (e.g. lentils and peas), whole [3]··· (e.g. bread and pasta), [4]··· (e.g. almonds and hazelnuts) and at least 400 grams of fresh [5]··· and [6]···.
4 A maximum of 10% of your daily calories should come from [7]···, about half a can of fizzy drink!
5 Try not to eat more than 5 grams of [8]··· a day.

8 Check your answers in pairs and decide if your diet fits the recommendations.

FAST FINISHERS Write a meal plan for a day of healthy eating.

Do all exercises in your notebook

KNOW YOUR FOOD

When you buy food, do you read the nutrition facts label? No? Well, perhaps you should! It gives you key information to help you buy healthier food.

This label is for a low-fat yogurt from the UK. There is a list of nutrients on the left, and quantities across the top. The final column is the 'Guideline Daily Amount' (GDA) of the nutrient. Sometimes there is a colour scheme: green means healthy and red means unhealthy. For example, this yogurt is low-fat, but it contains an unhealthy amount of sugar.

Energy

The energy in the label is given first in metric kilojoules (kJ) and then in kilocalories (kcal). Generally, an adult man needs about 10,500 kJ (2,500 kcal) a day and an adult woman needs about 8,400 kJ (2,000 kcal). Where our calories come from is also very important.

Nutrition information			
Typical values	per 100 g	per 1/4 pot	% based on GDA
Energy	250 kj	320 kj	
	60 kcal	76 kcal	3.8%
Protein	5 g	6.1 g	13.6%
Carbohydrate	7 g	8.6 g	3.7%
of which sugars	7 g	8.6 g	9.6%
of which starch	nil	nil	-
Fat	1.5 g	1.9 g	2.7%
of which saturates	1.0 g	1.1 g	5.5%
monounsaturates	0.5 g	0.5 g	-
polyunsaturates	nil	nil	-
Fibre	nil	nil	nil
Salt	0.2 g	0.3 g	5.0%
of which sodium	trace	0.1 g	4.2%
Vitamins & minerals			
Calcium	170 mg	210 mg	26%

Protein, carbohydrates, fat, fibre and salt

There's a lot of protein in meat and fish but also in nuts and beans. The healthiest sources of carbohydrates are wholemeal bread, pasta and fruit and vegetables. Protein, carbohydrates and fat are where we get most of our energy. Too much salt and fat, especially saturated fat, is bad for us. However, we do need some types in our diet.

Vitamins and minerals

We need vitamins and minerals to be healthy and stay that way. Some vitamins are organic; we store them in our bodies. But we need to get others, like Vitamin C, from the food we eat. We also need to get some minerals, like calcium, from our food.

So, the next time you go shopping and you see something that looks nutritious and healthy, have a look at the nutrition facts label. It will help you to be sure.

Do all exercises in your notebook

ANSWER KEY

Pages 86-87

1 *Student's own answers*

2
1 a low-fat yogurt
2 76
3 It's good for you because it is low-fat, but it also contains an unhealthy amount of sugar.
4 calcium
5 wholemeal bread, pasta and fruit and vegetables

3
1 True
2 False
3 Doesn't say
4 False
5 True

4
1 c
2 a
3 d
4 e
5 b

5
1 sources
2 Wholemeal
3 amount
4 store
5 key

6 *Student's own answers*

7
1 calories
2 fats
3 grains
4 nuts
5 fruit
6 vegetables
7 sugars
8 salt

8 *Student's own answers*

Remind students to do all the exercises in their notebook

LESSON FOCUS

Language in context Nutrition

Core values Healthy eating

Resources

Teacher's i-solutions, Student's Book audio

Preparation Several nutrition facts labels enlarged for all the class to see

→ See pages 36-37 **Literature**

Warmer

Show the nutrition labels to the class and ask if they know what they are. Ask the students to discuss in pairs or small groups if they would eat the foods or not and why.

1 Draw students' attention to the nutrition labels you showed them in order to answer the questions.

READING TOOLS

Get students to read the **Reading tool** and tell them their first reading task will ask them for specific information.

2 2.39 (See page 179 for transcripts) Do the first question together but stop students as soon as the first student has the answer. Give them a time limit for the task (1-2 minutes) and tell them they will have more time to read in detail in the next exercise. Ask how they knew where to find the answers.

3 Give them more time to do this exercise and the next, and help them with any vocabulary.

4 Encourage students to guess the meanings and check in pairs. Check that they know what word forms they are.

5 You could put students in pairs, one student facing the board and other facing away. Put the answers on the board for the first student and have them read out the sentences with a 'beep' sound for the gap, while the student facing away has to guess the words.

6 Encourage students to use the new vocabulary in their answers.

CORE VALUES Healthy eating

7 Check that students remember the food and nutrition words before they start.

8 You could ask them to think of one way in which their diets fit the recommendations and one way in which they don't.

FAST FINISHERS Students can complete this exercise alone or in pairs.

FURTHER PRACTICE

Workbook pages 80-81

Remind students to do all the exercises in their notebook

CONTINUOUS ASSESSMENT Students can understand vocabulary related to nutrition in a text about nutrition facts labels.

9.4 Writing

A report on your school canteen

Focus on quantifiers

1 **Complete the sentences so they are true for you. Compare your answers in pairs.**

a few a little a lot of no not many not much plenty of

1 Our school canteen has ··· space for everyone to sit.
2 There are ··· windows.
3 There are ··· healthy things to eat.
4 There are usually ··· vegetables.
5 There is ··· food that I really like.

2 **Read the text and choose the best summary in pairs.**

1 The canteen needs to improve its food a lot, but the facilities are OK.
2 The canteen is OK, but they recommend some changes.
3 The canteen facilities need to be improved, but the food is OK.

Report on the Summer Hill Secondary School canteen

Aim
The aim of this report is to evaluate the food and facilities at our school canteen.

The food
In general, the food is quite good. It's healthy and there's always more than one option. But sometimes there's a lot of meat and it's often a bit salty and cold. Also, the broccoli is often overcooked, so it's mushy and a little bland.

The facilities
The facilities are mostly good. There's lots of light and plenty of tables. The only problem is that the chairs aren't very comfortable.

Recommendations
The meat should be served hot and with less salt. The vegetables should be cooked less. Also, I think it's a good idea to replace the chairs.

Did you notice?

3 **Read the text again and find the following things.**

1 The phrase the writer uses to start the report.
2 An adjective that means a food is too soft.
3 An adjective that's the opposite of *flavoursome*.
4 Two quantifiers that are synonyms of *a lot of*.

NOW YOU! → Workbook page 82

4 PLAN **You are going to write a report on your school canteen. If you don't have a school canteen, imagine one.**

Aim
(Use the sentence from the model.)
The food
Start with a general comment. Then make specific comments. Is the food bland / salty / undercooked / etc ?
The facilities
Is there space for everyone? Is it bright? Is it comfortable? Are the chairs and tables OK?
Recommendations
Suggest changes to the things criticised

WRITING TOOLS
When you make critical comments, try to be gentle, specific and constructive. Always make recommendations about how to correct the problem.

5 WRITE **Use your plan to write your report. Remember to use quantifiers.**

6 CHECK **Read your report and check it follows your plan. Check that your recommendations are clear.**

REVIEW TASK 3 Mind maps

- Add sentences to your mind maps to give examples of each grammar structure you have learnt.
- Finally, add idioms and expressions.
- You can use these mind maps to study. Put them up on a wall where you can see them.

Do all exercises in your notebook

ANSWER KEY

Page 88

1 *Student's own answers*

2 2

3 **1** The aim of this report is to…
2 mushy
3 bland
4 lots of, plenty of

4 *Student's own answers*

5 *Student's own answers*

6 *Student's own answers*

LESSON FOCUS

Focus on Quantifiers
Writing A report on your school canteen
Review task 3 Complete the mind maps with example sentences and idioms and expressions

Resources
Teacher's i-solutions, Student's Book audio

Warmer

Describe a type of food using quantifiers students already know and have them guess the food: *It has a lot of protein and carbohydrates, some meat and maybe a slice of tomato between two pieces of bread (a hamburger).* Students continue in pairs or small groups.

Focus on quantifiers

1 If there isn't a school canteen, ask them to imagine one by thinking about a café or restaurant they sometimes eat at. Discuss what things students agree on and try to emphasise the positives.

2 Give students time to read the model and reach a consensus about their answer. Point out that you will look at vocabulary in the next exercise.

Did you notice?

3 To help students with the adjectives, ask what happens to broccoli or other vegetables when they're overcooked.

4 PLAN Remind the students of their comments in exercise 1. Encourage them to include answers to the questions in their plans.

WRITING TOOLS

Get students to read the **Writing tool** and then check each other's plans to see if they include effective, constructive criticism.

5 WRITE Before students start writing, make a checklist on the board of any elements related to content, structure, language and style that they should bear in mind.

6 CHECK Once students have checked their own reports, they can check each other's.

REVIEW TASK 3 Mind maps

Encourage students to write example sentences that are clear, personal and interesting to them so that they will help them to remember the relevant language.

Remind students to do all the exercises in their notebook

FURTHER PRACTICE

Workbook page 82

 CONTINUOUS ASSESSMENT Students can use quantifiers to write a report.

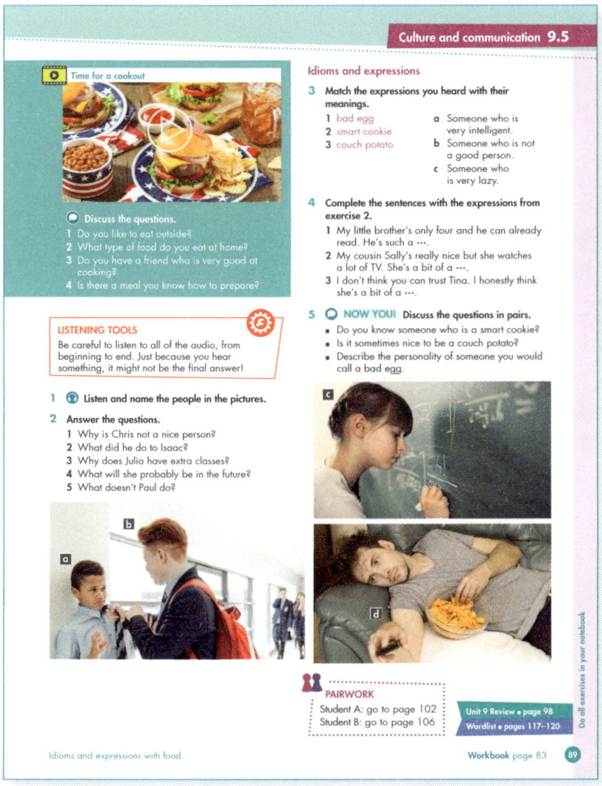

Culture and communication 9.5

Time for a cookout

Discuss the questions.
1 Do you like to eat outside?
2 What type of food do you eat at home?
3 Do you have a friend who is very good at cooking?
4 Is there a meal you know how to prepare?

LISTENING TOOLS
Be careful to listen to all of the audio, from beginning to end. Just because you hear something, it might not be the final answer!

1 Listen and name the people in the pictures.

2 Answer the questions.
1 Why is Chris not a nice person?
2 What did he do to Isaac?
3 Why does Julia have extra classes?
4 What will she probably be in the future?
5 What doesn't Paul do?

Idioms and expressions

3 Match the expressions you heard with their meanings.
1 bad egg
2 smart cookie
3 couch potato
a Someone who is very intelligent.
b Someone who is not a good person.
c Someone who is very lazy.

4 Complete the sentences with the expressions from exercise 2.
1 My little brother's only four and he can already read. He's such a ···.
2 My cousin Sally's really nice but she watches a lot of TV. She's a bit of a ···.
3 I don't think you can trust Tina. I honestly think she's a bit of a ···.

5 NOW YOU! Discuss the questions in pairs.
- Do you know someone who is a smart cookie?
- Is it sometimes nice to be a couch potato?
- Describe the personality of someone you would call a bad egg.

PAIRWORK
Student A: go to page 102
Student B: go to page 106

Unit 9 Review • page 98
Wordlist • pages 117–120

Do all exercises in your notebook

Idioms and expressions with food

Workbook page 83

89

ANSWER KEY

Page 89

1 **a** Isaac **b** Chris **c** Julia **d** Paul

2
1 He's always saying mean things to people. Any chance he gets to do something bad, he does it. He is a bully.
2 He pushed him in the corridor.
3 Because she's so far ahead of the rest of the class.
4 A famous inventor.
5 He doesn't do any exercise or help around the house.

3 1 b 2 a 3 c

4
1 smart cookie
2 couch potato
3 bad egg

5 *Student's own answers*

FURTHER PRACTICE AND UNIT ASSESSSMENT

Unit 9 Review **Student's Book** page 89
Workbook page 83
- Reflect on your learning page 83
- Grammar reference and practice pages 92 and 96
- Wordlist and exercises pages 101 and 104

Tests available to download and edit from the **Richmond***Learning***Platform**

→ See pages 40-41 **Assessment**

LESSON FOCUS
Idioms and expressions Food
Listening Short monologues
Speaking Describing people using idioms and expressions

Resources
Teacher's i-solutions, Student's Book audio, Culture video and worksheets

Time for a cookout

Video and worksheet available on the Richmond*Learning***Platform**
- In pairs, ask students to complete the *What I know...* exercises on the **Culture video worksheet**.
- Show students the **Culture video** and ask them to complete the *What I learned...* exercises on the worksheet.
- In pairs, students compare answers.
- In small groups, tell students to complete the *What I wonder...* exercises on the worksheet.

Warmer

Watch the Culture video and discuss the questions with the whole class. If you don't have video facilities, simply discuss the questions.

LISTENING TOOLS

Get students to read the **Listening tool** and tell them that they will need to apply it in the next listening task.

1 2.40 (See page 180 for transcripts) Play the first conversation and check that students listened to the end to find out the name of the bully. Play the rest of the audio for the students to complete the exercise.

2 Replay the audio for any answers students can't do from memory.

Idioms and expressions

3 Check if students can identify who was described as which in the monologues. Use the pictures to guide them in understanding the expressions.

4 To help students remember the expressions, encourage them to draw pictures of the food.

5 NOW YOU! Give students more food expressions for describing people they know: for example a *good egg, a tough cookie, a big cheese*.

PAIRWORK **Student's Book** pages 102 and 106
See **Teacher's Book** page 166 for more information.

→ See pages 30-33 **Mediation**

Remind students to do all the exercises in their notebook

Unit 9 Review

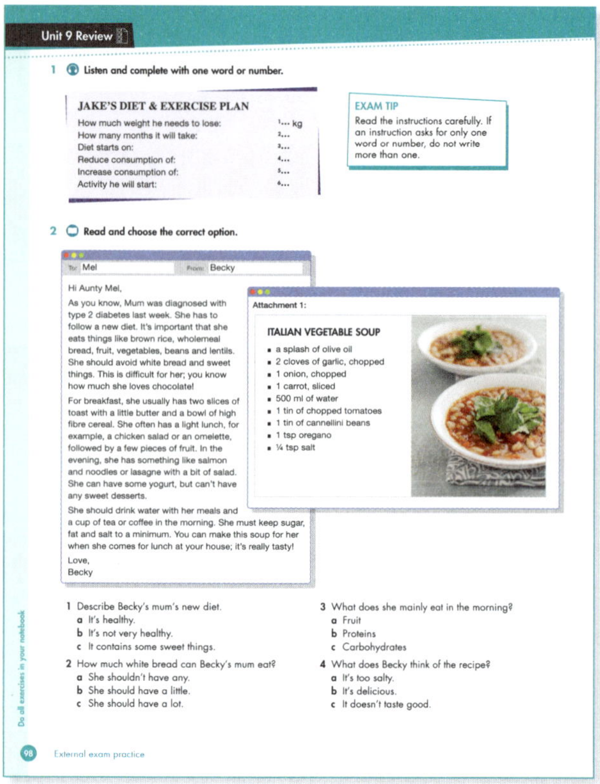

Unit 9 Review

1 Listen and complete with one word or number.

JAKE'S DIET & EXERCISE PLAN

How much weight he needs to lose: 1... kg
How many months it will take: 2...
Diet starts on: 3...
Reduce consumption of: 4...
Increase consumption of: 5...
Activity he will start: 6...

EXAM TIP
Read the instructions carefully. If an instruction asks for only one word or number, do not write more than one.

2 Read and choose the correct option.

To: Mel From: Becky

Hi Aunty Mel,

As you know, Mum was diagnosed with type 2 diabetes last week. She has to follow a new diet. It's important that she eats things like brown rice, wholemeal bread, fruit, vegetables, beans and lentils. She should avoid white bread and sweet things. This is difficult for her; you know how much she loves chocolate!

For breakfast, she usually has two slices of toast with a little butter and a bowl of high fibre cereal. She often has a light lunch, for example, a chicken salad or an omelette, followed by a few pieces of fruit. In the evening, she has something like salmon and noodles or lasagne with a bit of salad. She can have some yogurt, but can't have any sweet desserts.

She should drink water with her meals and a cup of tea or coffee in the morning. She must keep sugar, fat and salt to a minimum. You can make this soup for her when she comes for lunch at your house; it's really tasty!

Love,
Becky

Attachment 1:

ITALIAN VEGETABLE SOUP
- a splash of olive oil
- 2 cloves of garlic, chopped
- 1 onion, chopped
- 1 carrot, sliced
- 500 ml of water
- 1 tin of chopped tomatoes
- 1 tin of cannellini beans
- 1 tsp oregano
- ¼ tsp salt

1 Describe Becky's mum's new diet.
a It's healthy.
b It's not very healthy.
c It contains some sweet things.

2 How much white bread can Becky's mum eat?
a She shouldn't have any.
b She should have a little.
c She should have a lot.

3 What does she mainly eat in the morning?
a Fruit
b Proteins
c Carbohydrates

4 What does Becky think of the recipe?
a It's too salty.
b It's delicious.
c It doesn't taste good.

Do all exercises in your notebook

98 External exam practice

Student's Book page 98

ANSWER KEY

See page 181 for transcripts

1 2.46
1 5
2 6
3 Tuesday
4 fats
5 vegetables
6 running

2 **1** a
2 a
3 c
4 b

Pairwork

Unit 9 • Student A

1 Look at the picture of vegetable soup. Write down the ingredients you think are used to make it, their quantities and the three steps of the recipe.

2 Read your recipe for vegetable soup to Student B and check if you were correct.

3 Student B will guess the recipe for French toast. Then discuss the recipes with Student B. Which of the two dishes would you like to cook? Which would you like to eat? Which is healthier? Why?

French toast: Ingredients
- 3 eggs
- 1 cup of milk
- 2 tablespoons of sugar
- 3 slices of bread
- 1 tablespoon of butter
- 1 teaspoon cinnamon powder
- honey, strawberries and blueberries

Preparation
1 Mix the eggs and milk. Then add the cinnamon powder and sugar.
2 Put bread slices into the mixture.
3 Melt the butter in a saucepan and cook the bread until brown.
4 Serve with honey, strawberries and blueberries.

Do all exercises in your notebook

Student's Book page 102

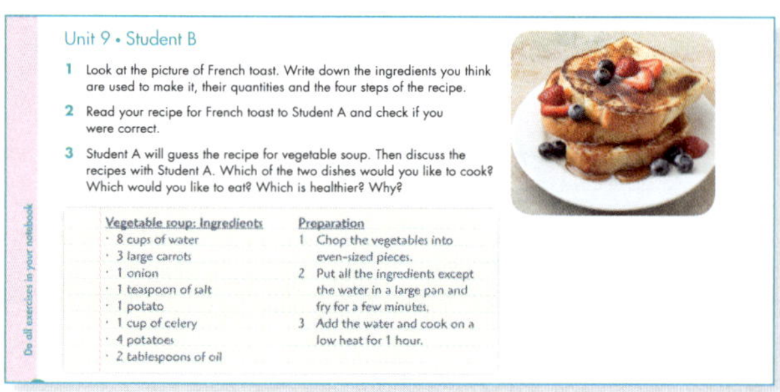

Unit 9 • Student B

1 Look at the picture of French toast. Write down the ingredients you think are used to make it, their quantities and the four steps of the recipe.

2 Read your recipe for French toast to Student A and check if you were correct.

3 Student A will guess the recipe for vegetable soup. Then discuss the recipes with Student A. Which of the two dishes would you like to cook? Which would you like to eat? Which is healthier? Why?

Vegetable soup: Ingredients
- 8 cups of water
- 3 large carrots
- 1 onion
- 1 teaspoon of salt
- 1 potato
- 1 cup of celery
- 4 potatoes
- 2 tablespoons of oil

Preparation
1 Chop the vegetables into even-sized pieces.
2 Put all the ingredients except the water in a large pan and fry for a few minutes.
3 Add the water and cook on a low heat for 1 hour.

Do all exercises in your notebook

Student's Book page 106

CEFR MEDIATION DESCRIPTOR

- **Facilitating collaborative interaction with peers**
Students can collaborate in simple, shared tasks, provided that other participants speak slowly and that one or more of them help him/her to contribute and to express his/her suggestions.

- **Describing a recipe**
Tell Student A and B that they each have a photo of one dish and the recipe for the other. See if they can guess what they have to do (guess the recipe for the photo and check their partner's guess of their recipe.) Give them time to write first and to discuss preferences at the end.

Remind students to do all the exercises in their notebook

Grammar reference

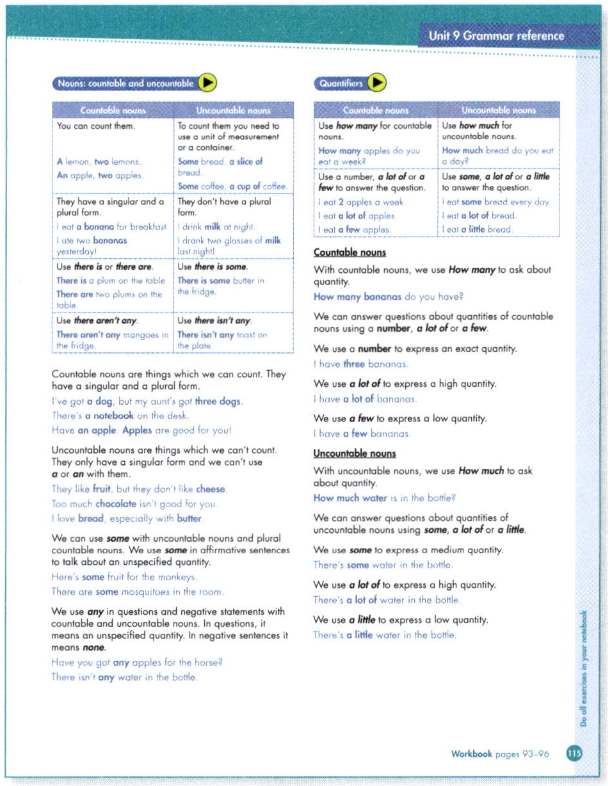

Unit 9 Grammar reference

Nouns: countable and uncountable

Countable nouns	Uncountable nouns
You can count them. **A** lemon, **two** lemons. **An** apple, **two** apples.	To count them you need to use a unit of measurement or a container. **Some** bread, **a slice of** bread. **Some** coffee, **a cup of** coffee.
They have a singular and a plural form. I eat **a banana** for breakfast. I ate two **bananas** yesterday!	They don't have a plural form. I drink **milk** at night. I drank two glasses of **milk** last night!
Use ***there is*** or ***there are***. **There is** a plum on the table **There are** two plums on the table.	Use ***there is some***. **There is some** butter in the fridge.
Use ***there aren't any***. **There aren't any** mangoes in the fridge.	Use ***there isn't any***. **There isn't any** toast on the plate.

Countable nouns are things which we can count. They have a singular and a plural form.

I've got **a dog**, but my aunt's got **three dogs**.
There's **a notebook** on the desk.
Have **an apple**. **Apples** are good for you!

Uncountable nouns are things which we can't count. They only have a singular form and we can't use ***a*** or ***an*** with them.

They like **fruit**, but they don't like **cheese**.
Too much **chocolate** isn't good for you.
I love **bread**, especially with **butter**.

We can use ***some*** with uncountable nouns and plural countable nouns. We use ***some*** in affirmative sentences to talk about an unspecified quantity.

Here's **some** fruit for the monkeys.
There are **some** mosquitoes in the room.

We use ***any*** in questions and negative statements with countable and uncountable nouns. In questions, it means an unspecified quantity. In negative sentences it means ***none***.

Have you got **any** apples for the horse?
There isn't **any** water in the bottle.

Quantifiers

Countable nouns	Uncountable nouns
Use ***how many*** for countable nouns. **How many** apples do you eat a week?	Use ***how much*** for uncountable nouns. **How much** bread do you eat a day?
Use a number, ***a lot of*** or ***a few*** to answer the question. I eat **2** apples a week. I eat **a lot of** apples. I eat **a few** apples.	Use ***some***, ***a lot of*** or ***a little*** to answer the question. I eat **some** bread every day. I eat **a lot of** bread. I eat **a little** bread.

Countable nouns

With countable nouns, we use ***How many*** to ask about quantity.

How many bananas do you have?

We can answer questions about quantities of countable nouns using a **number**, ***a lot of*** or ***a few***.

We use a **number** to express an exact quantity.
I have **three** bananas.

We use ***a lot of*** to express a high quantity.
I have **a lot of** bananas.

We use ***a few*** to express a low quantity.
I have **a few** bananas.

Uncountable nouns

With uncountable nouns, we use ***How much*** to ask about quantity.

How much water is in the bottle?

We can answer questions about quantities of uncountable nouns using ***some***, ***a lot of*** or ***a little***.

We use ***some*** to express a medium quantity.
There's **some** water in the bottle.

We use ***a lot of*** to express a high quantity.
There's **a lot of** water in the bottle.

We use ***a little*** to express a low quantity.
There's **a little** water in the bottle.

Do all exercises in your notebook

Workbook pages 93–96 115

Student's Book page 115

Wordlist

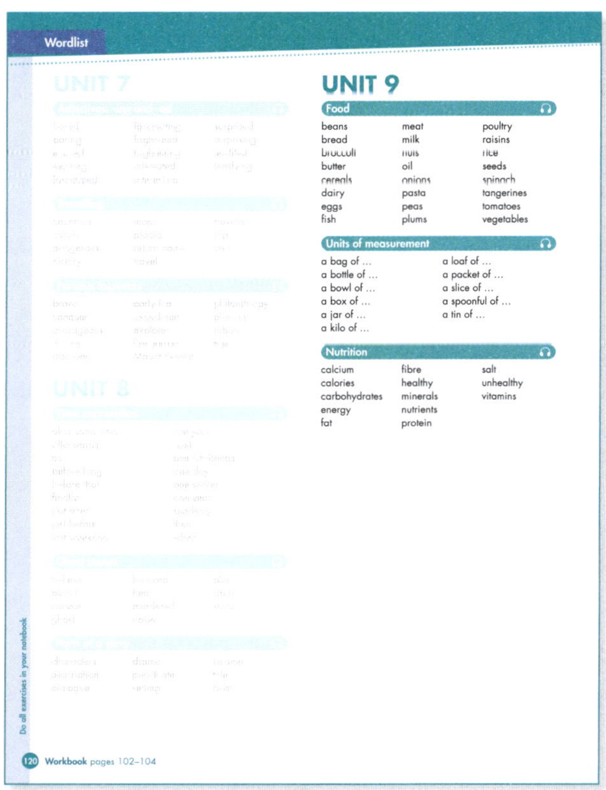

Wordlist

UNIT 7

UNIT 8

UNIT 9

Food

beans, bread, broccoli, butter, cereals, dairy, eggs, fish, meat, milk, nuts, oil, onions, pasta, peas, plums, poultry, raisins, rice, seeds, spinach, tangerines, tomatoes, vegetables

Units of measurement

a bag of …
a bottle of …
a bowl of …
a box of …
a jar of …
a kilo of …
a loaf of …
a packet of …
a slice of …
a spoonful of …
a tin of …

Nutrition

calcium, calories, carbohydrates, energy, fat, fibre, healthy, minerals, nutrients, protein, salt, unhealthy, vitamins

Do all exercises in your notebook

120 **Workbook** pages 102–104

Student's Book page 120

2.71 2.72 2.73

Remind students to do all the exercises in their notebook

Track 1.1 Get started! page 7, exercise 1
Starting a new school year is good and bad. Obviously, it's sad that the summer is over, but it's also cool to see all your friends again. In the school year, we study so much that we forget to enjoy it too. We're still kids, after all. Human brains change so much as we grow – one year you're terrible at something, and the next year it's no problem! I think it's pretty interesting.

Track 1.2 Get started! page 8, exercise 1
I spent this summer with all my family, all of them! I've got 15 cousins so that's a lot of people! My aunts and uncles live far away, so we all travelled to the same place for two weeks. Some people came on motorbikes. My aunt came on hers and she took me for a ride. I was really nervous at first, but my family always know what to say to make me feel better about myself!

Track 1.3 Get started! page 9, exercise 1
I had a good summer, but my parents didn't! They work a lot because they've got their own business. I don't think that I would like to have my own business in the future; it's a lot of stress and not a lot of holidays! I wouldn't like to work in an office either. I like to talk to people, not look at a computer all day. I would like to help people. Maybe I'll be a firefighter.

Track 1.4 Unit 1, page 10, exercise 1
1
Man 1: Hey! How's the basketball?
Man 2: It's great! Hurry up, you're late!
Man 1: I know! What's the address?
Man 2: It's 27 Stadium Street.
Man 1: OK. See you soon.
2
Young girl: I can't find my mum and dad!
Policeman: What's your name?
Young girl: It's Lauren.
Policeman: OK, Lauren. What's your mum's phone number?
Young girl: It's 684 537 912.
Policeman: Right. How old are you?
Young girl: I'm 8 years old.
3
Woman: Hello! I'm Emily, from BTC News, and this is Thomas Austen.
Man: Hello, Emily. Nice to meet you.
Woman: Nice to meet you, too.
4
Teen girl: Wow! Player number 7 is great!
Man: Yup. He's called Bob Tibballs.
Teen girl: His surname is Tibballs?
Man: Yes! T-I-B-B-A-L-L-S.
5
Mum: We can't find our daughter!
Woman: What is your daughter's name?
Dad: Lauren Wigan.
Woman: How do you spell Lauren?
Dad: L-A-U-R-E-N
Receptionist: May I have everyone's attention, please…

Track 1.5 Unit 1, page 10, exercise 2
Girl: That was a great game, Dad. The team played really well! What's the coach's name?
Man: It's Sam.
Girl: But what's his surname?
Man: It's VEASEY. He's Sam Veasey.
Girl: How do you spell that?
Man: V–E–A–S–E–Y.
Girl: Sam Veasey. He looks very young. How old is he?
Man: He's 33 years old.
Girl: Can we come to see the next game?
Man: Yes, I think that's a great idea, actually!
Girl: Oh! And could I invite my friend Tina, please?
Man: Sure, if her parents are OK with it. What's Tina's mum's phone number?
Girl: It's 932 466 82. Or we could go by her house – she lives nearby.
Man: Oh yes. What's the address?
Girl: It's number 32, Green Street.

Track 1.6 Unit 1, page 11, exercise 3
Boy: Hello! I'm Jack Collins. What's your name?
Girl: Hi, my name is Marie Thompson.
Boy: How do you spell your surname?
Girl: It's T-H-O-M-P-S-O-N.
Boy: How old are you?
Girl: I'm 12 years old. And you?
Boy: I'm 11.
Girl: What's your phone number?
Boy: It's 327 178 065. What's your address?
Girl: It's 54 Cobbler Street.
Boy: That's near my house!

Track 1.7 Unit 1, page 11, exercise 5
Introducing yourself
1
Boy 1: Hey! I'm Roger.
2
Man: Nice to meet you. My name is Ross White.

Introducing other people
1
Boy 2: Lucy, this is my friend David. David, this is Lucy.
2
Man: Mr Evans, I'd like to introduce Miss Woodson.

Greeting
1
Girl 2: Good morning, Mr Smith. How are you today?
Man: I'm very well, thank you, Sophie. And you?
2
Girl 1: Hi, Billy. How are you doing?
Boy 1: Not too bad. How's it going?

Saying goodbye
1
Girl 2: See you later!
2
Girl 1: It was nice to see you.

Track 1.8 Unit 1, page 12, exercise 1

Argentina	Colombia	Japan
Australia	France	Peru
Belgium	Germany	Spain
Brazil	India	Switzerland
Canada	Ireland	Turkey

Track 1.9 Unit 1, page 12, exercise 2
The USA, American
Colombia, Colombian
Mexico, Mexican
China, Chinese
Japan, Japanese
Portugal, Portuguese
Argentina, Argentinian
Brazil, Brazilian
Italy, Italian
England, English
Ireland, Irish
Spain, Spanish
New Zealand, from New Zealand
Greece, Greek
The Netherlands, Dutch

Track 1.10 Unit 1, page 12, exercise 3
1
I'm Jaime Ramírez. That's J-A-I-M-E R-A-M-I-R-E-Z. I'm from Mexico City, in Mexico. I'm 18 years old. My phone number is 55 5450 170. Oh! And my address is number 11, Santos Street.
2
Hi. I'm Hendrika Jansen. That's H-E-N-D-R-I-K-A J-A-N-S-E-N. I'm from Amsterdam, in the Netherlands. I'm Dutch. I'm 16 years old. My phone number is 20 672 560 and my address is number 75, Albert Street.
3
I'm Li Wei Ying. That's L-I-W-E-I-Y-I-N-G. I'm from Beijing, in China. I'm Chinese. I'm 32 years old. My phone number is 10 6512 079 and my address is number 23, Renmin Street.
4
Hi! I'm Osvaldo Santos. That's O-S-V-A-L-D-O S-A-N-T-O-S. I'm from Lisbon, Portugal. I'm 12 years old. My phone number is 21 346 123 and my address is number 17, Farol Street.
5 and 6
Greek woman: Hello! I'm Aleka Karras. That's A-L-E-K-A K-A-R-R-A-S. I'm from Athens. I'm Greek. What's your name?
English woman: My name's Trish Henry. T-R-I-S-H, H-E-N-R-Y. I'm English – I'm from London Nice to meet you.
Greek woman: And how old are you, Trish?
English woman: I'm 40 years old. And you, Aleka?
Greek woman: I'm 45.
English woman: What's your phone number and address?
Greek woman: My phone number is 694 034 857 and my address is number 2, Toro Street. And yours?
English woman: My phone number is 020 7980 442 and my address is number 48 Waterloo Street.

Track 1.11 Unit 1, page 13, exercise 5
Listen and repeat.
1 I
2 I'm fine.
3 Nice to meet you.
4 I'm from Ireland. I'm Irish.

Track 1.12 Unit 1, page 14 and 15, exercise 2
1
This is Liam Hemsworth. He's Australian, but he lives in California. He's a film and television actor and is the star of the action film Independence Day: Resurgence. He also appeared in The Hunger Games. He is the younger brother of Luke and Chris Hemsworth. Liam says that the brothers are competitive, but they are also supportive. He likes surfing, his favourite food is pizza and he's a vegan.
2
This is Lorde. She's from Auckland, New Zealand. She's a singer-songwriter and record producer. She's famous for the hit song 'Royals', but she's also known for The Hunger Games, like Liam Hemsworth! She recorded the soundtrack. She has two Grammy Awards, a Brit Award and ten New Zealand Music Awards. She likes lots of different kinds of music: jazz, folk, pop, R&B and hip-hop. Her favourite food is tuna sashimi.
3
These are the Williams sisters, Venus and Serena. They're from Florida, in the USA. They're professional tennis players and between them, they have won over 100 titles and eight Olympic gold medals. Like the Hemsworth brothers, the Williams sisters are rivals and good friends. Serena's favourite hobbies, apart from tennis, are reading, watching films and spending time with family and friends. Venus likes fashion and listening to music, and her favourite food is cherry pie.

Track 1.13 Unit 1, page 17, exercise 1
1
Hi, I'm Trish. I'm 13 years old and I'm American. My hobby is cooking. I like Chinese food, so I sometimes try to make it for the family dinner. Some things are difficult to cook, but practice makes perfect! My favourite part is eating the food, of course!
2
Hello, I'm Jacob. I'm 13 years old. Where am I from? I'm South African. My hobby is Capoeira. It's a combination of martial arts and dance from Brazil. We practise every day, from Monday to Friday. Sometimes I get tired but I never throw in the towel!
3
Hey, my name's Joanna. I'm from England. How old am I? I'm 14. My hobby is table tennis. It's great! I play with my cousin. He's from Wales but he lives in England. I want to be an Olympic table tennis player. Well, you have to reach for the stars!

Track 1.14 Unit 1, page 17, exercise 3
My name's Sarah. I'm from England. I like dancing to hip-hop. It's not easy to learn the dance moves, but practice makes perfect! Hip-hop's main instruments are drum machines and synthesisers. I like hip-hop lyrics about politics and family. My best friend is Lisa. She's from Ireland. She's 13 years old, like me! Lisa plays the guitar really well. She likes reggae. She practises every day and she never throws in the towel. She wants to be famous. I believe she can do it. Reach for the stars, Lisa!

Track 1.15 Unit 2, page 18, exercise 1

first	seventh	thirteenth
second	eighth	twentieth
third	ninth	twenty-first
fourth	tenth	thirtieth
fifth	eleventh	fortieth
sixth	twelfth	fiftieth

Track 1.16 Unit 2, page 18, exercise 2
1
Boy: Is your birthday on Tuesday?
Girl: Yes. My birthday is on Tuesday the 12th.
2
Girl: What day is it today?
Boy: It's Sunday.
Girl: Is it Sunday the 3rd?
Boy: No, it isn't. Today is Sunday the 10th.
3
Girl: When is the football match?
Boy: It's on Monday. Monday the 18th.
4
Boy: Are our exams on Thursday the 21st?
Girl: No, they aren't. They're on Thursday the 28th.
5
Boy: Have you got lunch at your grandma's house on Friday?
Girl: No. That's on Saturday. Saturday the 30th.

Track 1.17 Unit 2, page 18, exercise 3
Listen and repeat. Put your fingers on your throat when you speak.
/θ/, third, fifth, Thursday
/ð/, there, these, then

Track 1.18 Unit 2, page 20, exercise 1
1 Half past twelve.
2 Six o´clock.
3 A quarter past ten.
4 A quarter to eleven.

Track 1.19 Unit 2, page 20, exercise 2
1
Girl: What time is the exam tomorrow?
Woman: It's at half past one. Don't be late!
2
Girl: What time is the basketball match?
Boy 1: It's at seven o'clock. See you there!
3
Boy 1: What time is Geography class?
Boy 2: It's at a quarter past eleven, after Maths.
4
Girl 2: When is the party?
Girl 1: It's tomorrow, at a quarter to nine.

Track 1.20 Unit 2, page 20, exercise 3
1
Girl: When was your baby cousin born?
Boy: He was born on the 11th of February at half past eleven.
2
Boy: What time is it, Mum?
Woman 1: It's half past six. Come on! The school bus leaves soon!
3
Woman 2: Excuse me, what time does the restaurant open?
Man: In the summer it opens at a quarter past two, Madam.

Track 1.21 Unit 2, page 21, exercise 5
Boy: Have you seen the new timetable? It changes in the summer.
Girl: Yes! The first double class on Monday is History, right?
Boy: Yes. History class is on Monday from nine o'clock to eleven o'clock. But on Wednesday, our first double class is English.
Girl: OK. English class is on Wednesday at nine o'clock.
Boy: When is Music?
Girl: Music is on Tuesday, from a quarter past eleven to a quarter past one.
Boy: That's great!
Girl: When is the Geography class?
Boy: It's almost the last class of the week. Geography is on Friday from a quarter past eleven to a quarter past one.
Girl: OK. That's a nice Friday! It's double PE at nine o'clock, too! PE, Geography, then English!
Boy: What is the last class on Wednesday?
Girl: At half past two? It's Art. Art is the last class on Monday, too.
Boy: I like the new timetable. Wait, what's on Thursday after the break?
Girl: Ahh, it's History class – from a quarter past eleven to a quarter past one.
Boy: And after that?
Girl: Oh, on Tuesday and Thursday at half past two, it's Science.
Boy: Great! Tuesday and Thursday? I love Science!

Track 1.22 Unit 2, pages 22 and 23, exercise 2
Multiple intelligences
We all think of some people as intelligent and some not. But what is intelligence? Is it the ability to do well at school? Is it the capacity to understand complex concepts? Is it just common sense? Can we define it? Howard Gardner says that people are intelligent in eight different ways. And they're all equally important!

1. These people are a little shy and individualistic. But they're self-aware too.
2. Someone with this intelligence is adventurous and energetic. Maybe their favourite class is Science. They like animals and plants.

3. If you've got this intelligence, you're talkative and creative. You like poems and short stories, and your favourite subject is probably English.
4. People with this intelligence are very imaginative and creative. They like colours and shapes, and their favourite class is probably Art.
5. These people are very sociable and friendly. They like working in groups, and they're not shy.
6. If this is your dominant intelligence, you are ingenious and analytical. Your favourite class is Maths, and you probably like computers.
7. A person with this intelligence might like musical instruments. Music is probably their favourite subject. They are patient and persevering.
8. This intelligence means you are very active. You're sporty and your favourite subjects are probably PE and Drama.

Track 1.23 Unit 2, page 25, exercise 2

Welcome to Springtown Public School. This year is very special. We have a full calendar of school events and celebrations. In January there's the Back to School Party. It's our first important event of the year! In February there's our Sports Tournament. There will be basketball, soccer and volleyball competitions. The third special event is in March: the traditional Ecological Campaign. Then our Spring Festival is in April, and Teacher's Day is in May. Don't forget my gift!

In June we have Children's Day. And after that, there is the Arts and Crafts Show in July. In August we break for the summer holidays, but make sure you get back just in time for the Book Club in September. We want to know what you read on your holidays! The Science and Technology Fair is in October. We take time out in November to rest, because as usual, time flies and suddenly December is here with the last school celebration, the End of Year Concert.

Track 1.24 Unit 2, page 25, exercise 3

1

Hello, I'm Oliver. I'm from Manchester, in England. We have six short holidays in a school year: Christmas, Easter and the summer holidays, and the half-term holidays in October, February and May. The summer holidays start on the 24th of July this year, just in time for the warm weather! Then we go back to school on the last day of August.

2

Hi, I'm Andrea. I'm from Texas, in the USA. We have three holidays in a school year: Christmas Break and Spring Break, then the best holidays are in the summer. They're the longest holidays, so you can really take time out from studying! We start the summer break on the last day of May. This year, the summer holidays finish on the 20th of August.

3

Hi, I'm Kirsten. I'm from Melbourne, in Australia. We have four holidays in a school year, one in each of the seasons: autumn, winter, spring and summer. The summer holidays start on the 15th of December this year. It feels very short. Time flies when you're having fun! Then we go back to school at the end of January. Don't be confused! Remember our seasons are the opposite of seasons in the Northern Hemisphere!

Track 1.25 Unit 3, page 28, exercise 2

The body

1 arm	**6** chest	**11** knee
2 elbow	**7** stomach	**12** heel
3 shoulder	**8** waist	**13** foot
4 mouth	**9** hip	**14** toe
5 neck	**10** leg	

The head

15 tongue	**18** hair	**21** ear
16 tooth	**19** eyebrow	**22** nose
17 eye	**20** eyelash	**23** cheek

Track 1.26 Unit 3, page 29, exercise 4

1 Wink one eye.
2 Stand on tip toes.
3 Touch your nose.
4 Wiggle your fingers.
5 Scratch your neck.
6 Stick out your tongue.
7 Bend your knees.
8 Pull your left ear.
9 Stretch your right leg.
10 Swing your arms from side to side.

Track 1.27 Unit 3, page 29, exercise 5

Listen and repeat.

/s/ cheeks, hips
/z/ elbows, eyes
/ɪz/ eyelashes, faces

Track 1.28 Unit 3, page 29, exercise 6

In pairs, decide if these words finish with a /s/, /z/ or /ɪz/ sound. Listen and check.

1 necks	**4** noses
2 ears	**5** legs
3 chests	**6** appearances

Track 1.29 Unit 3, page 30, exercise 1

Boy: This is my cousin, little baby Maggie! Maggie's lovely. It's nice to hold her because she's plump! Her hair is short and blonde, and her eyes are blue, like mine!
Girl: This is my brother, Paul. He's short for a child of ten, but he's really cute. He's quite skinny for his age, too. He makes me laugh all the time! His hair is red, like mine, but it's straight and his eyes are green.
Boy: This is my friend, Amy. She's medium height, like me. She's a teenager now and she's very pretty and slim. She's got long, wavy hair and hazel eyes.
Girl: This is my guitar teacher, Steve. He's a very tall young man and he's handsome and athletic. He's bald and he's got brown eyes.
Boy: This is my grandma, Sue. She's tall, like all our family. She's an elderly woman now. She's beautiful and slim and she's got wavy, grey hair and grey eyes, too!

Track 1.30 Unit 3, page 30, exercise 2

Woman: OK. Let's see. Ahh yes, this is a photo from my 40th birthday! There's Melissa. She's my daughter. She's

8 years old. She's short and slim. She's got wavy, blonde hair and brown eyes. She's such a funny girl! David is my cousin. He's 32 years old. He's such a friendly guy! He's tall and thin. He's got brown hair, as well as a beard and moustache, and his eyes are brown. That's me on the other side of Melissa. I'm Barbara. I think I'm a happy person. I'm medium height and slim. I've got brown eyes, too. My hair is short and curly, but I'd love to have long hair! I like to dye my hair different colours. At the moment, it's orange!

Track 1.31 Unit 3, page 31, exercise 3

The woman with blue eyes and short, black hair is Sarah.
The lady with light brown eyes and long, straight, black hair is Jenny.
The man with green eyes and short, brown hair is David.
The woman with hazel eyes and long, wavy, light brown hair is Paula.
The woman with brown eyes and short, dark brown hair is Anita.
The lady with green eyes and long, red hair is Maria.

Track 1.32 Unit 3, page 32 and 33, exercise 2

Can you judge a book by its cover?

Look at the photos of these people. What do you see? An elderly woman with a shy smile, a man who probably isn't very interested in appearance, and a man with a face that inspires trust.

Who are they really? The woman is Rita Levi-Montalcini, 1986 winner of the Nobel Prize in Physiology or Medicine. The man with the beard is Austrian artist Gustav Klimt, famous for his beautiful gold leaf paintings. The man with the white hair is ex-criminal Frank Abagnale. His story is the basis of the Leonardo DiCaprio film Catch Me If You Can.

We often make judgements about people based on their appearance. An attractive politician has more chances of winning an election. People with more dominant facial features are usually more successful in business and we prefer nurses with soft facial features, because it makes us feel more comfortable. But obviously not all attractive people make good politicians and not all soft-featured people are kind and caring. Sometimes our initial judgements are very wrong.

So, why do we make them? Well, it's an evolutionary advantage to make quick judgements. It helps us to recognise people who may be dangerous.

But this doesn't mean that it's a good idea to believe your first impressions. People are usually much more complex than you first think.

Track 1.33 Unit 3, page 35, exercise 1

My mum? Hmm. Well, her name is Mia. She's tall and slim. Her hair is curly and red, and her eyes are brown. She's a scientist; she works at a laboratory. She works long hours, but she's always happy to give me a hand with my Science homework! She's really talented and she's won lots of awards for her research. I want to be like her in the future.

She doesn't sound anything like my dad. His name is Robert. He's short and plump. He gives the best hugs! His hair is brown. It's quite long and wavy. He's a shy person, but he's all ears if you want to talk about your problems. He's a musician and he's really family-oriented. He just loves to spend time with my brothers and me! My dad really is all heart.

Track 1.34 Unit 4, page 37, exercise 3

1 Gloria is wearing white trainers and a flowery dress.
2 Martin is wearing a checked shirt and blue jeans.
3 Maggie is wearing a tartan dress and black high-heeled shoes.
4 Carla is wearing a blue dress with colourful spots.
5 Roy is wearing a short-sleeved shirt with a pattern and brown shoes.
6 Marianne has got blue goggles on her head and is wearing a swimsuit with blue and white stripes.
7 Monica is wearing a light grey suit and glasses.
8 Robert is wearing dark blue jeans and a stripy T-shirt.

Track 1.35 Unit 4, page 38, exercise 1

Rob: Look! There's my grandad, Matthew. He's wearing a yellow T-shirt.
Alice: What's he doing?
Rob: He's reading the newspaper.
Alice: Oh! I see. He is wearing sunglasses.
Rob: Yes. There's Grandma. She's looking at photos. She isn't drinking milk; she's drinking juice.
Alice: Is that your mother? The lady wearing a purple hat? What is she eating?
Rob: Yes, that's her! She's eating dessert. Mum's brother is my uncle Theo. He's wearing a black shirt and light blue jeans. He's talking on his phone.
Alice: Who is this woman? She's wearing an orange dress. She's listening to music.
Rob: That's my aunt Lucy.
Alice: Who are the girls in the sea? Are they your cousins? What are they doing?
Rob: They aren't in the sea. That's the swimming pool. That's my sister Kate and my cousin. They are playing. Kate is throwing a ball.
Alice: What is your father doing?
Rob: Dad? He's taking photos.
Alice: Oh yeah. He's wearing a patterned T-shirt and shorts. Hey, what is your brother looking for?
Rob: Joe? I think he's looking for his marbles, again!

Track 1.36 Unit 4, page 39, exercise 3

Alice: OK. So, your grandad's name is Matthew. Lucy is your aunt and Theo is your uncle, but **what are your parents' names?**
Rob: My mum's name is Isabel and my dad's name is Michael.
Alice: OK. So… your brother is Joe and your sister is Kate… what's your grandma's name?
Rob: Her name is Rose. And you missed my cousin. Her name is Petra. And that's everyone!
Alice: Well, I guess I'm ready to meet them now!
Rob: OK, let's go!

Track 1.37 Unit 4, page 39, exercise 4

Listen and repeat.

asking	ring	taking
doing	song	wearing

Track 1.38 Unit 4, page 40 and 41, exercise 3

Going green

These people from different countries around the world are working together to protect the environment. They are joining efforts and energies to teach the rest of the world a lesson: we can all help! They're all part of a project called Go Green. Let's see what these people are doing in order to save our planet.

My name is Sara. I'm 15 years old and I'm from Medellin, Colombia. My family is huge.
I've got lots of brothers, sisters and cousins. We're planting trees at the local park. All the kids from our neighbourhood are helping us with this project too.

My name's Mike and I'm a teacher from Liverpool, in England. I'm 26 years old. I know that water is an important natural resource, so I'm having 5-minute showers so that I don't waste it. I'm also teaching my students about how to protect animals by buying ecological products.

We are the Smith family. We are from Glasgow, Scotland. Our family is small: my wife, my son Theo and me. We are riding our bikes to school and work. That way, we don't pollute the air. Also, we are helping to keep the streets clean by picking up the rubbish.

I'm from Cienfuegos, Cuba. My name's Monica and I'm 14. My brother Danilo and I are working with the Go Green project in my city. We know that plastic is non biodegradable, so we're not using plastic bottles. We're only using metal flasks or ceramic cups for our drinks. And we're teaching my family and neighbours about how to recycle correctly.

Track 1.39 Unit 4, page 43, exercise 2

1

Boy 1: I'm sorry my exam results were bad.
Man: Well, at least it was only a practice exam.
Boy 1: I'll study really hard for the real one, I promise.
Man: OK, Will. You can do better than this– but you have to pull your socks up if you don't want to fail.

2

Woman 1: No, Jennifer! You don't use it responsibly! I'm taking your phone away until the weekend.
Girl: Muuuum!
Woman 1: I know you're angry, but put yourself in my shoes. You didn't answer your phone for hours and I was worried about you.
Girl: But I was at Carla's house!
Woman 1: I didn't know that, because you ignored my calls!
Girl: I'm sorry, Mum. I'll be more sensible next time.

3

Boy 2: Mum! The teacher emailed me the exam results!
Woman 2: And...?!
Boy 2: I can't look. Can you open the email please?
Woman 2: The problem with you, Harry, is that you worry too much about your exam results. But OK, I'll look. You did it! You passed! I take my hat off to you.
Boy 2: Thanks, Mum! Phew!
Woman 2: Next time, try not to worry so much, all right?

Track 1.40 Unit 4, page 43, exercise 3

1 You can do better than this – but you have to pull your socks up if you don't want to fail.
2 I know you're angry, but put yourself in my shoes. You didn't answer your phone for hours and I was worried about you.
3 You did it! You passed! I take my hat off to you.

Track 1.41 Unit 5, page 46, exercise 1

1

Man: You look really cold.
Woman: It's snowing out there!
Man: Do you want to put my gloves on?
Woman: No thanks, dear. I'm not going back outside!

2

Girl: It's getting hot in here. Can you open the window?
Boy: Sure. Oh look! It's sunny outside.
Girl: Yeah! What a beautiful day!
Boy: Let's go out for a walk.

3

Woman 1: It's freezing!
Woman 2: I know! But I've got the fire going!
Woman 1: Oh, great!
Woman 2: Why don't you stand a bit closer to get warm?

4

Young man: Hi Mum, we're on our way home.
Mum: You're so late! What's the problem?
Young man: Sarah is driving very slowly. It's really foggy!
Mum: I see! Well, be careful. See you soon!

5

Boy: Look! It isn't raining anymore.
Young man: Oh! Well, do you want to go for a walk?
Boy: OK, but it's still really cloudy.
Young man: Well, let's take our umbrella just in case.

6

Boris: Wow, this weather is terrible!
Pam: Terrible? What do you mean?
Boris: Well, look how the leaves are blowing everywhere!
Pam: I don't mind. I love windy days.

Track 1.42 Unit 5, page 46, exercise 2

See previous track

Track 1.43 Unit 5, page 47, exercise 3

Boris: Wow, this weather is terrible!
Pam: Terrible? What do you mean?
Boris: Well, look at my scarf. It's so windy!
Pam: Yeah! I love windy days!
Boris: Why? It's chilly and unpleasant!
Pam: No, it's beautiful! Look at the leaves falling from the trees. Red, yellow, orange and brown!
Boris: They're everywhere! I think they're making me sneeze. Achoo!
Pam: No, Boris. You're sneezing because you've got a cold!
Boris: Urgh. Autumn is not my favourite season!

Track 1.44 Unit 5, page 47, exercise 4
Listen and repeat.

/ɪ/, chilly, spring, windy, winter
/iː/, leaves, people, sneeze, trees

Track 1.45 Unit 5, page 47, exercise 7

Man 1: Hi, I'm Steve. I live in Rio de Janeiro. It's really hot and sunny here today. It's fantastic!
Woman 1: Hello, my name's Amanda. I'm in London today and it's absolutely freezing! It's cloudy too. I think I'll stay indoors today!
Man 2: Robert here! I'm in Buenos Aires today. It's summer here at the moment – it's a nice day but it's a little windy!
Woman 2: I'm Sarah. I live in New York City. The weather is usually pretty good, but today it's foggy and cold. Urgh! I'm not a fan of the winter!

Track 1.46 Unit 5, page 48, exercise 2

Amanda: Hey, aren't you Laura Smith's cousin?
Tom: Yes, and you're her friends, right?
Amanda: Yeah! We go to the same school.
Patrick: And we live in the same neighbourhood.
Tom: Oh! I see.
Patrick: Do you live in this neighbourhood, too?
Tom: Yeah. I live on Calvert Street. Laura lives there, too.
Amanda: We know that street.
Patrick: That's right! We go to Calvert Sports Club every Saturday.
Amanda: Sometimes we go with Laura, too.
Tom: What sports do you play?
Patrick: We play table tennis.
Tom: What sport does Laura do there?
Patrick: She plays table tennis, too.
Amanda: Yeah, and we always do judo together. Do you do any sports?
Tom: No, I don't. I'm not into sports. I never go to the gym, but I ride my bike a lot.
Patrick: What do you do in your free time?
Tom: I meet my friends. We have a rock band.
Amanda: Wow! Really?
Tom: Yeah. I play the guitar and I sing, too. Laura sometimes sings with us as well.
Amanda: Really?
Tom: Well, I have to go to band practice now. It was nice to meet you both.
Patrick: Nice to meet you, too!

Track 1.47 Unit 5, page 50 and 51, exercise 3
Make the most of your Easter!

Spring is here and the Easter holidays are coming. More and more students are staying in camps over the Easter holidays, so if you want to do something fun this spring, here are a couple of great ideas.

Outdoor Adventure

This camp is all about enjoying the countryside and appreciating nature. On the first morning, we go canoeing and then explore the area in the afternoon. We spend the first night in a comfortable cabin. On the second day, we wake up early, pack our bags and walk through the beautiful countryside. We stop for a picnic lunch and then put up our tents in the late afternoon. We stay for the rest of the week and go hiking in the area. We stop at caves and waterfalls, and we usually see lots of deer in their natural habitat. You also learn how to find a good campsite and light a fire. You'll love it!

Sports Camp

At sports camp you can try lots of different sports. Our sports facilities include rugby fields, squash and tennis courts, an Olympic-size swimming pool and even a climbing wall. We've got all the equipment you need. We start your week with a general introduction. On the first day, we play squash and tennis, and then go outside for games of rugby and hockey. The next day, we do fencing – you wear protective clothing and it's perfectly safe. Then, in the afternoon we take you to the pool to scuba dive. After that, you choose the sports you want to play for the rest of the week. Stay with us and discover your new hobby!
Do you like the sound of one of these camps? Why not sign up now?

Track 1.48 Unit 5, page 53, exercise 1

Mum: Hi my love! How's summer camp?
Boy: Hey, Mum. Actually, it's great! There are so many activities!
Mum: Oh wonderful! What kind of activities?
Boy: Well, we play basketball from two o'clock to four o'clock every day.
Mum: Oh! And do you do any other sports?
Boy: Yes! We ride bikes! Usually from five o'clock to six o'clock. If it's raining, we play table tennis indoors. That's available from half past five to half past seven. I won the table tennis competition last night.
Mum: That's wonderful! You must be so happy.
Boy: Yeah. I'm on cloud nine!
Mum: And how about social time? Have you got some friends?
Boy: Yes! We eat breakfast together every morning, from nine o'clock to half past nine. Then, in the evenings, John plays the guitar and we dance and sing from half past seven to half past nine.
Mum: Great! I'm so glad you're having a good time!

Track 1.49 Unit 5, page 53, exercise 2

Welcome to Parkland Summer Camp! There are lots of fun things to do here. In the mornings, the weather is usually rainy and cloudy, so after breakfast we do indoor activities like painting or watching TV. But it's usually sunny and hot in the afternoons, so we do lots of sports. We even have special tandem bikes - bikes for two people! Some kids are nervous about learning to cycle on a tandem bike but really, it's a breeze. In the evenings it can be foggy and cold, so we play music and dance or sing. It's a great way to break the ice! Come over and visit us and see for yourself!

Track 2.1 Unit 6, page 54, exercise 1

Man: John
Woman: Go straight ahead for two blocks and turn left. It's on your left, across from the park. I'm sure you'll find something to buy there; it's got lots of different shops inside!
Woman: Alison

Man: Go straight ahead, past the school. Turn left and walk for two blocks, up Dean Street. It's on the corner, next to the museum. You can report your stolen money to the police officers there.

Woman: Vicky

Man: Go to the roundabout and turn right down Sun Avenue. Go straight ahead and it's on your right, in front of the car park. They have rooms available all the time, and the breakfast is delicious.

Man: Matt

Woman: Go to the traffic light, turn right and go straight ahead. Turn left at the corner and it's second on your left, behind the hospital. It's got clothes for men and women, and nice shoes too!

Track 2.2 Unit 6, page 55, exercise 4

1

John: Excuse me, is this the way to the music shop?

Man: Yes. Go past the shopping centre. Then walk across the park. It's on the corner of Dean Street and Sun Avenue, next to the hairdresser's.

2

Alison: Excuse me, where's the post office?

Woman: Go straight ahead, past the school and the clock tower. It's on your right, across from the church.

3

Vicky: Excuse me, how do I get to the museum?

Man: Well, go to the roundabout and turn right onto Sun Avenue. Go past the park and it's on your left, between the car park and the police station.

4

Matt: Excuse me, is there a church near here?

Woman: Yes. Go to the traffic light and turn left. Go straight ahead and take the second right. It's on your left, behind the hotel.

Track 2.3 Unit 6, page 56, exercise 1

Reporter: Dr Sam Richards is an expert on sharks. He lives and works in the north of Australia from January to June every year, and then for the rest of the year he lives with his family in New York City. Dr Richards, what's a typical day like for you in Australia?

Dr Richards: Well, I usually get up at 4am. I have a short, cold shower to wake myself up. I often have fruit and juice for breakfast. I hardly ever drink coffee. Then I go by boat to a place called Raine Island to find tiger sharks.

Reporter: What happens when you find the sharks?

Dr Richards: I capture the sharks very carefully. Then I place small transmitters on their tails. It's not dangerous because I turn them on their backs and they relax in that position. I sometimes take pictures of them. After that, I spend the rest of the day studying the transmitter signals. It's really interesting!

Reporter: Do you have lunch on the island?

Dr Richards: I never have lunch, actually. I love my job, so time flies. I prefer to continue working while I can.

Reporter: When do you stop following the sharks?

Dr Richards: When I'm really hungry. I go back home and eat dinner at about 6pm. I often have a big dinner.

Reporter: What do you usually do after dinner?

Dr Richards: I always read my notes from the day.

Reporter: What time do you go to bed?

Dr Richards: At 8pm, or sometimes even 7pm. I have to get up very early!

Track 2.4 Unit 6, page 56, exercise 2

See previous track

Track 2.5 Unit 6, page 56, exercise 3

Listen and repeat.

/e/ bread, breakfast, egg, ever, friends, pleasure, yes

Track 2.6 Unit 6, page 56, exercise 4

Reporter: So, Dr Richards, for the second half of the year you live with your wife and children in America. I imagine your routine is different when you're there!

Dr Richards: Yes. It's totally different! I often get up at 9am and have a big American breakfast with bacon, eggs and toast or sometimes pancakes. I spend the entire morning writing replies to my emails. After that, I read the newspaper and sometimes listen to the radio. Then I have lunch with my wife and children. We usually go out to nice restaurants, though, to be honest, I prefer homemade food. In the afternoon, I write and send reports to the office. I usually have a snack with my friends in the late afternoon.

Reporter: And then?

Dr Richards: I go to the gym. Sometimes I play squash after exercising. Back home I often have dinner at 8.30pm and I always have a long, warm shower. Finally, I phone my parents before going to sleep.

Reporter: Do you watch TV at night?

Dr Richards: Hmm, hardly ever. I prefer to read a good book.

Reporter: Well, Dr Richards, it's been a pleasure to talk to you today. Thank you!

Dr Richards: You're welcome. Thank you!

Track 2.7 Unit 6, page 57, exercise 5

In Australia, Dr Richards usually gets up at 4am, sometimes takes pictures of the sharks, never has lunch and always reads his notes after dinner. In the USA, he often gets up at 9am, usually goes out to nice restaurants, sometimes plays squash after exercising and hardly ever watches TV.

Track 2.8 Unit 6, page 57, exercise 7

1

My colleague Frank is good at his job. He's very punctual, too. We have to be in the office at 9am every day and Frank is always one of the first to arrive. He's worked here for four years and he's never late.

2

I love my cousin Susie! She's kind and patient, and lots of fun too. She lives quite far away, though, so I don't see her very often. In fact, we only see each other on Christmas Day at my grandmother's house.

3

I have a difficult job here at Summerhill School, as my day is very busy. However, the students are the most important part of my job and I make sure I have time for them. I make time to stop and talk to the students in the hallways when I can.

4

My neighbour's dog Spike doesn't like the postman. Every day the postman runs to the door, delivers the letters, and runs back to his van. I think he's afraid of Spike. And I don't understand it because Spike never barks at anyone, except the postman! He barks at him every day!

Track 2.9 Unit 6, page 58 and 59, exercise 2
Wonder where the best jobs are?

Man: Myriam is an archaeologist. She works around the pyramids at Chichen Itza, in Mexico. She usually rides her bike to work, but she never gets to work late. Sometimes, Myriam and her team dig to find ancient artefacts.
Woman: Thomas is a professional photographer. He takes photos for travel magazines and he usually works in the desert. His favourite site is Petra, in Jordan. He often spends his days photographing this ancient city of rock.
Man: Mao Su is a video game designer. He's making a video game that's based on the Great Wall of China. He always makes sketches of the wall in the morning. Then he goes home and works on the game. Mao loves his job.
Woman: Elias is an electrical engineer in Rio, Brazil. Every afternoon, he goes to the statue of Christ the Redeemer. He tests each bulb and then checks that the generators are working. Sometimes he carries out electrical repairs.
Man: Micaela is a history professor in Rome. She's an expert on the Colosseum; she studies its design and construction. She often visits the monument for her research and film-makers sometimes consult her when they need information about Roman civilisations.
Woman: Juana is a painter. She lives near Cuzco, in Peru. She always takes the first train to an area near Machu Picchu because she likes the light in the morning. She never has breakfast at home.
Man: Jahan is a tour guide at the Taj Mahal, in India. He always walks to work. Tourists come from all over the world to visit this ancient palace. He hardly ever has time to rest!

Track 2.10 Unit 6, page 61, exercise 1

1

I'm Renato. I'm on a boat in Venice. I'm here with my family. Where I live in South Africa, canals and rivers are few and far between, so it's exciting to be on a boat! I'm going to take lots of photos so I remember the canals when I'm back home.

2

I'm Samantha and this is my brother, Todd. We're from England. We're waiting in the car for Mum and Dad. We're visiting our gran in Scotland for a few days. I've had lots of exams at school this month, so a relaxing holiday at Gran's house really fits the bill.

3

I'm Lian. I'm on a train in China with my family. There are so many amazing things to see here! The culture is very different to where I live, in the USA. For example, people here make a lot of noise in restaurants! Oh well, when in Rome, do as the Romans do!

Track 2.11 Unit 7, page 64, exercise 1

Freya Stark was born in Paris. She was an explorer and travel writer. She was interested in travelling and making maps of the places she visited.
Stark's trips were sometimes frightening because she was the first European to visit many of these distant countries. She wrote more than 20 books about travel, history and culture. The books also include maps, drawings and surprising stories.

Track 2.12 Unit 7, page 64, exercise 2

The explorer Marco Polo was born in Italy. His life was very exciting! He was a good friend of Kublai Khan, the great leader of the Mongols. Polo was fascinated by Khan's stories, and he included them in a book, The Travels of Marco Polo. In it, he tells tales of terrifying events such as finding cannibals. People were very surprised by his adventures, and some people think his stories weren't true. Well, they certainly weren't boring!

Track 2.13 Unit 7, page 65, exercise 4

Roald Amundsen was born on July 16th, 1872, in Norway. When he was a little boy, he was fascinated by stories about explorers and was interested in tales of adventures. He was the first person to travel to both the North Pole and the South Pole. Many of his trips were dangerous. One of the most exciting moments in Amundsen's life was when the Inuit people taught Roald and his team how to use dog sleds to travel faster.

Track 2.14 Unit 7, page 66, exercise 1

Edward Drinker Cope and Othniel Charles Marsh were two famous American palaeontologists in the mid-1800s. Both of them were dinosaur fossil hunters and they were great rivals. Arthur Lakes was a teacher and geologist from Colorado. Their rivalry over the discovery of fossils in Colorado started the Bone Wars. The big question is – who was the discoverer of the Colorado bones? Cope? Marsh? Or Lakes?

Narrator: THE BONE WARS!
Man 1: So, who exactly discovered the Colorado Bones? Where were you last month, gentlemen?
Man 2: I was in Colorado looking at dinosaur fossils.
Man 3: No, you weren't! I was in Colorado looking at the fossils!
Man 1: So, tell me, was the fossil big?
Man 2: Yes, it was. I was surprised to see such an enormous fossil!
Man 3: No, it wasn't. It was very small!
Man 1: Gentlemen, just tell the truth! Who was the discoverer of this fossil?
Man 2: It was me, of course!
Man 3: No, it wasn't! You are a liar!
Man 4: Actually, it was me. I'm Arthur Lakes and I discovered the fossil!

Track 2.15 Unit 7, page 67, exercise 3
Listen and repeat. Do the words *was* and *were* sound weak or strong?

1 I was excited.
2 Where were you yesterday?
3 Yes, I was.
4 No, you weren't.

Track 2.16 Unit 7, page 68, exercise 1

1 Vasco de Gama was born in the Portuguese city of Sines. He was one of the most famous ocean explorers in history. He was most famous for discovering the sea route to India.

2 One of history's most important archaeologists was Englishwoman Gertrude Bell. She was born in 1868 in County Durham, in the north of England. She was famous for her work in the Middle East.

3 Another important explorer was the American, Daniel Boone. He was famous for establishing the first colony in Kentucky. He died in 1820.

Track 2.17 Unit 7, page 68 and 69, exercise 2
Edmund Hillary

Sir Edmund Hillary was a mountaineer, explorer and philanthropist. People remember him as the first man to climb Mount Everest, but he wasn't alone on his adventure. A man called Tenzing Norgay, a Sherpa from eastern Nepal, was with him on this expedition. After climbing Everest with Norgay, Hillary became a friend of the Sherpa community for the rest of his life.

Edmund Hillary was born in Auckland, New Zealand, in 1919. He was a shy child and was fascinated by books. He was interested in mountain climbing from the age of 16, when he went on a school trip to Mount Ruapehu. As a young man, he was also a beekeeper. He did beekeeping in the summer, so he was only able to climb in winter. This was a big advantage for his later career.

On the 29th May 1953, Hillary and Norgay conquered the 8,850 metres of Mount Everest. They were the first people to climb the highest mountain in the world, and suddenly they were famous! After climbing Everest, Hillary was a member of various other expeditions, including an unsuccessful trip to find a mysterious animal called the Yeti. Later, he also went on expeditions to the North and South Poles. He was the first person in history to reach both Poles and the top of Everest.

Hillary was not only daring and courageous, but also kind-hearted. Once, one of the Sherpas said, 'I wish my children could have an education.' This wish had a big impact on Hillary and thanks to his efforts, there are now many more schools and hospitals in the Himalayas.

When Hillary died, aged 88, he was one of New Zealand's most loved and respected public figures. His face appears on stamps and on the country's $5 banknote. There are also many things named after him, including a rugby trophy, a walking track, and even a ridge on New Zealand's highest mountain.

Track 2.18 Unit 7, page 71, exercise 1

Hi, I'm Lisa. One day, when I was eight years old, I was in the garden playing with my cousin Rick. There was a beehive hanging just above us from a tree. I was over the moon! Beehives are so interesting! We decided to climb up the tree to reach the beehive. Suddenly, we were face to face with a thousand angry bees! It was really frightening! Why did we decide to climb up that tree? It beats me! Fortunately, we were able to escape the bees because there was a pond nearby and we jumped under the water, but it was terrifying!

Track 2.19 Unit 7, page 71, exercise 2

1

One day, my sister and I were in the woods. We were walking along. Suddenly, I was face to face with a bear! It was huge and terrifying!

2

A famous writer from Ireland was at our school last week. It was so interesting. There was a story competition and I was the best in my class. I was over the moon!

3

Last winter, I was on holiday with my family in Canada. We were skiing in the mountains. There was an avalanche and I was in trouble. I was terrified. How did my dog find me? It beats me!

Track 2.20 Unit 8, page 72, exercise 1

1

Last weekend, I went camping with some friends. We arrived just before lunch and we put up our tent. As we started to make lunch, we heard a strange noise. I thought it was a bear and I was really scared, so I climbed up a tree. But when I looked down, I saw it was only a goat! It walked towards the food, but it didn't eat any. Instead, it ate a sock from my backpack!

2

My grandma lives in a big old house in the country. One day, when I was younger, I was at her house. We had dinner and told each other ghost stories. After some time, I went to bed. As I sat in bed, I saw the curtain moving. It was strange because the window was shut. Suddenly, it flew open! I shouted out to my grandma. But when she arrived, she didn't believe me. I still don't really know what happened.

3

My cousin and I like the same things. Right now, for example, we're both learning to play the guitar. One Christmas, I bought him a book. We started opening presents. Before long, his turn came to open my present to him. Then he said, 'But this present is for you.'

I showed him the label with his name on it. 'Oh,' he said. 'I think I got you the same present as you got me!'

Track 2.21 Unit 8, page 72, exercise 2

See previous track

Track 2.22 Unit 8, page 73, exercise 3
Listen and repeat.

/t/, laughed, missed, watched
/d/, enjoyed, happened, realised
/ɪd/, hated, sounded, started

Track 2.23 Unit 8, page 73, exercise 4
In pairs, decide if the *-ed* words end with a /t/, /d/ or /id/ sound. Listen and check.

They walked and climbed until they reached the top. They waited, but no one arrived. He wanted the sandwich but she really needed it, so he handed it to her.

Track 2.24 Unit 8, page 73, exercise 7

This happened to me a couple of years ago. One day I was working alone down on the farm and it started to get dark, so I thought I'd better go back home. Suddenly, the cows all started mooing and running around the field. I couldn't keep them quiet or still, and I didn't know what was making them so nervous. Then I saw something in the sky! I didn't know what it was, but it got closer and closer...

Track 2.25 Unit 8, page 74, exercise 1

Dt. Gregson: Did you wear your diamond necklace tonight, Mrs Templeton?

Mrs Templeton: No, I didn't. I thought it would be too heavy, but I showed it to everyone before dinner. Then, when we finished eating, the lights went out and it disappeared!

Dt. Gregson: I see. Where did you go after dinner, Miss Olive?

Miss Olive: I went to my aunt's room to look for her medicine.

Dt. Gregson: Mmm… and you, Mr Parker, why did you leave the room?

Mr Parker: Because I wanted to go to the kitchen to get another bottle of champagne for my aunt.

Dt. Gregson: Is that true, Mrs Templeton? Did you ask Mr Parker for more champagne?

Mrs Templeton: Not exactly. I asked him to get more red wine, not champagne. But it's true that I told him to go to the kitchen.

Dt. Gregson: And you, Mr Davies. Mr Smith saw you hiding something in your jacket after the lights came back on. What did you hide?

Mr Davies: Uh… well, it's glue for my wig. I didn't want Mrs Templeton to know that I wear one.

Mrs Templeton: Oh, Mr Davies my dear, I knew about that!

Track 2.26 Unit 8, page 74, exercise 3

Narrator: Miss Scarlet disappeared before the lights went off. Where did she go? Later, Detective Gregson heard someone talking on the phone about their new, expensive flat in London…

Dt. Gregson: So, Miss Scarlet, where did you go when the lights went off?

Miss Scarlet: I went to the bathroom. Mr Davies saw me there.

Dt. Gregson: Mr Davies, did you see Miss Scarlet go to the bathroom?

Mr Davies: Oh yes! That's exactly what I saw. I also saw Mr Smith on the telephone.

Dt. Gregson: Mr Smith, who did you talk to?

Mr Smith: Err, I spoke to my friend.

Dt. Gregson: Hmm! And did you buy an expensive flat in London last week?

Mr Smith: Err, yes, I did.

Dt. Gregson: Well then, tell us, why did you steal Mrs Templeton's necklace?

Mr Smith: I… I did it because… because… well, because Mrs Templeton owed me a lot of money! More than a year of my salary! When I asked her to pay me, she told me she didn't have any money… and then she bought this necklace! Can you believe it? It wasn't fair at all!

Track 2.27 Unit 8, page 75, exercise 5

Last night I went to the supermarket to buy some flour and a meat pie. When I was finished at the supermarket, I ran home because I wanted to be on time to watch a show on TV. I ate my dinner and watched the show. Suddenly, I heard the TV presenter say, 'And the right answer this week came from Pat Robbins!' I was the winner of the competition on the show and I won a trip to Wales!

Track 2.28 Unit 8, page 75, exercise 7

See previous track

Track 2.29 Unit 8, page 76 and 77, exercise 2

The Canterville Ghost, adapted from the story by Oscar Wilde

When Mr Otis moved to England from America and bought Canterville Chase, everyone told him he was making a mistake because it was haunted. In fact, when Lord Canterville sold the house to Mr Otis, he felt it was his duty to mention the ghost.

'My Lord,' answered Mr Otis, 'I will take the house with the furniture and the ghost. I come from a modern country, where we have everything that money can buy.'

So, Mr Otis moved to Canterville Chase with his family. When they arrived, Mrs Umney, the housekeeper, took them into the library. She pointed to a red stain on the floor. She said, 'This is the blood of Lady Eleanor of Canterville, who was murdered on that very spot by Sir Simon of Canterville, in 1575. The blood stain cannot be removed.'

'That is nonsense,' cried Washington Otis, Mr Otis's son. 'Pinkerton's Champion Stain Remover will clean it up in no time,' he said. Before the terrified housekeeper could stop him, he cleaned the stain.

'I knew Pinkerton would do it,' he exclaimed triumphantly, as he looked at his admiring family. Then, a terrible flash of lightning lit up the room and Mrs Umney fainted.

One night, Mr Otis heard a curious, metallic noise in the corridor outside his bedroom. He opened the door and right in front of him there was a terrifying old man. His eyes were red; long, grey hair fell over his shoulders; his clothes were dirty and ragged, and he had heavy, rusty chains hanging from his wrists.

'My dear sir,' said Mr Otis, 'I really must insist you oil those chains. Here, I have brought you some Rising Sun Lubricator!' Mr Otis put a bottle down in front of the ghost and returned to bed. For a moment the Canterville ghost remained motionless in anger. Then, knocking the lubricator over violently onto the floor, he flew down the corridor, crying noisily.

Track 2.30 Unit 8, page 79, exercise 1

Detectives Jones and Miller: Good afternoon, Detective Smith.

Dt Smith: Good afternoon, Detective Jones, Detective Miller.

Dt Miller: Are you working on a case, Smith?

Dt Smith: Yes. I'm just finishing my report. It's not a big case, but it's unusual. My client was worried about her new boyfriend. She suspected that he had a skeleton in the closet, but she didn't know what it was.

Dt Jones: And what did you find out?

Dt Smith: Well, I discovered that he spent fifteen years in prison for bank robbery, and he was released last year. And he didn't tell his girlfriend!

Dt Miller: That certainly is a skeleton in the closet! Well, let me tell you about a case I had last month.

Dt Jones: Go on, Detective Miller. Let's hear it!

Dt Miller: There was a robbery over at the Johnsons' house. You know, that billionaire? Well, someone stole all his wife's jewellery – pearl necklaces, diamond rings – a fortune! Everybody involved was suspicious, and I wasn't making any progress in the investigation. I had a strange feeling about the son, so I took a shot in the dark and made up a story about how he committed the robbery. And what do you know? I was right and he confessed!

Dt Jones: Wow. That was lucky!

Dt Miller: What about you Jones? Got any interesting cases to tell us about?

Dt Jones: I had a strange case last month. Someone kidnapped a French poodle – you know, one of those little dogs with curly hair. They asked for a thousand pounds! All the accusations pointed to these two brothers. The older brother confessed to the crime, and the younger brother was set free.

Dt Smith: What an easy investigation!

Dt Jones: Not exactly. It turns out the younger brother was the one who really kidnapped the dog. The older brother was innocent, but he confessed because he wanted to protect his younger brother. It's true what they say… blood is thicker than water!

Track 2.31 Unit 8, page 79, exercise 3

See previous track

Track 2.32 Unit 9, page 82, exercise 1

Breakfast is important!

Breakfast gives you energy to start the day, and there are many options to choose from. You can have some cereal with milk or an egg and some bread. If you don't know what to eat for breakfast, open the fridge. Maybe there is some yogurt. If there isn't any, look again. Is there any fruit? Have some! Cut an apple, a kiwi or a banana into pieces and mix it with some muesli and milk. Some coffee, some cheese and some toast can be a nice alternative too. The important thing is to have something nutritious to start the day!

Track 2.33 Unit 9, page 83, exercise 4

Eating well

1. The grain group includes bread, pasta, cereals and rice. There are two kinds of grains: wholemeal and refined.
2. There isn't any meat in this group! Instead, there are onions, tomatoes and peas. There is also broccoli and spinach. Plums, raisins and tangerines are some of the fruits you can eat in this group. Remember to drink some fruit juice too!
3. All products made from milk are part of this group. So, there isn't any rice or pasta in this group.
4. Solid fats, like butter, come from animals. Liquid fats, like oil, usually come from plants and fish. Some oils are cholesterol-free. But there aren't any cholesterol-free solid fats.
5. There are lots of different kinds of meat, poultry and fish here. Nuts, seeds, beans and eggs also go in this group.

Track 2.34 Unit 9, page 83, exercise 7

Girl: Mmm! What a delicious picnic! Is there enough bread?

Boy: Don't worry, there's a lot of bread. How many bananas are there?

Girl: Let me see. There are 3 bananas. Do you want one?

Boy: Yes, please. Is there any yogurt?

Girl: Sorry, no. There isn't any yogurt, but there is some cheese.

Boy: Great! Can I have some? I really like cheese.

Track 2.35 Unit 9, page 84, exercise 1

Snack pizza:

Ingredients

four slices of bread, wholemeal is best, but white bread if you prefer
a jar of your favourite tomato sauce
half an onion and two tomatoes
two slices of ham, chopped into pieces
a block of cheese

Track 2.36 Unit 9, page 84, exercise 2

Preparation

1. Chop the onion and tomatoes.
2. Spread the tomatoes and tomato sauce on the bread.
3. Grate the cheese and add it.
4. Put the onion and ham on top of the cheese.
5. Cook the pizzas in the microwave.

Track 2.37 Unit 9, page 84, exercise 3

Listen and repeat. Is the first word or the second word stressed?

1 animal fat
2 breakfast cereal
3 chocolate cake
4 dairy products
5 fruit juice
6 olive oil

Track 2.38 Unit 9, page 85, exercise 6

Jane: What have we got for lunch?

Larry: Yeah! I'm hungry. Is there any bread?

Jane: Yes, there's a loaf of bread.

Larry: What about jam. Is there any jam?

Jane: There's a jar of jam.

Larry: Are there any eggs?

Jane: No, there aren't any eggs.

Larry: Is there any cheese?

Jane: Yes, there's some cheese. There are four slices.

Larry: Is there any juice?

Jane: Yes, there are two bottles of juice. There's also some spinach, a mango, a tin of sweetcorn and a bottle of olive oil.

Larry: OK! What can we make with all that?

Jane: Well, we can use the bread and cheese to make sandwiches!

Track 2.39 Unit 9, page 86 and 87, exercise 2

Know your food

When you buy food, do you read the nutrition facts label? No? Well, perhaps you should! It gives you key information to help you buy healthier food.

This label is for a low-fat yogurt in the UK. There is a list of nutrients on the left, and quantities across the top. The final column is the 'Guideline Daily Amount' (GDA) of the nutrient. Sometimes there is a colour scheme: green means healthy and red means unhealthy. For example, this yogurt is low-fat, but it contains an unhealthy amount of sugar.

Energy

The energy in the label is given first in metric kilojoules (kj) and then in kilocalories (kcal). Generally, an adult man needs about 10,500 kilojoules (2,500 kilocalories) a day and an adult woman needs about 8,400 kilojoules

(2,000 kilocalories). Where our calories come from is also very important.

Vitamins and minerals

We need vitamins and minerals to be healthy and stay that way. Some vitamins are organic; we store them in our bodies. But we need to get others, like Vitamin C, from the food we eat. We also need to get some minerals, like calcium, from our food.

Protein, carbohydrates, fat, fibre and salt

There's a lot of protein in meat and fish but also in nuts and beans. The healthiest sources of carbohydrates are wholemeal bread, pasta and fruit and vegetables. Protein, carbohydrates and fat are where we get most of our energy. Too much salt and fat, especially saturated fat, is bad for us. However, we do need some types in our diet.

So, the next time you go shopping and you see something that looks nutritious and healthy, have a look at the nutrition facts label. It will help you to be sure.

Track 2.40 Unit 9, page 89, exercise 1

1

There's a boy in my class who's just not a nice person. He's always saying mean things to people and I saw him pushing Isaac in the corridor today. Any chance he gets do something bad, he does it. Chris is a bully and generally a bad egg.

2

My friend Julia is really intelligent. She has extra Maths classes with Mrs Henry because she's so far ahead of the rest of the class. She'll probably be a famous inventor in the future. She's such a smart cookie!

3

My older brother Paul is so lazy! He just lies around watching TV all day and playing computer games with his friend Adam. He doesn't do any exercise and he eats a lot of junk food. And he won't help around the house. He's a real couch potato.

Track 2.41 Unit 1 Review, page 90, exercise 1

Boy: Hi Ellie.
Girl 1: Oh hi, Jamie. Hey, thanks for the help with the French homework.
Boy: No, problem. Is this your Dutch friend, Julia?
Girl 1: No, this is Yota. She's from Greece.
Girl 2: Pleased to meet you.
Boy: Nice to meet you, too.
Girl 1: Yota's a big sports fan. She loves tennis, skateboarding and basketball. I don't really like sports but I love to roller-blade! So, we're going roller-blading in the park.
Boy: Which one, Stanley Park?
Girl 1: Stanley Park hasn't got any ramps so we want to go to Victoria Park, near the supermarket.
Boy: Oh, I know the one. Are you good?
Girl 1: I'm not bad. I'm good at going forwards but going backwards is difficult.
Boy: Oh well. Practice makes perfect!
Girl 1: That's what they say. Yota can do jumps!
Girl 2: Well, I practise a lot! Hey, when's the bus to the park?
Girl 1: What time is it now?
Boy: It's 10.17.
Girl 1: Ahh, it's in 3 minutes! Let's run!
Boy: Well, have a great time and I'll see you next week.
Girl 1: Thanks, Jamie. See you!

Track 2.42 Unit 3 Review, page 92, exercise 1

Girl: Mum, I've invited five friends to come over on Saturday. Is that alright? We've got a project to do.
Mum: Yes, that's fine. Who's coming?
Girl: Do you remember Amina from my primary school?
Mum: Oh yes, I know Amina. She's the shy one, isn't she?
Girl: Yes. She's lots of fun but she doesn't like talking to people she doesn't know. And Scott's coming too.
Mum: Is Scott the boy with red hair who's a bit plump?
Girl: No, that's his brother. Scott is quite slim.
Mum: Amina and Scott, that's two. Who else is coming?
Girl: Well, there's a new girl called Jessica that you don't know. She's very kind and friendly. Everyone likes her - she's all heart.
Mum: She sounds lovely.
Girl: She is! Then Dale's coming too. Do you know him? He's the one who goes hiking and camping at weekends. He does lots of activities and likes to try new things.
Mum: Oh yes, I know Dale. Yes, he's very adventurous. What about Yasmin, is she coming too?
Girl: She is. But not with her sister this time.
Mum: Oh, that's a pity. Her sister's so cute. Oh well, I like Yasmin. She can be a little loud but she's a lot of fun.
Girl: I know. She's a bit of an extrovert!

Track 2.43 Unit 4 Review, page 93, exercise 1

1 Who is Tyler's uncle?
Boy 1: Hey James, thanks for coming to my party.
Boy 2: Hi Tyler, thanks for inviting me! I like the sunglasses! Hey, is your uncle here, the one who's a game designer? I'd love to meet him.
Boy 1: Yes, he's over there, next to the wall.
Boy 2: Oh, is that him with the spotted shirt?
Boy 1: No, that's my cousin. My uncle's wearing a stripy shirt.
2 Which photo are they looking at?
Boy: That's a nice photo of you, Jenny. Is that your sister?
Girl: No. I'm an only child. That's my mum!
Boy: Wow! She looks really young.
Girl: She is quite young. So's my dad. He's taking the photo.
Boy: And that's your grandma. You and your mum have the same curly hair.
Girl: And so does my grandma. But hers is blond.
3 What is Olivia doing to help the environment?
Teen boy: Hi Olivia. You look angry. What's the matter?
Teen girl: Well, I'm getting really annoyed about how much plastic we consume and what it's doing to the environment. We all need to pull our socks up and stop being so wasteful. We use so many plastic bottles every day. It's terrible!
Teen boy: Why don't you reuse them? Or make them into something, a plant pot maybe?
Teen girl: That's a good idea but there are still millions more and we throw so many away. I volunteer with a local clean-up group. We collect rubbish from public places, sort it and take it to the recycling centre.
4 What is Belinda wearing today?
For work I wear a suit and high heels or sometimes I wear

a smart dress. I travel a lot and I have to look professional. In my spare time, like today, I do a lot of exercise to keep fit. So, as you can see, right now I'm wearing sports clothes and trainers. I go swimming regularly too!

Track 2.44 Unit 6 Review, page 95, exercise 1

1 You will hear two people talking about their town. Where is the gym?

Man: Hey Becky, where are you going?

Woman: I'm going to the shopping centre for some new trainers because mine are really old.

Man: I'll walk with you. I'm going to the gym.

Woman: Oh, is that the shop next to the bookshop?

Man: No, that's a sports clothes shop. The gym's behind the shopping centre.

2 You will hear a girl talking about her routine. What time does she get up on Saturday?

During the week, I have to get up early for school. I usually get up at seven, but I sometimes lie in until a quarter past seven. At the weekend, I can sleep a bit longer, but I can't sleep too much because I always help my mum in her flower shop. The shop opens at a quarter past nine and I get up an hour before that.

3 You will hear a man talking about his travels. Where does he go?

My friends and I love to travel. We work hard and save up our money so we can see the world. There are so many amazing places to see! One of my favourites is Machu Picchu. But normally, my friends and I hardly ever go back to the same place. I hope I can continue travelling throughout my life. I would like to be a travel writer one day!

4 You will hear a man talking. Which country is he in?

Hi, my name's Benny and I'm from Egypt, land of the pyramids! I often travel for work and this week I'm in the UK. I'm in a small town on the south coast. Egyptian restaurants are few and far between around here so I'm trying the local food – fish and chips. The people here usually put vinegar on their chips so I'm giving it a go too. When in Rome, do as the Romans do!

5 You will hear two people talking. Where is Patricia going?

Man: Hi Patricia. I love your hair!

Woman: Thanks! I cut it short.

Man: It really suits you.

Woman: Well, thank you! I play a lot of football, so it makes life easier when it's short.

Man: Ahh. Do you have time to come for a coffee?

Woman: No, sorry, I'm going to go and buy some sausages for lunch. Maybe tomorrow?

Man: OK. Bye!

6 You will hear a woman talking about her town. Who is she?

I live in a great little town in the south of England. It's popular with tourists. This is important for my job. I always have lots of customers, especially at the weekend. I usually park outside the train station and I never have to wait for more than a few minutes to pick up my first passenger. It's a wonderful place to live, too, because it's so close to the sea. Sometimes, I take my children to the beach and we play football and eat ice cream.

Track 2.45 Unit 8 Review, page 97, exercise 1

1 What did the teacher ask the class to do a project on?

Girl: What are you laughing about?

Boy: Do you remember last week we studied animals and we did that project on dolphins?

Girl: Yeah. That sounded interesting!

Boy: Well, this week we're studying countries in the UK, and our teacher asked us to do a project on Wales.

Girl: Did he mean the country Wales?

Boy: Exactly. But David thought he was talking about the animal, so he did the whole project on that.

Girl: Oh no!

2 What did the girl buy her brother for his birthday?

Boy: How was your brother's birthday?

Girl: It was good. He really liked his present.

Boy: Did you get him that T-shirt you looked at?

Girl: No. I bought him a comic book that he really likes. He's really excited now because they made a film of it and the DVD is coming out soon.

3 What moved in the boy's room last night?

Boy: Do you believe in ghosts?

Girl: No. Why? Did you see one?

Boy: Well, last night I was in bed reading. I put my book down on the floor near my bed and I turned the light out. Just as I closed my eyes, I heard a noise in the room.

Girl: What was it?

Boy: I don't know. But when I turned on the light, my book was on the table.

Girl: Are you sure you didn't put it there?

4 Who stole the diamonds on the detective show?

Boy: Did you watch that detective show I told you about last night?

Girl: Inspector Harris? Yes, it was great!

Boy: I watched the beginning of it but then I fell asleep. I was so tired. Did you find out who stole the diamonds? You can tell me – I can't watch it again anyway.

Girl: OK. It was the artist. I thought it was the security guard.

Boy: Oh really? So it wasn't the cleaner? He seemed very suspicious.

Track 2.46 Unit 9 Review, page 98, exercise 1

Hi I'm Jake and I'm a bit of a couch potato. I don't do enough exercise and I eat a lot of unhealthy foods. My doctor says I need to lose about five kilos. I'm going to lose the weight slowly and responsibly over the next six months. I start my new diet and exercise plan on Tuesday. There are three parts to it. The first is to reduce the quantity of fats I eat. The second is to eat more vegetables. The third part is to start running. I need to do more exercise!

Track 2.47 Wordlist, page 117, unit 1, Greetings and introductions

Greetings

Good morning.	I'm very well, thank you.
Hey!	It was nice to see you.
How are you doing?	Not too bad.
How are you today?	See you later!
How's it going?	

Introductions

I'd like to introduce …	Nice to meet you.
I'm …	This is …
My name is …	This is my friend, …

Track 2.48 Wordlist, page 117, unit 1, Countries and nationalities

Argentina, Argentinian
Australia, Australian
Belgium, Belgian
Brazil, Brazilian
Canada, Canadian
China, Chinese
Colombia, Colombian
England, English
France, French
Germany, German
Greece, Greek
India, Indian
Ireland, Irish
Italy, Italian
Japan, Japanese
Mexico, Mexican
The Netherlands, Dutch
New Zealand, from New Zealand
Peru, Peruvian
Portugal, Portuguese
Spain, Spanish
Switzerland, Swiss
Turkey, Turkish

Track 2.49 Wordlist, page 117, unit 1, Hobbies and interests

Hobbies	**Interests**
basketball	action films
listening to music	animated films
reading	classical music
roller-blading	comedy
spending time with friends	fashion
surfing	folk music
swimming	jazz
watching films	pop music
	R&B
	series

Track 2.50 Wordlist, page 117, unit 2, Dates

Days	**Months**
Monday	January
Tuesday	February
Wednesday	March
Thursday	April
Friday	May
Saturday	June
Sunday	July
	August
	September
	October
	November
	December

Track 2.51 Wordlist, page 117, unit 2, Time

a quarter past
a quarter to
break
half past
It's at ...
late
lunchtime
midnight
o'clock
timetable
What time is ...?
What time is it?

Track 2.52 Wordlist, page 117, unit 2, Personality adjectives

active
adventurous
analytical
creative
energetic
friendly
imaginative
ingenious
intelligent
patient
persevering
self-aware
shy
sociable
sporty
talkative

Track 2.53 Wordlist, page 118, unit 3, Body parts

arm
cheek
chest
ear
elbow
eye
eyebrow
eyelash
foot
head
heel
hip
knee
leg
mouth
neck
nose
shoulder
stomach
tooth
toe
tongue
waist

Track 2.54 Wordlist, page 118, unit 3, Body actions

bend
pull
scratch
stand on tiptoes
stick out your tongue
stretch
swing
touch
wiggle
wink

Track 2.55 Wordlist, page 118, unit 3, Physical appearance

Body

athletic
fat
little
medium height
plump
short
skinny
slim
tall
thin

Face

beautiful
cute
freckled
handsome
pretty
Hair
bald
blonde
curly
grey
red
straight
wavy

Track 2.56 Wordlist, page 118, unit 4, Clothes

belt
boots
cap
coat
dress
gloves
hat
jacket
jeans
jumper
shirt
shoes
shorts
skirt
socks
suit
sunglasses
swimsuit
tie
trainers
trousers
T-shirt

Track 2.57 Wordlist, page 118, unit 4, Patterns

checked
dark
flowers
flowery
light
pattern
patterned
spots
spotty
stripes
stripy
tartan

Track 2.58 Wordlist, page 118, unit 4, The environment

conservation
endangered animals
endangered species
green
natural resource
non-biodegradable
plant trees
plastic
pollute
pollution
protect the environment
recycle
rubbish
save our planet
waste
water shortages

Track 2.59 Wordlist, page 119, unit 5, Weather and seasons

Weather

chilly
cloudy
cold
foggy
freezing
hot
raining
snowing
sunny
windy

Seasons

spring
summer
autumn
winter

Track 2.60 Wordlist, page 119, unit 5, Outdoor adventure and sports

Outdoor adventure

cabin
campsite
canoeing
cave
countryside
hiking
light a fire
natural habitat
nature
put up a tent
tent
waterfall

Sports

climbing wall
court
equipment
facilities
fencing
field
hockey
Olympic-size pool
rugby
scuba dive
squash
tennis

Track 2.61 Wordlist, page 119, unit 5, On the farm

barn
blossom
carrots
crops
eggs
farm animals
farmstay
field
fresh milk
fruit trees
grow
lettuces
look after the animals
milk
plant
seeds
vegetable garden
wake up early

Track 2.62 Wordlist, page 119, unit 6, Places in a city

bakery
bookshop
bus station
butcher's
car park
clothes shop
gym
hairdresser's
hospital
hotel
museum
music shop
police station
post office
school
shopping centre
stadium

Track 2.63 Wordlist, page 119, unit 6, Directions

across from
behind
between
Excuse me, where's the ...?
go past
go straight ahead
How do I get to the ... ?
Is this the way to ...?
near here
next to
on the corner of ... and ...
on your left
on your right
take the first left
take the second left
take the third left
take the first right
take the second right
take the third right
turn left
turn right
walk across

Track 2.64 Wordlist, page 119, unit 6, Historical monuments

all over the world
ancient
artefact
city
civilisations
construction
design
history
palacev
pyramid
repairs
research
rock
statue
tour guide
tourists
travel
visitors

Track 2.65 Wordlist, page 120, unit 7, Adjectives: *-ing* and *-ed*

bored
boring
excited
exciting
fascinated
fascinating
frightened
frightening
interested
interesting
surprised
surprising
terrified
terrifying

Track 2.66 Wordlist, page 120, unit 7, Travelling

countries
culture
dangerous
history
maps
places
return home
travel
traveller
trips
visit

Track 2.67 Wordlist, page 120, unit 7, Famous explorers

brave
conquer
courageous
daring
discover
early life
expedition
explorer
first person
Mount Everest
philanthropy
pioneer
tribute
trip

Track 2.68 Wordlist, page 120, unit 8, Time expressions

after some time
afterwards
as
before long
before that
finally
just after
just before
last weekend
last year
next
one Christmas
one day
one winter
one year
suddenly
then
when

Track 2.69 Wordlist, page 120, unit 8, Ghost stories

believe
blood
curious
ghost
haunted
hear
murdered
noise
plot
stain
story

Track 2.70 Wordlist, page 120, unit 8, Parts of a story

characters
description
dialogue
drama
punctuate
setting
tension
title
twist

Track 2.71 Wordlist, page 120, unit 9, Food

beans
bread
broccoli
butter
cereals
dairy
eggs
fish
meat
milk
nuts
oil
onions
pasta
peas
plums
poultry
raisins
rice
seeds
spinach
tangerines
tomatoes
vegetables

Track 2.72 Wordlist, page 120, unit 9, Units of measurements

a bag of …
a bottle of …
a bowl of …
a box of …
a jar of …
a kilo of …
a loaf of …
a packet of …
a slice of …
a spoonful of …
a tin of …

Track 2.73 Wordlist, page 120, unit 9, Nutrition

calcium
calories
carbohydrates
energy
fat
fibre
healthy
minerals
nutrients
protein
salt
unhealthy
vitamins

Get started!

Page 6

1 *Student's own answers*

2 **1** school
2 case
3 on
4 around
5 in

3 **1** am / 'm
2 do not / don't
3 are
4 visiting

4 **1** job
2 Helping
3 nurses
4 good

5 *Student's own answers*

6 *Student's own answers*

Page 7

1 **1** year
2 study
3 Human
4 something
5 interesting

2 **1** Close
2 listen
3 Open
4 borrow
5 look
6 repeat

3 **1** e **2** c **3** a **4** b **5** d

4 **1** on
2 under
3 in
4 on
5 over

5 **1** highlighter
2 marker
3 exam
4 clock
5 desk

6 *Student's own answers*

Page 8

1 **1** cousins
2 aunts and uncles
3 hers
4 my

2 **1** d **2** c **3** e **4** a **5** b

3 **1** ours
2 mine
3 theirs
4 hers; his
5 yours

4 *Student's own answers*

5 **1** sister's car
2 dog's ball
3 aunt's motorbike
4 parents' boat
5 James and Mike's cousin

6 *Student's own answers*

Page 9

1 **1** business
2 stress
3 an office
4 a computer
5 a firefighter

2 **1** b **2** d **3** e **4** c **5** a

3 **1** a
2 the; a
3 an
4 The; a
5 an

4 *Suggested answers:*

School	Station	Outdoors	Office	Hospital
teacher	firefighter	gardener	journalist	doctor
librarian	police officer	archaeologist	lawyer	nurse

5 My name is George Franklin. I'm English and I'm from Manchester. My favourite subject at school is French, the classes are on Mondays and Wednesdays. My teacher's name is Marianne, she's from Paris.

6 *Student's own answers*

Unit 1

Page 10

1 **1** b
2 d
3 e
4 c
5 a

2 **1** Sam Veasey
2 V-E-A-S-E-Y
3 33 years old
4 932 466 82
5 32 Green Street

Page 11

3 **1** e
2 f
3 k
4 j
5 a
6 d
7 i
8 h
9 c
10 b
11 g

4 *Student's own answers*

5 **Introducing yourself**
1 informal
2 formal
Introducing other people
1 informal
2 formal
Greeting
1 formal
2 informal
Saying goodbye
1 informal
2 formal

6 *Student's own answers*

Page 12

1 *Student's own answers*

2

Country	Nationality
The USA	American
Colombian	Colombian
Mexico	Mexican
China	Chinese
Japan	Japanese
Portugal	Portuguese
Argentina	Argentinian
Brazil	Brazilian
Italy	Italian
England	English
Ireland	Irish
Spain	Spanish
New Zealand	from New Zealand
Greece	Greek
The Netherlands	Dutch

3 **1** Jaime Ramírez; Mexican; 18; 55 5450 170
2 Hendrika Jansen; The Netherlands; 20 672 560; 75 Albert Street
3 Li Wei Ying; Chinese; 32; Renmin St
4 Osvaldo Santos; Portugal; 21 346 123; 17 Farol Street;
5 Greece; Greek; 45; 2 Toro St
6 England; English; 40; 020 7980 442

1 a
2 d
3 f
4 b
5 e
6 c

Page 13

4 **1** is / 's
2 It is / It's / My name is / My name's
3 Are
4 I'm / I am
5 are
6 Ireland
7 American
8 She is / She's

5 *Student's own answers*

Page 14

1

basketball	classical	action	cherries
rollerblading	folk	animated	ice cream
surfing	jazz	comedy	pizza
swimming	R&B	series	sashimi

2 **Name(s):** Liam Hemsworth
Nationality: Australian
Profession(s): film and television actor
Famous for: *Independence Day: Resurgence* and *The Hunger Games*. Also, younger brother of Luke and Chris Hemsworth
Likes: surfing, pizza

Name(s): Lorde
Nationality: from New Zealand
Profession(s): singer-songwriter and record producer
Famous for: Royals and the soundtrack for *The Hunger Games*
Likes: jazz, folk, pop, R&B, hip-hop, tuna sashimi

Name(s): Venus and Serena Williams
Nationality: American
Profession(s): tennis players
Famous for: winning over 100 titles and eight Olympic gold medals
Likes: Serena: reading, watching films, spending time with family and friends
Venus: fashion, listening to music, cherry pie

3 **1** False. She's from New Zealand.
2 True
3 False. She is also a record producer.
4 False. He has two brothers.
5 False. They are good friends.
6 True.
7 False. His favourite food is pizza.
8 False. They have eight gold medals between them.

Page 15

4 **1** vegan **2** rivals **3** supportive **4** hit **5** Apart from

5 *Student's own answers*

6 *Student's own answers*

7 *Student's own answers*

8 *Student's own answers*

Page 16

1 **1** and; Lorde
2 but; Liam Hemsworth
3 Like; the Williams sisters
4 Apart from; Venus Williams
5 also; Liam Hemsworth

2 **1** She is 11.
2 She lives in Montreal, in Canada.
3 She speaks English and French.
4 Ice hockey, reading and spending time with her friends
5 Her favourite food is poutine.

3 *Student's own answers*

4 **1** Hello everybody, my name's Karen.
2 I'm 11.
3 I'm a big fan of…
4 Canada is really cold in the winter.
5 Oh, and…

5 *Student's own answers*

6 *Student's own answers*

7 *Student's own answers*

Page 17

1 **1**
Name: Trish
Country: America / the United States of America / the USA
Favourite part of hobby: eating the food
2
Name: Jacob
Nationality: South African
When he practises: every day from Monday to Friday
3
Name: Joanna
Age: 14
Who she plays with: her cousin

2 **1** b **2** c **3** a

3 **1** I'm **2** It's **3** perfect **4** She's **5** throws **6** stars

4 *Student's own answers*

Unit 2

Page 18

1 *Student's own answers*

2 Sunday, 10th October: Today
Monday, 18th October: Football match
Thursday, 28th October: Exams
Saturday, 30th October: Lunch at Grandma's

3 *Student's own answers*

4 **1** February **2** 25th **3** 1st **4** October **5** March **6** 4th

5 *Student's own answers*

Page 19

6 **1** aren't/are not; are/'re
2 is; isn't/is not
3 are; aren't/are not
4 am/'m; I'm not/I am not
5 isn't/is not; is/'s
6 isn't/is not; is/'s; is/'s

7 *Student's own answers*

8 *Student's own answers*

Page 20

1 **1** half past twelve
2 six o'clock
3 a quarter past ten
4 a quarter to eleven

2 **1** the exam; half past one
2 the basketball match; seven o'clock
3 Geography class; a quarter past eleven
4 the party; a quarter to nine

3 **1** a **2** a **3** b

Page 21

4 **1** in; false. (It started in 2001.)
2 on; false. (It's at the end of January or the beginning of February.)
3 at; true
4 on; true
5 at; false (In the far south, the latest it goes down is around eleven o'clock.)

5 Monday 9:00 History
10:00 History
14:30 Art
Tuesday 11:15 Music
12:15 Music
14:30 Science
Wednesday 9:00 English
10:00 English
14:30 Art

Thursday	11:15 History
	12:15 History
	14:30 Science
Friday	9:00 PE
	10:00 PE
	11:15 Geography
	12:15 Geography

6 **1** Science
2 Art
3 On Monday at nine o'clock and on Thursday at a quarter past eleven
4 On Monday at a quarter past eleven and on Friday at nine 'clock
5 At eleven o'clock

7 *Student's own answers*

Page 22

1 *Student's own answers*

2 *Student's own answers*

3 **1** Intrapersonal
2 Naturalistic
3 Verbal-linguistic
4 Spatial
5 Interpersonal
6 Logical-mathematical
7 Musical
8 Bodily-kinaesthetic

4 **1** shy
2 self-aware
3 patient
4 creative
5 sociable

Page 23

5 Susan – Interpersonal
Mike – Intrapersonal
Silvia – Musical
Sam – Bodily-kinaesthetic
Bobby – Verbal-linguistic
Hiroko – Spatial
Helen – Logical-mathematical
Tony – Naturalistic

6 *Student's own answers*

7 *Student's own answers*

Page 24

1 **1** d **2** c **3** a **4** e **5** b

2 **1** Diana, a student at Sligo Secondary School
2 Their teacher wants them to write an email to their pen pals about their school day.

3 *Student's own answers*

4 Paragraph 1 – b
Paragraph 2 – d
Paragraph 3 – c
Paragraph 4 – a

5 *Student's own answers*

6 *Student's own answers*

7 *Student's own answers*

Page 25

1 *Student's own answers*

2

January Back to School Party	**February** Sports Tournament	**March** Ecological Campaign	**April** Spring Festival
May Teachers' Day	**June** Children's Day	**July** Arts and Crafts Show	**August** Summer holidays
September Book Club	**October** Science and Technology Fair	**November** No events	**December** End of Year Concert

3 **1** **Country:** England
Summer holidays start: the 24th of July
2 **State:** Texas
Summer holidays finish: the 20th of August
3 **Country:** Australia
Summer holidays start: the 15th of December

4 **1** b **2** c **3** a

5 *Student's own answers*

Unit 3

Page 28

1 **1** arm
2 elbow
3 shoulder
4 mouth
5 neck
6 chest
7 stomach
8 waist
9 hip
10 leg
11 knee
12 heel
13 foot
14 toe
15 tongue
16 tooth
17 eye
18 hair
19 eyebrow
20 eyelash
21 ear
22 nose
23 cheek

2 *Student's own answers*

3

Singular	Plural
ear	ears
foot	feet
tooth	teeth
arm	arms
eye	eyes

Page 29

4 1 eye; h
2 toes; b
3 nose; f
4 fingers; d
5 neck; c
6 tongue; g
7 knees; a
8 ear; e
9 leg; j
10 arms; i

5 *Student's own answers*

6 1 /s/
2 /z/
3 /s/
4 /ɪz/
5 /z/
6 /ɪz/

7 *Student's own answers*

Page 30

1 1 little
2 plump
3 blonde
4 short
5 cute
6 skinny
7 height
8 slim
9 wavy
10 handsome
11 He's
12 elderly
13 slim
14 grey

2 *See table below*

Page 31

3 1 Jenny
2 Maria
3 Anita
4 Sarah
5 Paula
6 David

4 1 your
2 Their
3 They
4 My
5 His
6 He
7 She
8 Her
9 it

5 a Dana
b David
c Sam and Tom

6 *Student's own answers*

Page 32

1 *Student's own answers*

2 *Student's own answers*

3 1 a 2 a 3 b 4 a

4

Noun	Adjective
comfort	comfortable
complexity	complex
judgement	judgemental
success	successful
shyness	shy
trust	trustworthy

5 1 comfortable
2 shy
3 trustworthy
4 judgemental

Page 33

6 *Student's own answers*

7 *Student's own answers*

Page 34

1 1 versatile; wide
2 talented; short
3 brilliant; silly

2 1 c
2 a
3 e
4 b
5 d

3 *Suggested answer:*
Her mother Jenny because she's got two children and is very good at her job as head of a design company

4 1 a bit
2 quite
3 absolutely
4 extremely
5 very

5 *Student's own answers*

6 *Student's own answers*

7 *Student's own answers*

Name	Height	Age	Opinion	Body	Hair	Eyes
Melissa	short	8	funny	slim	wavy, blonde	brown
David	tall	32	friendly	thin	brown	brown
Barbara	medium height	40	happy	slim	short, curly (dyed orange)	brown

Page 35

1 Mia
1 b
2 a
3 a
4 a
5 a

Robert
1 b
2 b
3 b
4 b
5 a

2 1 c 2 a 3 b

3 *Student's own answers*

Unit 4

Page 36

1 **Clothes:** coat, dress, jacket, jeans, jumper, shirt, shorts, skirt, socks, suit, swimsuit, trousers, T-shirt
Footwear: boots, shoes, trainers
Accessories: belt, cap, gloves, hat, sunglasses, tie
1 belt
2 coat
3 T-shirt
4 cap
5 jumper
6 socks
7 shirt
8 boots
9 gloves
10 trousers
11 tie
12 skirt
13 trainers
14 swimsuit

2 **1** these
2 That
3 those
4 this
5 That
6 those
7 that
8 this

Page 37

3 **1** trainers; flowery
2 checked; jeans
3 tartan; shoes
4 spots
5 shirt; pattern
6 swimsuit; stripes
7 light
8 dark; stripy

4 *Student's own answers*

Page 38

1 **1** is
2 is
3 isn't
4 Is
5 is
6 eating
7 is
8 listening
9 Are
10 are
11 aren't
12 are
13 is
14 is

2 **a** Brother Joe
b Aunt Lucy
c Mum
d Grandpa Matthew
e Uncle Theo
f Sister Kate and cousin
g Grandma
h Dad

Page 39

3 **1** Rose
2 Uncle
3 Aunt
4 Michael
5 Isabel
6 Petra
7 Brother
8 Sister

4 *Student's own answers*

5 *Student's own answers*

6 **1** is riding
2 am tying
3 is writing
4 are taking
5 is running
6 is sleeping
7 are drinking
8 are swimming

Page 40

1 **1** rubbish
2 water shortages
3 endangered animals
4 plastic
5 pollution

2 *Student's own answers*

3 *Student's own answers*

4 **1** Sara
2 Mike
3 All of them
4 Monica
5 Sara; the Smith family

5 **1** picking up
2 pollute
3 huge
4 non-biodegradable
5 natural resource
6 waste

6 **1** waste; Student's own answers
2 huge; Student's own answers
3 natural resource; Student's own answers
4 non-biodegradable
5 pollute; Student's own answers
6 picking up; Student's own answers

Page 41

7 *Student's own answers*

Page 42

1 **1** d **2** a **3** b **4** c

2 **1** Greenwatch
2 To protect their future by developing student awareness of conservation.
3 Clean-up Days, talks at school assemblies and a blog.
4 They are inviting local artists to sell their products made from recycled materials at an upcycling market.

3 **1** so that
2 in order to
3 so
4 by

4 *Student's own answers*

5 *Student's own answers*

6 *Student's own answers*

Page 43

1 *Student's own answers*

2

	Name	Problem	Solution
1	Will	His exam results were bad.	He'll study hard for the real one.
2	Jennifer	She didn't answer her phone for hours.	She'll be more sensible next time.
3	Harry	He worries too much.	Next time he won't worry so much.

3 **1** socks
2 shoes
3 hat

4 **a** I take my hat off to you.
b Put yourself in my shoes.
c Pull your socks up.

5 *Student's own answers*

Unit 5

Page 46

1 c, f, b, a, e, d

2 **1** cold
2 snowing
3 hot
4 sunny
5 freezing
6 foggy
7 raining
8 cloudy
9 windy

Page 47

3 **1** True.
2 True.
3 True.
4 False. Boris is sneezing because he's got a cold.
5 False. It's autumn.

4 *Student's own answers*

5 *Student's own answers*

6 *Student's own answers*

7

Person	City	Weather today
Steve	Rio de Janeiro	hot and sunny
Amanda	London	freezing and cloudy
Robert	Buenos Aires	a nice day but a little windy
Sarah	New York	foggy and cold

8 *Student's own answers*

Page 48

1 **1** go
2 live
3 Do
4 lives
5 play
6 does
7 plays
8 Do
9 ride
10 do
11 meet
12 have
13 sing
14 sings

2 *Student's own answers*

3 **1** Patrick and Amanda know Laura.
2 Laura, Amanda and Patrick go to the same school. / Laura, Amanda and Patrick don't go to different schools.
3 Patrick and Amanda go to the sports club every Saturday.
4 Tom doesn't do any sport. / Tom doesn't do a lot of sport.
5 Tom sings in his band.

4 *Suggested answers:*
1 How do Patrick and Amanda know Laura?
2 Where does Tom live?
3 Where do Patrick and Amanda go every Saturday?
4 Does Laura play table tennis?
5 Do Laura and Tom sing together?

Page 49

5 **1** Jimmy never plays table tennis
2 Jimmy sometimes plays basketball.
3 Jimmy always rides his bike.
4 Jimmy sometimes plays the guitar.
5 Jimmy never reads a book.
6 Jimmy always listens to music.

6 *Student's own answers*

7 *Student's own answers*

Page 50

1 **1** rugby field
2 climbing wall
3 hiking
4 fencing
5 deer
6 campsite

2 *Student's own answers*

3 *Student's own answers*

Page 51

4 *Student's own answers*

5 **1** cabin
2 canoeing
3 cave
4 waterfall
5 tent
6 tennis court
7 equipment
8 scuba dive

6 Outdoor Adventure
1 False. You sleep in a cabin for the first night.
2 True
3 True
Sports Camp
4 True
5 False. You play six sports in the first two days.
6 True

7 *Student's own answers*

8 *Student's own answers*

9 *Student's own answers*

Page 52

1 **1** have
2 wake up
3 is milking
4 go out
5 are planting

2 *Suggested answers:*
1 I'm having (a great time)
2 (the fruit trees) are blossoming
3 (the weather) is warm
4 (every day) we wake up around 6:00am

3 **Weather:** warm, sunny, foggy
Breakfast: eggs, toast, fresh milk
Farm: farmstay, barn, animals, cows
Crops: fields, seeds, fruit trees

4 **1** Dear Sally,
2 Bye for now!
3 I'm having a great time
4 barn
5 blossom

5 *Student's own answers*

6 *Student's own answers*

7 *Student's own answers*

Page 53

1 **1** Basketball from two o'clock to four o'clock.
2 Breakfast from nine o'clock to half past nine.
3 Ride bikes from five o'clock to six o'clock.
4 Table tennis from half past five to half past seven.
5 Dance and sing from half past seven to half past nine.

2

	Mornings	Afternoons	Evenings
Weather	rainy and cloudy	sunny and hot	foggy and cold
Activity	indoor activities, painting or watching TV	sports like cycling on tandem bikes	play music and dance or sing

3 **1** cloud; b
2 ice; c
3 breeze; a

4 *Student's own answers*

Unit 6

Page 54

1 John is going to the shopping centre.
Alison is going to the police station.
Vicky is going to the hotel.
Matt is going to the clothes shop.

2 **1** clothes shop
2 gym
3 bakery
4 bus station
5 butcher's
6 car park
7 bookshop
8 school
9 post office
10 shopping centre
11 hospital
12 stadium
13 police station
14 music shop
15 hairdresser's
16 museum

Page 55

3 **1** turn left
2 go straight ahead
3 walk across
4 go past
5 turn right

4 **1** music shop
2 Go past
3 walk across
4 post office
5 Go straight ahead
6 museum
7 turn right
8 Go past
9 church
10 turn left
11 Go straight ahead

5 **1** next to
2 between
3 behind
4 across from

6 **1** There is; There isn't
2 Is there; there isn't
3 There are; There aren't
4 Are there, there are

7 *Student's own answers*

Page 56

1 **1** False
2 False
3 False
4 True
5 Not mentioned
6 True

2 **1** gets up
2 has
3 goes
4 captures
5 never has / doesn't have
6 has/eats dinner
7 reads
8 goes to bed

3 *Student's own answers*

4 c, f, d, e, g, a, h, b

Page 57

5 **1** usually
2 sometimes
3 never
4 always
5 often
6 usually
7 sometimes
8 hardly ever

6 *Student's own answers*

7 **1** a **2** b **3** a **4** a

8 *Student's own answers*

Page 58

1 **1** Chichen Itza, Mexico
2 Petra, Jordan
3 The Great Wall of China, China
4 Christ the Redeemer, Brazil
5 The Colosseum, Italy
6 Machu Picchu, Peru
7 Taj Mahal, India

2 *Student's own answers*

Page 59

3 **1** b
2 a
3 b
4 b
5 a
6 a
7 a

4 **1** b **2** c **3** d **4** e **5** a

5 *Student's own answers*

6 *Student's own answers*

7 *Student's own answers*

Page 60

1 *Student's own answers*

2 **1** before
2 after
3 after

3 **1** Samantha
2 Kylie
3 To welcome Kylie to Edinburgh

4
1 till
2 get back
3 loads of
4 spooky

5 c, b, d, a; *Student's own answers*

6 *Student's own answers*

7 *Student's own answers*

Page 61

1 **1** Venice; South Africa
2 Scotland; England
3 China; USA

2 **1** c
2 a
3 b

3 **1** fits the bill
2 when in Rome, do as the Romans do
3 few and far between

4 *Student's own answers*

5 *Student's own answers*

Unit 7

Page 64

1 1 interested
2 frightening
3 surprising

2 1 exciting
2 fascinated
3 terrifying
4 surprised
5 boring

3 *Suggested answers:*
1 I am excited. Travelling is exciting.
2 I am terrified. Fighting cannibals is terrifying.
3 I am fascinated. Kublai Khan's life is fascinating.
4 I am bored. My daily life is boring.

Page 65

4 1 (Roald Amundsen) His name was Roald Amundsen.
2 (July 16th, 1872) He was born on July 16th, 1872.
3 (Norway) He was born in Norway.
4 (North Pole and South Pole) He was the first person to travel to both the North Pole and the South Pole.
5 (Inuit people, dog sleds) One of his most exciting moments was when the Inuit people taught him how to use dog sleds to travel faster.

5

	Freya Stark	Marco Polo	Roald Amundsen
1 I was born in 1872.			✓
2 I was frightened by the cannibals!		✓	
3 We were able to travel by dog sled.			✓
4 I was the first European to visit some distant countries.	✓		
5 People were very surprised by my terrifying adventures.		✓	
6 There were maps and drawings in the books I wrote.	✓		
7 I was fascinated by stories about explorers when I was young.			✓

6 *Student's own answers*

Page 66

1 1 were
2 was
3 who was
4 Where were
5 weren't
6 was
7 Yes, it was.
8 No, it wasn't.
9 Who was
10 wasn't

Page 67

2 1 Who was
2 Where was
3 Were
4 Was

3 1 weak 2 weak 3 strong 4 strong

4 1 was
2 was
3 Were
4 was
5 Were
6 was

5 *Suggested answers*
1 He was in Mongolia in 1923.
2 Her surname was 'Anning'.
3 Yes, they were.
4 Mary Anning was.
5 Yes, they were.
6 Dinosaurs were real and they were reptiles.

6 *Student's own answers*

Page 68

1 1 Vasco de Gama. Nationality: Portuguese; Profession: Ocean explorer; Was famous for: discovering the sea route to India.
2 Gertrude Bell. Nationality: English; Profession: archaeologist; Was famous for: her work in the Middle East
3 Daniel Boone. Nationality: American; Profession: explorer; Was famous for: establishing the first colony in Kentucky.

2 *Student's own answers*

3 1 Who was he?
2 Early life
3 Expeditions
4 Tributes
5 Philanthropy

4 1 b 2 c 3 d 4 a

Page 69

5 1 b 2 b 3 a 4 a 5 b

6 *Student's own answers*

7 *Student's own answers*

Page 70

1 **1** After; Christopher Columbus
2 Charles Darwin; but
3 Martin Luther King Jr.; so
4 J.K. Rowling; later
5 As; Malala Yousafzai

2 b, e, a, d, c

3 **1** c **2** b **3** a **4** d

4 *Student's own answers*

5 *Student's own answers*

6 *Student's own answers*

Page 71

1 **1** She was eight years old.
2 She was in the garden.
3 She was with her cousin Rick.
4 It was a beehive.
5 Yes, it was.

2 **1**
1 were
2 was
3 terrifying
2 **1** was
2 interesting
3 **1** was
2 were
3 terrified

3 **1** c **2** b **3** a

4 *Student's own answers*

Unit 8

Page 72

1 **1** b **2** a **3** b

2
1 **1** Last weekend
2 Just before
3 But when
2
1 One day
2 After some time
3 Suddenly
3
1 One Christmas
2 Before long
3 Then

Page 73

3 *Student's own answers*

4 /t/ - walked, reached
/d/ - climbed, arrived
/ɪd/ - waited, wanted, needed, handed

5

Infinitive	Past simple
buy	bought
come	came
eat	ate
fly	flew
get	got
go	went

Infinitive	Past simple
have	had
hear	heard
put	put
see	saw
sit	sat
think	thought

6 **1** didn't know
2 didn't leave
3 didn't want
4 didn't have
5 didn't matter
6 didn't want
7 didn't exist
8 didn't think

7 *Student's own answers*

8 *Student's own answers*

Page 74

1 **1** thought
2 showed
3 finished
4 went
5 wanted
6 asked
7 told
8 saw
9 came
10 knew

2 *Student's own answers*

3 **1** did you go when the lights went off?
2 you see Miss Scarlet go to the bathroom?
3 did you talk to?
4 you buy an expensive flat in London last week?
5 did you steal Mrs Templeton's necklace?

Page 75

4 **1** Where did you go yesterday afternoon? Student's own answers
2 Did you see an interesting film last week? Student's own answers
3 What did you buy the last time you went to the shopping centre? Student's own answers

4 Did you visit your family last summer? Student's own answers
5 What did you do last night? Student's own answers
6 Did you have Maths class before English today? Student's own answers

5 1 He went to the supermarket last night.
2 He bought some flour and a meat pie.
3 Yes, he did. He ran home because he wanted to be on time to watch a show on TV.
4 He ate his dinner.
5 Yes, he did.
6 He won a trip to Wales.

6 1 flour; made
2 hair
3 Claus
4 flew; bear

7 1 (whales) c (Wales)
2 (flower) a (flour)
3 (knight) d (night)
4 (write) e (right)
5 (ate) b (eight)

Page 76

1 *Student's own answers*

2 1 The Otis family is from America.
2 Because the house was haunted.
3 It was the blood of Lady Eleanor or Canterville.
4 He heard a curious, metallic noise.
5 He saw a terrifying old man.

3 *Suggested answers:*
1 An American buys a haunted house and moves there with his family, but the family are not scared of the ghost. They suggest practical solutions to the problems and this upsets the ghost.
2 No
3 Sir Simon of Canterville
4 He is angry; Because Mr Otis is not scared of him.

4 *Student's own answers*

Page 78

1 1 was; lived; some time ago
2 decided; One stormy night
3 opened; saw; Just as
4 went; were; Suddenly

2 *Student's own answers*

3 b, e, d, c, a

4 *Student's own answers*

5 *Student's own answers*

6 *Student's own answers*

Page 79

1 *Student's own answers*

2 *Student's own answers*

3 1 c; ii
2 a; iii
3 b; i

4 *Student's own answers*

Unit 9

Page 82

1 1 cereal
2 milk
3 egg
4 bread
5 yogurt
6 apple
7 kiwi
8 banana
9 muesli
10 coffee
11 cheese
12 toast

2

	Breakfast ideas	
A	kiwi	banana
An	egg	apple
Some	cereal milk bread yoghurt	muesli coffee cheese toast

3 **Countable:** carrot, egg, pear, onion, sausage, tomato
Uncountable: cake, jam, juice, meat, pasta, rice

Page 83

4 1 are
2 isn't any
3 are
4 is
5 some
6 some
7 isn't any
8 Some
9 aren't any
10 are

5 *Student's own answers*

6 *Student's own answers*

7 *Student's own answers*

Page 84

1 1 slices
2 jar
3 half
4 two
5 slices
6 block

2 1 e
2 b
3 d
4 a
5 c

3 **1** animal
2 breakfast
3 chocolate
4 dairy
5 fruit
6 olive

4 **1** two spoonfuls of
2 two spoonfuls of
3 two slices of
4 a tin of
5 three slices of

5 *Student's own answers*

Page 85

6 **Ingredients**
1 slices
2 tin
3 loaf
4 bottle
5 cup
Preparation
1 the mustard on a slice of bread
2 the apple
3 the turkey and the apple on the bread
4 another slice of bread and the slice of pineapple

7 **1** Is
2 any
3 loaf
4 jar
5 aren't any
6 some
7 slices
8 bottles
9 a
10 tin
11 bottle
12 sandwiches

8 *Student's own answers*

Page 86

1 *Student's own answers*

2 **1** a low-fat yogurt
2 76
3 It's good for you because it is low-fat, but it also contains an unhealthy amount of sugar.
4 calcium
5 wholemeal bread, pasta and fruit and vegetables

3 **1** True
2 False
3 Doesn't say
4 False
5 True

4 **1** c **2** a **3** d **4** e **5** b

5 **1** sources
2 Wholemeal
3 amount
4 store
5 key

6 *Student's own answers*

7 **1** calories
2 fats
3 grains
4 nuts
5 fruit
6 vegetables
7 sugars
8 salt

8 *Student's own answers*

Page 88

1 *Student's own answers*

2 **2**

3 **1** The aim of this report is to…
2 mushy
3 bland
4 lots of, plenty of

4 *Student's own answers*

5 *Student's own answers*

6 *Student's own answers*

Page 89

1 **a** Isaac
b Chris
c Julia
d Paul

2 **1** He's always saying mean things to people. Any chance he gets to do something bad, he does it. He is a bully.
2 He pushed him in the corridor.
3 Because she's so far ahead of the rest of the class.
4 A famous inventor.
5 He doesn't do any exercise or help around the house.

3 **1** b **2** a **3** c

4 **1** smart cookie
2 couch potato
3 bad egg

5 *Student's own answers*

Unit Reviews

Unit 1

1 1 b
2 c
3 a
4 a
5 b

2 *Student's own answers*

3 *Student's own answers*

4 *Student's own answers*

Unit 2

1 1 b
2 b
3 c
4 a
5 c
6 a
7 b
8 a

2 *Student's own answers*

3 *Suggested questions:*
1 What school subjects are you good at?
2 What's your favourite subject?
3 What time is your first class on Monday?
4 When's your last class on Friday?
5 What's the date today? / What date is it today?
6 When's your birthday?
Student's own answers

Unit 3

1 1 f
2 g
3 d
4 a
5 c

2 1 c
2 b
3 a
4 b
5 a

Unit 4

1 1 b
2 c
3 b
4 b

2 *Student's own answers*

Unit 5

1 1 like
2 sunny
3 don't
4 ice
5 every
6 play
7 Do
8 evening

2 *Student's own answers*

3 *Student's own answers*

Unit 6

1 1 a
2 b
3 a
4 b
5 c
6 b

2 *Student's own answers*

3 *Student's own answers*

Unit 7

1 1 a
2 b
3 c
4 b

2 *Student's own answers*

Unit 8

1 1 b
2 a
3 b
4 b

2 1 was
2 decided
3 as
4 thought
5 was/got
6 Did

3 *Student's own answers*

Unit 9

1 1 5
2 6
3 Tuesday
4 fats
5 vegetables
6 running

2 1 a
2 a
3 c
4 b

Track 1
Unit 1, page 4, exercise 1

Lola: Hi, can I help you?
Mark: Errrr yes. I can't find my class. I think I'm lost. It's my first day at this school, you see. I'm new here.
Lola: Oh right. I'm Lola. And this is my friend, Rita.
Rita: Hey!
Mark: Nice to meet you. My name's Mark Walters. I'm from Ireland. As I said, it's my first day and I'm a little nervous.
Rita: Walters? That's like my name. How do you spell your surname?
Mark: It's W-A-L-T-E-R-S.
Rita: We have the same surname! How strange. And you're Irish? My cousins are from Ireland. They are younger than me. How old are you?
Mark: I'm twelve.
Rita: I'm fourteen! How many brothers and sisters have you got?
Mark: I haven't got any sisters, but I've got two brothers.
Rita: That's exactly the same as my family in Ireland. You know, I think we could be cousins! I've got to tell my parents about this. What's your address?
Mark: It's 24 Church Street.
Rita: Church Street? I live at 26 Church Street.
Mark: No way! Next to the stadium?
Rita: Yes! There is a basketball match this evening. Do you want to come and watch it with us?
Mark: I'd love to. It's my favourite sport. My phone number is 345 788 002. Can you call me after school?
Rita: Of course! Oh, that's the bell. Come with me and I'll show you to your room. We're in different classes, of course. What's your teacher's name?
Mark: Errr Mrs White, I think.
Rita: Great, she's really friendly........

Track 2
Unit 1, page 4, exercise 2

See previous track

Track 3
Unit 1, page 5, exercise 8

1

Receptionist: Hello, School reception. How can I help you today?
Michaela: Oh yes, hello. My name's Michaela. I want to join the sports club. Can I do this here?
Receptionist: Yes, Michaela, you can. I need you to give me some details. What's your surname?
Michaela: It's Baker.
Receptionist: How do you spell that?
Michaela: It's B-A-K-E-R.
Receptionist: And how old are you, Michaela?
Michaela: I'm nearly thirteen. My birthday is next month in fact.
Receptionist: So, you're twelve. Good. What's your phone number?
Michaela: It's 456 124 098.
Receptionist: Sorry, I couldn't hear you. Did you say 456 124 050?
Michaela: No, it's 456 124 098.
Receptionist: Great, that's it. You are signed up. The first meeting of the sports club is on Monday at 4pm. We look forward to seeing you there.
Michaela: Thank you!

Speaker 2 – Anthony

Receptionist: Hello, School reception. How can I help you?
Anthony: Hello. I want to join the French club. My teacher said that I needed to call and give you my details.
Receptionist: Yes, that's correct. What's your name?
Anthony: It's Anthony. I'm thirteen years old.
Receptionist: And what's your address, Anthony?
Anthony: It's 27 Glynne Street. It's near the school in fact.
Receptionist: 27 Glynne Street. How do you spell that?
Anthony: It's G-L-Y-N-N-E street.
Receptionist: Thanks Anthony. Now, French club starts at 6pm on Tuesday.
Anthony: Great, my grandad can bring me home when it's finished.
Receptionist: What's his name?
Anthony: It's Mike.
Receptionist: And his phone number?
Anthony: It's 334 667 000.
Receptionist: Great, Anthony. See you on Tuesday.

Track 4
Unit 1, page 5, exercise 9

See previous track

Track 5
Unit 1, page 8, exercise 2

International School, Sports club blog

Welcome back to school. It's a new school year and time to join a club. Here are our sports club's newest members.

Alex

Hey! I'm American and I was born in Florida, USA. I'm fifteen and I speak three languages: English, Spanish and French. My dad is a professional surfer and I love surfing too. When I'm not surfing, I like listening to music, but I only listen to classical. I haven't got any brothers or sisters, so I like spending time with friends.

Jenna

Hi, I'm thirteen years old and I'm Irish. I like football (my favourite football team is Manchester United) but my favourite sport is skiing. I'm a big fan of rollerblading too. I usually go to the park with my younger sister at the weekend. I'm a vegan. My favourite food is anything with vegetables.

Kosuke

I'm fourteen and I'm from Japan. I speak two languages. I love playing and watching all sports, but I especially love baseball. Apart from sports, I like listening to music, especially folk and R&B. My favourite singer is Ed Sheeran. I know the words to all of his songs. My other hobbies are reading and watching action films. I go to the cinema with my family every Saturday.

Track 6
Unit 2, page 12, exercise 4

Chris: Wow, it's September already! Hey, when do classes start, Tina?

Tina: On the 13th. I'm really excited about going back to school. Are you?
Chris: Yes, I am. We start on the 12th and I can't wait. It's a pity that we aren't in the same school!
Tina: I know. Are you free on Wednesday to study together?
Chris: No, I'm not. What about Saturday?
Tina: I've got lunch at my friend's house.
Chris: Hmm, Tuesday then?
Tina: Yes, OK. Dad says that Mrs Watson is my English teacher this year. She's the best. I thought she was English but, in fact, she's Irish. She's really friendly.
Chris: That's great. My favourite teacher is Mr Wang. He's Chinese. He knows everything about Maths! That reminds me, we've got an exam on the 27th of October.
Tina: Oh, I think we've got exams too on the 26th of November. I'll check with my teacher when classes start.
Chris: Good idea! Oh, and guess what? My friends and I are all in the same class this year too!
Tina: That's cool. My best friend Katia is coming to my school this year.
Chris: Katia? I think I know her! Is she German?
Tina: No, she isn't. Her name is German or Russian. But she's Peruvian. Her family are from La Paz.
Chris: Really? Do you want to bring her to my birthday party?
Tina: When is it?
Chris: Saturday the 10th at 2pm.
Tina: She's on holiday, but she's back here on the 9th. That's this Friday. I'll ask her.
Chris: Great. I have to go. See you later!
Tina: Bye!

Track 7

Unit 2, page 12, exercise 5

See previous track

Track 8

Unit 2, page 14, exercise 3

Conversation 1

Kit: Hey Ned. Where's our English class?
Ned: English? It's in Room 34.
Kit: Is that the room by the library?
Ned: No, it isn't. It's near the gym.
Kit: It starts at a quarter to eleven, right?
Ned: No, it starts at a quarter past ten.
Kit: We need to hurry!
Ned: Kit! It's only nine o'clock! It's PE class now!

Conversation 2

Lily: I can't wait for the weekend, Rob. It's my birthday.
Rob: Oh! Happy birthday, Lily. It's my birthday soon too. When were you born?
Lily: On the 13th of April, 2005.
Rob: Ahh. I was born on the 13th of May 2006.
Lily: Wow. That's my brother's birthday too! But he was born in 2008. Hey, can you come to my birthday party on Saturday?
Rob: Oh, I'm sorry Lily. I've got volleyball on Saturday so I can't. It's a really important match, you see.
Lily: No problem, Rob. Good luck!

Conversation 3

Ted: Hey, Magda. Where's our school trip this year? Is it a football stadium? I love football.
Magda: I know! And I like art. But it isn't a football stadium or an art gallery. It's something I think we all like, really. It's the zoo.
Ted: Oh, is it?
Magda: Yes, but it's a Science excursion with a guide. We learn all about the animals, where they're from and how they live – including the strange ones!
Ted: Oh, good! Science is my favourite subject! When is it?
Magda: It's on the 10th of January.
Ted: Oh no! I can't go. I'm in Greece with my family until the 12th.
Magda: Oh well. Next time!

Track 9

Unit 2, page 14, exercise 4

See previous track

Track 10

Unit 2, page 16, exercise 2

Schools around the world

My name is Yolanda. I'm from Rosario, in Argentina, and I really like reggae music and photography. My dad's a professional photographer and he says my photos are really good! My school timetable is a little different because I live in the Southern Hemisphere. The school year starts in March and our summer holidays start in December. Classes start at a quarter past seven and finish at one o'clock. My favourite subject is Music and I love playing the guitar. It takes time to learn, but I'm patient and persevering.

I'm Ayako and I'm from Kyoto, in Japan. I'm crazy about numbers and computers so my favourite subjects are Maths and IT. I guess you could say that I am analytical. I'm also quite shy and I prefer working on my own. I usually go to clubs in the evening or to 'juku', a school where students can do extra study. I always get good marks in exams.

My name is Aegeus and I'm from Athens, in Greece. I'm really good at sports. I love swimming, tennis and ice-skating. My favourite subject is PE and I also like Drama. My mum says that I am really active and a bit too talkative. I also love meeting new people. I don't go to school. I have classes at home with my sister and my mum is our teacher. It's great but I don't always pass my exams!

Track 11

Unit 3, page 22, exercise 3

Mum: Is that your Science homework, Ross?
Ross: Yes, it is.
Mum: Is it for tomorrow?
Ross: No. It's for Tuesday, but I want to do it now because Monday afternoon is football practice.
Mum: Oh, OK. Who's your Science teacher this year?
Ross: It's Mr Cortes. He's really energetic and nothing's ever boring. He's preparing us for the Science and Technology Fair in March.
Mum: But it's only November.
Ross: Yes. He wants to make sure we're ready in time.
Mum: And what's your homework about?

Ross: It's about the human body, from our head to our feet. It's really interesting.
Mum: Tell me something interesting from your class then!
Ross: Well, mum, did you know that our feet absorb more than 10,000 kilos of force every day?
Mum: Wow, that's a lot.
Ross: Yes, and it's more if you've got shoes with high heels! Our knees take a lot of stress too. And everybody's knees are different, just like our fingerprints.
Mum: Wow! That is interesting! Now let me tell you something about your body. That's your stomach talking and it says it's time to have dinner.
Ross: Oh, that's another thing. Our stomachs produce about 2 litres of acid every day to help us digest our food.
Mum: Come on then, Ross. Let's give your stomach something to digest.
Ross: Actually, now I think of it, I'm really hungry, Mum!

Track 12
Unit 3, page 22, exercise 4
See previous track

Track 13
Unit 3, page 24, exercise 3
Sally: Hi Tom. What's that in your wallet?
Tom: This? Oh, it's a photo of my best friends.
Sally: Oh, do they go to this school?
Tom: No, they don't. They go to different schools. I really miss them! The photo is from last summer at camp.
Sally: Tell me about them.
Tom: Well, with the straight, red hair and blue eyes on the left is Sophia. We're very alike in character. She is adventurous and friendly, just like me!
Sally: And who's that?
Tom: That's Hugo. People say we look very similar because he's got short brown hair and blue eyes too. And he's tall and athletic just like me. He's always smiling. Actually, he's really funny and he makes us laugh. He's good at sports too. He loves basketball and he's got a match to play every weekend.
Sally: Sounds just like you! And who's that in the middle? The girl with long, dark brown hair and hazel eyes?
Tom: That's Maria. She's really pretty. She's also the happiest person I know. She's never in a bad mood or angry. She's the youngest by a few months. She's from Peru.
Sally: And who's that boy with short black hair?
Tom: Oh, that's Martin. He's actually really tall but you can't see that in the photo. He's quite shy around people – he doesn't like big groups. Not like me – I'm the most talkative person I know! Look, I've got more photos here. This is Rachel. She's also really pretty and......

Track 14
Unit 3, page 24, exercise 4
See previous track

Track 15
Unit 3, page 26, exercise 2
People you admire
My dad and role model
Everybody has somebody that they admire in their lives. It could be a close friend or a family member. For me, it's my dad, Fernando. He's very responsible, persevering and trustworthy. He works a lot because he's a doctor. Doing the best for his patients is very important to him. Everybody says that I look like him. I'm tall and I've got hazel eyes too. I hope I'm as successful as him when I grow up.
Jaime, Spain

A successful uncle
My uncle, Charles, is an English architect. He's ingenious and creative. He is well known for his remarkable buildings all over the world. We don't look anything alike. He's got short red hair that's a bit curly and he's medium height. But everybody says our personalities are very similar. My family and I spend every summer with him in England and I hope to work in his office in the future.
Mustafa, Turkey

The best teacher
My English teacher, Julie, is amazing. She's American and she's very tall. She is energetic and imaginative and we always have fun in class. She is also very patient and she doesn't get angry if we make mistakes. She speaks Arabic, English and French. Her husband, David, is from the USA too. He's a lawyer and also teaches law classes at the university.
Adele, France

Track 16
Unit 4, page 31, exercise 6
Mum: OK Carla, it's time to clean out your room. You have so many things in here that I can't see the bed! There are more clothes outside the wardrobe than in it.
Carla: But Mum, everything here is special. I don't want to throw anything away.
Mum: Hmmm. Let's see. There must be something. What about these dark brown boots? They look quite old.
Carla: But they are my favourite! And they're from Grandma. She gave them to me for my birthday when I was ten.
Mum: That was three years ago, Carla. It's time to get new ones.
Carla: Oh OK, you're right.
Mum: Good. Now what about this stripy jumper? It looks very small.
Carla: It is. I got that from cousin Rob but I don't really wear it anymore.
Mum: OK. What's this? Is this your sister's flowery dress?
Carla: Errrrr, yes. I need to give it back to her. I don't like it anyway.
Mum: OK, that's three things. Now what else?
Carla: Well, I don't wear this tartan shirt anymore, but my best friend, Lizzie, gave it to me.
Mum: Why don't we give it to your aunt? I'm sure that she'd like it. She wears a lot of tartan dresses and skirts.
Carla: That's a great idea.
Mum: See, isn't this fun?
Carla: Actually, it is. What about these jeans, Mum? I know they're expensive, but I don't like them.
Mum: I bought you those last week, Carla!
Carla: Oh yes, I forgot. I'll keep them, of course!

Track 17

Unit 4, page 31, exercise 7

See previous track

Track 18

Unit 4, page 33, exercise 7

Peter: Sonia, you have so many pictures on social media. Who are all these people?

Sonia: Well, I love taking photos. I'll show you some of my favourites. See this one of the two girls smiling?

Peter: You mean the picture in the park?

Sonia: Yes, the girl with long, straight blond hair is my best friend Rose. She's a year older than me. She's wearing a dark blue jacket. She's in Italy at the moment. She's going to school there and studying Italian. I really miss her. She loves watching movies and reading books, just like me.

Peter: Who's the other girl in the photo with her?

Sonia: That's me.

Peter: Oh, I didn't recognise you. And what about this picture?

Sonia: That's my friend Roy at school after PE class with a friend of his. Roy's wearing the light green and yellow stripy shirt and holding the football. He's a big football fan. In fact, I think he's watching a match right now. But he prefers playing really.

Peter: And this picture of the man in the office?

Sonia: Oh, that's my uncle John. That isn't an office – it's his old house. He's a graphic designer, you see, and he works from home. He's living with us at the moment though, because she's looking for a new house.

Peter: Who's that in the flowery dress? They look like they are in their garden.

Sonia: That's my cousin Karen with her daughter. They're actually at school planting flowers. Karen's a teacher here. She's teaching a class at the moment. That's reminds me. We'd better go to class!

Track 19

Unit 4, page 33, exercise 8

See previous track

Track 20

Unit 4, page 34, exercise 2

Four tips to help the planet

The planet is in trouble, but what can we do? Do you want to help save it? If so, read on to learn about the small changes that you can start making today.

Tip 1: Recycle and reduce waste

Use different coloured bins to classify the rubbish in your house so that recycling is easy. Take short showers and turn off the tap while brushing your teeth. Turn off lights when you leave the room and teach your family to do the same. This helps to save our natural resources.

Tip 2: Plant a tree

Planting trees helps fight against deforestation. Find out if you can plant trees in your local park or in your own garden. Trees help clean the air and they provide food and oxygen. Small things like building a house for wild birds in your garden can help to protect endangered species.

Tip 3: Drive less

Walking, taking the bus or cycling instead of driving a car can help to reduce air pollution. This not only helps the environment but you get more exercise as well. You can also suggest to your family that you share your car with neighbours or friends.

Tip 4: Think about what you buy

Make a list before you go to the supermarket so that you don't buy things you don't need. When you go shopping, use reusable bags instead of plastic bags. Keep these bags in your car so that you don't forget them. Buy food that is locally grown and in season. Follow our four easy tips and start saving the planet today!

Track 21

Unit 5, page 40, exercise 3

Speaker 1 – Alexander

Winter in Iceland starts at the end of October and not in December like in most of Europe. There are 26 weeks of winter and on the first day in my city, there's free meat soup on the streets. As you can imagine, it's freezing here in winter. It's always snowing and very windy. Sometimes we can't go to school! The shortest day is in December and it's four hours long. The sun comes up at midday and it goes down just after three o'clock. Sometimes it's so cloudy that it can stay dark all day. You have to wear a lot of clothes to keep warm. Everybody wears hats and coats. Some people think that you don't need sunglasses but they are important to protect your eyes from the cold.

Speaker 2 – Sandy

Summer in Australia is different to a lot of other countries. Our summer starts in December, not June, like other places. It ends in February. This means that a lot of people usually celebrate holidays like Christmas and New Year on the beach instead of indoors. The weather here can depend on the part of the country. In the north, it's usually hot and sunny but it can also rain. In the south, it can be cold and chilly. We usually wear shorts, swimsuits and T-shirts in the summer and a jacket in the evening if it gets colder. There's so much to see and do here; it truly is the best place in the world to spend the summer!

Track 22

Unit 5, page 40, exercise 4

See previous track

Track 23

Unit 5, page 41, exercise 7

Receptionist: Hello, Chester Sports Experience. How can I help you?

Woman: Yes, hello. I'm just calling for a bit of information.

Receptionist: Yes. What would you like to know?

Woman: Have you got a camp this July?

Receptionist: Yes, we have. There's one that starts on the 12th of July and ends on the 13th of August.

Woman: OK. Where exactly is it? I don't really know anything about the area of Chester.

Receptionist: It's very easy to find. The address is 32 Albert Road. It's next to the park.

Woman: Right. What kind of activities do the children do? It's for my son, you see. He loves sports.

Receptionist: We do a range of different sports, including tennis, volleyball and swimming.

Woman: Oh, great. He'll love that. You say it starts in July. What's the weather like then?

Receptionist: It's usually sunny and quite hot so campers should wear hats and sun cream at all times.
Woman: Got it. What kind of food do you serve at lunch?
Receptionist: We have lots of options. Has your son got any allergies?
Woman: No. But there are a lot of things he doesn't like to eat. At home he usually just has sandwiches for lunch and pasta for dinner.
Receptionist: Well, there are always options of sandwiches, pasta and pizza.
Woman: Oh, he loves pizza. So how much does the summer camp cost for the month?
Receptionist: It's £120 per week and £400 for the whole month.
Woman: Great! Thanks for your help. I'll talk to my family and see what they think.
Receptionist: OK, no problem. Bye for now!

Track 24

Unit 5, page 41, exercise 8

See previous track

Track 25

Unit 5, page 44, exercise 2

Safari Summer Camp

Do you love adventure? Then come to Serengeti Park! Our two-week summer programme in the heart of the Ngorongoro Conservation Area in Tanzania is an excellent opportunity to visit Africa, learn valuable life skills and make new friends.

Contributing to the local community

At Serengeti Park, you share a small cabin with five other campers. When you arrive, we organise team-building activities for you to get to know each other. We then spend a week visiting a nearby village to work on community service projects like helping out at schools and health centres. It's a great way to meet the locals and share life experiences.

Food

Tanzanian cuisine is fabulous and we offer traditional dishes, as well as your favourite food from home. There are buffet breakfasts and lunches, and for dinner there are a range of hot dishes, including vegetarian options.

Adventure

We spend the second week of the programme exploring. You can canoe on the Grumeti River or go on a ride through the conservation area, one of the best animal sanctuaries in the world. Here you can observe all kinds of wildlife, like elephants, zebra and even lions. Don't forget to bring your camera and your sunglasses. It gets very sunny here in the summer months.

Lessons for life

As well as adventure and a feeling of contributing something to a community, Serengeti Park offers valuable life lessons. You learn teamwork and leadership skills, and we also teach you some basic outdoor survival skills and ways you can help protect the environment. If all of that sounds interesting to you, click here for information about prices and dates.

Track 26

Unit 6, page 48, exercise 3

Speaker 1

Boy: Excuse me? I'm a little lost. Can you help me?
Girl: Of course. What are you looking for?
Boy: The museum. I want to see the new exhibition. I hear it's excellent.
Girl: It is ! Go straight ahead and turn right. It's across from the bakery. It's very close, about a ten-minute walk from here.
Boy: Thanks.
Boy: Oh, hello again! You're right. The exhibition is great! Hey, do you know where the park is
Girl: Sure. It's not far. Go past the roundabout and walk across Alban Road. It's between the gym and the music shop.
Boy: Great, thanks!

Speaker 2

Woman: Excuse me, is there a place I can send a letter around here?
Man: Yes, the post office is near here. It's just next to the school.
Woman: How do I get there?
Man: Go straight ahead and go past the traffic lights. Then turn left when you see the bus station. Keep walking for about five minutes and you'll see it. It's next to the hospital. You can't miss it!
Woman: Thanks!
Woman: Excuse me? Is there anywhere to stay around here?
Man: Sure, there are a lot of hotels in town. There's a great one on Main Street. The restaurant there is great and the staff are really friendly. It's not that expensive and it has a swimming pool too.
Woman: It sounds perfect. How do I get there?
Man: It's quite far. Walk across Main Street and take the bus. Get off at Sunset Avenue and you'll see it. It's across from the post office.
Woman: Thank you for your help.

Track 27

Unit 6, page 48, exercise 4

See previous track

Track 28

Unit 6, page 50, exercise 3

Presenter: Welcome to Radio 10. We're here on this glorious summer's day with Liam, who is travelling around Ireland on foot. Liam, can you tell us why you're doing this?
Liam: Well, after my last year of school, it seems like a good idea to learn more about my country before I start university. And walking is the best way to see as much as I can! I don't usually walk much at home in Dublin, but I'm enjoying it a lot!
Presenter: Can you tell us about a typical day?
Liam: I get up early every morning around 6am. I have a shower and I have breakfast. I don't read the newspaper or go online because I don't have time. Then I get dressed and start walking. I usually walk all day but I stop for lunch at 1pm. In the evening, I have dinner and after that, I often watch a film. I usually go to bed around 9pm.
Presenter: What's the best thing about doing the walking tour?

Liam: You meet a lot of people and make new friends on the way. I meet people from Ireland and all over the world every day. They're often very interested in my travel experiences. I sometimes send them emails when I have time to tell them about my progress.

Presenter: What's the worst thing?

Liam: Hmmmm, I'd say missing my family. It's strange not seeing them every day. I phone them every evening and we catch up on each other's news. But generally, I¡m enjoying travelling alone. It gives me time to think.

Presenter: Thanks Liam. Best of luck with the rest of your project. Next up, we have ....

Track 29

Unit 6, page 50, exercise 4

See previous track

Track 30

Unit 6, page 52, exercise 2

Cool jobs in amazing places!

These three places are magnificent and important historical monuments. We interviewed the lucky people who get to work in or near these ancient places to find out what they do.

The giant rock structures of the pyramids of Giza, in Egypt, are over 4,500 years old, and one of them, the Great Pyramid, is the only one of the Seven Wonders of the Ancient World that still exists. Natalie works as a tour guide for a company that organises sightseeing tours around them. She usually starts work at 8am and finishes at 8pm. She loves meeting new people, but she says that it can get very hot walking around in summer. From May to October she usually takes a break in the afternoon.

The Hagia Sophia in Istanbul, in Turkey, was built in 537 AD. At different times a church, a mosque and a museum, the building has a rich history, and millions of people visit its spectacular dome and towers every year. Deniz works there as an archaeologist. He always discovers something new and at the moment he is studying a very old statue which he thinks is an important artefact. Deniz loves learning about his city's history but he doesn't like it when it gets crowded with tourists.

Angkor Wat, near the city of Siem Reap, in Cambodia, is the world's largest religious monument. Built by an ancient civilisation as a palace dedicated to the god Vishnu, its 400 square kilometres include around 70 temples. More and more people visit every year. Sita is an artist who lives nearby. She spends her time painting and drawing the temples. She never gets bored because there is always something new to explore, but she often gets lost among the temples and the jungle.

Track 31

Unit 7, page 58, exercise 4

Polly: I have nothing to do. My sisters are at a school play and my parents are on holiday. I don't have any homework. There aren't any exciting programmes on the TV. No surprise there. I have nothing to do! It's so boring without anybody here! Let's see. What can I do? Oh, I know. I'm in the kitchen so I can make a snack....Done....What next? Oh, I can read that new book on explorers that mum bought last weekend. Lara said it was frightening but I don't get frightened that easily! Now where did I put it. Here, it is...... Oh! Look at the time. It's midnight. Time goes so fast when you are interested in a book. This book is a lot scarier than I thought. It's full of stories about ghosts and monsters. I don't believe in them of course but..... What was that noise? Oh, I don't like being alone. There it is again! It's coming from the wardrobe! Help!

Danny: Polly? Polly? Are you there?

Polly: That sounds like Danny. Danny? Is that you?

Danny: Yes, I'm at the front door. Can you let me in?

Polly: Coming. Oh, Danny, I'm so happy to see you. I thought you were a ghost or a monster.

Danny: Don't be silly Polly. They don't exist.

Polly: What are you doing here so late at night?

Danny: Oh, well. I was on my way home and it started to rain. I saw your house and decided to come in.

Polly: Come in and I'll tell you all about this book I'm reading. ..... There's that noise again!

Danny: Let me investigate........ Polly! Come up here and look. It's just your cat. It was stuck in the wardrobe!

Polly: Oh, right. I knew that.

Track 32

Unit 7, page 58, exercise 5

See previous track

Track 33

Unit 7, page 60, exercise 1

Presenter: You're listening to FM Radio 4. I'm Cathy Smith and welcome to the quiz – Do you know your history? Today's contestants are Emma and Lucas. Here's the first question for you, Emma. Who was the leader of the first voyage around the world?

Emma: Was it Ferdinand Magellan?

Presenter: That's correct. For an extra point. Where was he born?

Emma: He was born in Italy.

Presenter: That is incorrect. Next contestant. Lucas, what do you think?

Lucas: It's Portugal. He was born in Portugal.

Presenter: Correct! Well done, Lucas. You win two tickets to see the new fossil exhibition at the Museum of History. Who are you going to take with you to see the exhibition?

Lucas: My father. He loves dinosaurs. Thank you so much.

Presenter: And here's our next question. In what year was Neil Armstrong on the moon?

Emma: I know! He was there in 1968!

Presenter: That was very close but it's not right. Sorry, Emma. Lucas, what do you think?

Lucas: It was 1969.

Presenter: Yes, that's the correct answer! You win a free pass to twenty art galleries and museums in the city.

Lucas: Are you saying I can visit all of them free all year?

Presenter: Only in certain months. Your pass is for April only.

Lucas: Wow! Thank you!

Presenter: OK. Final question. In what year did Amelia Earhart fly across the Atlantic Ocean

Emma: I know! It was 1920.

Presenter: Wrong again Emma, I'm afraid. Lucas?

Lucas: It was in 1928.

Presenter: Correct! You win a copy of this fabulous...

Track 34

Unit 7, page 60, exercise 2

See previous track

Track 35

Unit 7, page 62, exercise 2

Adventures in the wild

Bessie Coleman

Bessie Coleman was a courageous woman and a pioneer pilot. Born in 1892 in Texas, she was one of 13 children and had to work to help her family while she was still at school. She was a very good student and she was particularly good at Maths. But what she really wanted to do was to fly. It wasn't easy to go to flight school in the USA at that time, but Bessie was persistent. She saved money to go to France to get her licence, and she was successful. In 1920 she became the first woman of Native-American and African-American origins to get a pilot licence, and she was soon famous for her daring tricks in US air shows. Her dream was to open a flight school for people who weren't able to pay for it. She was in an accident when trying out a new plane in 1926 and died at the age of 34. She is still remembered by her nickname: Queen Bess.

Tom Avery

He is a brave, professional climber who was born in December 1975 in London. When he was eight years old, his favourite book was about the inspiring life of Captain Robert Scott. When Avery was 16, he was the leader of a number of climbing expeditions in Wales and Scotland. In 2002, he was the youngest British person to get to the South Pole on foot. In 2005, he was head of an expedition to the North Pole. He wasn't the first to do this, but he was the fastest. His journey took about 37 days. Avery tells of this thrilling adventure in his book To the End of the Earth. Today, he gives talks in schools and is planning to sail around the world.

Track 36

Unit 8, page 66, exercise 2

Speaker 1 - Oliver

Last spring, I went camping with my mum and dad and my younger brother Tommy. We drove all day so when we finally got to the campsite, we were very tired and it was dark. Just after we arrived, we put up our tent and went to bed. We didn't notice anything unusual. But when we woke up in the morning, we saw that we were not in the campsite at all. We were in somebody's front garden!

Speaker 2 - Isabella

I love taking photos and I always have my camera with me. One day, my friend and I visited an old castle. We spent the whole day exploring the rooms and taking photos. There wasn't anybody else there. The next day, we were very excited to see the photos. But when we looked at them, we were terrified. In each photo, there was a woman dressed in black just behind us. We never went back to the castle again!

Speaker 3 – Julia

I love collecting things from the past like old books and pictures. One day, I was at my local bookshop, one that sells really old books, when suddenly a book fell off the shelf! I picked it up and opened it. It was a novel by an Italian woman called Rita and inside there was a letter from her. The man in the shop let me take it home for my mother to translate because she was born in Italy. When she read it, she got a big surprise. It turns out that Rita was actually my great grandma!

Track 37

Unit 8, page 66, exercise 3

See previous track

Track 38

Unit 8, page 68, exercise 1

I remember that summer like it was yesterday! My family and I decided to go to Australia on June 15th. It was our fifth trip there because we love it, and my birthday is on June 16th, so it was a treat for my birthday. Normally we stay in hotels, but this time my mum found us a typical Australian house to stay in. It was in a quiet area near the beach and it had a big swimming pool at the back. My younger brother wasn't happy because he wanted to go camping, but I thought it was great.

One morning, I decided to go for a swim alone. Just before I jumped in, I saw something move suddenly by the side of the pool and enter the water. I thought it was a bird or a mouse but when I looked closer, I saw that it was a huge snake! I screamed and I threw my shoe at it. I was terrified. My dad ran over and asked me what was wrong. I pointed to the water and he screamed too! The woman next door called a snake catcher and he took it away. He told us that we were lucky because it was a very dangerous snake. Afterwards, my parents bought me a new pair of trainers as a present. I spent the rest of the holiday in my room reading a book and I didn't swim again for the entire holiday.

Track 39

Unit 8, page 68, exercise 2

See previous track

Track 40

Unit 8, page 70, exercise 2

The adventure of the Mazarin Stone

When Dr Watson arrived at Sherlock Holmes's house, he found his friend sitting in his armchair by the window. He said hello but there was no answer. Then a voice greeted him from behind.

'Doesn't it look like me?' asked the detective. He explained that the wax effigy of him in the chair was part of a plan to catch a dangerous diamond thief called Count Negretto Sylvius, and he told Watson to go and give the name to the police.

The Count soon arrived and found the door open. He saw the effigy in the chair and tried to attack it. He soon realised his mistake, and the real Sherlock Holmes explained that he knew that the Count and his accomplice had a diamond called the 'Mazarin Stone', and that information from his investigations could put them both in prison. He then offered the Count a choice: the diamond or prison. He told the Count to invite his accomplice into the house to discuss the options as he went into his bedroom with his violin.

The accomplice came in and the two men immediately started planning to trick Holmes. Hearing the violin music and assuming their conversation was secret, they planned to escape. The Count took the diamond out of a secret pocket and lifted it up to the light by the window to show his accomplice. Suddenly a hand reached up from the chair and took the diamond from the Count.

'Thank you!' said Holmes. 'Let me explain. You saw me go into my room with my violin. What you didn't see is that I have a record player and a second door in my bedroom. I put on some violin music and came out of my room through the second door, behind the curtain. Then I sat in the chair and replaced the effigy. And now I believe I hear the police coming to arrest you.'

Adapted from 'The Adventure of the Mazarin Stone', by Sir Arthur Conan Doyle

Track 41

Unit 9, page 77, exercise 7

Presenter: Welcome to the Good Food Guides. Today, we are talking about your favourite snacks, those small meals that you like to eat when you feel tired and hungry. Our first caller is Lisa. Lisa, what is your favourite snack and when do you like to eat it?

Lisa: Well, the snack that I eat the most is quite a common one. It's eggs on toast. Some people like to add sausages or bacon but I prefer to keep it simple. Sometimes I add some cheese though. It's delicious.

Presenter: And do you eat it in the morning?

Lisa: No, I don't eat it for breakfast like everybody else. I like to eat it as an afternoon snack.

Presenter: Interesting! Thanks Lisa. OK, our next caller is Jim. Tell us about your favourite snack, Jim.

Jim: Hi! My favourite thing to eat is a small snack of banana and yogurt. In fact, there are always bananas in my fridge. I couldn't live without them. I really like them, and the snack reminds me of my grandad. He made it for me a lot when I was very young.

Presenter: What a lovely memory! Thanks, Jim. Next, we have Diana. Hi Diana.

Diana: Hi there! My favourite snack is hot chocolate and biscuits. I like my hot chocolate really strong and the biscuits have to be chocolate too. I usually have it at night, just before bed. It helps me to sleep!

Presenter: Fascinating! That's all we have time for today, unfortunately. Tune in next week to.....

Track 42

Unit 9, page 77, exercise 8

See previous track

Track 43

Unit 9, page 78, exercise 1

Gary: Hmm, that smells great. What are you cooking Mum? I'm so hungry!

Mum: I'm cooking an omelette. Grandma and Grandad are coming for lunch and it is Grandad's favourite recipe. He taught me how to cook it when I was your age, you know.

Gary: Did he? Can you teach me?

Mum: Of course. Wash your hands and you can help me prepare.

Gary: OK. Ready! So, what do I do first?

Mum: First, check the box of eggs in the fridge. Do we have six?

Gary: Hmmm, yes we do.

Mum: Great. Now put the eggs in a bowl and mix them together. Then add the milk and some salt and pepper.

Gary: How much milk do I add?

Mum: Just a cup. Here, there is enough in this bottle. Now mix everything together. That's it – you're good at this!

Gary: I think I like cooking Mum!

Mum: Now, you need to grate the cheese. While you do that, I'll chop the ham and the green onions.

Gary: Finished! What now Mum?

Mum: Now, add the chopped ham and onions to the egg mix. Be careful, we don't want to waste anything. That's it. Now, put the grated cheese on top of the egg mixture. Add a little more salt and pepper and that's it.

Gary: That's it? Can we eat it now?

Mum: Of course not, Gary! We have to cook it first.

Gary: How long do we cook it for?

Mum: About thirty-forty minutes. If we put it in the oven now, it will be ready in time for lunch. Then the last thing to do is to serve it with a fresh salad or fruit.

Gary: Delicious! But what can I eat now?

Track 44

Unit 9, page 78, exercise 2

See previous track

Track 45

Unit 9, page 80, exercise 2

Where does our food come from?

One of the biggest changes in food production was the development of farming. People could now stay in one place and cultivate the food they needed. But it took a long time to grow the food and sometimes it went bad or insects ate it. Over time, science helped make big improvements in farming. Scientists invented chemicals to protect the plants and help them grow better, and they also invented ways of changing plants and vegetables so we could store them for longer. These plants are called GMOs or 'genetically modified organisms'. However, many people believe that these chemicals can damage the environment and wildlife, and that GMO foods are bad for humans. That is why ecological farming is becoming more popular. But what is it?

Ecological or 'Eco' farming means that the farm works in a way that is good for the environment. There is no artificial intervention in the production of eco food – no chemicals, no hormones and no genetic modification. Then there is bio food, which just means there is no genetic modification. And finally there is organic food. This means that no chemicals were used to grow the food, although GMOs are sometimes involved.

Supermarkets are also becoming more conscious of the source of their products.

Labels on food can tell us a lot about where the food comes from. Take eggs, for example. Eggs have two numbers printed on them, the date and a number from 0 to 3: 3 means the chicken lived in a cage; 2 means that it lived indoors; 1 means that the chicken was able to walk around freely, and 0 means that it was free and it was also fed organic food.

So, next time you shop, stop and consider your choices about the type and the amount of food you buy. Do you know where your food comes from?

Track 46
Wordlist, page 98, unit 1, Greetings and introductions
See Student's Book transcript, Track 2.47

Track 47
Wordlist, page 98, unit 1, Countries and nationalities
See Student's Book transcript, Track 2.48

Track 48
Wordlist, page 98, unit 1, Hobbies and interests
See Student's Book transcript, Track 2.49

Track 49
Wordlist, page 98, unit 2, Dates
See Student's Book transcript, Track 2.50

Track 50
Wordlist, page 98, unit 2, Time
See Student's Book transcript, Track 2.51

Track 51
Wordlist, page 98, unit 2, Personality adjectives
See Student's Book transcript, Track 2.52

Track 52
Wordlist, page 99, unit 3, Body parts
See Student's Book transcript, Track 2.53

Track 53
Wordlist, page 99, unit 3, Body actions
See Student's Book transcript, Track 2.54

Track 54
Wordlist, page 99, unit 3, Physical appearance
See Student's Book transcript, Track 2.55

Track 55
Wordlist, page 99, unit 4, Clothes
See Student's Book transcript, Track 2.56

Track 56
Wordlist, page 99, unit 4, Patterns
See Student's Book transcript, Track 2.57

Track 57
Wordlist, page 99, unit 4, The environment
See Student's Book transcript, Track 2.58

Track 58
Wordlist, page 100, unit 5, Weather and seasons
See Student's Book transcript, Track 2.59

Track 59
Wordlist, page 100, unit 5, Outdoor adventure and sports
See Student's Book transcript, Track 2.60

Track 60
Wordlist, page 100, unit 5, On the farm
See Student's Book transcript, Track 2.61

Track 61
Wordlist, page 100, unit 6, Places in a city
See Student's Book transcript, Track 2.62

Track 62
Wordlist, page 100, unit 6, Directions
See Student's Book transcript, Track 2.63

Track 63
Wordlist, page 100, unit 6, Historical monuments
See Student's Book transcript, Track 2.64

Track 64
Wordlist, page 101, unit 7, Adjectives: *-ing* and *-ed*
See Student's Book transcript, Track 2.65

Track 65
Wordlist, page 101, unit 7, Travelling
See Student's Book transcript, Track 2.66

Track 66
Wordlist, page 101, unit 7, Famous explorers
See Student's Book transcript, Track 2.67

Track 67
Wordlist, page 101, unit 8, Time expressions
See Student's Book transcript, Track 2.68

Track 68
Wordlist, page 101, unit 8, Ghost stories
See Student's Book transcript, Track 2.69

Track 69
Wordlist, page 101, unit 8, Parts of a story
See Student's Book transcript, Track 2.70

Track 70
Wordlist, page 101, unit 9, Food
See Student's Book transcript, Track 2.71

Track 71
Wordlist, page 101, unit 9, Units of measurement
See Student's Book transcript, Track 2.72

Track 72
Wordlist, page 101, unit 9, Nutrition
See Student's Book transcript, Track 2.73

Unit 1

Page 4

1 **1** T **2** T **3** F **4** F

2 **1** Ireland
2 Walters
3 twelve
4 two
5 24 Church Street
6 basketball
7 345 788 002

3 **1** a **2** a **3** b **4** b **5** b

4 **1** It is 345 334 889.
2 I am 11.
3 It's 18 Segovia Street.
4 My name is Agatha.
5 It is J-A-N-S-S-E-N.

5 **1** d **2** e **3** b **4** c **5** a

6 *Student's own answers*

Page 5

7 **Conversation 1**
1 How are you doing
2 Not too bad
3 It was nice to see you
4 See you later

Conversation 2
1 Good morning
2 How are you today
3 I'm very well, thank you
4 I'd like to introduce
5 Nice to meet you

8 **Speaker 1**
Michaela's surname; Her age;
Her phone number
Speaker 2
His age; His address

9 **1** M **2** M **3** A **4** M **5** A **6** A

Page 6

1 **1** Spain
2 France
3 Australia
4 Colombia
5 Japan
6 Ireland
7 Belgium
8 Greece

2 **1** Spanish
2 French
3 Australian
4 Colombian
5 Japanese
6 Irish
7 Belgian
8 Greek

3 **1** Mexico
2 Portuguese
3 Argentina
4 Turkey
5 Dutch
6 England

4 **1** am; am
2 are; is
3 is; is
4 is; is
5 are; are

5 *Student's own answers*

Page 7

6 **1** is; am
2 are
3 is; is
4 is; is
5 are
6 are; are

7 **1** is Justyna
2 is twenty-five
3 is Polish; is in England
4 are George and James
5 are fourteen
6 are English
8 are in Ireland

8 **1** What is your name?
2 Where are you from?
3 When is her birthday?
4 What is his address?

9 **1** is
2 is
3 is
4 is
5 are
6 am
7 is
8 is
9 Are
10 am
11 is
12 are not
13 are
14 is

Page 8

1 **1** cherries - Cherries are a type of food, but the other two are types of sport.
2 comedy - Comedy is a type of film, but the other two are types of music.
3 series - A series is a type of TV show, but the other two are types of food.
4 French – French is a nationality and a language, but the other two are countries.
5 R&B - R&B is a type of music, but the other two are types of film.

2 Age; Nationality; Favourite sport

3

Name	Age	Nationality	Favourite sport
Alex	15	American	surfing
Jenna	13	Irish	skiing
Kosuke	14	Japanese	baseball

4 **1** English, Spanish and French.

2 He's a professional surfer.
3 Classical music.
4 Manchester United.
5 No, she isn't.
6 Anything with vegetables.
7 English and Japanese.
8 Ed Sheeran.

5 1 singer
2 club
3 vegetarian
4 cinema
5 member

Page 10

1 *Student's own answers*

2 *Student's own answers*

3 *Student's own answers*

Page 11

1 1 c 2 a 3 b

2 1 throw in the towel
2 practice makes perfect
3 reach for the stars

Unit 2

Page 12

1 1 Saturday 2 Monday 3 Thursday 4 Wednesday 5 Friday 6 Sunday

2 1 November
2 January
3 July
4 April
5 October
6 February
7 August

3

3rd third	7th seventh	11th eleventh
12th twelfth	15th fifteenth	20th twentieth
22nd twenty-second	30th thirtieth	31st thirty-first

4 1 different schools
2 Chris

5 1 b 2 a 3 b 4 c 5 c 6 b

Page 13

6 *Student's own answers*

7 1 Is
2 is
3 Are
4 I'm
5 am
6 Is
7 isn't
8 are
9 aren't
10 aren't

8 1 No, it isn't. It's sunny.
2 Yes, he is. He's our best friend.
3 No, I'm not. I'm in first year.
4 No, they aren't. They are easy.
5 Yes, she is. She's from Paris.

9 1 Is John the English teacher?
2 Are Mick and Tom surfers?
3 Is Miss Lee thirty years old?
4 Are we there?
5 Is climbing an outdoor sport?

10 1 Rick and Luna aren't Brazilian.
2 We aren't 13 years old.
3 Kim isn't American.
4 I'm not in your class at school.
5 It isn't Saturday today.

11 1 Are you 15 years old?
2 The exam isn't on Monday.
3 Are Jane and Sam at school today?
4 We aren't in the photo.
5 Is Julia from Germany?

Page 14

1 1 seven
2 half past six
3 a quarter to twelve
4 a quarter past four
5 nine
6 half past twelve

2 *Student's own answers*

3 1 b 2 a 3 b

4 1 English class is in the room near the gym.
2 PE class starts at nine o'clock.
3 Rob was born in May.
4 Rob can't go to Lily's party because he's got volleyball.
5 Ted's favourite subject is Science.
6 The school trip in on the 10th of January.

Page 15

5 1 on 2 at 3 at 4 on 5 at 6 in

6 1 The first PE class is on the 13th of September.
2 This Friday the musical Cats is on.
3 The class party is on Thursday at lunchtime.
4 The school basketball match is on Saturday at 1pm.
5 The first meeting of the debating club is on Tuesday, the 20th of October at 5pm.

7 1 clock
2 late
3 lunchtime
4 Geography
5 midnight
6 Music

Page 16

1 1 analytical
2 persevering
3 shy
4 active
5 sociable

2 1 Ayako
2 Yolanda
3 Aegeus

3 1 c; f 2 d; e 3 a; b

4 1 F. It's in the Southern Hemisphere.
2 T
3 F. She isn't very sociable and she is quite shy.
4 T
5 T
6 F. He has classes at home.

5 1 marks
2 good at
3 pass
4 timetable
5 on my own

Page 18

1 *Student's own answers*

2 *Student's own answers*

3 *Student's own answers*

Page 19

1 1 take time out
2 time flies
3 just in time

2 1 time flies
2 just in time
3 take time out

Unit 3

Page 22

1 1 chest
2 mouth
3 shoulder
4 elbow
5 hip
6 stomach
7 knee
8 toe
9 heel
10 hair
11 eyebrow
12 nose
13 ear
14 eyelash
15 cheek
16 tooth
17 neck
18 tongue

2 1 toes; foot
2 nose; ears
3 teeth; mouth; tooth
4 hair; head
5 elbow
6 stomach

3 head; feet; heels; knees; stomach

4 1 Tuesday
2 energetic
3 March
4 body
5 feet
6 knees
7 acid
8 Ross

Page 23

5 1 f 2 d 3 b 4 c 5 a 6 e

6 1 stretch; arm
2 scratch; neck
3 swing; arms; head
4 touch; nose
5 stick out; tongue

7 1 bodies
2 feet
3 arms
4 legs
5 shoulders
6 eyelashes
7 teeth
8 stomachs

Page 24

1 1 elderly woman
2 grey
3 wavy
4 blue
5 tall
6 athletic
7 short
8 babies
9 little
10 bald
11 cute
12 long
13 straight
14 short

2 1 elderly
2 young
3 slim
4 grey
5 hazel
6 beautiful
7 bald
8 handsome

3 1 Sophia
2 Hugo
3 Maria
4 Martin

4 1 different
2 adventurous; friendly
3 funny; sports
4 happy; Peru
5 tall; shy

Page 25

5 1 she; She
2 your; It's
3 I; we; our
4 My; she
5 Your; my
6 My; they; their

6 **1** My brother is very adventurous and he is very athletic.
2 At the moment, it's bright pink
3 They are hazel with some green in the centre.
4
5
6 You know him.

7 *Student's own answers*

Page 26

1 **1** successful
2 trustworthy
3 judgements
4 comfortable
5 complex

2 **1** My dad and role model
2 A successful uncle
3 The best teacher

3 **1** b **2** a **3** e **4** d **5** c

4 **1** **Personality:** He's very responsible, persevering and trustworthy.
Appearance: He's tall and he's got hazel eyes.
2 **Personality:** He's ingenious and creative.
Appearance: He's got short red hair that's a bit curly and he's medium height.
3 **Personality:** She's energetic and imaginative. She's also very patient.
Appearance: She's very tall.

5 **1** they **2** their **3** he **4** his **5** Her **6** They

Page 28

1 *Student's own answors*

2 *Student's own answers*

3 *Student's own answers*

Page 29

1 **1** b **2** c **3** a

2 **1** give her a hand
2 are all heart
3 am all ears

Unit 4

Page 30

1 **1** cap
2 sunglasses
3 socks
4 suit
5 shirt
6 trainers
7 swimsuit
Secret word: clothes

2 **1** boots
2 shorts
3 coat
4 gloves
5 belt

3 **1** b **2** c **3** c **4** a **5** c

Page 31

4 **1** patterned **2** stripy **3** light **4** tartan **5** spotty **6** flowery

5 **1** He's wearing a dark blue T-shirt.
2 He's wearing light blue jeans.
3 He's wearing brown trousers.
4 She's wearing a long-sleeved red T-shirt.
5 She's wearing a stripy T-shirt.
6 She's wearing grey trainers.
7 She's wearing a checked shirt.

6 **1** b **2** d **3** c **4** e **5** a

7 **1** F **2** F **3** F **4** F **5** T **6** T

Page 32

1 **1** am staying
2 is teaching
3 aren't speaking
4 are you doing
5 Are you living
6 am not studying

2 **1** sitting
2 tying
3 getting
4 riding
5 studying

3 **1** He's playing (the) piano.
2 She's playing tennis.
3 She's taking a photo.
3 They're watching a film.

4 **1** Sunita is getting up.
2 are having lunch.
3 a quarter past three; grandma isn't taking; is getting the bus.
4 four o'clock; Sunita isn't doing; is going shopping with
5 a quarter to eight; are going to the cinema; is studying for an exam

5 **1** Is it raining? Student's own answers.
2 What are your friends doing now? Student's own answers.
3 Are you listening to music? Student's own answers.
4 Where are you sitting right now? Student's own answers.

6 **1** A: Is; listening
B: Isn't listening; is reading
2 A: are; doing
B: am finishing

3 A: is watching
B: we are cooking
4 A: Are; making
B: am frying

7 1 Karen; d
2 Rose; a
3 Roy; c
4 John; e
5 Sonia; b

8 1 In the park
2 Studying Italian
3 At school
4 Watching a football match
5 At home
6 Looking for a new house
7 At school
8 Teaching a class

Page 34

1 1 endangered animals
2 plastic
3 water shortages
4 pollution
5 rubbish

2 **a** 4 **b** 3 **c** 1 **d** 2

3 **1** b **2** b **3** a **4** c

4 b

5 **1** a **2** b **3** a **4** a

6 *Student's own answers*

Page 36

1 *Student's own answers*

2 *Student's own answers*

3 *Student's own answers*

Page 37

1 1 shoes
2 hat
3 socks

2 1 take my hat off to them
2 pull my socks up
3 put themselves in my shoes

Unit 5

Page 40

1 Across
1 freezing
4 snowing
5 windy
Down
2 raining
3 cloudy
4 sunny

2 1 cold; raining
2 freezing; snowing
3 windy
4 foggy
5 hot; sunny

3 1 freezing, snowing, windy, cloudy, cold
2 hot, sunny, rain, cold, chilly

4 1 October
2 meat soup
3 4
4 wear
5 December
6 on the beach
7 north
8 shorts

Page 41

5 1 warm; spring
2 hot; sunny; summer
3 chilly; autumn
4 freezing; winter

6 *Student's own answers*

7 **b**

8 1 July
2 13th
3 32 Albert
4 tennis
5 volleyball
6 swimming
7 sandwiches
8 pasta
9 pizza
10 400

Page 42

1
1 Daniel doesn't play the guitar.
2 My dad works at the weekends.
3 I don't get up until half past eight.
4 They don't go to the same school.
5 We take a break from classes at one o'clock.
6 Pete and Ricardo don't live there anymore.

2
1 I do
2 he doesn't
3 they do
4 she does
5 we do

3
1 Do; know
2 live
3 don't go
4 have
5 don't meet
6 study
7 don't have
8 eat
9 don't/doesn't like
10 do; want

4
1 Do you
2 Do they
3 Where do you
4 What do you do
5 How do you get
6 What does he have
7 When does class/What time does class

Page 43

5
1 Penny always does her homework on time.
2 I never play table tennis with my brother because he is better than me.
3 My family and I sometimes eat out at a restaurant at the weekends.
4 I try to go to bed early but it never happens.
5 We always have pizza on Thursdays after guitar practice.

6
1 sports
2 basketball
3 bike
4 music
5 read

7
1 never
2 always
3 sometimes
4 always
5 sometimes
6 never

8 *Student's own answers*

Page 44

1

Outdoor adventure camp	Sports camp	Both
adventure	climbing wall	canoe
cabin	pool	equipment
tent	rugby field	camper

2
1 Contributing to the local community
2 Food
3 Adventure
4 Lessons for life

3
1 It's in the Ngorongoro Conservation Area, in Tanzania.
2 It's two weeks.
3 They stay in cabins.
4 Six.
5 They serve a buffet breakfast.
6 They can canoe on Grumeti River or go on a ride through the conservation area.
7 They can see elephants, zebra and lions.
8 They learn teamwork, leadership and basic outdoor survival skills.

4
1 c
2 a
3 d
4 e
5 b

5
1 protect
2 outdoor
3 dishes
4 wildlife
5 get to know

Page 46

1 *Student's own answers*

2 *Student's own answers*

3 *Student's own answers*

Page 47

1
1 She's on cloud nine!
2 to break the ice
3 It's a breeze.

2
1 am on cloud nine
2 break the ice.
3 is a breeze.

Unit 6

Page 48

1
1 bus station
2 music shop
3 stadium
4 police station
5 school
6 museum
7 hairdresser's
8 hospital
9 church
10 gym

2

Clothes shop	Bookshop	Bakery	Butcher's
coats	magazines	bread	chicken
socks	novels	cakes	sausages

3 Speaker 1: a; d
Speaker 2: a; d

4 **1** straight
2 right
3 Go
4 between
5 Turn
6 next to
7 Walk
8 across from

Page 49

5 *Student's own answers*

6 **1** walk
2 turn
3 past
4 to
5 ahead
6 from
7 between

7 **1** across from
2 next to
3 behind
4 between

8 **1** Is there
2 there is.
3 There is
4 Are there.
5 there aren't
6 there is

9 **1** b **2** b **3** c **4** c **5** a

10 *Student's own answers*

Page 50

1 **1** does
2 flies
3 studies
4 works
5 finishes
6 meets
7 cries
8 catches

2 **1** gets
2 has
3 leaves
4 goes
5 has
6 walks
7 takes
8 phones
9 watches
10 has

3 **1** a **2** b

4 **1** F
2 T
3 F
4 NI
5 T
6 T
7 NI
8 T

Page 51

5 **1** sometimes takes
2 usually rides
3 never goes
4 often does
5 always has
6 hardly ever has

6 *Student's own answers*

7 **1** George always gets up early.
2 He never goes to the gym.
3 He usually spends his days at historical sites.
4 He sometimes finds interesting objects from ancient times.
5 He hardly ever has lunch at home.
6 He never thinks his job is boring.

8 c

Page 52

1 **1** pyramid, rock
2 church, tower
3 jungle, palace

2 *Student's own answers.*

3 **1** Natalie
2 Deniz
3 Natalie; Sita
4 Deniz
5 Natalie
6 Deniz; Sita

4 **1** A
2 AW
3 G
4 HS
5 A

5 **1** temples
2 sightseeing
3 crowded
4 building
5 break

Page 54

1 *Student's own answers*

2 *Student's own answers*

3 *Student's own answers*

Page 55

1 **1** I love Japanese food but sushi restaurants are few and far in between in my town.
2 I'm buying that dress. I have a party on Saturday and it fits to the bill perfectly.
3 It's tradition here to celebrate New Year's on the beach. You know what they say, when you're in Rome, do as the Romans do.

2 **1** fits the bill
2 few and far between
3 when in Rome, do as the Romans do

Unit 7

Page 58

1 **1** excited
2 surprised
3 fascinated
4 bored

2 **1** interesting
2 fascinating
3 interested
4 boring
5 frightening
6 terrified

3 **1** fascinating
2 interested
3 excited
4 terrifying
5 boring

4 **1** bored **2** terrified **3** surprised

5 **1** d **2** c **3** a **4** b **5** e

Page 59

6 **1** was
2 was
3 were
4 were; were
5 was

7 **1** was
2 was
3 were
4 weren't
5 was
6 were
7 wasn't
8 was
9 weren't
10 were

8 **1** I wasn't excited about the party.
2 It was an interesting trip to the museum.
3 He wasn't born in Spain.
4 We were surprised by the news.
5 The film wasn't as good as they said.
6 Joe and David weren't fascinated by the old maps like I was.

9 *Student's own answers*

Page 60

1 **1** a **2** b

2 **1** T
2 T
3 F
4 T
5 F
6 T
7 F
8 T

3 **1** Were
2 Were
3 was
4 were
5 were
6 Was
7 wasn't
8 were

4 **1** Were
2 Was
3 was
4 was
5 Were
6 was

5 **1** Who was; was
2 When were; were
3 Where was; was

Page 61

6 **1** explorer
2 expedition
3 adventures
4 discovered
5 discoveries

7 **1** Where was he
2 Was he born in the
3 Was he always
4 Who was
5 Were they
6 What were the books

8 **1** He wasn't very famous in the beginning.
2 No, they weren't.
3 We were in the kitchen when we heard the terrifying noise.
4 The trip was dangerous and long. It took half a year to get there.
5 Were you in class yesterday?
6 Where were they when we needed help?
7 Sally was fascinated by their stories.
8 Yes, it was / No, it wasn't.

9 *Student's own answers*

Page 62

1 Childhood: as a child, at the age of 12
Achievements: is famous for, was the first person to
Career: climber, palaeontologist
Personality: brave, shy

2 Text 1
1 2
2 3-5
3 9-11

Text 2
1 15
2 16-17
3 20-24

3 **1** TA **2** BC **3** BC **4** TA **5** TA **6** BC

4 **1** She was born in 1892.
2 She was in France.
3 Yes, she was.
4 No, he wasn't.
5 He was 16.
6 It was about 37 days.

5 **1** daring
2 persistent
3 inspiring
4 successful
5 thrilling

6 **1** inspiring
2 successful; persistent
3 daring; thrilling

Page 64

1 *Student's own answers*

2 *Student's own answers*

3 *Student's own answers*

Page 65

1 **1** a **2** c **3** c

2 **1** is over the moon
2 It beats me
3 was face to face

Unit 8

Page 66

1 **1** b **2** c **3** a **4** c **5** a **6** b **7** a **8** b

2 **1** True **2** True **3** False

3 **1** spring
2 tired
3 after
4 camera
5 castle
6 suddenly
7 Italian
8 grandma

Page 67

4 **1** start; started; R
2 study; studied; R
3 go; went; I
4 eat; ate; I
5 stop; stopped; R
6 believe; believed; R
7 think; thought; I
8 laugh; laughed; R
9 realise; realised; R
10 leave; left; I

5 **1** saw
2 didn't think
3 realised
4 jumped
5 got
6 didn't matter
7 went
8 heard

6 **1** went
2 started
3 didn't know
4 came
5 sat
6 fell
7 had
8 woke up

Page 68

1 **1** b **2** a **3** a

2 **1** James's birthday
2 quiet
3 beach
4 before
5 suddenly
6 screamed
7 shoe
8 trainers
9 didn't swim

3 **1** said
2 looked
3 didn't recognise
4 asked
5 sat
6 didn't want
7 told
8 thought
9 knew
10 finished

4 *Student's own answers*

Page 69

5 **1** No, we didn't.
2 Yes, she did.
3 Yes, I did.
4 No, they didn't.
5 Yes, it did.

6 **1** did; look
2 did; see
3 Did; steal
4 did; get
5 did; try

7 **1** When did; see
2 What time did/When did; get
3 What did; do
4 Where did; hide
5 How did; find
6 Who did; meet

8 **1** Wales
2 flew
3 meet
4 ate
5 buy
6 made

Page 70

1 **1** mistake
2 detective
3 curtain
4 diamond
5 investigate

2 **1** himself
2 diamond
3 Sherlock Holmes

3 **1** T
2 T
3 F. He attacked the effigy of Holmes.
4 F. They started planning to trick Holmes.
5 T
6 F. He put some violin music on the record player.
7 T

4 **1** c **2** a **3** d **4** e **5** b

Page 72

1 *Student's own answers*

2 *Student's own answers*

3 *Student's own answers*

Page 73

1 **1** blood is thicker than water
2 a shot in the dark
3 a skeleton in the closet

2 **1** a skeleton in the closet
2 Blood is thicker than water
3 a shot in the dark

Unit 9

Page 76

1 **1** biscuit
2 cereal
3 kiwi
4 peach
5 bread
6 yogurt
7 cheese
8 mango
9 strawberry
10 butter

2 **Countable:** biscuit, kiwi, peach, mango, strawberry
Uncountable: cereal, bread, yogurt, cheese, butter

3 **1** coffee
2 toast
3 milk
4 mangoes
5 pasta
6 cheese
7 grapes

4 *Student's own answers*

Page 77

5 **1** is
2 are
3 is
4 is
5 any
6 some
7 some

6 **1** How many
2 How much
3 little
4 How many
5 A few

7 **a** 3 **b** 2 **c** 1

8 **1** F. She sometimes likes to have some cheese with it.
2 F. She usually eats it in the afternoon.
3 T
4 F. Jim's grandad made the snack for him.
5 T
6 F. Diana eats her favourite snack at night.

9 *Student's own answers.*

Page 78

1 cheese, eggs, fruit, ham, milk, onions, pepper, salad, salt

2 **1** eggs
2 milk; salt; pepper
3 cheese
4 ham; onions
5 cheese
6 salad; fruit

3 **1** a bowl of strawberries
2 a slice of ham
3 a bag of oranges
4 a box of eggs
5 a spoonful of oil
6 a tin of sardines
7 a loaf of bread
8 a bottle of apple juice
9 a jar of pickles
10 a packet of raisins

4 **1** a loaf of
2 loaves of
3 a bag of
4 tins of
5 a box of
6 slices of
7 a kilo of
8 a bottle of

Page 79

5 **1** spoonful
2 put
3 Chop
4 Spread
5 grate
6 Add

6 **1** Is; any
2 many
3 Is
4 much
5 Is; any
6 Are; any

7 **a** slices; 1
b bottles; 5
c some; 6
d spoonful; 3
e boxes; 2
f an/one; bag; 4

8 *Student's own answers*

Page 80

1 **1** label
2 energy
3 source
4 store

2 **a** 3 **b** 1 **c** 2

3 **1** c **2** c **3** a **4** a **5** b **6** b

4 **1** vegetables
2 farms
3 environment
4 improvements

5 *Student's own answers.*

Page 82

1 *Student's own answers*

2 *Student's own answers*

3 *Student's own answers*

Page 83

1 **1** a bad egg
2 a smart cookie
3 a couch potato

2 **1** a smart cookie
2 a couch potato
3 bad eggs

Unit 1

1 **1** am; am
2 is; is
3 is
4 is; is
5 are
6 are; are

2 **1** What; *Student's own answers*
2 When; *Student's own answers*
3 Where; *Student's own answers*
4 Which; *Student's own answers*
5 Why; *Student's own answers*

Unit 2

1 **1** Are you English?
2 Is he Chinese?
3 Is it Tuesday?
4 Are they at the cinema?
5 Are we finished?

2 **1** in **2** on **3** At **4** At **5** In

Unit 3

1 **1** knives
2 women
3 children
4 eyelashes
5 feet
6 bookshelves

2 **1** The Hulk; he; his; he
2 Superman; His; it; He
3 Wonder Woman; She; her
4 Iron Man; It; he
5 Spider-Man; he; It

Unit 4

1 **1** a **2** b **3** a **4** b **5** b **6** a

2 **1** He is wearing sunglasses.
2 I am studying for an exam.
3 We are recycling paper.
4 They are planting trees.
5 Are you wearing a coat?
6 Is she reading a book?

Unit 5

1 **1** I play the guitar.
2 You don't have a cat.
3 They live in the same street.
4 Does he do yoga?
5 She doesn't meet her friends after school.

2 **1** I always walk to work.
2 I sometimes see my cousins; Sometimes I see my cousins.
3 I never drink milk.
4 I'm always early to school.
5 He's never late.

Unit 6

1 **1** c **2** e **3** f **4** d **5** b **6** a

2 **1** I always have breakfast.
2 I hardly ever go to bookshops.
3 I often go to the shopping centre.
4 I sometimes walk to school.
5 I never eat sweets at home.

Unit 7

1 **1** A Who B was
2 A: Was B: was; were
3 A: Was B: wasn't; was
4 A: When B: was
5 A: Was B: wasn't; was
6 A: Were B: weren't; were

2 **1** ed **2** ing **3** ed **4** ed **5** ing **6** ing

Unit 8

1 **1** had
2 went
3 arrived
4 met
5 saw
6 told
7 ate
8 came
9 sat
10 didn't like
11 heard
12 slept

2 **1** d **2** f **3** a **4** c **5** b **6** e

Unit 9

1 **1** There is a banana on the table.
2 There is some milk in the fridge.
3 Too much chocolate is bad for you.
4 She's got some fruit.
5 There's a little butter in the fridge.
6 I haven't got any money.
7 There aren't any oranges.
8 We've got a lot of meat.

2 **1** many; *Student's own answers*
2 much; *Student's own answers*
3 much; *Student's own answers*
4 much; *Student's own answers*
5 many; *Student's own answers*

Unit 1

1
1 nice
2 Colombia
3 basketball
4 rollerblading
5 fashion
6 morning
7 Irish
8 French
9 France
10 comedy
11 going
12 Greece
13 swimming
14 surfing
15 series

Unit 2

1 January; February; March; May; June; August; October; November; December
Missing months: April, July, September

2 Monday; Wednesday; Thursday; Saturday
Missing days: Tuesday, Friday, Sunday

3
1 c
2 e
3 b
4 d
5 a

4
1 active
2 intelligent
3 creative
4 sociable
5 patient

Unit 3

1
1 little; short
2 skinny; thin
3 curly; wavy
4 light
5 young

2
1 ear
2 shoulder
3 eyebrow
4 tooth

3
1 wink
2 bend
3 stretch
4 stand
5 stick

Unit 4

1
1 gloves; jacket
2 shorts; swimsuit
3 socks; shoes
4 cap; hat

2
1 stripes
2 T-shirt
3 spotty
4 pollution
5 plastic

Unit 5

1
1 windy
2 cloudy
3 sunny
4 foggy

2
1 spring
2 Winter
3 autumn
4 Summer

3

Camping	Sports	On the farm
cabin	hockey	barn
campsite	scuba dive	crops
tent	squash	egg

Unit 6

1 A 1: me
B 2: bakery 3: near 4: Go 5: next

2
1 palace
2 artefacts
3 pyramids
4 tour guide
5 research

Unit 7

1
1 trip
2 dangerous
3 pioneering
4 tribute
5 first person
6 all three options are correct
7 excited
8 frightening

Unit 8

1 1 c 2 a 3 f 4 b 5 d 6 e

2
1 day
2 long
3 Suddenly
4 Finally
5 Afterwards

Unit 9

1
1 kilo
2 loaf
3 bag
4 bottle
5 tin
6 jar
7 packet

2

Fruit	Vegetables	Dairy	Other animal products	Nutrients
plums	broccoli	butter	fish	carbohydrates
tangerines	peas	milk	meat	vitamins

3
1 healthy
2 fat
3 protein
4 fibre
5 minerals

Notes and ideas

Notes and ideas

Richmond ®
58 St Aldates
Oxford OX1 1ST
United Kingdom

Publishing Director: María Lera
Managing Editor: Catherine Richards
Development Editor: Ben Pincus
Editorial Team: Joanne Fairgrieve, Natalie Krol, Jayne Marshall, Siobhàn O'Connor, Nicola Strutt

Video: MTJ Media
Audio: EFS Television Production Ltd. Motivation Sound Studios

Art Director: José Crespo
Art Coordination: Rosa Marín, Javier Tejeda
Cover: EMC Design Ltd.
Design and layout: ColART Design

Technical Director: Jorge Mira Fernández
Technical Coordination: Rocío Lominchar Romero
Photo Researcher: Amparo Rodríguez

Photos:
ARCHIVO SANTILLANA

Printed in Brazil
ISBN: 978-84-668-3388-2

The editors would like to thank all those teachers and consultants who provided invaluable help and insight with their participation in this book.